TRUE TO NATURE

TRUE TO NATURE

CHRISTOPHER PARSONS
looks back on 25 years of wildlife filming
with the BBC Natural History Unit

FOREWORD BY DAVID ATTENBOROUGH

For Desmond
to whom we all owe so much

First published in 1982
Second impression June 1982

ISBN 0-85059-530-4

Design by Tim McPhee
Produced for the publishers, Patrick Stephens Limited,
Bar Hill, Cambridge, CB3 8EL, England,
by Book Production Consultants, Cambridge.

Typeset by King's English Typesetters Ltd, Leeds
Printed and bound in Great Britain by William Clowes
(Beccles) Limited, Beccles and London.

FRONT ENDPAPER
Pacific Ridley turtles mass-nesting on Nancite beach,
Costa Rica.

HALF TITLE SPREAD
David Hughes at work in the Namib for his film Strange
Creatures of the Skeleton Coast.

TITLE SPREAD
Martin Saunders filming a wild mountain gorilla in Ruanda
for Life on Earth.

BACK ENDPAPER
Thompson and Skinner filmed the feeding and courtship of
many British spiders, including these crab spiders; the small
one is the male.

Contents

'To see the scarlet ibis birds of Trinidad whirling in clouds over the blue mud-banks, and to know that they are real, is to be made aware how beautiful the world is and how little of it one has seen. It is to be filled with longing and discontent: and discontent is the beginning of wisdom.'

Peter Black – after viewing one of the first natural history films to be shown on colour television.

Foreword

The British are famous – perhaps even notorious – for their devotion to wildlife. Many of the great naturalists who laid the foundations of zoology in the 19th century were British – Bates, Wallace and, above everyone, Darwin. They were professionals, inasmuch as the profession of zoologist existed in their time. But Britain's amateur naturalists have also made major contributions. The smallest of this country's mammals was discovered in the 18th century by a Hampshire parson, Gilbert White, who also indefatigably dragged the ponds of his parish during the winter to find out whether or not swallows hibernated under water. The first dinosaur remains to be identified, for which that now famous name was coined, were collected by a Sussex doctor, Gideon Mantell. The first true bird sactuary of modern times was created by a Yorkshire squire when, in the 1820s Charles Waterton enclosed his entire estate with a high wall, built special nesting holes for the birds and forbade entrance to any who might disturb them.

This passion for the natural world, which can so easily become an obsession, is still widespread throughout British society. It leads the richest and the poorest, the humblest and the noblest, to stand for hours up to their waists in chilling salt marshes watching wildfowl, to tramp for miles across bleak moorlands just to glimpse a rare flower in bloom, to spend night after night counting migrant birds as they fly across the face of the moon.

So maybe it should not come as a total surprise that the world's biggest group of film-makers and broadcasters, devoted solely to the job of making natural history programmes for radio and television, should be found in Britain; nor that the British public should greet such programmes so enthusiastically that they are among the most successful of all broadcasts in this country.

The BBC Natural History Unit was formally founded in 1957 in Bristol. That it should have been established there was due partly to the fact that the BBC, then as now, had a policy to encourage particular specialisations in its production centres outside London; and partly because the outstanding producer of natural history programmes at that time, Desmond Hawkins, was living and working in that part of England.

The Unit quickly recruited splendid contributors to its television programmes from among the ranks of the passionate amateurs – a distinguished soldier, Field Marshal Lord Alanbrooke, who spent all his spare time devotedly filming birds; a Hampshire small-holder, Eric Ashby, who, with inexhaustible patience, filmed the animals of the

New Forest; a biology teacher, Ernest Neal, who discovered that it was possible to accustom wild badgers to artificial light and so watch and photograph them throughout the night; and, above all, a portrait painter and wildlife artist who had already created a national reputation as a broadcaster on natural history and who became the primary figure in the Unit's output, Peter Scott. No wonder that the Unit's programmes were an immediate and nationwide success.

I have to confess a particular interest in these events for at the time I was producing animal programmes in London. It was by no means uncommon in those days for infant programme empires to wage aggressive territorial war on one another, but it is a measure of the kindliness of the Bristol Unit that no attempt was ever made to demand a monopoly of natural history programmes or to insist that I either joined the Unit or turned my attentions to other subjects. Instead, it was amicably agreed that, for the first few years at least, Bristol would concentrate on European natural history while I pursued my own preoccupation with filming in the tropics. Indeed, though in later years I began to contribute to the Unit's output as a writer and narrator, I have never been a member of its production staff.

Only one founder member of the Unit still works for it, Christopher Parsons. He is presently its Head and under his leadership, the Unit has produced a larger number of programmes of greater scope and higher quality than ever before. He is also the author of this book and no one could describe with more first-hand authority than he the story of this unique institution. What he has written reveals a great deal about the way in which natural history programmes are made. But I suspect that it does more. It constitutes an important – and quintessentially British – chapter in the story of broadcasting.

David Attenborough.

January 1982

Introduction

The popularity of wildlife programmes on radio and television should come as no great surprise to anyone. I believe it's only natural for humans to take a close interest in other forms of life; indeed, just a few thousand years ago this was the very essence of survival. You *had* to know about the habits and the senses of the animals you preyed on; for that matter, it was important to have similar information about animals that might prey on you. The same considerations applied to plants and fungi; your health depended on being able to distinguish between plants good to eat and those which were poisonous; and you had to know where to find them and in what seasons. Although it is now more important for urban man to be aware of the risks of picking up a power cable than a venomous snake, I suspect that the comparatively small number of generations involved in our transition from hunter-gatherer to worker-commuter means that there is a lot in our genes which still disposes us to be closer to nature than we realise. All we need is a little stimulation.

In my own case, this came from an upbringing in a sheltered Devon valley, which, although within sight and sound of the Blitz, remained untouched by the ravages of war. Next door to us was a farmyard; from here a deep-rutted lane with high, thick hedges curved down to the meadows nearby and then up through a patchwork of small fields on the hill opposite. On the steepest field, which could not be worked by horses, there were rabbits everywhere. Even in our large rambling garden I occasionally glimpsed, from behind the living-room window, a doe rabbit on regular visits to her kittens hidden just underground in the herbaceous border. Myxomatosis had not yet hit the valley, nor were chemicals being used against insects; so not only the luxuriant hedgerows but our own garden borders were vibrant with insect life. Red admirals, peacocks, clouded yellows, painted ladies – all danced and sipped at both wild and cultivated flowers and, in some years, I watched entranced as, on blurred wings, humming-bird hawkmoths darted and stopped instantly in space before their feeding flowers.

Ten years later, whilst on holiday with my uncle at his house in Uxbridge, I watched a television transmission for the first time and instantly became totally fascinated with the medium. After university and National Service, it was my good fortune that the West Region of the BBC began to develop wildlife television just when I was looking for a job, thus giving me an opportunity to combine my two major interests. As a result, I was ready and waiting when the BBC formed the Natural

History Unit at Bristol in 1957; and now, 25 years later, I find I am the only member of the Unit to have stayed the whole course. This continuity, perhaps, gives some validity to a book of reminiscences but there is a danger that, by writing a personal account of my own experiences, I might appear self-important. Although I have been connected with over 600 natural history programmes in one capacity or another as film editor, production assistant, producer or series editor, that total is insignificant compared with the radio and television output on this subject from Bristol since Desmond Hawkins produced the first of the radio series, *The Naturalist*, in January 1946. That number is probably in excess of 5,000 programmes!

This, then, is not a history of the Natural History Unit but a personal celebration of 25 extremely happy and exhilarating years. Some important output of the Unit has not been mentioned at all; other programmes appear only briefly, because I was not intimately involved with these. Colleagues such as Richard Brock, John Sparks and Barry Paine have all been with the Natural History Unit many years and their world-wide adventures would fill many books. Jeffery Boswall, who joined the Unit soon after its formation, has made a special study of wildlife broadcasting in Britain and I hope that one day he will write a history which will include a proper account of the development of the Natural History Unit. Until then I hope this book of memories will give some insight into the processes of making wildlife programmes and at the same time convey the pleasure I have had in trying to communicate my own fascination with natural history through the medium of television.

Christopher Parsons

Chapter 1

The bay where time stood still

The narrow beach stretched endlessly ahead, lifeless under a grey, clouded sky. A soft wind frisked the waters of the bay, masking the rhythms of the sea so that only tired waves beat on the shore. It was early evening and as the light began to drain in the west I sensed an almost uncanny lull in the elements, the chatter of water gradually subsiding like a full auditorium in anticipation of a great performance. Indeed we had come to witness something of that kind – a natural spectacle due to occur this very evening when the tide was high and the moon was full. It was a performance which took place every year about this time and it had probably done so on these and similar shores for over 300 million years. We had just arrived to see it for ourselves on this carefully chosen day – Wednesday, June 1 1977.

Six of us had made the long journey from London to Philadelphia by air and then southwards by road to the eastern shores of Delaware Bay; a three-man BBC film crew, my assistant, Pam Jackson, the programme presenter, David Attenborough, and me. We had come to film a key sequence in a mammoth television series about the ancestry of life entitled *Life on Earth*. Tonight, if the predictions came true, we should be able to witness the mass spawning of strange marine creatures which had changed little since a prehistoric age (before life moved on to land from the sea). Two other men had joined us before the long walk down that deserted beach: a hired electrician with a set of battery lights – for we should be filming after dark – and a tall American biologist named Carl Shuster who was a leading authority on the animals we had come to see. Carl was confident but concerned: we had built an entire six-week filming schedule in the USA around the date which he had forecast would be right for our sequence at Delaware Bay – but that prediction had been made well over a year ago from his office in Washington DC.

*   *   *

I had been in the federal capital during the early stages of our research for the series, visiting the US Fish and Wildlife Service and various biologists in the Smithsonian Institution. It was there that I enquired if anyone knew of the present whereabouts of one Dr Carl Shuster, whose papers on the horseshoe crab, *Limulus polyphemus*, I had recently discovered. 'Crab' was a misnomer for although its horseshoe-shaped carapace did give it some resemblance to a strange type of crab, it belonged to a different and ancient lineage which stretched back to the days of the trilobites – an extinct class of armoured marine invertebrates which swarmed in the seas of 400–500 million years ago. The horseshoe crab could, indeed, be regarded as a living fossil for it has another link with the past in its larval form, which is popularly known as a 'trilobite larva' on account of the superficial resemblance to that extinct creature. So, as our series attempted to trace the evolution of life on earth through living species, the horseshoe crab and its larvae were of prime importance.

'Well, that guy's around somewhere in Washington', the man in the Crustacean Section at the Smithsonian had said. 'I came across his name in a report only the other day . . . let me see . . .'. He reached for some directories. 'I think he's an ecologist with the Federal Power Commission now . . .'. He dialled a number on the telephone and eventually got through to Dr Shuster's office and introduced himself.

'The reason I'm calling is that I have a Mr Christopher Parsons from the British Broadcasting Company . . .'.

'Corporation', I said.

'. . . pardon me, British Broadcasting Corporation . . . he would like to come and talk to you'. He capped his hand over the mouthpiece and asked, '3:30 today all right?'

'Fine', I said, and it was fixed. Later on I took a cab to the tall concrete block that housed the Federal Power Commission and made straight for Dr Shuster's office. The room was heavy with shelves bearing books and thick reports. Dr Shuster looked under pressure but he rose from behind his desk and welcomed me warmly with a large, firm hand.

'I know of your work on *Limulus*', I said.

'Oh, yes', said Dr Shuster, as if this was only a formality. 'I presume you want to talk to me about that report on the dam at . . . .'.

'I've come about horseshoe crabs', I interrupted him. Dr Shuster looked at me disbelievingly. 'I'm from the BBC Natural History Unit at Bristol – it's a specialised production group which makes about a hundred radio and a hundred television programmes each year for the British networks. I'm here as executive producer of a new major natural history series which we hope will be in the same league as *The Ascent of Man* and *America*'. I knew both series had been shown on the Public Broadcasting System. The comparison seemed to make a good impression so I went on to outline the scope of our series and said that the production team was currently in touch with biologists at over 500 universities and other scientific institutions throughout the world.

'And as we require a sequence on horseshoe crabs for programme two, I've come to the fountain head', I concluded. Dr Shuster's face had slowly taken on a broad smile. Clearly horseshoe crabs were the last thing that people came to talk to him about nowadays and for a television producer to raise the subject was about as rare an occurrence as a meteorite hitting the White House. He reached behind him for a box of scientific papers.

'Of course, it's many years ago that I studied *Limulus* and wrote these, but if there's anything I can help you with . . .'.

'There certainly is', I said. 'I know from the literature I have read that they emerge from the water to mate and lay their eggs in the sand at certain conditions of tide and moon. I need to know the best location for filming the largest concentration of them – and exactly when to do it!'

'That shouldn't be difficult, it's almost certainly here'. He jabbed at a map on the desk, indicating part of the eastern shore of Delaware Bay. 'That stretch along there is the prime site. Why, they could be so thick on the shore you could walk along the top of them for miles – just like a sidewalk!'

I pointed out that we would not only need to choose the right location but also select the right day – or possibly two days – so that we could plan the filming into a tight schedule next year. Moreover, we wished to avoid shooting the entire sequence at night so we would like to find an evening when the horseshoe crabs began to appear in large numbers even before darkness fell. Carl Shuster did not possess lunar tables for the following year but he promised that my requirements could be met and in due course he would write to me in England with the details. As I rose to go to the door I said, 'By the way, if you should find it possible to take a few days off and be with us during the filming, I'm sure it would be most helpful'. The expression on Carl Shuster's face left no doubt that he would be there come hell or high water.

*   *   *

Carl, as he quickly became known the following year, was already making a reconnaissance in the Cape May area when I arrived on May 30 with my assistant, Pam Jackson. We had flown in advance of the rest of the party so as to pinpoint the exact spot on the beach and plot the sequence of shots required, for I knew that when the spawning activity occurred we would have to work very fast and there would be no time for indecision. After sleeping off the effects of jet-lag, we met Carl at his hotel the next morning and set out to inspect the beach. He was in good spirits and reported that all looked well, for there had already been many horseshoe crabs the previous evening and the peak activity should occur on the day of filming. We parked the car near the beach – I was glad to see that we could drive the film equipment so close – and started walking southwards along the shore. There was a scavenging party of gulls ahead and, as we drew close, they flew away leaving a horseshoe crab struggling helplessly on its back.

Carl picked it up by its long spike of a tail and handed it to me. It looked so archaic that it was like holding a piece of prehistory. Most of the animal was protected under a broad domed shield about 10 inches wide, from which two compound eyes protruded, and at the back was a smaller hinged plate. Underneath seven pairs of legs and some pincers waved furiously about so it looked like a strange mechanical toy animal picked up before its clockwork had run down. We placed it at the edge of the water and it immediately headed out into the bay. Within a mile we rescued dozens of horseshoe crabs in this way, casualties from last night's spawning when waves had overturned them and the receding tide had left them stranded. However, many others had not survived and now lay dessicated after mutilation by the gulls.

We arranged to meet again at six o'clock that evening, this time with the film crew and David Attenborough, who by then would be well

A stranded horseshoe crab. The circular pattern in the sand was made by the spiky tail as the animal attempted to right itself.

'Carl picked it up by its long spike of a tail.'

*Pam Jackson
rescuing a stranded
horseshoe crab.
There were dozens
of casualties from
the previous night.*

rested from the long journey. Carl had forecast that the first horseshoe crabs would emerge from the water well before sunset and this would enable us to find a good male specimen for David to hold and talk about as he introduced the sequence. So we all walked on down the beach, eventually stopping at an arbitrary spot where we would begin filming – an optimistic procedure indeed when there was no sign at all of our subject material.

Low in the western sky the clouds momentarily parted and the yellow sun spilled through, showing there was still some time before it dipped below the horizon. For a few seconds the rays were reflected on the grey waters catching, I noticed, a round, glistening stone in the shallows. I saw another. Curious, I thought, I had not realised there were so many large stones just off-shore. Then I saw that they were moving – difficult to detect at first amongst the lapping waves. The recognition made me shudder involuntarily – the water was full of them. Our horseshoe crabs had arrived.

Carl said, 'They are males mainly – waiting for the females. They patrol the shallow water out there, waiting for their opportunity as the females come in to spawn. Then they'll swim up behind a female and hang on tight to her with their specially adapted claws'. He waded into the water to look for a good-sized male and brought it out by the tail.

We filmed a couple of takes of David's short statement to camera and then quickly took the inter-cutting close-ups of claws and eyes before the light changed too much. It was fading fast now but there was no

15

more sound film work to be done and so we could react quickly to the changing scene, moving the camera easily as new arrivals appeared at the water's edge. Even in the short time that we had been filming David, several pairs of crabs had started spawning nearby, each female digging whilst her clinging male released his sperm from behind as soon as the eggs were laid. We took the camera to the water's edge, looking along the tideline where horseshoe crabs were appearing as far as the eye could see. It was now only in daylight that we could give some impression of the scale of the spectacle for after dark our battery lights would enable us to film only small groups. So Maurice Fisher, the cameraman, worked fast taking every possible angle as more and more crabs arrived on the scene. There was something quite eerie about it all. Within a few yards of us there were hundreds of crabs and yet there was

The horseshoe crabs began to arrive – like grey stones at the water's edge.

OVERLEAF

LEFT

More parties arrive,
several males
surrounding a
larger female.

*Horseshoe crabs
were appearing as
far as the eye could
see.*

TOP RIGHT
*After dark the crabs
formed a living
cobbled road along
the tideline.*

BOTTOM RIGHT
*Surrounded by
grains of sand, a
tiny horseshoe crab
egg develops in the
Oxford Scientific
Films studio.*

no sound from them, apart from the water washing over their backs. In no way could this phenomenon be described as a sexual orgy; but there was a feeling of natural relentlessness in the way that more and more crabs kept appearing to take their places at the water's edge – it was a scene that was both primitive and inevitable.

To emphasise the concentration of crabs we filmed David walking along the shore for long distances in the last light of day, and then after dark with a lantern. At some places we stopped to look at congested groups with males jostling for position near a large female. So strong was their mating urge that there were often four or five lined up behind a single female. Within an hour there was a solid band of crabs along the tideline, forming a living cobbled road. Their numbers were beyond belief.

The following day, we drove to Washington for our next assignment, but first I had to call at Dulles International Airport to despatch a very important package to England. It contained two plastic containers full of sand and horseshoe crab eggs collected from the spawning beach. This was the subject material for the second part of our sequence. After being given the flight number and the waybill number of the package, Pam Jackson telephoned the production organiser of the *Life on Earth* series to confirm the provisional arrangements we had already made. It was 11 in the evening at Bristol and Derek Anderson was at home waiting for the call. The following morning he would ensure that the containers with the eggs were picked up from the BBC Shipping Department at London Airport and rushed to the studios of Oxford Scientific Films at

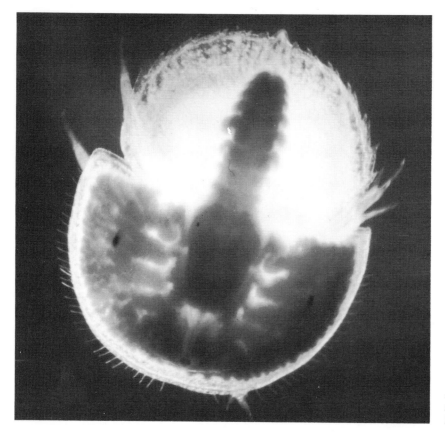

*A 'trilobite' larva
soon after
hatching.*

Long Hanborough near Witney. There Peter Parks would place them in
a miniature aquarium, simulating the conditions of the beach at Delaware Bay. For the next month he would film their development in
marvellous detail on his optical bench; and, finally, when the next high
tide at Delaware Bay reached the buried eggs on the beach to disturb
and release the hatching larvae, Peter would re-create similar conditions
on a small scale in his studio to complete the sequence.

It was just one tiny piece in the huge film jigsaw that we were putting
together for our three-year project. At the end of two more years we
would have worked in 39 different countries, filmed over 650 species
and covered over 1⅓ million miles. As yet we had no idea if our series
would be successful although we did know that it was undoubtedly the
most ambitious and complex natural history series ever undertaken by a
broadcasting organisation. As I drove back the 25 miles from Dulles
Airport to our hotel in Washington, I wondered how many million
viewers would eventually see that extraordinary scene at Delaware Bay
and the miraculous development of those tiny eggs, which even now
were starting on their long journey to England. Certainly the answer
would not be known for many years. How different, I thought, from
those days of more than 20 years ago when we were often not sure what
wildlife film we would have ready for transmission just a month ahead.
But that was long before there was a Natural History Unit at Bristol. . . .

Chapter 2

Welcome to Bristol

The letter from the Administrative Assistant stated quite clearly that I should report to the Senior Administrative Officer on November 21 1955 at 10:00 am, but I was convinced that a mistake had been made in the time. After all, I reasoned to myself, it was inconceivable that an organisation which began broadcasting at 6:30 each morning should not be humming with activity in all departments by 9:15. So, playing safe and not wishing to make a bad impression on my first day's employment with BBC West Region, I mounted the steps of Broadcasting House, Bristol, at nine sharp.

The Commissionaire was friendly but unimpressed by my eagerness. He fumbled amongst his papers apologetically but obviously he had not yet been given a list of the day's visitors and their appointments. 'Of course, there's not many around in Admin until after half-past-nine', he admitted. 'I'm sure they really did mean 10 o'clock'.

Broadcasting House, Whiteladies Road – the headquarters of the BBC West Region in 1955, now BBC Bristol Network Production Centre.

He showed me into a waiting room furnished with leather armchairs and a table on which were copies of *Radio Times* and *The Listener*. I had already read the week's editions from cover to cover the previous evening but I picked up the *Radio Times* again and thumbed through the pages, noting the radio and television programmes originating that week from West Region. I had begun this habit at home in Devon when, as a schoolboy, I first became addicted to natural history programmes on the Home Service and noticed that many of them were produced in the west. The habit continued through university days and during National Service, most of which was spent not far away at RAF Yatesbury in Wiltshire. For years the same names appeared over and again – Desmond Hawkins, producing radio series such as *The Naturalist* and *Birds in Britain*; Bill Coysh producing *Country Questions*. In the last year I had noticed that the old familiar pattern was changing. A new name – Tony Soper – had been credited at the end of some radio programmes and Desmond Hawkins' name also now appeared at the conclusion of Peter Scott's wildlife programmes on television. During the past few months, these television programmes, too, had been changing: they were now transmitted at fortnightly intervals under the title *Look* and yet another new name concluded the production credits – that of Brandon Acton-Bond. I sensed that my arrival was part of this pattern of change which, no doubt, was caused by West Region re-organising itself to meet the new challenge of television.

If these developments were accompanied by a quickening of tempo

Peter Scott and Desmond Hawkins at the Severn Wildfowl Trust on the occasion of an edition of The Naturalist *about geese in December 1947.*

within the BBC at Bristol there was at least no sign of it at 9:30 on that November morning. Outside, in Whiteladies Road, the traffic stopped and started at the busy crossroads and pedestrians hurried by on their way to the shops and the university a few hundred yards down the road. Few would be aware that they were passing the headquarters of the BBC's West Region, for there was little evidence of the paraphernalia of broadcasting to be seen behind the windows and iron first-floor balconies of the elegant early Victorian buildings where it was housed. Indeed there had not been a sign of a microphone or a camera on my previous visit over two months ago; on that occasion I had been particularly apprehensive, having been summoned to an appointments board after submitting an application for the job of Assistant Film Editor, West Region Film Unit.

The advertisement had miraculously appeared in *The Daily Telegraph* one morning after I had spent a miserable evening alone in my room at the Officers' mess at Yatesbury contemplating the pros and cons of teaching mathematics at a school in Bath and a career in electronic research with a firm in Essex. Both had been offered to me following recent interviews. Although for many years my main interests had lain in natural history, music and films, I had been persuaded to take a science degree as an insurance policy and this had led to a commission in the RAF as an education officer teaching basic electronics to air wireless fitters. Now with National Service nearly completed I had to choose a job – fast. Yet nothing that came up attracted me – until that advertisement in the *Telegraph*. After listing the usual professional requirements for an assistant film editor, the advertisement concluded, 'An interest in, and a knowledge of natural history an advantage'. I knew that my chances would depend on that last phrase; how many experienced assistant film editors, I wondered, could tell the difference between a song thrush and mistle thrush or distinguish between a stoat and a weasel? I might have the edge there but I could certainly not offer any experience in a professional film cutting room, although I had been closely involved in films made by the RAF Station Film Unit, particularly in the editing and sound dubbing stages. I doubted whether anybody at the BBC would seriously consider this as even relevant.

To my surprise I was asked to attend an appointments board. It was rather a formal affair, the four board members sitting behind a long, highly polished table. A solitary chair on the opposite side of the table signalled where each candidate was required to sit. To begin with there were some pleasantries and general inquiries from the chairman, who was from Appointments Department, but, in less than five minutes, I was unveiled as a complete imposter by someone from London who appeared to be of high rank in the Film Department. He then appeared to wash his hands of the whole affair and, as far as I was concerned, that was the end of my brief association with the BBC. However, the interview was prolonged (for politeness, I naively thought at the time) by two other members of the board who seemed intent on putting me at my ease. One of them was particularly interested in my bird-watching experiences on the Exe Estuary as well as badger-watching in the New Forest, while the other probed into my adventures into writing music for university revues, a few years as a church organist, and 18 months' spare-time activities running a busy RAF Station Theatre. Something in this conversation must have struck the right chord for, to my complete astonishment, several weeks later I was offered the job on a trainee basis at a salary of £520 per annum.

So, on this my second visit to Broadcasting House, Bristol, I waited impatiently for 10 o'clock – and with not an entirely clear conscience. Perhaps, after all, I *had* managed to conceal the truth from the board; perhaps they hadn't realised just how little time I had actually spent handling film and how clumsy and slow I was compared to the real professionals. Now would come the dreaded moment of truth. In less than 10 minutes I would be led into a gleaming film cutting room furnished with all the latest power-driven editing equipment and supervised by an unsympathetic film editor who had just arrived from one of the top London film studios. 'Lace this up for me', he would say, handing me a large roll of 35 mm film and nodding in the direction of a complex piece of machinery, and I wouldn't know where to begin. Or perhaps, 'Splice these scenes together would you, old chap', rather patronisingly, and I wouldn't know how to operate the latest type of film joiner.

My imagination was prevented from creating further horrific situations by the sudden opening of the waiting room door and the arrival of what appeared to be another new recruit. An older man than I, he had a confident, well-travelled air about him; he drew a tin of tobacco from his pocket followed by a packet of cigarette papers and with a few deft movements of his fingers rolled a cigarette – an act which seemed strangely incongruous with his well-groomed appearance. We were just about ready to strike up a conversation when the door opened again and we both were summoned to meet Mr Mair.

In spite of his warm welcome, Mr Mair, a slight, pale-faced Scot, was less impressive than the office in which he worked. It was a large, gloomy room, well carpeted and furnished with huge leather chairs into which my companion and I sank after the introductions. George Shears, it turned out, was the new film cameraman; he announced that he had just come from World-Wide Pictures. Obviously the RAF camp at Yatesbury was not in this league so I decided to let this uncomfortable topic rest for the time being. Mr Mair's next remark did nothing to improve my confidence.

'I'm sorry to have to tell you . . .', he began gravely, peering at me from behind his enormous desk, 'I'm sorry but our new film editor, Bob Higgins, for whom you will be working, cannot be released from London until the New Year'.

There was a slight pause while Mr Mair studied me intently to watch the effect of this devastating news. My mind raced wildly ahead weighing up the advantages and disadvantages of this unexpected situation. If I was to be alone in the cutting room I might have a chance to try out all that complicated machinery while no one was looking and perhaps get in a little practice; on the other hand I might be thrown in at the deep end and found wanting on the very first day.

'Unless you have any questions, I suggest we go down to your rooms and meet the others', said Mr Mair, leading us to the door. We followed him down several corridors and eventually into an open alleyway between the canteen and a large studio. At the rear of the studio building a small room had been converted into a new, shining office, every item of which must have just been unpacked. Desks, chairs, in and out trays, wastepaper bins, carpet, filing cabinets – all were apparently untouched, unmarked and unused. Seated behind a typewriter at one of the desks was a rosy-faced young woman with all the appearances of a hen clucking over a clutch of day-old chicks.

'This is Jose Ford, the Film Unit secretary', announced Mr Mair; 'and this, Mr Shears, is your assistant, Mr Greenhalgh.'

We turned and looked into the corner of the room, where a small figure had been sitting on a shiny metal camera box lovingly inspecting a 35 mm Camiflex camera in mint condition. Billie Greenhalgh rose to meet us without noticeably increasing his height in any way, for he turned out to be one of the shortest men I had ever met. Sporting a thin, neat moustache, heavy spectacles and his oiled hair brushed perfectly straight back, Billie immediately registered as a cheeky, wise-cracking character.

Then came the great moment I had been waiting for. Mr Mair walked towards an adjoining room and reached for the light switch, for the room was in total darkness.

'This is where *you* will spend most of your time, no doubt', he said in a somewhat apologetic voice.

For a few seconds I surveyed the scene with incomprehension; and then I looked around again in utter disbelief. The room bore a closer resemblance to a prison cell than to the picture I had in my mind of how a modern cutting room should look. No gleaming sophisticated editing machines; no power rewinds, no synchronising benches, no elaborate joiners for splicing film shots together. Instead there was a simple table made of wood and hardboard. On it were a pair of hand rewinds for film spools, a pair of scissors, an ancient film splicer, a bottle of film cement and a battered 16 mm animated viewer of the type used by amateur filmmakers. To complete the equipment there was a home-made wooden-framed cloth bin with a horizontal bar of pins for hanging up film shots. Everything in sight was the sort of makeshift equipment that I had been using as an amateur. It was difficult to know whether to feel disappointed or thoroughly relieved.

'Don't worry, there's better equipment due here soon'. A new cheerful voice came from the open doorway and I turned to find a tall man who, by all appearances, conducted business in a brisk, military manner. This was Patrick Beech, the Assistant Head of Programmes, and one of his principal tasks was to build up and run the television output of the region; the establishment of a Film Unit was one of the key stages in this process. However, all of Pat Beech's wiles, charm, and not a small amount of administrative short-circuiting, had failed to synchronise the arrival of staff and all the necessary equipment.

I soon discovered that there were fewer than a dozen people in the building engaged full-time in television duties, for most of the staff – and indeed most of the technical facilities – were concerned with the production and administration of radio output. This came as more of a surprise than it should have done because an examination of a current *Radio Times* showed only a page devoted to television programmes each

day and this always appeared *after* several pages devoted to radio programmes. Moreover, although BBC television transmitters covered 90 per cent of the population there were only about 40 hours of transmissions per week with peak figures reaching around five million viewers during the three-hour evening session. In fact, much larger audiences were listening to popular radio programmes such as *The Goon Show, Take It From Here* and *Any Questions* (which was produced from Bristol) and twice as much of the BBC's income was still being spent on radio than on television. The balance was swiftly changing, however, and West Region, with a long history of enterprise and innovation in radio broadcasting, would not allow television to arrive without a respectable share of the action. However, because West Region's bids were made from premises which were essentially radio-orientated, the means by which it approached the new medium were necessarily basic, invariably inventive and, as I was to discover behind the scenes, occasionally comic.

The metamorphosis which was still taking place within the walls of Broadcasting House at Bristol had been quite rapid. At the time the BBC's standard method of first exploiting the television potential of a new area was to allocate to the region concerned a television outside broadcasts kit, consisting of a mobile control room (MCR) with its various vehicles to carry the electronic cameras, cables, microphones, generators, radio links, etc. And so MCR 6 – and its attendant engineers – arrived at its own base at a deserted airfield near Bristol in early 1953 and for many years the facilities it provided were shared by West Region and Welsh Region.

The number of MCRs posted out to various regions, as well as a large fleet in London, reflected the great importance that the BBC attached to television outside broadcasts (OBs) at the time. In fact, OBs accounted for nearly a quarter of the television output. The first full-time production appointment to be made at Bristol was, therefore, quite logically an outside broadcast producer, Nicholas Crocker. Formerly a Radio OB producer Crocker – responsible for early editions of *Any Questions* amongst other things – had been sent up to London for television training before the MCR arrived.

West Region soon began to offer a steady stream of subjects to S. J. Lotbiniere ('Lobby'), the Head of Outside Broadcasts in London, and through sheer determination, very hard work and a wonderful pioneering spirit the Bristol-based engineers got their OB cameras into an extraordinary variety of strange and difficult locations. But this type of broadcasting had severe limitations: only five minutes of film in each programme was permitted (usually to enable the electronic cameras to move from one location to another while the film sequence was being shown) and this had to be shot and edited by the London-based Film Unit as well as transmitted from a Telecine machine at Lime Grove. Moreover, many other programmes which West Region wished to produce required a studio as well as film and no one was more anxious to have these facilities in Bristol than Desmond Hawkins, the radio features producer, who, since 1946, had been associated with pro-grammes about natural history from the West Region.

Desmond Hawkins' regular series *The Naturalist* and *Birds in Britain* were transmitted on the Home Service on Sundays, usually after the one o'clock news, and regularly brought to the microphone a number of well-known naturalists including Maxwell Knight, Ludwig Koch, James Fisher and Peter Scott. It was Scott who was to play the key front-of-camera role in making successful Desmond Hawkins' ventures into television which included some outside broadcasts from the Wildfowl Trust at Slimbridge.

The first studio programmes were produced in London but later on the largest radio studio at Whiteladies Road was used (after it was vacated by decanting the BBC West of England Light Orchestra into a converted theatre near the centre of Bristol). Studio A, as it later became known, was not a television studio in the strict sense since it had neither permanent lighting nor vision and sound control rooms, but a large set of double doors enabled the MCR to draw up outside so that engineers could run their cameras in to shoot against an improvised set. Film still had to be projected through a telecine machine in London.

In spite of the makeshift methods required to get them on the screen, Peter Scott's wildlife programmes were extremely successful. During 1954 they appeared somewhat irregularly, often quite late on a Saturday evening. During the summer of 1955 they were given a series title – *Look* – and, at the end of September, new programmes were being transmit-ted at fortnightly intervals on Wednesdays. For a tiny production team it was a daunting task – not made any easier by having to start the series before proper film editing facilities became available at Bristol. For the newly-arrived Assistant Film Editor (Trainee), C. E. Parsons, it was disconcerting to say the least; there was no proper cutting room equipment to work with and no film editor to train under. Nevertheless even an untrained pair of hands could be put to good use and in no time at all I found myself helping with the preparation of sound tracks.

There were none of the normal professional facilities for making film sound tracks at Bristol in 1955 so West Region did its best with what it

Ludwig Koch, a frequent broadcaster from Bristol in the 1940s and 50s. His recording of the curlew introduced each edition of The Naturalist *and all his wildlife recordings laid the foundations of the Natural History Unit's sound library.*

had available in its radio studios. A 16 mm projector and screen were set up in the control room of one of the studios and, using several dozen effects discs played on a bank of turntables, a skilled assistant studio manager would match sound to picture. My role was to stop and start the projector while each section was carefully rehearsed and the order of discs plotted. These would eventually be played in 'live' on transmission.

For the final rehearsals the film projector was taken into the television studio and set up in front of a translucent back-projection screen. On the other side of this was a television camera – the fourth and spare camera, normally only available in case of breakdown with the other three. This camera enabled the film sequences to be viewed on a monitor close to Peter Scott and his guest so that they could speak their commentary. Another monitor in an adjoining sound cubicle allowed the grams operator to polish up the sound effects. As projectionist I was cued

James Fisher, distinguished ornithologist and broadcaster, regularly introduced Birds in Britain *as well as appearing on many other programmes from Bristol.*

through a pair of headphones on which I also heard the producer's instructions to cameramen and floor manager. Although this taught me something about studio routines and disciplines it soon became rather boring and I was grateful to be allowed into the 'Scanner' or mobile control room for the transmission of my second *Look* programme; for when we went on the air the 'show print' of the film sequences was run on a telecine machine in London and my services were no longer required.

MCR 6 had roughly the dimensions of a furniture van, though not so high. It was packed with electronic apparatus and a comparatively small amount of room had been left at one end for production staff and engineers. Facing a row of picture monitors linked to each of the three cameras, four people sat behind a raised desk. On the left was the producer's secretary, stopwatch in one hand, scribbling notes and timings on her script with the other. Next to her was the *Look* producer,

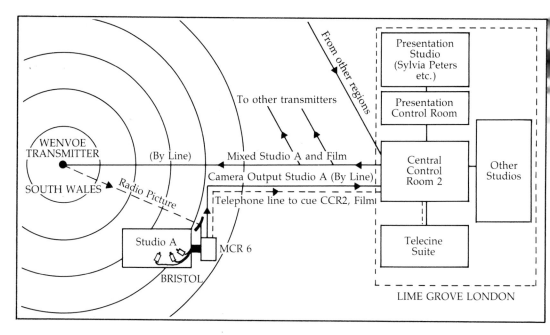

Diagram labels: From other regions / To other transmitters / Presentation Studio (Sylvia Peters etc.) / Presentation Control Room / WENVOE TRANSMITTER / (By Line) / Mixed Studio A and Film / Central Control Room 2 / Other Studios / SOUTH WALES / Radio Picture / Camera Output Studio A (By Line) / Telephone line to cue CCR2, Film / Studio A / MCR 6 / Telecine Suite / BRISTOL / LIME GROVE LONDON

Brandon Acton-Bond, and in front of him on the desk were the buttons and faders necessary to cut or mix from one camera to another. On Brandon's right were the senior sound engineer, with his set of faders, and the senior television engineer. In front of them all, huddled like troglodytes under the monitors and racks of electronic apparatus, sat three engineers controlling the pictures from the three cameras; they were known simply as 'Racks'. The entire scene was dimly lit, cramped, and very warm.

I was given a square foot of space in a corner behind the producer and stood there transfixed, hardly daring to breathe whilst the final minutes before transmission ticked by. There seemed to be about six different conversations going on at once: the producer was talking through his headset to one of the cameramen, the senior engineer was talking to one of his 'racks' engineers, the producer's secretary was on the telephone to someone in London and, coming out of loudspeakers, were the floor manager's instructions to Peter Scott mixed up with the sound of the London programme currently being transmitted. This was visible on yet another monitor which was showing the 'radio' picture direct from the Wenvoe transmitter in South Wales.

A few minutes before the programme was due to begin a telephone rang and Mavis, the producer's secretary, answered. It was the central control room in Lime Grove informing us that the previous programme was over-running and we would be starting a minute-and-a-half late. For a short while everyone relaxed a little but, as Mavis suddenly announced, 'One minute to go', the tension built up again as the cameramen lined up their opening shots and the make-up girl applied a touch of powder to Peter Scott's shining forehead.

The studio set represented Peter Scott's combined studio and living room and an easel, at which Peter would be doing lightning sketches

For several years in the early 1950s there was no telecine machine for showing film at Bristol. Furthermore, there was no good quality return line available from London to preview film so Peter Scott had to rely on pictures from the Wenvoe transmitter during live broadcasts from Studio A.

during the broadcast, was a standard part of this. Usually, each edition began with a Scott drawing of a subject relevant to the programme and on this the opening titles were electronically superimposed. So, as everyone got ready, Camera 1 focused on the drawing on the easel while Cameras 2 and 3 framed up caption cards on which were written 'LOOK' and 'Introduced by Peter Scott'. Suddenly Sylvia Peters appeared on the radio picture monitor and most of the conversation in the scanner subsided. As the close-up of Sylvia Peters faded, Mavis, still in touch with London on the telephone, said, 'Cue grams', and the strains of the *Look* signature tune were heard as Camera 1's shot of the Scott drawing appeared in place of Sylvia Peters.

'Superimposing 2 – coming to 3', intoned Brandon, his fingers on the faders.

'On 3', added Brandon. 'Change on 2', prompted Mavis as the floor manager took away the caption card in front of Camera 2 to reveal another one underneath. The procedure was repeated for two more cards and eventually Camera 2, its caption work complete, swiftly moved towards Peter Scott's guest in time for his introduction.

After a few minutes the studio conversation turned to the film that the guest speaker had shot and Mavis furiously turned the little handle attached to her telephone set. She was calling the central control room at Lime Grove again so that telecine could be warned. After a few seconds someone answered and she was able to say, 'Stand by Telecine'. Eventually Peter Scott spoke the key sentence which, it had been agreed, would immediately lead to the first film. Mavis said, 'Cue telecine', and everyone hoped that the message was being relayed to the operator at his machine 120 miles away. Peter Scott talked on and Mavis said into the telephone, 'Mix on first frame'. At Lime Grove the vision mixer would in theory be watching the numbers of the leader appear on a monitor as the machine ran up to speed – 8, 7, 6, 5, 4 and then black until the first frame of action. As soon as he saw the film begin he would mix from the picture being sent up the line from the Bristol studio to the picture from the telecine machine.

About 10 seconds after the cue we saw the radio monitor change from Peter Scott to film. 'On film', said Mavis, and in the studio the floor manager silently drew Peter's attention to the monitor. This was essential to enable Peter and his guest to speak their commentary. Back in the MCR there was noticeable relief all round as soon as the film began. 'On film for 6½ minutes', Mavis said down the telephone and put the receiver down. The programme was now in the hands of Scott, his guest and London telecine.

Through a series of telephone cues the programme switched from film to the Bristol studio and back twice more until the closing studio sequence began in which the credits were superimposed on another Scott drawing, the signature music cued in, and the programme finally faded out. I then tried to move out of my cramped position in the corner, but no part of my body wished to respond. I had remained motionless for so long, hardly daring to move a muscle, that my limbs seemed to be locked solid. The experience of watching a live broadcast for the first time was so exciting to me that until then I had not even noticed my discomfort.

Chapter 3

Learning with Look

The following morning Tony Soper asked me if I would like to go filming with him. This was a surprise. I had no idea that I would be allowed out on location whilst on the editing staff.

'Where?', I enquired, wondering if I was to get a 25-mile trip up the road to Slimbridge as a special treat.

'Norfolk', Tony replied, 'tomorrow, leave about nine. OK?'

      *   *   *

Although he now directed most of his energies towards television, Tony Soper was still officially *radio* staff. He thought this was a huge joke and during the long journey from Bristol to Norfolk told me about events of the preceding years which had led to this situation. He had begun his BBC career as a junior engineer at the Plymouth studios – another part of West Region – but with the help of Frank Gillard, the Head of West Region Programmes, he had been posted to Bristol as a studio manager so that he could be closer to the radio programmes that the Features Producer, Desmond Hawkins, was currently producing. Tony therefore then managed to get himself assigned to most of these wildlife productions and, indeed, became so successful at this over a period of time that he became Desmond's unofficial assistant. At first Desmond did not realise what was happening but after a while the coincidence of Tony appearing as studio manager on *all* his programmes was too much; when challenged, Tony admitted he was rigging the schedules! By early 1954 when the first television programmes with Peter Scott began, Tony was indispensable and it was then that West Region acquired the 16 mm viewer, film rewinds and joiner which, when the Film Unit was formed, still represented the only equipment in the cutting room.

The first wildlife television programmes had been built around Peter Scott's own expedition films shot in Iceland, Greenland and South America. They were the colour films with which he lectured in order to raise money for the Wildfowl Trust he had recently founded at Slimbridge. The films were too long for the half-hour allocated for each programme so that they had to be modified and shortened using a specially made copy. The only time allowed in London for this was half a day per programme so Tony did most of the work himself at Bristol, taking the print to the professional editor for such tidying up as could be done in a few hours. This procedure took place at monthly intervals through 1954, first with Peter Scott's films and then, as these ran out,

A black woodpecker feeds its young – a scene from Heinz Sielmann's Woodpeckers.

Heinz at work inside his hide. His sophisticated techniques for filming woodpeckers in their nesting holes caused a sensation on BBC Television when the film was shown in January 1955.

with films by other contributors such as Ernest Neal, Humphrey Hewer, Dick Bagnall-Oakeley, Roger Tory Peterson and Viscount Alanbrooke.

Then, in January 1955, came a film which needed no editing. It had been seen by Peter Scott the previous year when he was attending the International Ornithological Congress at Basle in Switzerland. It was such an outstanding wildlife film that Peter had urged Desmond Hawkins to invite the German director over to England to show it on his programme. This Desmond had done, and in turn he was so impressed by the film that he sensed it would make a great impact on television viewers. He therefore took the unusual step of arranging a press preview before the programme was transmitted. Scott's and Hawkins' judgement was correct; the film impressed the critics and the public and a tremendous filip was given to Scott's wildlife programmes. The director was Heinz Sielmann; his film was *Woodpeckers*.

Although Sielmann was making other wildlife films which could be shown in Scott's series from time to time, most of the programme material for *Look* continued to come from amateur sources. But, as Tony Soper pointed out, the comparatively small number of films available on wildlife subjects which were suitable for television was fast running out. Some programmes would have to depend on material from more than one source and Tony himself soon hoped to film wildlife subjects specially for television. All this would require much more than the half-day per programme allowed in a London cutting room and so the preparation of material for *Look* had been one of the duties that had been included in the job description for the new assistant film editor.

'It's a bit of a joke, really', Tony said. 'You're the only part of the production team that's officially television staff'. It was reassuring to be considered already as part of the team.

Lime Grove Studios were used for the first wildlife television programmes produced by Desmond Hawkins.

We arrived at our hotel near Blakeney in Norfolk late in the afternoon and it was already dark. A biting wind was blowing in from the North Sea, but the hotel was warm and gave a mellow welcome with its Christmas decorations, coloured lights and an ample dinner of Norfolk turkey. Broadcasting, I mused over the brandy, seemed to be a congenial and comfortable profession.

I saw things in a different light after breakfast the next morning. The wind had dropped a little but it still had a cold cutting edge which boots, thick socks, a duffle coat and two sweaters did not easily blunt. Dick Bagnall-Oakeley, a teacher and the man whom we were to film, was similarly attired but he seemed unconcerned by the cold. He was well used to such conditions for he would spend hours each winter weekend stalking and watching the great variety of migrant birds to be found in and around the marshes and coastal dunes nearby. A naturalist of note, he had broadcast several times on Desmond Hawkins' radio programmes and in recent years he had specialised in filming birds *Away from the Nest* – the title used for a television programme in which he had shown some of his films. Most bird photographers used hides at nest sites, but Bagnall-Oakeley stalked his birds, usually on his stomach, behind hedges or through reed beds. More of his films – this time of birds in winter – were to be shown in a *Look* programme soon after Christmas and what Tony wanted to do was to show how Dick Bagnall-Oakeley got his material. So we drove a few miles from the hotel to a suitable marshy area where the hoar frost was as thick as snow and the frozen mud puddles scrunched and tinkled under our feet. Dick got out his 16 mm Bolex camera and fixed on the pistol grip, which made it easier to operate, supported by his elbows, in a crawling position. Under Tony's instructions, Billie Greenhalgh filmed Dick from several angles, sometimes following him deep into the reed beds in the hope of framing a shot with Dick in foreground and wild birds in the background.

A few days later in a viewing theatre at Lime Grove, I saw the 'rushes' – the print of the negative exposed in the camera – with Tony, Brandon Acton-Bond and Bob Higgins, the film editor who was soon to be my boss. Bob turned out to be much older than I had anticipated; he was a dapper little man, meticulous about his dress and appearance and proud of his long association with the film business. Brandon I had met briefly before, and had watched him directing operations in the studio at Bristol, but I had been careful to keep out of his way for I had noted that in moments of stress, he did not suffer fools gladly and could draw on a colourful vocabulary when the situation warranted it. At all other times, however, I soon discovered that he was the gentlest of men and a sensitive and thoughtful producer, although it was not always easy to read the thoughts going around in his extremely creative mind.

The theatre lights dimmed and a duffle-clad Parsons appeared on the screen holding the identifying take-board with the roll and scene number. All the shots of Dick Bagnall-Oakeley stalking his bird subjects were satisfactory, although after ten minutes they became somewhat boring. However, a selected few, preceding Dick's own film, would provide a useful visual accompaniment to Dick's studio commentary on how he operated in the field. Dick's film was then projected and, although it was a trifle shaky and roughly edited at times, it was breathtakingly beautiful for it was in colour. This was the camera

Heinz Sielmann and Peter Scott wait for a cue during rehearsals for the historic presentation of Woodpeckers.

original, normally used for natural history lectures, and from which a duplicate monochrome negative would be made to make a print for television. It seemed a crime that we should thus degrade such beautiful images but in 1955 colour television, although technically possible, was no more than a distant landmark in our brave new electronic world. 'Never mind, old son!', said Bob, reading my thoughts. 'What the viewers don't see, they won't miss'.

During the screening Bob took notes of Tony's identifications and Brandon's instructions for re-editing. Most of the film was of winter bird visitors to East Anglia; fieldfares and redwings gorged themselves on holly bushes heavy with berries; various finches, including bramblings, sifted through the debris of an old corn rick; and in the reed beds and tidal marshes, rare grebes and waders dived and probed for hard-earned meals. There was some concern about the timetable for editing, as there was only just over a week before Christmas, and the programme would be on the air on January 4. Moreover, Bob was still finishing off other programme commitments and would be staying in London until well into the New Year.

On the way out of the theatre Bob pulled me to one side and said, 'Look we're in a hell of a fix, old son. I can't possibly look at that stuff until after Christmas and I couldn't tell a grebe from a duck anyway. I'll have to come in on Boxing Day – can you get up here and give me a hand?'. I agreed that, trains permitting, I would be at Lime Grove on Boxing Day morning.

The film cutting rooms at Lime Grove were arranged in rows on either side of a long corridor on the top floor of the building. When I stepped out of the lift on Boxing Day this part of Lime Grove was almost deserted and I had no difficulty in finding Bob – all I had to do was walk towards the clackety sound of his editing machine which was the only one in use. He looked relieved to see me. 'What a way to spend a Christmas, old son – dammit, I've been going mad here trying to sort out fieldfares from redwings.'

'Oh that's quite easy', I said confidently. 'Let me see. For a start you should be able to see the red flanks just under . . .'. I stopped as I reached the machine. Of course, how stupid, the work print or 'cutting copy' was in black and white. 'Er, what I mean is, there's a distinctive pale stripe above the eye of the redwing, and it's smaller than the fieldfare which has a grey head and . . .'. Covered in confusion I peered into the lens in front of the film gate. I stared at the indistinct image until I resolved it as a group of birds in a bush.

'The pedal's by your right foot if you want to run it', said Bob. 'Guide the film through from the bottom with your left hand'. The machine stood on a pedestal and was in essence a projector gate through which the film could be run either backwards or forwards. A bright light was housed at the rear of the machine and this shone forward through the film so that the image, enlarged by a lens, could be viewed by the operator from a standing position. The intermittent claw and shutter mechanism, which made it possible to study the action, produced the distinctive clattering noise which echoed down the corridor.

I pressed on the foot pedal cautiously. Nothing happened. I tried a little harder and with a jerk the machine erupted into action like a

miniature pneumatic drill. Almost immediately the noise changed, there was an unpleasant scrunching noise from the film entering the machine and I saw a line of sprocket holes flying up through the screen. I took my foot off the pedal, there was silence once more and Bob rescued the mutilated film and attempted to smooth out the creases. Patiently he inserted the film into the gate again, showed me where I had gone wrong and I tried again. This time I could at least see Bob's identification problem. The image was small and flickery, the birds tiny. I thought I could distinguish both redwings and fieldfares in the shot, but I wasn't sure. To me it seemed to be a hopeless piece of machinery for the task in hand and I felt that I could have managed much better with the little animated viewer and film rewinds I had at Bristol. I even cautiously suggested this to Bob in case there was such a device at Lime Grove, but he was quite appalled at the idea.

When Look *began as a regular series in June 1955, the Bristol Studio A was in operation – although with no purpose-built control room as yet. Designer Desmond Chinn prepared this set to represent Peter Scott's own studio at Slimbridge.*

'You can't cut on a pair of hand rewinds', he protested. 'Besides, this is a perfectly good machine. Just takes a bit of getting used to that's all. It's this damned 16 mm film – like bootlaces – and these bloody birds!'

The disparaging remark about the 16 mm gauge was repeated to me in various terms during 1956 by the older film editors that I met. They had been trained – and had worked most of their lives – with the professional gauge – 35 mm – and 16 mm film had such an amateur status that it was almost degrading for some even to touch it. Bob did not take that extreme view but obviously he did not feel so comfortable in handling 16 mm film as he did 35 mm. Although some 16 mm film was being used for documentary and newsreel work, all the film inserts for drama productions as well as outside broadcasts were shot on 35 mm – for only then could a satisfactory match of quality be achieved with the electronic pictures. Moreover, most of the work in the cutting rooms was on sequences rather than complete films because the BBC Film Department was very much a supply department – films made for television were rarities. Although a *Look* programme might contain up to 20 minutes of film sequences within a total duration of 30 minutes, film was still considered as being of minor importance in television and this largely accounted for the small amount of editing time allocated to the programme (not necessarily a condescending attitude by London towards the region).

In that lonely cutting room at Lime Grove on Boxing Day, there were no interruptions while we worked on Dick Bagnall-Oakeley's film. We speeded up the operation by taking over another machine in the adjacent cutting room. This was a forerunner of what is now a very sophisticated line of editing tables which are in general use for both 16 mm and 35 mm editing and on which the film travels horizontally from one plate to another. Motor-driven, the film passes over a set of rotating prisms through which a strong light projects the image on to a small screen at the back of the table. Although Bob regarded it with a certain amount of suspicion, I found it easy to operate and the projected image clear enough for me to identify the birds quickly and with certainty. Bagnall-Oakeley's film, being already edited for lecture purposes, did not need major re-organisation so the small amount of tidying up was easily achieved by early afternoon.

Heinz Sielmann and Peter Scott with Vicky the fox during rehearsals for Look No 1 – Foxes – *another film made by Heinz.*

Next the duplicate negative, taken from the original colour film, had to be cut to match the cutting copy, but this had to be done with great care so that the negative itself did not become scratched or dirty. Normally this procedure is now made relatively easy through consecutive numbers which appear at intervals of every foot on the negative (every 40 frames on 16 mm film); these are printed through on to the cutting copy. Unfortunately, the stock used for making duplicate negatives at that time did not bear edge numbers and this made it very difficult to match negative to print. In action close-ups one could usually find a frame with a very distinctive blur, but with distant scenes in which no difference between successive frames could be discerned with the naked eye – or even with a lens – the task often seemed impossible at first.

By early evening, we were over half way through the negative cutting when I reached a shot which I could not match at all. It was a medium-distant shot of a Slavonian grebe swimming in the middle of a very calm stretch of water. No reed beds, no sky, no other birds were visible. The entire frame was filled with the surface of the water and the grebe, but because there was no wind, and therefore no ripples, the grebe presented a perfect mirror image of itself in the water. The length of this shot used in our assembly was considerably less than the original in Bagnall-Oakeley's film so we had to shorten the duplicate negative. The problem was where and how because, however much Bob and I stared at the film, we could not find any mark on the film or change in the image which enabled us to match it. After about 15 minutes of total frustration, Bob finally became exasperated.

'Dammit man, the bird's not doing anything – it's just sitting there, so it doesn't matter what part of the negative we put in!'

Just over a week later the programme was transmitted from Bristol with Dick Bagnall-Oakeley as Peter Scott's guest. As usual the work print was used in the studio for rehearsals while Bob took the graded show print to the telecine machine at Lime Grove. The transmission time drew nearer and I became somewhat tense for this was the first programme which I had actually helped to prepare; much of the film had actually passed through my fingers and I couldn't help feeling a mixture of pride and concern that all would be well. Not that there was any need to worry for Bob had telephoned me to say that he had seen the show print in the viewing theatre at Lime Grove and it had looked crisp and good.

The transmission began and I was surprised to see how well the film looked even though it was in black and white. Then up came the shot of the Slavonian grebe and immediately I sensed that something was wrong. The shot was not scratched, there was no mis-cut as far as I could see and yet there was *something*. Before I could work it out the scene had ended and Peter Scott was already identifying the next bird on the screen. A few seconds later the appalling truth dawned on me. There was indeed a mistake and I knew what it was; what's more, I felt sure it was my fault.

As the transmission ended I went into the studio where Peter and Dick were quickly joined by Brandon and Tony. Apart from my blunder, the show had gone smoothly and everyone was paying complimentary remarks to each other in the glow of satisfaction which comes with having got to the end of a programme without major disasters. I kept to the back of the group, slightly ashamed at having let the side down, but Tony noticed me and made an unnecessary compliment about my small contribution.

'The film was all right then?' I asked weakly.

'Sure', said Tony. 'You'll be doing it all yourself down here at Bristol from now on I should think. Come and have a drink.'

Later, and still quite incredulous, I asked Brandon if he had noticed anything wrong with the film.

'No . . .', Brandon looked at me quizzically. 'Quite a good print I thought. Didn't you?'

'Oh yes', I said in a matter-of-fact tone. 'Just wanted to be sure you were happy with it'. And I decided to let the matter rest. No one else noticed, so why worry them with my problem? For only I seemed to have realised that we had just transmitted one of Dick Bagnall-Oakeley's film shots upside down and backwards! Because the Slavonian grebe had a perfect mirror image in the still water, grebe and image were almost indistinguishable. However, one small detail had given the game away. Although there was no wind on the water, tiny leg movements of the otherwise stationary bird had caused the faintest of ripples around it. And that was what was wrong; for the ripples weren't radiating *out* from the bird – they were travelling *inwards* towards it!

Chapter 4

Facing the future

By the beginning of spring 1956 there was no doubt that the *Look* series was a great success; the newspapers printed complimentary comments, the day after transmission members of the public were often heard discussing the programme on buses and in pubs, and many viewers began to make a regular date with *Look*. The biggest problem now was to find new material quickly enough to satisfy our hungry television monster and there was a great feeling of relief when the series ended its first long run in June 1956. Peter Scott was not available to introduce the last edition so Maxwell Knight, who regularly introduced *The Naturalist* on the Home Service, stepped in; he was no stranger to the programme as he had been a guest in an edition on *Tracks and Signs* at the beginning of the year. Maxwell Knight's own guest was to be Frances Pitt, another well-known naturalist whose regular newspaper articles had a wide appeal. The programme, entitled *Animals as Friends*, was to include Miss Pitt's own film of various wild animals she had tamed as pets, as well as some of the wildlife around her home in Shropshire.

Winwood Reade, new Features assistant in 1956 and later Television producer.

True to form, and no doubt encouraged by Tony, she planned to bring with her a selection of animal friends to make, as she put it, 'personal appearances'. Winwood Reade, a comparatively new recruit to the Features office, viewed this prospect without enthusiasm; as production assistant for the past five months she had been assigned the duties of animal handler, a fairly regular job since it was found that a live animal in the studio always proved to be good value. A few weeks previously she had been the only person in the office the evening that Captain W. R. Knight telephoned from the station to announce that he, his nephew/actor Esmond Knight and 'Mr Ramshaw' had arrived for the following day's programme and they would like to know where Mr Ramshaw was staying please. As Mr Ramshaw was a golden eagle, this did pose a problem but Winwood eventually found a satisfactory room in the cellars of Broadcasting House and the eagle was installed in a suitable cage which Captain Knight considered to be escape-proof. Warning notices were posted on the door for the house staff who visited that part of Broadcasting House in the early hours each day but, nevertheless, there was considerable consternation when it was discovered that Mr Ramshaw had made a bid for freedom and was creating havoc in the stores. This was nothing to the storm of protest that arose amongst the office cleaners during and after the time of the polecat. Polecats are members of the weasel family and have a particularly pungent odour; it was unfortunate that Tony had seen fit to accommodate the star of the programme in the Features office, for its memory lingered on for weeks after its triumph on television. A ferret was also required at the same time and, as the animal in question was of a particularly nervous and jumpy disposition, Winwood stoically kept it on her desk so that it would get used to human company for long periods and the sudden movements of people coming and going.

Winwood had said from the outset that she didn't mind handling birds and mammals and getting bitten, scratched, clawed and pecked as long as she never had to look after a snake. This was no problem until the day that Frances Pitt arrived for her programme accompanied by various cardboard boxes and cages. It was the custom to make use of a radio studio on the morning of each edition of *Look* to discuss the form of the programme, view the film on a projector, and rehearse any 'business' with animals. On this occasion, Miss Pitt started chattering away whilst undoing her boxes and in one swift movement opened a lid, fished around the bottom and swung round handing the contents to Winwood. In this case it was a fine grass snake which Winwood suddenly found herself holding, and much to her surprise discovered that it was not really too bad after all. In fact, it cured her fear of handling snakes, for, as others with such a phobia have found, a snake is dry and rather pleasant to hold and not a bit slithery or slimy. However, unlike the harmless grass snake, two other pets belonging to

A polecat attacking an adder – a scene from another Heinz Sielmann film shown on Look.

Frances Pitt were capable of inflicting quite serious lacerations in their impish way. They were household pets: Mac, the blue and yellow macaw, and Jolly, the raven – veterans of some 26 and 35 years respectively. Miss Pitt was considerate enough to warn Winwood of the hazards of handling these birds and mainly looked after them herself during rehearsals. However when the live transmission began in the evening, Winwood discovered to her horror that the birds were still in their boxes and Frances Pitt was signalling to her to get them out – a feat she nevertheless managed to perform just off screen without losing a single finger.

Technically, Frances Pitt's film was shaky, scrappy and full of jump-cuts – a term used for a join between two shots of the same subject at approximately the same angle and filmed with the same lens. Nevertheless, some of the subject material – of albino moles and squirrels and the old raven – was of such interest, especially when commented on by the grand old lady, that Tony judged that the programme would be popular. With Frances Pitt in charge he was quite right but her film highlighted the fact that we were beginning to reach the bottom of the barrel when it came to available amateur wildlife material.

If *Look* was to return to the screen regularly – and there was plenty of support from the public and the television planners alike for this – the Bristol staff would have to search further and further afield for film, in some cases compiling programmes on a given subject from several different sources; and they would also have to start shooting and

RIGHT
Whilst West Region developed wildlife television programmes in the early 1950s, David Attenborough was also making a success of his Zoo Quest *series. Here he is seen on the first of these, making wildlife recordings at night in Sierra Leone.*

producing films themselves. This was something particularly dear to Tony Soper's heart for he had always had aspirations as a wildlife director-cameraman. The opportunities for this so far, however, were decidedly limited. *Look* was to return to the screen in October – just four months' time – and as Brandon was being drawn more and more towards drama, Tony would virtually be responsible for producing the next series.

There was another incentive for the Bristol group to begin originating their own wildlife films as soon as possible: a young features producer in London had been making a tremendous impact with an occasional series made overseas – initially in association with personnel from London Zoo on collecting trips. The first series of six programmes had been made in Sierra Leone and had begun just before Christmas 1954 – a few weeks before Sielmann's woodpecker film. The second series, filmed in British Guiana (now Guyana), was on the air when *Look* began its first run the following September.

The success of *Zoo Quest*, as each series was called, undoubtedly lay mainly in the hands of its producer, David Attenborough, who, at short notice, had stood in for the original presenter, Jack Lester, who became ill almost immediately after the first series began. Lester, Curator of Reptiles at London Zoo, should have appeared in the studio each week, linking the film sequences which Attenborough had obtained on location with his cameraman, Charles Lagus. Attenborough's gift as a storyteller was plainly evident; together with his boyish charm and enthusiasm, it meant that he would retain the dual role of presenter and producer for many successful series to come. The first *Zoo Quests* were presented from the studio but, as the original animal-collecting idea for zoos became less important, the programmes became complete expedition films. In each case, however, the talents of the film cameraman involved, Charles Lagus (in later series, Geoff Mulligan), contributed greatly to viewers' involvement with the adventure on the screen. Many *Zoo Quest* programmes did not have a particularly high content of animal behaviour, for this was not always possible in the three months available for each expedition, but the simple professionalism with which they were filmed squeezed out the maximum value from the animal footage that was obtained.

On the other hand, *Look* programmes, although rich in wildlife film creamed out of thousands of feet of amateur material, lacked some of the elements vital to the success of *Zoo Quest*. Quite often, the camerawork was so erratic that editing the material involved more ingenuity than creativity and it was difficult to build effective sequences rather than a succession of short incidents. The exceptions, of course, were the films made by Heinz Sielmann. *Woodpeckers* had been only 18 minutes long but was a masterpiece of film craft which set the standard for years to come. Yet, although they made excellent contributions to *Look*, Sielmann's films had not been produced for television, for they were exceptionally well-made educational films distributed by the Bavarian Institut für Film und Bild.

So, as the first series of *Look* closed in June 1956, our little team at Bristol was beginning to sense its future direction: if Sielmann's film craft was to be emulated we should at the same time tailor our work to suit the medium as Attenborough had done. Nobody was too sure what the future programmes would look like but they would probably resemble neither Sielmann's films nor *Zoo Quest*, although much could be learnt from both. Such aspirations were tempered by the reality of the situation, however, which was that Tony had in his possession a clockwork Bolex camera with some telephoto lenses, a tripod, a small amount of money for film and two weeks' free time in which to do some filming before returning to prepare for the next series. He was also short of assistance on location but this problem was quickly solved for, as soon as the idea was mooted that Tony would go to Fair Isle to film fulmars for a *Look* programme, written by James Fisher, Winwood and I volunteered to give up two weeks' holiday for the privilege of being in the team.

Charles Lagus filming driver ants.

We drove in Tony's car to Aberdeen and caught the boat bound for Lerwick in Shetland. The next stage of the journey was a road trip south

over the windswept and treeless main island to a little hotel close to a
jetty from which departed the weekly boat to Fair Isle. *The Good
Shepherd* was the islanders' only regular link with the main island and,
each week, it came over to pick up supplies and ornithologists visiting
the bird observatory. It was about the size of a lifeboat and a similar
function was required of it for negotiating a notorious tide race which
soon became evident as we rocked and rolled southwards so violently
that lashing oneself on board was the only guarantee of a safe passage.

After five exhausting hours we chugged into the little bay at Fair Isle
where we were welcomed on the jetty by Ken Williamson, the warden at
the observatory. With us on board were several bird-watchers, some of
whom were already beginning to worry about the return trip. But lured
on by promises of hot soup our little party extricated its trappings from
the boat and walked shakily up the hillside track towards the little
cluster of huts which was the observatory headquarters. Fair Isle is one
of the most important of a chain of bird observatories around Britain's
coasts with facilities for trapping and ringing migrant birds. The ringing
activities would normally be at peaks during the spring and autumn
migrations but there were always a few stragglers to be found in the
summer and, of course, thousands of seabirds to be seen breeding on
the cliffs.

After settling into our clean but austere rooms, we walked further up
the track which led towards the interior of the island before branching
off towards the cliffs on our left. Sheep grazed on the grassy slopes
which led down towards the sea and which sometimes ended precipi-
tately and sometimes curved steeply towards gullies from which came
the echoing sounds of breakers and seabirds' cries. On the crevices and

ledges immediately below us, and performing an aerial ballet in front of
us, were the birds that we had come to film. To the uninitiated, fulmars
– or fulmar petrels to give them their full name – have a superficial
resemblance to gulls for they are white and grey in colour. Observed
closely, their distinctive tubular nostrils are enough to identify them as
petrels but a few moments spent watching them flying show clearly that
these masters of the air currents are not gulls. For the most part, they
scarcely move their rather narrow, rigid-looking wings, using instead
the updrafts and eddies from the cliff-face to soar and weave with
effortless grace. Mesmerised by them, we would stand at the cliff edge
following a single bird as it soared upwards until it was almost level,
then banked down to the sea before rising again in a figure of eight flight
path. Occasionally there would be a few flaps made almost apologetically before a new updraft was found to slope soar once more. Then one
would make an ungainly landing near its mate on a tiny ledge and
hobble closer, uttering loud guttural cackling noises. Other pairs close
by would echo their calls and soon the chorus would swell for a few
seconds before dying away to mix with the sound of restless surf drifting
up from the rocks below.

Winwood reminded us that there was a job to be done and we
clambered down the grassy slopes cautiously, looking for nest sites
which were accessible. Most of the fulmars were nesting on tiny ledges
far below the cliff-tops but, occasionally, one of the grassy tongues that
rolled down towards the gullies allowed us to approach quite close to,

49

ABOVE
*Tony Soper filming
flight shots of
fulmars.*

ABOVE RIGHT
*The author
recording fulmars
at their nest . . .
situated 30 feet
below.*

and almost level, with a pair of fulmars who had not been able to obtain
one of the choicest sites. Eventually Tony found a site to his satisfaction,
where he could get close-ups with his longest telephoto lens. Winwood
and I helped him erect the rudimentary framework for his hide – four
uprights and some cross pieces that made the shape of an upright box
3½ feet square and 5 feet high and secured in position by guy ropes.
Then the canvas cover was put on, the bottom weighted by large stones
to prevent it flapping in the wind. Usually such a hide is erected in
stages over a longer period of time so that nesting birds have time to get
used to the unusual sight, but here in the middle of a seabird colony –
and with the hide many feet from the next – there was no danger of the
birds deserting.

Early next morning, Tony was installed in his hide and I set off far
along the cliff-top to start my work which was to record various seabird
noises, in particular the sound of the fulmars. I had a greater choice of
nest site than Tony for, provided I could manoeuvre myself into a
position to conceal the microphone near a nest, I did not have to find a
safe place for a hide as the microphone cable could be run up to the cliff-
top where I could listen to everything on headphones in comfort. At first
nothing seemed more simple and more attractive than the task that had
been set me, but I soon discovered that Fair Isle was extremely windy
and it was difficult to find a position for the microphone which, even
with the help of a wind shield, did not produce more rumbles and
bumps than bird sounds. Nevertheless, the hours spent in waiting for
the wind to drop were amply rewarded by the constant activity on the
cliffs of the thousands of seabirds – fulmars, kittiwakes, guillemots,
puffins – and even the occasional seal in the sea below.

LEFT
*The fulmar petrel –
subject of Tony
Soper's first full-
length film for
Look.*

The idyllic days on Fair Isle passed all too quickly and we returned to
Bristol to find West Region even more vibrant with life and excitement
than usual. Some of this was due to high level staff moves which were to
be of momentous importance to the development of West Region over
the next two years. Firstly, the Controller of West Region, Gerald

A fulmar chick.

Beadle, was appointed Director of Television Broadcasting; then, the controller's job was filled by Frank Gillard, until then Assistant Director of Sound Broadcasting in London. He had been one of the best known voices on radio during the war, and, although I had not yet met him, to most of my colleagues he was an old friend returning home. He had joined the BBC as a producer at Bristol in 1941 but had then served as a war correspondent until he became West Regional Programme director in 1945, a post later re-designated head of West Regional Programmes and now held by Desmond Hawkins.

One of the key words which summed up the philosophy of the region at the time was 'ambidexterity' and this principle was never better illustrated than by the activities of the little group of people in the Features office which was already becoming a sort of self-styled natural history unit. The principle spread also to the cutting room, for one of the inevitable consequences of the pressures of work in Features was that I should become more and more involved in the selection and arrangement of programme material as well as the actual editing. All this activity created the need for an extra cutting room but as there was no official establishment for this or funds for equipment, these had to be acquired by various, often unofficial means. Undoubtedly, the growth at this time owed much to the efforts of the Assistant Head of Programmes, Pat Beech, who had special responsibilities for television and liked nothing better than a challenge, especially when it involved creating something out of nothing. Various bits of equipment were begged or borrowed from London and surreptiously loaded on to the back of vehicles travelling down to Bristol and what was known as 'the philosophy of nails' was stretched to the limit. This term referred to a system that the region had long employed for obtaining minor items of equipment, requests for which would normally have become bogged down for months in the bureaucracy of various finance and develop-

ment committee meetings in London. Gerald Daly, who had been the senior engineer on the site for many years, had discovered that minor items purchased during any given year and listed under the heading 'nails' never attracted any attention or caused any questions to be asked from those whose job it was to examine the books.

As autumn 1956 – and the new season of *Look* programmes – approached, there were further complications, for Peter Scott was due to travel to Australia for the Olympic Games just after the series began. As President of the International Yacht Racing Union, he had been invited to preside over the International Jury at Melbourne and it soon became clear that he would only be able to introduce the first few editions of *Look* in October; most of the other programmes would have to be introduced by either James Fisher or Maxwell Knight who regularly introduced the radio series *Birds in Britain* and *The Naturalist* respectively.

The fact that Peter Scott was going to Australia suggested an attractive idea – that he should at the same time film a wildlife expedition there to be shown in a future *Look* series. There was no one who would have loved to have joined him as director-cameraman more than Tony but this was quite impossible as he was now in charge of the series. There was one other cameraman in the BBC who was known to have the talents, experience and temperament for wildlife filming of the expedition type and this was Charles Lagus who had, so far, filmed three *Zoo Quest* series with David Attenborough. Fortunately the Australian idea attracted Charles, especially as he would be working largely as director-cameraman, and shooting in colour – not so much an investment for future colour television as a means of providing Peter with a source of new lecture material.

The first edition of the new *Look* series began impressively with a film on whales which was gathered from various sources – a compilation which set the style for a number of later editions. There was a good deal of press coverage for the return of the series and a short article by Tony Soper in the *Radio Times* referred to various future film projects including our recent Fair Isle expedition. The second programme was notable for a brave experiment in attempting to interest viewers in invertebrate pond life. Moreover, the illustrations were not film but *live* pictures shown through the aid of a special micro-projector which John Clegg of Haslemere Museum demonstrated in the studio. By today's micro- and macro-film standards the pictures were primitive but they had a novel fascination although, unfortunately, this did not prove strong enough to sustain an entire half-hour programme; it was a good idea, ahead of its time and the necessary technology. Thereafter the

Frank Gillard, appointed Controller, West Region, from July 1956.

series ran a more predictable course with film contributions from Scotland by Walter Higham, from Kenya by Mervyn Cowie (photographed by Bernard Kunicki) and from Spain by the famous bird photographer – Eric Hosking – turning to cinephotography for a while. By the beginning of 1957, a few more ambitious ventures were appearing in the series, including the programme on bird flight, which involved more complicated film compilation, and a film about Konrad Lorenz.

While the series was on the air the film taken by Scott and Lagus began to flood in from Australia, New Zealand and New Guinea. Because of Peter's interest in wildfowl a high proportion of it was of Australasian ducks and geese but they were unfamiliar species to Europeans and some scenes, such as the flocks of magpie geese on the ricefields of the Northern Territories, were quite spectacular. Charles Lagus' camerawork was excellent but it was supported by some very good film by Peter himself, using his 50 feet load Kodak Magazine. This was the camera which Kodak had presented to him in 1949 after an expedition to the North West Territories of Canada and he had used it to shoot film for all his subsequent expeditions. In fact, the Kodak camera had provided the material for Peter's first wildlife television programmes in 1954 and, without this, *Look* might never have been launched.

Almost at the same time as Peter returned from Australia, quite revolutionary things were happening in BBC television. The changes which took place in early 1957 are startlingly apparent when two editions of *Radio Times* for February 8 and 15 are compared. The television schedules, which until then had been modestly tucked away at the end of the radio programmes, suddenly appeared *first* under each day's lists. Further examination of the television programme pages showed that the old barren patch in the early evening when there were no programmes for an hour (known popularly as the toddler's truce) had disappeared. A continuous schedule of programmes was listed, including a brand new magazine called *Tonight*, introduced by Cliff Michelmore. There was more than a little reflected glory in that for Bristol since Cliff had strong West Region associations and had for two years regularly introduced the West Regional magazine, *Westward Ho!*

In spite of these major developments, I and several of my colleagues actually watched very little television at the time since we were working each evening until at least nine o'clock in order to keep the West Region film programmes on the air. For the same reason I was not as conscious as I should have been of the changes in British television as ITV spread throughout the country. For, although the BBC could still claim in late 1956 that they had 39 out of the top 40 television programmes in total audience terms, the truth was that out of the one-quarter of homes equipped to receive ITV signals, 62 per cent were switched to the commercial channel.

Nevertheless, as the pattern of television changed, and the industry began to expand at a remarkable rate, there were opportunities which West Region was determined not to miss. *Look* had proved that natural history had a regular place in the television schedules at peak viewing time. Moreover, others were beginning to take an interest in the potential of the Bristol group: the Head of Children's Programmes,

*Peter Scott, with
the Kodak camera
he used to shoot
his lecture films –
material for many
of the early
television
programmes from
Bristol.*

Owen Reed, who until recently had been a drama producer at Bristol, had indicated a requirement for a 15-minute fortnightly nature programme; Schools Television, too, were interested in the potential of the library of nature film being accumulated at Bristol. Unfortunately, with only a small staff available, it was not possible to satisfy these extra demands, especially as the radio output had been already increased by a quarterly magazine, *Naturalists Notebook*, and Ludwig Koch's *Bird Song of the Month*.

No doubt Controller, West Region, Frank Gillard, and Head of West Region Programmes, Desmond Hawkins, spent many hours discussing the tactics of how to increase the output of natural history programmes and acquire the necessary staff – a delicate matter if the ambidexterity of the region was to be maintained as television began to grow in importance. As Desmond had virtually created this type of output from Bristol it was only fitting that he should be the one to write the formal proposal to establish the BBC Natural History Unit at Bristol. In retrospect, it appears almost symbolic that it was just one week before *Radio Times* and the BBC television schedules had their new look that Desmond put pen to paper, setting out the proposals for a Unit which in a few years would achieve international status, and eventually become a BBC department in its own right.

Chapter 5

The Unit is born

During the spring of 1957, there was no doubt that something special was afoot. Although officially still part of the West Region Film Unit, I was to all intents and purposes a part of the little Features group which was already a self-styled 'natural history unit' and this title came to be used more and more as rumours grew that there were moves to make it official. There was little time to speculate on what might be going on behind the scenes; we were busier than ever with *Look* still on the air, all the Australasian material to edit for what was to be *Faraway Look* in the summer, new radio programmes and Tony's plans to mount a Euro-vision outside broadcast with James Fisher from Hagenbeck' Zoo in Hamburg. The original radio series. *The Naturalist* and *Birds in Britain*, kept going with support from the new trainee producer, Patrick Drom-goole (later to move into drama production and eventually become Assistant Managing Director of Harlech Television). With so much to do we scarcely noticed the comings and goings of people from high places in London; occasionally a VIP – or a group of them – accompanied by Frank Gillard or Desmond Hawkins would appear briefly at the cutting room door and then move on to another part of the Bristol complex talking earnestly all the while. Within a couple of months the Director of Sound Broadcasting, the Director of Television Broadcasting, the Chair-man and the Board of Governors and the Director-General himself were all at Bristol. Something was afoot all right, we said knowingly to each other over the canteen coffee.

   As we discovered much later, things had been moving amazingly swiftly, all prompted by the paper Desmond Hawkins had drafted early in the year which had been placed before Controller Frank Gillard on February 8. It was in the form of a BBC memorandum and was entitled 'BBC Natural History Unit' – possibly the first official BBC document to bear that title. And it was clear from the first paragraph that not only did Desmond believe that the regional ambidexterity, which he had done so much to encourage, should continue as a working principle in the new Unit, but also that this should be the key to the Unit's financing. The memo began: 'The West Region's self-styled Natural History Unit is, I imagine, the most developed example of ambidexterity in the Corpor-ation. For that reason it needs to have its future development based soundly on a joint appraisal of its function and its needs, made by the Sound and Television Services in concert. It is the concern, not of one service or the other, but of both . . .'.

   Desmond then sketched in the history of the small Bristol group,

pointing out that it consisted of some radio features production staff, one production assistant paid for by television, and an assistant film editor belonging to the West Region Film Unit. It was argued that because of the group's impressive output, professionals in the Natural History field were now looking to Bristol as the main centre for programmes, network planners also looked there for wildlife material, and staff with an aptitude in the subject were looking to West Region as a place to work. Nevertheless, shortage of staff meant that Bristol was neither able to accept Third Programme invitations, nor those from Schools and Children's Television – not to mention the desirability of following up the success of *Look* with a year-round weekly adult television programme. Desmond then went on to propose that: '. . . West Region should be formally recognised as having the responsibility of serving the Corporation's primary needs in Natural History for sound and vision programmes. For this purpose a Natural History Unit should be established and designated accordingly as the first point of reference for planning requirements and for outside contributors; and it should be self-sufficient for all its needs under the headings (a) Producer effort, (b) Library, (c) Film Editing'.

The proposed minimum establishment of eight included the absorption of four old posts; new posts included a 'Research Librarian/ Recorded Programme Assistant'. This person was to be in charge of the film library and also be responsible for making new wildlife sound recordings. At the time the BBC's Wildlife Sound Collection, based on the original work of Ludwig Koch, was housed in London in Sound Archives and the responsibility for its upkeep and the recording of new sounds rested with Eric Simms. Desmond's proposals required careful

James Fisher, Tony Soper and Herr Wegener – superintendent at Hagenbeck's Zoo. The Eurovision broadcast from Hamburg in 1957 set the style for later series such as News from the Zoos *and* World Zoos.

handling for, if the BBC Natural History Unit was to be based in Bristol it was clearly sensible that it should have the Wildlife Sound Collection under its wing. The question was, would London object? Desmond tactfully wrote: 'If DSB (Director of Sound Broadcasting) has misgivings about the future of Eric Simms, he is a strong candidate'.

A week later Frank Gillard sent Desmond's report to the Directors of Sound and Television Broadcasting so that they would have adequate time to consider it carefully before their forthcoming visit to Bristol, for they were already due to discuss the organisation and functions of West Region in broad terms. Apparently, the meeting went well but there were reassurances to be made – which Frank Gillard did in a memorandum a few days later. He was at pains to point out that the region was not asking for *exclusive* rights in the sphere of natural history. 'Indeed', he wrote, 'we should be glad, as a sort of headquarters, to take account, on our planning, of nature contributions from elsewhere which Central Controllers for Regional Programme Heads might be accepting or initiating and we should be glad to put our resources (eg Film Library) at the disposal of producers working on such programmes, as indeed we are doing at present. We see ourselves as the main single provider of nature programmes, and if it is desired, as the friendly co-ordinator of kindred contributions supplied from other centres'. Gillard went on to stress the urgency of the request for increased staff resources and gave support to Desmond Hawkins' plea for the setting up in the near future of a BBC Field Unit for nature film-making with a cameraman of its own.

It was Gerald Beadle who took the initiative in London; not only was the major part of the proposed development at Bristol in his television directorate but, as a recent Controller of West Region, he would obviously take a close personal interest in the matter. In a memorandum to his Deputy, Cecil McGivern, there was no doubt about his support for the general proposals in West Region: 'We believe that this is the most sensible and imaginative organisation yet put forward by a region which looks forward to an ambidextrous future, and might well be taken as a model, with of course local variations for other regions . . .'. And of Desmond's paper on the Natural History Unit: 'The other document concerning the Nature Unit is in fact a proposal of the kind I have always been rather keen on. It is a proposal for a regional devolution of a kind which is quite new in the Corporation's history, but it is the same kind of devolution which we are proposing for Midland Region in connection with Agriculture'.

There then followed a suggestion which, if it had been taken up, might have resulted in not only the Natural History Unit, but also the Television Service, developing in a different way over the next 20 years. Gerald Beadle wrote: '. . . the proposal doesn't necessarily mean an increase of staff but transfer from elsewhere. For example, an obvious candidate for Head of Unit is David Attenborough, whose post could be transferred from London Talks Department to West Region'.

At about this time – in early March 1957 – the rumour that this notion was being entertained actually reached down as far as the Bristol cutting room. There were mixed feelings about it. On the one hand David Attenborough was seen as the competitor, for his *Zoo Quest* series was enormously successful and full of natural history material. He had been filming these overseas programmes with a staff cameraman for three years so he had a distinct edge on West Region which had only recently managed to organise its first foreign television expedition by getting Charles Lagus attached to Peter Scott's trip to Australia – which was primarily for the Olympic Games.

On the other hand, in spite of this slight feeling of envy, we all admired Attenborough the presenter and the professionalism of his programmes. Within the London Talks Department he also produced *Travellers' Tales* – a series which had parallels with *Look* and which eventually led to the formation of the Travel and Exploration Unit in London. Occasionally some of the film subjects of *Travellers' Tales* contained enough wildlife material to be just as eligible for *Look* and there was always uneasiness at Bristol when this occurred. So on reflection, everyone agreed that there were many advantages in Attenborough moving to Bristol and the rumour continued, although in fact the idea had been abandoned very soon after it had first been set down on paper. Less than two weeks after Gerald Beadle had written his note, Cecil McGivern called David Attenborough in for an interview and put the idea about Bristol to him. Although grateful for the compliment, David declined the offer and hoped that he would not be pressed. He explained that although he had a zoology background, his interests were wide and he was happy in the London Talks Department. Moreover, he had bought his house in Richmond only three years ago, his children were entered for schools in London and he preferred to remain close to his parents' home.

It could be said that, although the putative Natural History Unit lost a leader during that talk between McGivern and Attenborough on March 18, we gained a special friend in London. For although others in positions of responsibility voiced concern about the developments in West Region, Attenborough always maintained that clashes and ill-feeling could be avoided by keeping up a friendly dialogue between Talks Department and the Natural History Unit, pooling information and reaching agreement on areas of responsibility. It is significant that in a number of documents written about the new Unit at Bristol over the next few months it was mentioned that, while '. . . the Unit will be the main source of supply of naturalist and wildlife subjects to the various programme services in sound and vision . . .' and '. . . it is particularly important that producers handling closely-allied subject matter should maintain detailed liaison with the Natural History Unit in order to avoid overlapping . . .'. It was also noted that '. . . close contact with the projects initiated by Mr Attenborough should be maintained'.

In spite of the disappointment over Attenborough's response to the idea of moving to West Region, the plan for the new Unit was moving ahead fast. It was enthusiastically supported by the Regional Advisory Council, and then unanimously approved by the BBC Board of Management in London, after Gillard and Hawkins had been called to make a detailed presentation of the proposal. The final endorsement came from the Board of Governors, who came to Bristol for a special meeting in April 1957. After that it was only necessary to obtain formal approval to increase the television establishment to the level proposed, although in an effort to move things along it was agreed to leave the delicate matter of the Research Librarian/Recorded Programme Assistant in abeyance as this might involve a transfer from London within the Sound Directorate.

At the end of June, an article by Desmond Hawkins in the West Region edition of *Radio Times* heralded the new five-minute television news for the west each night as well as 'new developments in wildlife programmes for which the region has a bigger task than ever before, as we are now responsible for the BBC's general output in this sphere of both sound and television'. A statement had also been issued to the national press but we were not conscious of any special interest in us at the time. In fact the only incident that made any impression on me was opening an internal envelope one day and finding a slip which simply stated that I was being transferred from assistant film editor, West Region Film Unit, to assistant film editor, Natural History Unit, with effect from July 8 1957. A few others in the Features office received similar notifications, and so by means of a handful of documents, and still without a leader, the BBC Natural History Unit formally but quietly came into existence.

At first the notification of transfer annoyed me intensely. The new establishment included a film editor and, as for over a year I had taken on full responsibility for all the wildlife film editing (although only paid as an assistant), and was receiving both screen and *Radio Times* credits, I felt that the BBC should at least have the decency to place me in an acting capacity as film editor. A discussion with Tony revealed that some staff had been administratively 'parked' in the most junior positions until the most senior post was filled. It was assumed that I would wish to compete for one of the junior production posts and I had been temporarily placed as the new Unit assistant film editor so that my old West Region Film Unit job could be filled behind me, as there was an urgent need for extra help in the general cutting room.

Finding suitable candidates for the senior production post proved difficult. Desmond Hawkins, wishing to build on the already consider- able respect which naturalists and zoologists had for Bristol programmes, hoped to find someone with an academic background or considerable experience as a naturalist as well as first-hand knowledge of sound and television broadcasting. Not surprisingly there were no obvious candidates now that Attenborough was out of the running and so a number of experienced general producers, who had worked in radio as well as in television, were invited to attend the board to be held on September 13. Shortly afterwards, it was announced that Nicholas Crocker, currently the West Region Television Outside Broadcast Producer, would take charge of the new Unit for a limited time as senior producer – news which I, for one, received with enthusiasm, for I had long respected his production talents.

Faraway Look was transmitted in the summer of 1957 and was the first television series to go on the air from the new Unit. The next series of *Look* was to be during the winter, and this allowed time for Nicky to take over the series so that Tony, with his ambitions as producer-cameraman, could develop other programmes: Tony had already set up some editions such as the fulmar programme, which was now ready for editing, another Heinz Sielmann film on wildlife in a summer meadow and a remarkable French film on the breeding of emperor penguins, filmed by Jean Prevost. We had already scored a success with Bill Sladen's film of Adelie penguins but Prevost's film of emperors was some of the most remarkable, and dramatic, material I had ever had on my editing desk. Emperors are the largest of all the penguins and able to endure the most appalling Antarctic conditions. After the egg is laid, the male takes it over, carrying it on top of his feet and under a fold of skin on his belly. There it is warmed for nearly two months while the male fasts and the female travels out to sea to feed. She returns in time to take over the chick and feed it and the young emperors are then reared during the Antarctic winter months. During incubation the males occasionally have to weather terrible blizzards and to prevent heat losses in temperatures which may drop to −40°C they form huge huddles, packing their bodies closely together against the wind. In winter, the juveniles adopt a similar strategy against the cold and Prevost had managed to film all of this outstandingly well.

Emperor penguins and their chicks. Filmed by Jean Prevost, an account of their breeding cycle during the Antarctic winter was a highlight of the second series of Look.

On the emperor penguin film, I was able to take a great deal of trouble with the effects sound track as the expedition had brought back excellent sound recordings, not only of the general colony but also close-ups of the various calls of adults and chicks. The latter were particularly important as the chicks had most engaging little chirruping calls which accompanied their head-bobbing displays, and these required careful synchronisation on 'laid' tracks; if two birds were calling simultaneously this necessitated the laying of two tracks – one for each bird. Gone were the old days when a studio manager merely played in an atmosphere disc on transmission; we were now taking much more trouble in producing an authentic sound track with 'beak synch' for we now had a primitive dubbing suite at Bristol where we could mix together carefully prepared tracks before transmission. In fact, the emperor penguin sound track was the most advanced on *Look* to date and the film certainly deserved all the time we could spend on it. The programme started the new series in January 1958 and *Radio Times* gave us a front cover picture as well as a full page article by Peter Scott about the new series. Penguins, in general, appeal to most people but emperor penguin chicks, with their attractive black-and-white head markings, must be the most enchanting of all; this, combined with the drama of the terrible conditions they face during their development, provided an unbeatable formula and the day after the programme's transmission viewers were talking in terms of another success equal to that of Sielmann's *Woodpeckers*.

It was, therefore, ironic that this programme, which provided so many opportunities for improved presentation, and for which at long last we had sufficient time and facilities, should be one of the last I was to edit; just prior to transmission I had been appointed to the post of television production assistant – a job which involved not only all manner of location work, preparation of scripts, supervision of record-ings and so on, but also actually directing sequences and often complete programmes. I soon found myself involved in all of these tasks but, because no film editor was immediately available to take my old place, I also had to spend some of the time editing my own work.

To begin with, at least, I was not sent out on my own; whether it was a reconnaissance for filming, or directing a film sequence or viewing film

for consideration for *Look*, it was always in the company of Nicky Crocker. Most cameramen sent their film to Bristol for viewing or brought it along themselves, but for one particular contributor there was never any doubt that we would ourselves go to the film-maker. That special person was Field Marshal Viscount Alanbrooke, a keen ornithologist and amateur wildlife cameraman who had been one of Peter Scott's original guests in 1954 before the *Look* series began. A year later he had appeared in *Look* itself with some of his bird studies of hobbies, bitterns and phalaropes, and more recently he had taken part in an ornithological expedition to the Coto Doñana in Spain with Eric Hosking and Guy Mountfort. So Nicky and I set off for Viscount Alanbrooke's home at Hartley Wintney in Hampshire where we had been invited for lunch. A very entertaining lunch it was, too, for – when gently encouraged – Alanbrooke recalled some of his more lively incidents in his long wartime association with Winston Churchill. It seemed incredible that this gentle, sincere man with his great passion for ornithology should also have been Chief of the Imperial General Staff and one of the principal architects of victory in the Second World War. His film of birds was technically good – all shot on a steady tripod, well

Field Marshal Viscount Alanbrooke in the Coto Doñana; an accomplished amateur cine-photographer, his bird studies featured in some early editions of Look.

exposed, in sharp focus and every scene running to a good length – but suffered from the same limitations as other well-known bird cine-photographers of the time: nearly all the material was at the nest, there was little establishing material of the habitat and no story. The film was no more than a succession of moving stills – delightful for ornithologists but of limited appeal to the general public. I was saddened by the realisation that this was probably the last time we would be able to use this great man's work, for his interest was in *taking* film of birds rather than *making* films about birds.

Shortly after visiting Viscount Alanbrooke, Nicky and I went to see another great amateur naturalist – H. G. Hurrell – who lived on the edge of Dartmoor near South Brent in Devon. 'HG', as he was popularly known, had also made a great impression in an early edition of *Look*, particularly with his film of pine martens. HG's filming was somewhat erratic – it was all hand-held camera work, and the shots tended to be rather short – but he had grasped one of the fundamentals of film-making, namely that it is largely about *action*. In fact, his films were so full of action of every conceivable kind that they left you breathless and it was to try to slow them down a little that Nicky took me down to Devon with the film crew for some additional shooting. It was all straightforward material – establishing shots of the house at the edge of the moor, the narrow Devon lanes and fields nearby, and HG looking after his various animals – but as uncomplicated as these short se-quences were, they brought home to me how long it takes to shoot just a few minutes of film: moving all the camera equipment from one position to another, lining up the shots, waiting for the rain to stop or the sun to come out, waiting for an aeroplane to pass overhead when it was a sound take – it all takes time.

Such days spent filming with Nicky were an excellent start to a useful apprenticeship and it was with a reasonable degree of confidence, therefore, that I gladly accepted his offer to direct the next filming session for *Look* a few weeks later. The main content of the programme was a film about pond life photographed by Alan Faulkner-Taylor. I had already edited this to the required 25 minutes, which left 4½ minutes for front and end titles and Peter's introductory sequences. Nicky agreed to my suggestion of filming Peter Scott's introduction on location and set me the task of finding a suitable photogenic pond or small lake, within an hour's drive of Bristol and Slimbridge.

I eventually found that Braydon Pond, near Malmesbury, seemed ideal for the purposes; it had a minor road, bearing little traffic, running down one side and on the other a track ran to some isolated houses from which there was easy access to a suitable filming spot by the waterside. One of the first things I had been told by Nicky was that a most important part of any reconnaissance is finding the best route for the film vehicles in order to get as close as possible to the actual filming point; no film crew want to carry their gear a foot further than absolutely necessary, and who can blame them, for they have plenty of heavy work to do during the course of a day, constantly moving from one camera position to another. It is still an important consideration today when film equipment is comparatively light and compact, but in the 1950s it was crucial to the crew's morale as the principal equipment used then

ABOVE
'Moorgate' – home
of the Devon
naturalist and film-
maker, H. G.
Hurrell.

ABOVE LEFT
'HG' preparing food
for one of his
animals.

was an extraordinary affair called the Camiflex double camera. It required two men to lift it and set it upon its tripod and once there it had all the appearance of an oversized sewing machine case. The case was in fact the blimp surrounding the camera and it was necessary to prevent the noise during filming from reaching the microphone; inside the case was not only the 35 mm film camera but alongside it a magnetic sound 'camera' which recorded on 35 mm sprocketed magnetic film. The two were mechanically linked and each could be loaded with just 400 feet of film which ran for 10 minutes 40 seconds at 25 frames per second. The recordist merely had a small control box linking his microphones with the camera. Nowadays the recordist carries his own tape-recorder, a pulse being recorded on a separate track on the ¼ inch tape for electronic synchronisation with the camera.

On the day of filming the weather was fine, much to my relief, but incredibly cold for it was very early in the year. A heavy frost lay on the ground and as we approached the lake I could see that most of it was frozen over. This was a setback for I had decided that I would ask Peter to disturb the water at the end of his introductory piece and the camera would then pan to the ripples so that I could dissolve into Alan Faulkner-Taylor's film. Well, that was a lesson for a start – always have an alternative plan. I conferred with Peter and he started working out his introduction. Meanwhile my old friends, George Shears and Billie Greenhalgh, were manoeuvring the huge camera into its opening position, while Howard Smith, the recordist, was making the connections to sound mixer, camera and microphone. Peter rehearsed his opening words a few times to me until we were both satisfied and I then signalled to the crew that we were ready to start. The previous evening I had gone through everything in my mind down to the exact words of command to the crew so that it would appear that I was confident and knew exactly what I was doing.

'Stand-by, Peter, please. Stand-by camera and sound', I intoned with a dry throat. Everyone settled down. 'Turn over', I said. George said 'Mark it!' and I held the clapper board up in front of Peter, repeating what was written on it, '*Look*, A Tale of Two Worlds, Scene 1, Take 1', and swinging the arm down to produce a loud clap before scuttling back to my position near the camera. I waited for George to tell me that the camera was up to speed. Seconds went by, nothing happened. Being over-anxious, and supposing that I had missed George's signal, I said loudly, 'Cue Peter!'

'No, no – wait!', George shouted irritably, 'Wait for speed'. A little deflated, and my false confidence already destroyed, I did as I was told. Several more seconds went by and I crept back behind the camera next to George.

'Bloody thing's hardly turning', he said. 'Look', pointing to the dial at the back of the camera which registered the frame speed. George stopped the camera, and little Billie pulled up a camera box so that he could step on to it and open up the cover. George, Billie and Howard all peered inside, fingering various components and shaking their heads sadly. The cover was snapped back down again.

'We'll have another try', said George. I went through the opening routine again, Peter waiting patiently for his cue. George watched the camera dial intently, I watched George's grim face for a flicker of hope and Peter watched me – still waiting for his cue. Peter was being extremely patient but, in spite of being well wrapped up in a sheepskin coat I guessed that he would be freezing in this static position by the lakeside. But the cue did not come and it seemed like minutes before George finally flicked the camera switch.

'Could we not send for another camera?', I asked in desperation, although I knew there was not another sound camera at Bristol and the winter days were too short to allow time for one to be sent from London. Nobody bothered to answer anyway, but I suspect the question made George even more determined to solve the problem on site. The batteries had been tested and had proved to be fully charged so the real problem it seemed was the very low temperature. The Camiflex, with its two linked mechanical systems took a lot of driving and, according to George, it was underpowered by its batteries at the best of times. At temperatures below freezing it appeared hardly to function at all. Nevertheless, having decided that the problem was linked to the low temperature, George was able to think of a solution.

'See those cottages over there?', he asked Billie, pointing to smoke emanating from a chimney behind some trees. 'Right, well see if you can get two rubber hot water bottles filled up and loaned to us for an hour or two, and get them back as fast as you can'. While Billie went on his quest the rest of us flapped our arms and stamped our feet to restore circulation and a flask of hot coffee did wonders to mellow the atmosphere which had rapidly degenerated during the last ten minutes. The hot water bottles eventually arrived, their precious heat protected between Billie's sweater and dufflecoat. George carefully packed them alongside the camera and closed down the blimp cover.

'Right, we'll wait for a few moments and see what happens', George said with detectable rising spirits. In spite of the discomfort, I suspected that George, the old professional, was quite enjoying cracking the problem. He turned on the camera and, as the speed started climbing, quickly turned it off again.

'We'd better look slippy while it's warm inside there', he said. 'Let's get into position'. Peter returned to his place at the edge of the frozen lake and we went through our routine again, the clapper board now indicating 'Scene 1, Take 3' – though not a word had been spoken yet by Peter. Again we waited for a sign from George that the camera had at last reached filming speed of 25 frames per second.

'It's going up', he whispered, 'but it's bloody slow'. At last he gave the sign and I dropped my arm so that Peter could see it out of the corner of his eye, before turning to camera:

'Two worlds. The world above the surface and the world below the surface of a pond.' I breathed a silent sigh of relief. At last it was going to plan. I only hoped that, with all the interruptions, Peter had remembered what he had planned to say.

'Not necessarily this pond by which I am standing on this very cold March morn . . .'.

'Film's run out!' squawked Billie from behind the camera. We all turned towards him and for a second poor Billie received all the hate we felt at that moment for the Camiflex and the designers of the double camera. So much film had been used in attempting to run the camera up to speed that we had wasted a complete 400 foot roll and we had still not achieved a single complete take.

Hurriedly the cover was lifted up and the magazine of exposed film taken off while Howard, with frozen fingers, laced up a new roll of magnetic recording stock. Meanwhile, the hot water bottles were removed and placed under the director's and presenter's clothing, ostensibly in the interest of heat conservation. Until now the light conditions had at least been tolerable, if somewhat flat, but I noticed that the sky was suddenly becoming heavier and I began to fear that unless the camera started working properly quite soon we would have a different sort of trouble – weather trouble.

At last the camera was reloaded, the hot water bottles replaced, and we were back to the starting positions again. 'Turn over', I said once more, after checking that Peter was ready. We succeeded in getting the clapper board on for 'Scene 1, Take 4' and waited for George's sign. We waited for a minute; the hot water bottles must have lost some of their heat. The camera speed was rising but at a frustratingly slow rate. A second minute went by but I was not yet too concerned as Peter's introduction was quite short and I knew that this time there must be seven or eight minutes left on the roll. At last George gave the thumbs up and I cued Peter.

'Two worlds. The world below the surface and the one . . . I'm terribly sorry, Chris . . . I'm afraid . . .'.

'KEEP ROLLING!', I shouted. 'Don't worry, Peter, just wait a few seconds and start again when you're ready . . . and keep on again and again if necessary'.

This time Peter's introduction was word perfect and I derived a great deal of satisfaction from saying 'Cut!' – the first time I had actually been permitted to reach that moment. There was a brief period in which everyone bathed in a glow of satisfaction from having achieved even a 30-second shot in the face of such adversity before we moved the camera position for the two other brief scenes to be filmed. Although there was half a roll of film left, George decided not to risk anything but a complete magazine and while the film was being changed the hot water bottles were refilled at the house nearby. Our task was finished an hour later and we hurried back to the nearest hotel for something to revive and warm spirit and body.

Within a few days I was editing the shots we had taken at Braydon Pond into Alan Faulkner-Taylor's film. The Unit now had a brand-new cutting room – installed in some prefabricated huts at the rear of one of the houses in Whiteladies Road which had previously belonged to the Ministry of Works. The new film editor from London had been appointed but as yet only an assistant was available to help run the cutting room. That in itself was a new luxury. It seemed so strange that after 18 exhausting months continually working against the clock and with inadequate equipment, I should be leaving the comparative comfort of that new cutting room as soon as it was created; and for what? Sitting at the editing table, one can so easily visualise what other directors and cameramen *should* have filmed, but didn't; the resulting frustrations, linked with a creative drive, make the goal of being totally responsible for one's own films quite irresistible. But one short experience with the crew had shown that in spite of the best laid plans, what actually gets on to celluloid is a compromise, and even that is achieved only with the united talents and efforts of many others. As I cut in the last sound shot of Peter Scott to complete *Look* No 44, *A Tale of Two Worlds*, I wondered, just for a few seconds, if it had been worth all the effort, the discomfort and the frustration. Yet already I was looking ahead to new opportunities; and with only a little effort I convinced myself that they couldn't all be as bad as that day at Braydon Pond.

Chapter 6

Out of Doors indoors

In the spring of 1958, there was a sudden increase in staff; the establishment for some of these new members of the Unit had been created in the previous year but, for a variety of administrative reasons, the posts could not be filled until April. I was particularly glad to greet Paul Khan, the new film editor, for his arrival would now permit me to move full-time into production. To my surprise, a few days later a second film editor, John Merritt, arrived. It had not been difficult to make the case for a second Unit cutting room on the grounds of our rapidly increasing output which included programmes featuring Armand and Michaela Denis and Hans and Lotte Hass. Both series had previously been presented from London but as Bristol was now supposed to have the main responsibility for Natural History there was a good argument – which Desmond Hawkins and his colleagues were not slow in presenting – for handing over both Denis and Hass.

The two series were regarded as being embarrassingly expensive and the Hass series in particular required considerable post-production support. So London was relieved of – and the Unit gratefully acquired – two Natural History man and wife teams who proved to be of great service to Bristol during the next few years. Not only were their programmes extremely popular but they could be conveniently included in the annual tally of programmes provided for the network by West Region at a time when the Natural History Unit was not yet capable of originating a high output of its own. Also, as every BBC Unit or Departmental Head will testify, there is nothing like having a successful ongoing series amongst your annual offers to the controllers to help maintain a healthy establishment.

Some of us were uneasy about the Unit being responsible for the Denis series, however. It was undeniable that Armand and Michaela were very popular with viewers and their films frequently contained excellent animal behaviour footage from Africa; but their personality double act – with alternating commentary – together with their 'pets in the warden's garden' routine made some of us uneasy. Moreover, the inference that they were always directly involved with the action on the screen was not, in our opinion, in line with the standards we were trying to set. In fact Armand produced his programmes in probably the only way possible for his prolific output: he used a team of cameramen to provide a steady flow of material. One or two of them would spend several weeks filming wildlife in a given area and then they would be joined by Armand and Michaela who would set up camp in order that

Armand and Michaela Denis with an Egyptian vulture fledgling.

Hans and Lotte Hass preparing for a dive in the Diving to Adventure series.

'continuity' shots of them could be filmed, as well as suitable material of Michaela with tame or orphaned animals – as likely as not by courtesy of the family of a local warden. On one occasion, some lion cubs reared by the late Joy Adamson were borrowed for an hour or two and filmed. Much later, the programme containing this sequence – which, incidentally, bore no reference to Joy Adamson – was on the air just at the time that Joy was attempting to interest various London publishing houses in the manuscript of *Born Free*. It is reported that, on seeing the programme, she was not amused.

Armand, a dynamic and charming Belgian giant, ran a very efficient film operation; he was a real professional who had been in the business since the 1930s when he had been a pioneer documentary film-maker in Africa. Above all, he knew that what had maximum appeal with the viewers was good animal pictures, although he later exploited his and Michaela's own personality appeal in programmes that were basically travelogues in the Far East. He nearly always knew when he had just got enough material for a programme and never wasted a sequence which could be used elsewhere. He put his programmes together in Africa and sent them back, accompanied by a pre-recorded narration, to an editor in London for post-production. Consequently, there was little that Nicky Crocker could do in an editorial sense on behalf of the Unit apart from accept or reject each programme, or at best make suggestions for minor amendments to the mixing of the sound track. In later series, the working arrangements were modified slightly and it was possible to suggest changes at an earlier stage in the production.

Dealing with Hans Hass was quite a different matter. His series were financed partly by Süddeutsche Rundfunk in Stuttgart and partly by the BBC, but some of the BBC contribution was in the form of post-production facilities for editing and sound recording. So Hans, and for some of the time Lotte too, came to England for several weeks at a time to take over a complete cutting room. Since the second Hass series was ready for editing in the spring of 1958 it fell to the newly-arrived Paul Khan to take on this work under the production supervision of Tony Soper. Paul was the ideal person to work with Hans for he treated his cutting room with the same care and reverence as a priest has for his church and he was meticulous in handling film – qualities which the Austrian film-maker respected. The tall, handsome Hans Hass was a scientist as well so it was not surprising that his film was supported by good documentation.

There were also new arrivals in the Natural History Unit offices upstairs. At last the problems over the transfer of the Natural History Sound Library from London had been resolved and the new post of Field Research and Library Assistant could be filled. The holder of the new post, also responsible for the film library, was Roger Perry – a dark, handsome and aristocratic young man who dressed immaculately and immediately sent ripples of heart flutter throughout the Bristol secretarial ranks. His close companion was another new recruit, Jeffery Boswall, also a young bachelor in his 20s. After it was discovered that he had a club in London, regularly met with friends in the House, and was an active officer in the Territorial Army, Jeffery acquired an image which has never changed. He has been one of the great characters – and one of the most distinguished members – of the Natural History Unit ever since.

Jeffery's first task was to take over the main responsibility for radio production of *The Naturalist* and *Birds in Britain*. He did this with immense enthusiasm and, in the case of *Birds in Britain*, with special pleasure for he was already a respected ornithologist and had joined the Unit after having worked for several years on the staff of the Royal Society for the Protection of Birds. Furthermore, he had himself broadcast on the series four years previously when he had given a talk on bird migration over the North Sea. Jeffery was fascinated by facts and figures, and this, together with his flair for organising events down to the last detail, proved to be an influential factor in much of his output. He had never been one to let a good anniversary pass by if there was a programme in it and he certainly began his career in the way he meant to go on. When Jeffery took over *The Naturalist* from Winwood Reade she was currently producing a group of four programmes on animal senses presented by W. E. Swinton. Jeffery immediately extended the series and produced a fifth programme on *Evolution of Senses* on the occasion of the centenary of the publication of Darwin's *Origin of Species*. Within a few months he had applied his organisational talents to his new profession with such success that he was able to broadcast live an edition of *The Naturalist* about bird migration from five radio-

Roger Perry (right) with recording engineer, Bob Wade, setting up the 36-inch parabolic reflector for recording bird song.

Jeffery Boswall, who took over the production of many of the Unit's radio programmes in 1958.

linked observatories at Fair Isle, Seahouses in Northumberland, Dungeness in Kent, St Agnes in the Isles of Scilly and Skokholm Island off Pembrokeshire.

Jeffery's arrival meant that Winwood could devote most of her time to television, in particular to the new monthly programme for children, *Out of Doors*. This was introduced by Bruce Campbell, and had various guest speakers and film items made specially for the programme, but the third edition, in June 1958, included an outside broadcast from Paignton Harbour in South Devon; what happened that day did not in itself make exceptional television but a long chain of events resulted from it which are directly linked to some of the output of the Natural History Unit today.

The story begins in 1957 when a Torquay school biology teacher, Leslie Jackman, wrote to the BBC at Bristol suggesting that there was television material to be found in the small public aquarium that he and a fellow teacher, David Halfhide, ran during the summer months at Paignton Harbour. At first the suggestion was received with little enthusiasm and a brief acknowledgement was sent, for it was not unusual to get letters from anybody who ran a museum or an exhibition on a commercial basis; television coverage, however small, would invariably lead to a sharp rise in future attendances. But Jackman's motives were not commercial. His little aquarium was entirely devoted to marine life from the rockpools and waters of Torbay, and as long as he could make a small profit to compensate for the many hours of effort it took to set it up each summer, he was quite happy. Thousands of holidaymakers came to Torbay each year and Leslie Jackman knew that most of them were oblivious of the abundance of marine life in the pools, amongst the seaweed or in the sand under their feet. But the aquarium had shown that the general public could find such things as netted dog whelks and prawns totally fascinating; and many admired the beauty of the common sea anemones in utter disbelief that such apparently exotic creatures lived on the rocks at well frequented beaches. Jackman used to watch his visitors filing round the tiny aquarium and he listened to their comments; if he could achieve this response on a small scale, how much more effective would it not be with millions of viewers on television?

So Leslie Jackman wrote to BBC Bristol once more. This time the letter reached the desk of Patrick Beech, Assistant Head of West Region Programmes. Plans were then well advanced for the new monthly children's television series so perhaps Jackman's offer had some relevance there, after all; Pat therefore invited him up to Bristol to discuss the matter with Winwood Reade. When the day came they saw him together and listened attentively whilst he recounted how the aquarium had come to be set up, what it had on display and how the public reacted to the exhibits. At first Pat and Winwood were not convinced that the static nature of the aquarium, with its emphasis on invertebrates, would have much to offer television. But then Jackman began to warm to his subject; perhaps he had learnt a few tricks as a schoolteacher about catching the attention of unenthusiastic children or perhaps he merely got carried away with his own enthusiasm. Making the point that there was in fact plenty of action amongst the occupants of his tanks he began to describe the amusing antics of cuttlefish at feeding time. He got out of his chair and began to prance around the room, imitating the movements of the cuttlefish, shooting out his arms to demonstrate the rapidity of the tentacles as the prey was caught. Pat and Winwood glanced at each other; perhaps there was more to this man after all?

A few weeks later, Winwood asked me if I would go down to Paignton with her to direct a number of short film sequences using the facilities available in Jackman's aquarium. Leslie took a close interest in all these problems for he, too, was beginning to see the possibilities of cine-photography in the aquarium and two days' experimental filming sparked off a long and successful programme-making relationship between us. But Winwood had additional plans for Leslie in her June *Out of Doors*. She had been so impressed with his enthusiastic and down-to-earth approach to his subject that she decided to take a chance and give him an item in her programme. We now had a permanent control room in the studio as well as our own telecine so the MCR could be sent to Paignton to provide a linked outside broadcast. The Paignton aquarium was too cramped, and the subject material too tiny, for the cumbersome electronic cameras to be used inside but there was another attractive possibility. Leslie obtained much of the marine life for his aquarium from local fishing boats, the skippers of which kept an eye out for suitable specimens each spring when Leslie was restocking his tanks.

It was therefore arranged that David Beauley – one of the skippers who had been especially helpful to Leslie – would bring in his boat at the time of transmission so that Leslie could then examine the catch and talk about it in front of the cameras. With no previous practice in television it was a brave thing for Leslie to undertake but, with the experienced Gwynne Vevers back in the studio to provide a reliable anchor, the programme went remarkably well. Amongst the Jackman family there was perhaps no greater admirer of the day's events than the youngest member of all – seven-year-old Rodger. As we shall see later, his first confrontation with television was to have a special significance.

There was do doubt that Leslie Jackman had potential as a presenter of natural history material for children; however, it was clear, too, that he could not do endless programmes on seashore life alone. He had a good general biological knowledge but what could his role be in the series? The answer was suggested by the evidence of his talents as a

Leslie Jackman with mounted specimens sent in by young viewers. His regular Club Room item in Out of Doors *was popular in the late 1950s.*

model maker and display artist which could be seen in the aquarium. These talents were also used professionally at school where he made special exhibits as teaching aids and encouraged his pupils to make their own drawings, paintings and collections of natural history items. Now it has to be said that Leslie was never the most well-organised, or the tidiest, person I have ever known and perhaps it was this, combined with his wide naturalist's interests, that suggested the part he was to play in *Out of Doors*. Leslie became the monthly host in the programme's Club Room – the set for which was a wooden shed of the type that some people have at the bottom of their garden. Inside were numerous shelves and an old table and the place was full of oddments and specimens of the kind that Leslie usually had cluttered around him at home. There were also materials which he needed to demonstrate things that the children could make or do themselves – cardboard, scissors, glue, bottles of various sizes, string, sealing wax, plaster of Paris and so on.

The Club Room became a regular item from January 1959 onwards and in due course badges were struck for children who wished to become members. To enrol they had to try to make for themselves whatever Leslie had demonstrated that particular month; this might be a series of bark rubbings, a collection of leaves, a plaster cast of a wild animal's footprint or some other exhibit which was then entered into a competition. In no time at all, Winwood and I were surrounded by a sea of drawings, paintings, blocks of plaster and cards on which were pasted leaves or bits of twigs, and we soon needed extra secretarial effort to send off the little circular metal badges (on which appeared a badger and the name of the programme) to all the competitors. In most cases, the competition called for a considerable amount of effort on the part of each child, including a visit to the countryside to collect materials, followed by at least an evening's work in drawing or mounting objects on card. Nevertheless, entries came in by the hundred and by the end of 1960 there were over 11,000 club members. In 1961 the numbers more than doubled.

Although I prepared most of the film items for *Out of Doors*, the fact that it was only a monthly programme meant that there was sufficient time also for me to search for, and supervise the editing of *Look* film sequences as well as assist in the studio production of these programmes. It was getting increasingly difficult to find new complete films for the series, although we did have the benefit of an arrangement with the Royal Society for the Protection of Birds Film Unit which provided at least one new programme each year. Nevertheless, there were short films available from foreign sources from time to time and these often provided the starting point for a film compilation on a given subject when we draw additional film from our steadily growing film library. For example, a film made by Harry Frith on the breeding cycle of the Australian mallee fowl suggested a programme about eggs and methods of incubation, for the mallee fowl has one of the most unusual patterns of behaviour in this respect. The hen lays her eggs in the bottom of a huge hole in the sandy ground which she and her mate have excavated to a depth of 3 feet and which may be 10 feet in diameter. This is filled with a mixture of sand and vegetation and built up to 2 or 3 feet above

ground level. The rotting vegetation warms up the eggs and, in combination with heat from the sun, this is enough for successful incubation without contact from the parents' bodies. The nest is closely supervised, however, and each day one of the parent birds – usually the male – uncovers the nest, tests the inside temperature with its tongue, and if this is not close to 92°F, corrects it by either scratching away or adding quantities of sand. Eventually the chicks hatch out underground and must burrow their way up to the surface. Harry Frith's film, although somewhat scrappily shot and edited, illustrated all the salient points of the story and provided a memorable finale to a richly varied programme.

On another occasion we compiled a programme about cephalapods – the group of molluscs that includes the octopus, squid, cuttlefish and nautilus. In this case, Nicky decided it would be amusing and instructive to have a live animal in the studio and as Winwood was producing *Out of Doors* it was now *my* job to provide and look after such a specimen. We had only a small glass-sided tank available so the animal would have to be either a cuttlefish or an octopus of modest size and my mind immediately went to Leslie Jackman and his aquarium at Paignton. Fortunately, the programme was to be tele-recorded on a Saturday evening in mid-October – just the time of the year when Leslie was usually closing down his aquarium and returning stock to the sea – so I telephoned to see if he could help.

'It just so happens that I've got two octopuses left', said Les. 'As a matter of fact, I was going to put them back in the sea this weekend'.

'Terrific', I replied, 'How can we get them here for the programme?'

As the years went by, many Look *programmes became complete films – the presentation by Peter Scott often being done at a relevant location. This picture shows Edwin Cohen being interviewed at his home in Hampshire for a* Look *programme based on the RSPB film of garden birds.*

'As it's a Saturday, I could drive them up to save you any trouble', Les answered, as helpful as ever. 'Besides, it would be nice to see a rehearsal in the studio. Do you mind if I bring Paul up, too?' (Paul, aged 11, was the elder of Leslie's two sons.)

So it was arranged that Oscar and Oswald, as they were eventually nicknamed, should be transported in large polythene bags, containing well-oxygenated seawater, and driven up to Bristol in Les' little Austin van. On the day of the recording I made sure that their temporary home in the studio was ready by mid-morning and then anxiously awaited Les' arrival. He was somewhat late.

'Everything all right?' I enquired anxiously, peering into the bottom of one of the transparent bags to see if there were any signs of movement.

'Oh yes, *he's* all right', said Les pointing to one of them; 'damn thing escaped, and we had to stop and get it back in the bag'. I looked disbelievingly at the bag which was tightly fastened at the top.

'Escaped from *that?*' I asked. 'Didn't you have it tied?'

'Of course – but they're real escape artists you know. An octopus can

A male mallee fowl tests the temperature of its incubation mound. Harry Frith's film of the behaviour of this Australian bird featured in one of the first compilation programmes in Look, *on incubation.*

squeeze its body through the smallest gaps and crevices imaginable. I don't know how they do it, but they do!' Les went on to tell me that he had been driving happily up the A38 between Bridgwater and High-bridge when Paul, sitting next to him, tapped him on the leg and pointed up to his shoulder. Les glanced round to see a tentacle waving about somewhere in the vicinity of Paul's right ear. The octopus had somehow escaped from the bag, which itself was in a container in the back of the van, scrambled forward and had just reached the back of the passenger seat and Paul's shoulder. Les hurriedly pulled into the verge and returned the octopus to its travelling bag before it could perform any more Houdini-type tricks. On the basis of this story, we decided that additional precautions would have to be taken with the octopuses' new home so, until studio rehearsals began, a lid was found for the top of the aquarium on top of which we placed a very heavy weight. Les stayed for a while after lunch to see the first rehearsal and then announced he would be leaving for Devon.

'What about the two octopuses?', I asked anxiously. 'Can't you wait until the recording is over this evening?'

'Oh, sorry, didn't you understand? We've closed the aquarium down so we don't need them anymore. But all you have to do is return them to the sea. The Bristol Channel isn't far away, is it?' I thought Les was being distinctly off-hand about the matter; maybe he was used to handling octopuses – I wasn't.

'Well, er, I suppose Clevedon isn't too far away – I'm sure I'll manage', I heard myself saying, but I wasn't at all confident. I never minded handling reptiles and snakes, spiders and most other types of invertebrates, but an octopus was another matter. For some peculiar reason I found the thought of handling Oscar and Oswald particularly revolting and I had already seen the difficulty Les had had in extricating them from the bag before putting them into the tank.

The guest speaker in the programme was Brian Boycott, a lecturer in Zoology at University College, London and, as the recording went smoothly, the studio crew had all packed up and gone home by nine o'clock. Nicky took Peter and Brian off for a drink and I stayed behind in the studio to collect the caption cards and scripts. I then drove my car to the nearest parking place by the studio so that I would have the least distance to carry my unusual load. I picked up the polythene bag, syphoned some water into it, and approached Oscar who was huddled in one corner of the tank, a couple of tentacles languidly stretched upwards. I looked at him, wondering how lively he was going to be and Oscar looked balefully at me, all the more unnerving because his eyes seemed so human. I dipped a hand cautiously into the tank just above Oscar and he sent a couple of tentacles snaking upwards to explore it. Gaining confidence I made a sudden thrust downwards, mindful of what I had been told about an octopus having a powerful beak; for a second I had the impression that I was grappling with something like an animated blancmange and then there was a convulsion and Oscar shot over to the opposite side of the tank to join Oswald. I looked around the deserted studio to see if there was any implement available that was going to be of use in getting either octopus under control, but I could see none. The octopus and I had continued to stare at each other for several minutes when the studio door suddenly swung open and Brian Boycott came in.

'Hello', he said, 'Having problems? I thought you might need a hand with them. What are you going to do with them?'

I replied that I was going to put them back in the sea – at Clevedon. Brian said that as he was staying overnight at a Bristol hotel, he had time to kill and would willingly accompany me. He suggested that as there were now two of us we should remove most of the water from the aquarium and then take it, octopuses included, to the boot of my car where we could cover the aquarium to prevent too much water sloshing around. Greatly relieved, I accepted the offer and we set off for Clevedon.

I had never actually been to Clevedon before so I didn't know quite what to expect. All I knew was that it had a seafront and a pier and was about 18 miles away. We drove slowly and steadily and arrived in the outskirts of the town after about 30 minutes. The place was dimly lit and deserted and there was no sign of the sea. We drove on through the centre of the town and eventually arrived on a road bordered by a wall. I stopped the car and looked over into blackness. There was no sound of seawash but I could smell the sea and I guessed that the tide was out.

'There's a pier here somewhere, I'm sure', I said to Brian on returning to the car. 'That may get us close enough to the water.' After another quarter of a mile we found the entrance to the pier – barred by huge, iron padlocked gates.

'I've an idea', said Brian, brightening. 'It's probably quite rocky round here, which means that there may be large tide pools quite close by. We can leave the octopuses in a pool and the tide will come in and soon they'll be able to swim off.' This seemed like an excellent idea so we retraced our route to the sea wall where we eventually found a slipway down to the beach. I had a torch in the car and a few minutes' exploration revealed that there were indeed some rocks nearby and a suitable pool for the octopuses. To my relief, Brian offered to remove Oscar and Oswald from the tank which he did expertly, accompanied by a loud rasping noise as their suckers were disengaged from the sides of the glass. Then, tentacles thrashing and winding around Brian's wrist and arm, the outraged Oscar and Oswald were carried to their temporary home for the night.

That, as far as I was concerned, was the last that I would ever see of the octopuses. However, a few days later a colleague who lived in Clevedon brought in a copy of his local paper – the *Clevedon Mercury*. On one page was a photograph of two dead octopuses on the beach being inspected by an elderly resident of Clevedon. The caption explained that octopuses were only rarely found so far up the Bristol Channel and their appearance was probably due to unusually mild weather. Of course, it may have been a coincidence. But the octopuses were found not far from the rock pool to which we had committed them; and those in the newspaper did look uncommonly like Oscar and Oswald. I suddenly found a soft spot for them, if indeed they were the subject of the photograph. It made me very conscious of the need, and the responsibility one had, for taking good care of all animal subjects before, during and *after* their performances in front of camera.

A small crowd gathered at the slipway near Clevedon Pier on Monday morning. Focus of attention were 16 tentacles, belonging to a pair of octopi washed ashore that morning.

Small boys watched round-eyed as Mr. C. Costello, of the U.D.C. seafront staff, pointed out the rows of suction cups along each "arm" of the octopi. "Plenty of these in the Mediterranean" said Mr. Costello, as he cleared away the "visitors." Then he glanced at the not-so-blue waters of the Channel. "It's very rare for one to be seen here" he commented.

The octopi—the larger of which measured about 18 inches across— were dead when a passer-by first saw them.

Photo: Peter Baker, Clevedon

Nicky directed the octopus programme as it was a fairly complicated show with an unusual number of short film sequences and a certain amount of 'business' in the studio. I was already being allowed to direct the more straightforward editions of *Look* as these were ideal programmes for a young director to gain experience in the studio. There was always a small set, usually only two artists were involved and there was only a limited amount of action possible; also the total transmitted time from the studio was never more than about eight minutes per programme and this was usually divided into three or four sequences so that the director did not have to sustain his concentration for long and, if necessary, could regain his composure during the long film sequence. I had stood behind Nicky many times while he was directing so I knew the procedures well when the time came for my debut in the control gallery. I was confident that I should now enjoy my first piece of studio direction.

The script for a *Look* programme was a simple affair: the title of the programme, the artists involved, a timetable of rehearsals and transmission, and the technical requirements – which were usually much the same week after week. Then followed the list of camera shots required, interspersed with the telecine film sequences and any instructions for superimposing title and credit captions. Although the camera moves were plotted in advance, such as 'Camera 2 : MS, track with Peter Scott as he moves from easel to introduce guest', the actual words were never written down as these were only finalised during the morning of transmission at a pre-camera rehearsal when the film sequences were also viewed in their final form. For my first programme, the guest was Leslie Brown, a distinguished ornithologist from East Africa who had made an exciting film about greater and lesser flamingos on Lakes Nakuru and Naivasha.

By the end of the morning everything had gone according to plan; as producer, Nicky had been in charge of the pre-camera rehearsal; Peter's introduction as well as the points to be discussed with Leslie Brown had been carefully worked out. After lunch I was still eagerly looking forward with innocent confidence to my first session in the director's chair – right up to the moment that I sat down and cleared my throat behind the talkback microphone. And then, I realised I wasn't confident at all – I was petrified. Looking back more than 20 years, the memory of those first few excruciating hours in the studio gallery still leaves me feeling uncomfortable – even embarrassed. How could such a simple piece of television appear to be so difficult?

'Right, chaps, stand-by in the studio, please, and we'll try a run-through. Opening mid-shot of Peter on Camera 1, captions on 2 and 3. Standby telecine.' The first directions come tumbling out almost automatically because I had rehearsed them silently so often. The telecine buzzes to signify the operator is waiting for a cue. There is a lot of shuffling around on the studio floor: cameras are being manoeuvred into position, a caption is sloping to the right and someone is trying to prop it into a horizontal position, Peter is checking a last minute point with Leslie Brown. As I am so anxious and nervous, I become irritated by the apparent slowness in getting the things organised. It's Ray Kite, the floor manager who's the first to know.

'Get Peter into his starting position for heaven's sake', I spit into the talkback microphone. Only Ray and the studio crew who are on headphones can hear this outburst. I look down through the gallery window to the studio below and can see Ray moving over towards Peter and having a word. The microphone is some distance away and I can't hear what is being said but Peter obligingly gets up and moves to his starting position. At last we seem ready to start. I breathe a sigh of relief and give a round of 'stand-by' to all and sundry for good measure. The telecine buzzes acknowledgement again.

Lesser flamingos on Lake Nakuru, East Africa. Leslie Brown's film of these birds was shown on Look.

'Cue telecine.' I wait for the leader to run through, 6, 5, 4, and silently count myself through the remaining black leader – '3 – 2' and say, 'Cue grams'. The first film shot appears on the telecine monitor and the signature tune starts.

'Superimpose 2 – hold it, fade 2; superimpose 3 – hold – fade 3; superimpose – damn, sorry we should have changed caption on 2. Right now then; fade Camera 2. Oh, hell the film's run out. Right, coming to Camera 1, oh yes, I see we're on Camera 1. Right, cue Scott. Sorry I should have cued him earlier. Now start to pull back Camera 1 as he walks . . . what's that? You can't? Why the hell not?'

Camera 1 is quietly trying to tell me that his tracking line isn't correct. Meanwhile Peter has taken the opportunity to go back over his opening lines and the senior television engineer is talking to the boom operator about the danger of getting the microphone in shot. In just a few seconds, chaos has set in. I suddenly realise that it is very hot and my palms are sticky. I collect my thoughts and realise that I've got to slow down and tackle the problems one by one. I help Camera 1 to line up the end of his tracking shot so that he can get his assistant to chalk suitable marks on the studio floor. Nicky, standing patiently behind me, bends over and murmurs: 'You could ask telecine to re-wind while this is going on so that you can try the opening routine again'. I accept his advice gratefully and by the time I have the opening shots rehearsed I see the '10' on the telecine monitor which shows they are ready to run again.

We go through the opening of the programme again and this time it works reasonably well but I am still too late cueing Peter and there is an uncomfortable pause between the end of the music and his first words. I'm beginning to relax a little when Nicky's assistant, Pamela, on my left, armed with script and stopwatches, tells me that we're already over-running this section of the programme by 1½ minutes. I realise that I've been so busy trying to get the cameras right that I haven't really been listening to what Peter and Leslie Brown have been saying. Nicky comes to the rescue again and whispers: 'You'd better tell them to cut the bit about making a raft – that can be mentioned when we see it on film'. I pass this on to Peter and Leslie via Ray Kite and we try the first interview bit again. This time we reach the end more or less on time and Peter says, 'Well, Leslie, let us now see the two species of flamingo which you have been filming'. Peter and Leslie look expectantly at their monitors but I've been caught out through not having given telecine a standby.

'I need a longer cue than that from Peter', I say indignantly to Ray. Peter knows this only too well, but I hadn't arranged an exact cue before the camera rehearsal. Peter suggests a line which we write down on the script and the first long film sequence is begun. Peter and Leslie rehearse their narration and meanwhile I go over the shots for the next brief studio sequence with the cameramen. When we reach it, every-thing goes fairly smoothly and I regain some confidence.

The second long film sequence gives me time to get ready for the brief closing routine. There are a couple of quick camera moves involved and I'm determined to learn from earlier mistakes and rehearse each shot separately and slowly. It nearly works but I'm too slow cueing the captions again and the film runs out before I can get the last credit on. It's Nicky's, and I think he will probably wish to dissociate himself from the programme anyway, but at the end, Nicky says it's not going badly for a first run. We all go down on to the studio floor for an inquest and to see how to cut some time out of the studio sequences.

After a tea break I rehearse the opening and closing routines alone before taking it from the top once again. The cues into film are still not very smooth but there are only two technical hitches this time and the programme comes out only 20 seconds overlength. Peter says he can manage to take that out of the opening and we all break for a meal. The programme is not going out live but is being tele-recorded up the line to London at 8:00 pm precisely. As far as I am concerned it is just as bad as being live, as I'm told the lines are open for only 30 minutes and there will be no second chance.

I'm far too worried to eat much and as Peter and Leslie have gone to the dressing room for make-up I return early to the gallery to make sure I know every part of the script – including all the notes scrawled during rehearsals. The camera crew return and line up the cameras and the senior television engineer is talking up the line to the tele-recording manager who is receiving the test signal from us. He confirms we will be going ahead on the hour. I look down and see Peter and Leslie arrive from make-up and go down to join them and wish them well. I should be saying something comforting to Leslie but I need it more than he does. It's now only two minutes to go and I've checked that everyone is ready. Telecine have shown me their '10' but it has been removed so that it doesn't burn onto the tube until I give the standby. Suddenly, we hear that London are ready. I give the standby and the reassuring buzz comes from telecine. The engineer, still on the telephone, says we can go and I cue telecine. Nicky puts a hand on my shoulder and says: 'Good luck, dear boy' and we're off.

There is now a completely different atmosphere in the gallery and, I suspect, on the studio floor. Everyone has wound themselves up for the show. I'm tense and I feel sick but there's a sense of excitement about too – the adrenalin is running. I hear myself giving the cues almost automatically; but everyone knows what to do and the studio seems to be running under its own momentum. Thirty minutes seem to fly by like ten, and I find myself relaying Pamela's information that there is time in hand and Peter can 'spread' a little on his closing remarks. I become so absorbed in how he does this that I nearly miss the last line when it comes and I'm late cueing grams. But the closing music comes up before the words are out of my mouth and I realise that not just the grams operator, but everybody from Peter to the camera dolly pusher, has been giving just that little bit extra – to get the new boy through his first show. At the end I tell everyone to wait while the senior television engineer checks with London that the tele-recording machine has been running to the end. After a few moments he gives the thumbs up and I say to everyone through the studio loudspeaker so that they all can hear: 'Thanks a lot everyone – see you in the bar later'. I reckon I owe them all that drink.

* * *

Under Nicky's patient tutelage, I soon got used to sitting in 'the hot seat' and gradually the feeling that I was helpless behind a runaway machine changed to that of a reasonably competent driver taking a lorry load of TNT over a bumpy road. The experience on those comparatively simple *Look* programmes was invaluable because, within a few months, I was to take over the production of several editions of the more complex *Out of Doors*, just at the time that Leslie Jackman's Club Room item was being introduced. Initially this was because Winwood was now preparing a special series of four television programmes on animal senses entitled *Their World* with Dr W. E. Swinton, but I subsequently acted as relief producer on several occasions during the next two years when Winwood was on holidays or absent through illness.

One of the most frequent guests on *Out of Doors* was the Devon naturalist, H. G. Hurrell. I always enjoyed driving down to Devon to see him at his home on the edge of Dartmoor for on each occasion one could be sure that he would have a new observation to tell you about or an interesting injured bird or mammal that he had somehow acquired.

It was therefore not difficult to find a suitable magazine item among HG's latest discoveries or endeavours. Sometimes the item would be built around some film that HG had himself taken, at other times I would take the film crew with me and shoot a sequence of HG observing or discovering something seasonal in the local lanes and fields. On one occasion early in the year, we filmed an item about the habits of moles and I asked HG if he could arrange to bring a live mole up to the studio. I wanted to see if we could demonstrate how quickly a mole can burrow underground once it had been brought to the surface. HG thought that if the mole was placed on a boxful of earth in the studio it would disappear in about two seconds flat but I had an idea that might provide an unusual shot. I asked Des Chinn, the designer at Bristol, to construct a wooden glass-fronted case about two feet high, three feet across and only two inches between the wooden back and the glass front. This was then packed as hard as possible with carefully sieved earth. The theory was that the mole, when placed at the surface, would quickly burrow downwards but because it was confined within such a narrow vertical section the camera – and viewers – would be able to follow its passage underground.

The scene in Studio A during an edition of Out of Doors. *Leslie Jackman, and guest, are in the Club Room set, left foreground.*

HG duly arrived with his mole on transmission day and kept it securely in his hand or in its travelling box during rehearsals. We did not attempt our underground demonstration too soon for fear that the mole

might not be easily retrieved or that it might not perform so well a second time once it had discovered that burrowing did not, in this instance, lead it away from the bright lights. So we decided to take our courage in our hands and save the special demonstration for the live transmission. When the moment arrived, HG placed the mole on top of the earth and for just a second or so it paused while we all held our breath in the gallery. Then, in a flash, it put its nose downwards and with amazing speed carved out a curved downward burrow which showed up beautifully in front of the camera. It was all over in under 10 seconds, but it was a convincing demonstration and a similar technique has often been used since then for filming underground creatures.

Having animals in the studio – especially wild ones on a live show – is always a risky business but, provided the animals are not terrified by the lights and cameras, their unpredictability often adds to the interest and improves the programme. Human beings are another matter, however, and on one or two occasions live editions of *Out of Doors* faltered badly when a guest either dried up completely or took it into his head to do something that had not been rehearsed. In one instance, a minor change in posture due to nervousness on the part of a guest was nearly enough to get us reported in the *Daily Mirror*.

The incident occurred during an item about red deer in Scotland. This consisted of a film sequence and an interview between Bruce Campbell and a Scottish expert on deer. Bruce had suggested that the gentleman should appear in his kilt and to this the guest willingly agreed. All went perfectly well during rehearsals and on transmission the item began as planned. Bruce did his introduction to Camera 2 and we cut to Camera 1 as the guest entered. Unfortunately as they both sat down in low chairs, the guest assumed an extremely awkward sitting position with his legs sprawled wide. Now, it's possible that the chair was uncomfortably low and it's also possible that Camera 1 on transmission was operating at a lower lens height than on rehearsals; whatever the factors involved the net result was that the unfortunate Scotsman provided the answer to that age-old question that, from time immemorial, seems to have worried everyone south of the border, namely what is worn – if anything – under the kilt. At least a large number of viewers *thought* they had discovered the answer.

In fact, I scarcely saw anything of this notable event for, after cueing the vision mixer to cut to the wide shot on Camera 1, I had glanced down at my script at the critical moment. I immediately heard a strangled cry from the senior television engineer on my right and looked up at the transmission monitor to see what was wrong. Our poor guest was certainly arranged in an undignified posture and there did seem to be a rather suggestive pale patch within the dark recesses of the upper legs and inner kilt. It cannot have taken more than a second to instruct the vision mixer to cut back to a mid-shot of Bruce in order that Camera 1 could then change lenses and give me a matching mid-shot of the guest – *above* his waist; nevertheless, the damage had been done – as I was to discover within a few seconds of the end-title music fading and the programme coming off the air. The telephone in the gallery rang, the secretary listened for a few moments and then passed the receiver to me, an odd smile on her face. It was a Scotsman complaining bitterly about the insult that his fellow countryman had just had to suffer at my hands on the screen. I had no sooner placated him and assured him that no harm was meant when the telephone rang again, this time from our own Publicity Office.

'What on earth have you been doing on *Out of Doors* today?', the female voice enquired.

'Why?', I asked, innocently.

'Well, the *Daily Mirror* has just rung us to say that they've had two scandalised ladies who have been watching the programme with their young daughters and they say that you've been showing the children pornographic pictures!'

This information was relayed to the other occupants of the gallery who now thought this whole affair was a huge joke. However, it occurred to me that our unfortunate guest was still blissfully unaware of all the fuss and I didn't see why he should have the embarrassment of reading all about it in the *Mirror* the following day. I carefully explained what had happened and indicated that whatever the viewers had reported they had seen was probably in the imagination. I then left Publicity to try and talk the *Mirror* out of following up the incident. Fortunately, the matter must have been overtaken by harder news or greater scandal and we were relieved to find no mention of the programme in the following morning's paper.

'Ah, it's such a pity', said one of the secretaries the next day, putting down her paper.

'What's the matter, you should be pleased we weren't made to look silly', I replied.

'No, I don't mean that', she said. 'But we never did have the opportunity to ask him. You know . . . under their kilts . . . I mean . , . .'
She put her hand up to cover her embarrassment. She finally got it out:
'Well, do they or don't they?'

Chapter 7

The Unknown Forest

When Bruce Campbell took up his duties as senior producer in April 1959, it was more like the return of an old friend than the arrival of a new boss. Bruce had taken part in many editions of *The Naturalist* and *Birds in Britain* and he was currently introducing *Out of Doors* each month; but his involvement with broadcasting had been more wide-ranging and of longer standing than his comparatively recent output from Bristol for he had taken an early interest in radio and had written his first script whilst still at school.

After the war Bruce had been one of the champions of Ludwig Koch and had drawn the attention of Max Nicholson, Chairman of the British Trust for Ornithology, to the possibilities of exploiting his bird recordings. The BBC subsequently purchased Koch's entire collection and Bruce, after becoming secretary of the BTO in 1948, served on the advisory panel of the Wildlife Collection with Julian Huxley. Ten years later Bruce and Desmond Hawkins met at the International Ornithological Congress in Helsinki and discussions began about the possibility of Bruce joining the Unit as senior producer. Although he had no experience as a producer, Bruce had shown himself to be truly interested in broadcasting and his impeccable ornithological background, together with his general involvement with various naturalists' organisations, provided just the right credentials for the leader of the Natural History Unit at the time. He was unable to take up his duties until April 1959 but kept in close touch with the forward plans whenever he visited Bristol. Meanwhile, Nicky was launching the first *News from the Zoos*, with James Fisher, a series which initially was to be one of the main responsibilities of the West Region Outside Broadcast Unit; and since Nicky was to return to his old post as OB producer, these zoo programmes effectively increased the animal output from West Region, even if the programmes did not strictly originate in the Natural History Unit.

After a crash six-week production course in London, Bruce was eager to seize any opportunity to offer new programmes on radio and television and in June 1959 something very special indeed turned up: the Royal Society for the Protection of Birds announced to the public that a pair of ospreys had successfully hatched a clutch of eggs at an eyrie at Loch Garten in Speyside, Scotland. This was one of the great ornithological events of the decade and Bruce was able to obtain a place in the television schedules for a special programme which he was to present and which he asked me to produce.

*Bruce Campbell,
Senior Producer of
the Natural History
Unit for three years
from April 1959.*

According to the reference books, ospreys had virtually been wiped out as breeding birds in Britain by the end of the 19th century. By the early 1950s, however, there had been several reports of ospreys around Speyside and even some attempts at breeding were rumoured. In 1955 George Waterston was appointed Scottish representative of the RSPB and he set about organising the protection of any birds making further attempts at breeding. In this he was helped particularly by the local landowner, Colonel J. P. Grant of Rothiemurcus, as well as many supporters and employees of the RSPB and the Nature Conservancy. Unfortunately, a series of disasters occurred, mainly through interference by egg collectors; in 1958, in spite of the fact that an eyrie at Loch Garten was closely guarded, an intruder climbed up to the nest, took the eggs and substituted some hen's eggs which had been painted to resemble osprey's eggs. Afterwards the birds made an unsuccessful attempt at another eyrie, also close to Loch Garten, and this was the site of the 1959 success. That year barbed wire was placed around the trunk of the nesting tree and the Natural History Unit co-operated closely with the team undertaking round-the-clock guard duties. Roger Perry and recording engineer, Bob Wade, had been on a long assignment recording several bird species in the district and arranged with the RSPB to place a microphone in a parabolic reflector within range of the eyrie. This not only enabled the BBC to obtain recordings of the ospreys but it also ensured that the nest could be guarded during hours of darkness, by listening for intruders on earphones in the specially erected hide nearby. In fact, it was through monitoring the sounds at the nest in this way that the hatching of the chicks was first detected and the RSPB knew of their success.

By the time that a decision had been made to produce a special television programme about the ospreys, Roger's work in Speyside was complete and the young birds were well developed although still on the nest. So there was already a full set of recordings available and, furthermore, Chris Mylne, the one-man RSPB Film Unit, had taken some good film of the birds through telephoto lenses. I soon suspected that the Scottish story was by no means simple and this was confirmed by Roger Perry, who had spent much time at Speyside talking to locals,

News from the Zoos *was launched in 1959. In this edition, from Paignton Zoo, James Fisher looks at a tree porcupine from South America with Bob Veeraswamy.*

Members of the public on their way to view the ospreys from the RSPB hide at Loch Garten in Speyside, 1959.

including the distinguished ornithologist Desmond Nethersole-Thompson – until 1954 official warden of the RSPB in the area. From such conversations it seemed that there had been some osprey activity which the RSPB Head Office did not know about and it was as late as March 1956 before Nethersole-Thompson disclosed in a letter to *The Scotsman* that his son, Brock, had located a breeding pair in 1954. Moreover, in 1956, Nethersole-Thompson's daughter found another nest at which she actually made some sound recordings with equipment borrowed from the BBC. I became intrigued by all this information and determined to piece it together, in order to give a proper account of what had *really* happened to the ospreys in Speyside since the early 1950s.

At first the news that I intended visiting and filming Nethersole-Thompson for the programme was received with considerable alarm at the RSPB headquarters in London but Bruce, with one foot in each camp as it were, was able to intercede on my behalf and when he gave the assurance that the disagreements between the RSPB and Nethersole-Thompson would not be the subject of a broadcast debate the objections subsided. Roger Perry returned to Scotland with me as guide and adviser and at Loch Garten we met Chris Mylne who had agreed to act as cameraman for the additional film I needed. After the news of the ospreys' success had been publicised, George Waterston decided to allow the general public to observe the birds from a specially erected hut at a safe distance from the eyrie. It was a courageous thing to do for some members of the RSPB were bitterly opposed to this but George took the view that, as the secret was out and all the locals knew exactly where the nest was, the RSPB might just as well organise the inevitable visitors properly and at the same time gain valuable publicity for the

An osprey lands at its eyrie – a view from the public hide at Loch Garten.

society. When Roger and I arrived there was already a constant stream of visitors who had parked at the roadside near the Loch and walked along a track, partly concealed by bushes and trees, towards the observation point.

The Return of the Osprey was transmitted on the afternoon of Sunday, August 23 1959; by a strange coincidence almost exactly 21 years later Hugh Miles' superb film on the Scottish ospreys, produced by the RSPB Film Unit, was also transmitted on a Sunday at the start of a new season of *The World About Us.* In the intervening years over 250 osprey chicks have been reared in Scotland – a wonderful record and a tribute indeed to George Waterston, his colleagues and their successors in the RSPB.

Bearing in mind Bruce's background and his particular interest in ornithology, it would have been all too easy for him to allow the Unit to slip into a production backwater, making programmes only for dedicated naturalists, but to his great credit he was ever conscious of the need to make programmes on a broad front and include some of wide, popular appeal. Certainly, he was always anxious to ensure that scripts were properly researched and checked so that no biological howlers went on the air and this did much to build up respect for the Unit in scientific and naturalists' circles; but he did not dismiss 'fringe' ideas for popular animal programmes even if they were not strictly wildlife subjects. So there was no lack of support when I suggested a short programme entirely devoted to one of H. G. Hurrell's latest animal projects – a series of intelligence tests on an Atlantic seal which HG and

94

his family had recently nursed back to health after its discovery in a distressed condition.

It was Tony Soper who first brought us the news of Atlanta the seal. She had been washed up on the mud in the Yealm Estuary in South Devon during a November gale in 1959 and had not been able to get back to the open sea. Atlantic grey seals are rarely seen on that part of the coast and so the arrival of this one provided a rich topic of conversation in the village of Newton Ferrers where two fishermen eventually decided to mount a rescue operation. Although the grey seal was only a few months old and little more than a pup, the rescue must have been quite dangerous for she had sharp teeth and, in her terror, was capable of inflicting terrible wounds. Unfortunately, the combined efforts of the locals, together with a vet and an RSPCA inspector, could not induce the poor seal to take any food and so one of the villagers did what many a local animal lover had done in a situation involving an orphaned or wounded animal – he phoned H. G. Hurrell. HG had a series of engagements at Plymouth that day but his two sons and daughter were able to answer the call and the elder son, Leonard, a doctor, made a good assessment of the seal's condition. He judged that the ugly gash on her back was a fairly superficial wound but the urgent need was to get the seal to accept some food; and because she had refused all previous offers of fish he suggested that food would have to be administered with a stomach pump. The Hurrell family were used to such challenges so without more ado the seal was loaded into the shooting brake and transported back to the family house at Wrangaton.

For three days the Hurrells fought to keep Atlanta alive by pumping into her a mixture of milk, margarine, fish meal and cod liver oil. Eventually, she began to take fish and in no time she was consuming 15 to 20 herrings a day. The original intention had been to release her back in the sea as soon as she was strong enough, but there were dangers in doing this now that Atlanta was beginning to get used to human company; she might easily become too trusting of humans and this could easily lead to her death at the hands of an unfriendly fisherman. So the Hurrells decided to keep her in spite of the appalling problems – and the expense – of feeding her. At least there were good facilities for exercising her as the family had built a swimming pool to celebrate Coronation year in 1953 and this was situated next door to Atlanta's enclosure. Most of the pool was six feet deep, which gave plenty of opportunity for diving, and at one end there was a ramp which was ideal for the seal to gain access.

HG soon had Atlanta swimming about the pool and diving for bits of herring. He always gave a signal to dive, speaking the word 'down' on each occasion, and quite soon noticed that the seal would respond to the spoken command without the visual signal. HG had always been interested in testing the intelligence of various creatures that he had looked after, as well as the wild birds which visited his bird-table, but here, he realised, was an animal subject *par excellence*. Within a few weeks, HG had taught Atlanta to push a balloon, and then a rubber ball, along the water in return for a reward of fish. From then on all kinds of activities followed – swimming through tyres, clapping her flipper to her side, and so on.

Tony Soper was well placed to keep an eye on activities at the Hurrell residence for his home was nearby at Plymouth; moreover, he had a special interest in seals himself having spent much of his spare time observing and tagging seal pups in Pembrokeshire. Tony had also undergone a diving course and had a new underwater housing for the Unit's Bolex camera, which he wanted to try out. So when an item about Atlanta was planned for *Out of Doors* it was natural that Tony should regard this as a heaven-sent opportunity to extend his underwater experience by getting into the pool with the seal. HG was very apprehensive about the whole business for Atlanta had never had a human being in the water with her before, let alone a strange-looking apparition in a rubber suit and face mask; he was afraid that the seal's vicious teeth could easily slash through the rubber and inflict a serious wound if she became frightened and turned on Tony.

On the filming day, Tony seemed unperturbed by the possibility of being savaged by a seal and, at one end of the pool, slipped into the cold Dartmoor water to await Atlanta. HG released her from her pen and she humped up the grass slope and slid silently into the other end of the pool. Immediately she sensed something in the water; perhaps the grey wetsuit gave the appearance of another seal, but whatever the reason, Atlanta suddenly dived under the surface and shot like a torpedo from a submarine straight towards Tony. For a second or so the onlookers were

Atlanta the seal waits expectantly in her enclosure at H. G. Hurrell's home.

transfixed in horror but, just a few feet away from Tony, Atlanta suddenly stopped and backed away. Clearly she had decided that the strange apparition was *not* a seal and for the remainder of the time that Tony was in the water Atlanta kept well clear of him. It was altogether an unhappy experience for Tony as not only would Atlanta not come close enough for satisfactory pictures but also the clarity underwater was not as good as it appeared from above. Nevertheless, the above water shots of Atlanta were entertaining and the seal caught the public's attention as soon as the item was shown on *Out of Doors*.

As the months went by, HG taught Atlanta to do many more 'tricks' – blowing horns, mouth organs, even hitting a toy piano with her flipper. But more remarkable was the relationship building up between seal and man and the level of communication between them. Gradually HG became able to control Atlanta's position anywhere in the pool by giving her precise directions using hand signals but speaking commands at the same time. After a time he was able to omit the hand signals, for the seal would respond with a high degree of accuracy to spoken commands only – 'Right', 'Away', 'Left' – and so on. It was these remarkable developments which suggested that Atlanta deserved a short film on her own, to which HG willingly agreed.

By 1961, when the film was made, sound filming equipment had improved considerably since my dreadful experience at Braydon Pond. Instead of the cumbersome double camera we were now using an

Arriflex mounted inside a comparatively light glass fibre 'blimp' and the *Atlanta.* sound recording was now being done on a portable quarter-inch tape recorder. Now we would film almost everything with synchronised sound since it was essential that the viewers should be able to watch HG giving the orders and Atlanta reacting to them in the same shot. Since HG walked around the entire pool at a fast pace while he was with Atlanta, two microphones had to be used: the first, a small personal one hidden under HG's pullover and the second placed near the pool to pick up all the splashes and other noises made by Atlanta during her 'performance'. And a performance it had begun to turn into for Atlanta's fame was spreading far and wide and HG was frequently being asked by visiting naturalists and reporters if he would demonstrate his seal's talents.

It was inevitable, therefore, that HG should get into something of a routine and the great difficulty was to stop him at the end of each 'experiment' so that a new camera set-up could be arranged for the next. It took several hours to film Atlanta's achievements before we came to the final sequences which were two diversions which the ever-inventive Hurrell family had recently introduced. The first was a see-saw. A plank about 12 feet long rested centrally on a large log near the edge of the pool. Atlanta was persuaded to clamber on to the end that stretched out over the water and HG would then step on to the other end. By carefully positioning himself and shifting his weight from one leg to the other he could swing Atlanta up and down, sometimes splashing her violently into the water. Atlanta really seemed to enjoy this for she was never in a hurry to get off and it appeared that she had a similar liking for the

98

second spectacular device that HG had arranged. This was a swing suspended from a metal bar mounted across a pole at the shallow end of the pool where there was a ramp. On one side the supporting pole was forked at the top and this was manhandled into position by HG and his son, Ken, after Atlanta had swum on to the swing seat which had been temporarily lowered into the water. By moving the pole slightly the swing would begin to move and Atlanta would go higher and higher – apparently enjoying every moment of it, for I am sure she could quite easily have slid off had she wished.

Although most of the action had been filmed on 'master' sound takes, it was necessary to film close-up 'cut-ins' of Atlanta as well as of HG, not only to give visual variety but also to enable us to condense the long sequences to about 15 minutes. After Paul Khan had edited the film, HG came up to Bristol to make a few extra explanatory comments on the soundtrack. Paul took an immense amount of trouble with the sound-track, carefully synchronising the tiniest water laps on the inserted mute cut-ins so that there would be the perfect aural continuity – just as if the programme had been recorded as a continuous outside broadcast. I had in fact tried to shoot the film rather like an OB as far as the limitation of a one-camera operation would allow – and so when HG announced a year later that Atlanta had progressed so far that she was worth another programme I decided I would try to shoot it with electronic cameras and thereby complete the programme in one day.

The outside broadcast equipment was set up the day before the recording and I arrived in the afternoon in time to help Valerie Pitts, who was to introduce the programme, get to know HG and Atlanta. The Hurrell family seemed completely shattered by the magnitude of the technical operation for the place was jammed with vehicles and there were over 20 engineers, riggers and drivers erecting rostra for the cameras beside the pool, laying cables back to the control vehicle, erecting aerials and so on. The largest vehicle of all, the mobile control room, had an ugly gash in its side – inflicted by a heavy boulder in one of the narrow lanes leading to the Hurrells' home. Otherwise everything seemed in good shape including Atlanta who, from the safety of her own tiny pool in the enclosure nearby, viewed all the activity through eyes filled with liquid amazement.

We stayed the night at a hotel in Ivybridge and next morning drove to our location in torrential rain. The ground was sodden, a few of the engineers were shuffling around in waterproofs, and a brisk wind drove the rain into our faces. Grateful for Mrs Hurrell's offer of hot coffee we went inside the house and telephoned the local meteorological office. We were told that the rain might die out for a while in the afternoon only to return again in the evening. There was nothing for it but to wait until after lunch and then take the first break for a recording. We went over the routine as best we could on paper and Valerie wrote out and memorised the opening and closing pieces to camera. Because so many of Atlanta's latest accomplishments were concerned with the under-standing of written and spoken words, we called the programme *School for a Seal* and had the title painted in white on a small blackboard to be placed beside the pool.

By mid-afternoon the rain had subsided to mist and light drizzle.

Atlanta going down the slide, filmed by Jim Saunders.

Valerie, who had spent most of her television career as a presentation announcer, was surprisingly unperturbed by the conditions; she had no head protection apart from a scarf but volunteered to start the recording even though the drizzle was quickly turning her hair into a limp, soggy mess. We began the opening routine and immediately a sudden gust of wind blew one of the captions into the pool. Undeterred, we kept going and I directed the three cameras as best as I could, shooting the programme as an almost unrehearsed event for I had instructed Valerie to suggest the order of most commands to HG so that there was no possibility of disbelievers claiming it was a well-rehearsed routine that Atlanta had learned to do exactly the same way each time. So Valerie selected the boards on which were written such commands as 'Clap', 'Down', 'Roll' and 'Slide' (each starting with a large distinctive capital letter), after which HG would show Atlanta the chosen word and the seal would invariably act on the written instruction. 'Slide' was made particularly impressive by the delay in achieving it – for Atlanta first had to swim down the pool, climb out on to the side, hump her way along the grass and up a wooden ramp to the top of a metal slide which ran to the edge of the pool. The instruction for this could also be spoken and by now Atlanta was able to recognise such words as 'Slide' in a long sentence spoken in the middle of a conversation.

I had been impressed when HG had demonstrated this the previous day and had suggested that, as the climax to the show, Valerie herself might try it. HG had been concerned that this might prove a flop as Atlanta was used only to his voice. However, he agreed to give it a try and as we approached the end of the programme we were all fascinated to discover if Valerie's instruction would be recognised by Atlanta. We

RIGHT
In later years one of Atlanta's more advanced accomplishments was to 'count' – recognising the spoken words 'one', 'two' and 'three' as well as circles on boards.

had arranged for Valerie to close the programme from the end of the pool near the seal's enclosure and as Atlanta swam towards her she said quietly, 'I wonder if you would mind doing the slide for me, Atlanta?'. There was no doubt about the response. Instantly Atlanta turned to her left, clambered out of the pool towards the ramp, climbed up it, and splashed down into the pool to give the programme a final flourish.

In spite of the appalling weather we had managed to record all the essential routines. I asked HG and Valerie if they would mind repeating two or three short sections which had not gone too well from a technical point of view and after the recording had been quickly spot-checked I opened the MCR door to thank the performers for their courageous efforts. I was quite unprepared for what I saw. I knew that the rain had begun to fall more heavily again but I did not expect to find that it was almost dark outside. The sensitivity of the monochrome cameras was such that the engineers had been able to produce excellent pictures which, when viewed from inside the MCR, gave no indication of the terrible conditions. I was reminded of that again when, on Christmas morning in the comfort of my living room, I watched the programme on its first transmission.

For some years the Unit had built up a tradition of presenting animal programmes of a lighter kind for Christmas so it was not surprising that the second Atlanta programme had been kept 'on the shelf' for the Christmas schedules. In a strange way the tradition probably began as a result of the transmission of Heinz Sielmann's woodpecker film in 1955. Soon afterwards, Denis Forman of Granada Television telephoned Desmond Hawkins for more information about Heinz Sielmann and his work and this so alarmed Desmond that he immediately rang Cecil McGivern in London. At the time, plans for the *Look* series were being formulated and it would have been disastrous if any new Sielmann films found their way to ITV, which was being launched in the autumn. So Desmond himself set off for Munich where he talked to officials of the Institut fur Film und Bild – the educational establishment for which Sielmann made his films. The result was a contract which gave the BBC exclusive television rights in the United Kingdom on all films belonging to the Institut; it was the biological subjects – and Sielmann's films in particular – which mainly interested Desmond but the deal included other material such as a batch of animated puppet films about well-known fables.

Desmond and Tony Soper considered the possibilities of these short films and decided that they were ideal vehicles for the talents of Johnny Morris – one of Desmond's greatest radio discoveries. Although a regular broadcaster on radio, Johnny's appearances on television were increasing – sometimes in programmes produced from Bristol. His distinctive brand of story-telling was also regularly featured as *The Hot Chestnut Man* in the children's magazine *Crackerjack*. So Johnny narrated the puppet film *Puss in Boots* – using his marvellous range of voices and developing a style which was soon to be used with real life action as well as animation. In 1957 the BBC acquired the United Kingdom rights to a prize-winning Swedish film made by Bertil Daniels-sonn about the adventures of a tufted duck. Simply entitled *Tufty*, the British version was produced by Tony Soper and narrated by Johnny

Morris. Again served up as a Christmas offering, it was enormously popular and started Tony and Johnny on a series of successes with programmes of a similar kind which Tony himself was to direct and film.

Johnny also played a large part in the success of the Unit's first home-made long television feature – a film about the wildlife of the New Forest, entitled *The Unknown Forest*. One of the reasons for making this programme was that I and a few of my colleagues had become concerned that our efforts were being almost entirely concentrated in one series – *Look*. This was doing well enough, Peter Scott was strongly identified with the series, and at a personal level he was very popular. But a strong personality identification with a series has disadvantages as well as advantages. It was evident there was no lack of support from viewers who had a commitment to wildlife or a strong interest in animals, but correspondence and direct contact with the general public indicated that the most regular viewers came largely from middle and upper-middle class sectors and older age groups. I began to suspect that Peter's own appeal, and the generally informal style of the programme, which had grown out of the television of the early 1950s when BBC still had a monopoly of the medium, did not do much to attract either the younger adults or the masses in the industrial areas who were currently deserting the BBC in millions as ITV transmitter coverage swept over the country. We needed to broaden the spectrum of our programme-making and explore new forms of presentation. Johnny Morris had already worked on the fringe of our output with Tony's Christmas films and had proved that his highly individual style of narration with its blend of humour and compassion worked for a wide range of age groups. True, his anthropomorphisms offended some people but I considered this a fair price to pay if we were thereby able to reach viewers who did not normally watch *Look*. Indeed, *The Unknown Forest* was specifically made for people who had no strong interest in wildlife, although of course we hoped to attract our regular viewers as well.

This approach was warmly supported by Bruce Campbell and Pat Beech but it would only work if the visual element of the programme was outstanding – Sielmann standard in fact. In 1959 we knew of no one in that league who was resident in Britain but this state of affairs was soon to change; and the first clue that we had a great talent under our noses came when Pat Beech noticed a short article about the photography of wild deer in the New Forest in an edition of *The Countryman*. The author mentioned that he had also taken some 16 mm film of wild deer and Pat therefore forwarded the magazine to me for immediate attention. We thought we knew of all the amateur and professional cameramen in the country who had ever filmed wildlife but here was a new name – Eric Ashby. By coincidence we heard of Ashby again within a few days through another source: a friend of his, one of the few people who had seen his films, wrote to Peter Scott about his work and Peter forwarded the letter to the Natural History Unit. I was busy with another programme at the time so I asked Roger Perry to call on Ashby as soon as possible. A few weeks later a beaming Roger appeared in my office puffing excitedly on his pipe and holding some cans of film.

'I say, old chap; you know that fellow Ashby who wrote the article in *The Countryman*? Well, I've seen most of his stuff and it's all rather splendid. Quite amazing, in fact. Come and have a look!' As we went down to the projection room, Roger said: 'The problem is most of the best stuff is taken at 16 frames per second – including some incredible shots of badgers'.

Eric Ashby waits patiently near a badger sett.

'Badgers?' I stopped dead, halfway down the stairs. 'You mean he's using lights?'

'No, that's what's so amazing. He's located setts where the badgers can be filmed in daylight. Foxes as well.'

I remember a strange mixture of emotions on hearing this news. It was remarkable and exciting that Ashby had been able to film wild badgers in daylight but I could not help feeling some personal disappointment as, for many months, I had been trying to condition a family of wild badgers in my father's garden to artificial lights for the purposes of filming. I knew that it would be a long, hard task to improve on the work of Dr Ernest Neal and Professor Humphrey Hewer whose film had been shown in an early Scott programme, but I had so far got my badgers used to the light from a 60 watt bulb. It was at this stage that Roger Perry made his dramatic appearance with Ashby's film.

As soon as I saw the film I knew that all my efforts had been a complete waste of time. Ashby had marvellous close-ups of badgers, digging, playing and feeding, many of the shots being taken some distance from the sett entrances. At home I could light only a very confined area immediately around the entrances to the sett. Now, when badgers first emerge in the evening they often sit back on their haunches and have a really good scratch. At home they would move out of sight into the undergrowth to do this and I could only hear the distinctive sound of them scratching. Ashby, however, had all this behaviour on film in close-up, and some of the shots were very amusing.

Roger said: 'I think you should have a talk to him, but I should warn you he is very, very shy and doesn't much like meeting strangers'. Nevertheless, Eric accepted my invitation to come to Bristol for the day and, on October 23 1958, arrived with more cans of film. He was indeed shy. A small, spectacled man in his early 40s, he was ill at ease and clearly wanted to get back to the forest he loved at the earliest opportunity. His nervousness diminished only when he began to warm to his favourite subject – the wild mammals of the New Forest.

Nicky and I watched his film spellbound for it seemed incredible that such superb work should have been done by an unknown 'amateur'. I then outlined my plan for a programme on the wildlife of the New Forest and stressed that 50 per cent of the production was already virtually 'in the can' if only Eric would agree to the BBC purchasing television rights in selected material. This he agreed to in principle so I then went on to propose that he should spend 1959 filming such additional sequences as might be required. Eric was a little less enthusiastic about this, pointing out that his small holding set a limit on the time available for filming and that work on wild mammals was so difficult that many filming attempts were completely fruitless. Nevertheless Eric agreed to try and film as much as possible of my 'shopping list' over the course of a year.

From time to time through 1959, Eric would post me a roll or two of film and each time I viewed his latest work I experienced the same kind

of excitement as opening a birthday present as a child. Eric never started running the camera unless he had an excellent close-up picture in the viewfinder and not a frame of film was wasted. Indeed, I had to remind him that he should occasionally film more distant, establishing shots to set the scene and create atmosphere and also allow the animals to move in and out of frame to facilitate editing. It was not until I visited Eric at his cottage near Ringwood that I fully realised just how slow and painstaking were his filming methods. Because his principal subjects were badgers, foxes and deer he had to use fieldcraft to stalk them, sometimes spending hours in approaching them downwind. Once within range special care was then taken to avoid any noise, including that from the camera. Unfortunately, the busy whirr of a Bolex camera, although comparatively inoffensive to birds, must sound like a large factory through the sensitive ears of a wild deer. So Eric was forced to operate with his camera encased in a home-made wooden 'blimp' filled with Kapok padding to absorb the mechanical noise during filming. Although quite efficient at reducing camera noise, this apparatus made normal operation quite impossible. The viewfinder was difficult to use and if any adjustment was required on the camera Eric would have to withdraw quietly to a safe distance from his subject before opening up the 'blimp'. I soon learned that 20 seconds of badger material was considered by Eric to be quite a successful evening's work.

The story of the film and Eric's shooting evolved together during the course of 1959. At the outset we had decided that the three principal animal species should be fallow deer, foxes and badgers – with squirrels and a variety of bird species providing additional sequences in all seasons of the year in the forest. I wanted to contrast the 'unknown' forest, which Eric was able to reveal with his camera, with the forest that

The three animal stars of The Unknown Forest – *badgers, foxes and fallow deer.*

most holidaymakers saw each summer. As Eric had no time for – and certainly little interest in – filming this part of the programme, I enlisted the help of a Bath cameraman, Bill Morris. I knew his work and admired his eye for countryside pictures so he would be ideal, not only to film the tourists in the opening and closing sequences of the film but to capture the atmosphere of the forest in the establishing shots which would supplement Eric's material.

When I invited Johnny Morris to write the narration, and outlined the shape of the film to him, he suggested that he should do it as if he were an owl – a wise old owl who could comment on the human visitors below and take a privileged view of the wildlife of the forest. I knew enough about Johnny's talents to be sure that this device would produce an entertaining narration, but it was also unconventional and likely to offend some of the regular viewers of natural history programmes who might think it in bad taste. But I was young and naïve and not over-concerned with such matters in my hurry to entertain as many people as possible with a new kind of wildlife film. So for my opening sequence I found a tame tawny owl and filmed it as if it were in a tree overlooking some picnickers.

The staff orchestra based at Bristol was the BBC West of England Light Orchestra and my circle of friends included a few of its players. For several years the principal trombonist was a delightful amusing charac-ter, with a perpetual toothy grin, by the name of Sidney Sager. Sidney was on the point of launching into a new and successful career as musical adviser, conductor and composer. He had already written music for solo instruments for some of Tony Soper's films and from the moment that I first mentioned *The Unknown Forest* there was never any doubt that Sidney would write the score for that as well.

By the time that music, narration and effects are all blended together on one sound track, the producer knows the worst and the best about his film. Various small modifications are possible in the final mixing stage – pieces of narration or music may be omitted, a few extra effects may be added at the last minute by playing in tapes or records – but it is then too late to make any major alterations. One may discover that a sequence appears too long or too short but nothing can be done without more work in the cutting room. At the beginning of a production one aims for perfection; but then you come face to face with reality. Time, money, facilities are limited; budgets have to be met and, in the end, it's always a compromise. So, after the final mix of *The Unknown Forest*, it was with no feeling of pride that I left the dubbing theatre. In fact, I was totally depressed for it was difficult for me to see any good in the programme at all whilst being so aware of its shortcomings – the behaviour there had not been time to film, the wrong decisions made in the cutting room weeks ago; and so on.

In spite of my misgivings, there was mounting evidence from col-leagues that the film had, in fact, turned out to be something rather special. Bruce Campbell, who had by then taken Nicky's place as senior producer, was enthusiastic about it and suggested trying it out at the Annual General Meeting of the RSPB in London. This was to be an important occasion for the Natural History Unit on another count: Desmond Hawkins would receive the Society's Silver Medal, an honour which he modestly considered to be recognition of the Unit's status as much as of his own endeavours.

I drove down to Ringwood and picked up Eric Ashby for the meeting at Great Smith Street. The audience loved the film and Eric was a hero. Our spirits rose and a few weeks later a print was sent up to the Controller of Television, Kenneth Adam. Back came the message: he liked it, it was 'an enchanting film' and it would be given a good mid-evening placing soon after Christmas. The transmission day was fixed for January 19 1961 with a preview for the Press two weeks before to which we coaxed the self-effacing Eric. Indeed, he provided the best possible publicity angle – the shy, unknown countryman who had shot a unique nature film. The press and audience response proved that we had not been wrong about his work; overnight Eric Ashby became one of the most well-known names in British natural history film-making. Letters came pouring in, most of them demanding an early repeat. Within a day or two, there was a pile of 350 letters extolling the beauty of Eric's photography; few had any complaints and these were mainly reservations about Johnny's commentary – opinion expressed rather more vehemently by a few critics who considered that it was outrageous that it should be so out of tune with the pictures.

In spite of the overwhelming public response, to *The Unknown Forest*, I became increasingly uneasy about Johnny Morris' narration which, though a brilliant example of his distinctive style, undoubtedly gave offence to some. On reflection I saw that at times it got dangerously close to sounding facetious. This was not Johnny's fault as much as mine; he was doing what he was brilliant at, but with unusual subject material. In my inexperience I was so full of admiration for his virtuosity that I was unable to stand back from his performance and produce it in the context of the rest of the film. As it was obvious that the programme would be repeated, it was suggested to me that it might be worth re-recording the commentary and asking Johnny to tone down some of the more personalised and colourful passages. Encouraged by the further suggestion that the BBC were seriously considering the film as entry for the coveted Italia Prize, this was duly done and the new version used for the repeat broadcast. Ironically, although it achieved good viewing figures again, this time it received a much lower Appreciation Index from the Audience Research Department.

In spite of its shortcomings, *The Unknown Forest* was an important bench-mark in the history of the Unit: we had discovered a new wildlife cameraman of great distinction, we had probably reached parts of the television audience that did not normally tune in to *Look*, and we had shown the television chiefs in London that in Bristol we could come up with a 'special' at a popular level that would hold its own against the ever growing competition on the Independent channel. And in that respect the programme did not come a day too soon. For the next month – on February 1 1961 to be exact – the first *Survival* programme was transmitted. There is nothing like a little competition to concentrate the mind and *Survival* was certainly to do that. And although that competition was to cause us some difficulties at times, it also had the effect of strengthening us – just as in the world of nature, competition in a changing environment eventually produces the fittest forms of life.

Chapter 8

In search of new talent

The discovery of Eric Ashby had been important for the Unit not only because he was a wildlife cameraman of considerable ability but also because he was an outstanding naturalist with a special interest in British mammals. Among the most difficult of all wildlife subjects, mammals usually made their appearance in *Look* programmes only through the talents of Heinz Sielmann; and many of his sequences were at least partially shot under controlled conditions. Ashby was a man who would not countenance such procedures even if the behaviour filmed was considered by experts to be effectively 'natural'; he insisted that all his film should be taken in the wild and it was inevitable that his output would therefore be low. In *The Unknown Forest*, which ran for 45 minutes, television had eaten up the fruits of his labours over a period of more than four years.

Nevertheless, Eric's next film was under way before *The Unknown Forest* was even transmitted. He had never been entirely happy with the style of presentation in that film and so I had promised him that any new material would all be set aside for an edition of *Look*. Eric wanted to continue with his work on badgers, foxes and fallow deer and, although it was difficult to see how he could improve on existing material at the time, I agreed to go along with this – waiting to see what his successes were before writing the final storyline for the programme. There had to be trust on both sides: on the one hand, I had enough faith in Eric's unique talents for providing enough wild mammal film to make a satisfactory programme in about a year's time and, on the other hand, he assumed that I would be able to shape a programme from his film and provide sufficient copyright payment to cover costs of the film stock at least. For there was no question of the BBC actually commissioning Ashby at that time: *Look* was run on a modest budget and payment to film-makers was on the basis of a few shillings for each foot of film used. The fact that the informal arrangement worked at all was primarily because Eric was a man of modest lifestyle who ran a small-holding in the New Forest and wished to spend the maximum number of hours per day studying the wildlife around him. As he was also a keen photographer, he saw the BBC as a convenient source of modest revenue to underwrite his film costs which would then allow him to be more ambitious with his hobby. His principal worry about the arrangement was that the publicity about the wildlife of the forest might cause too many tourists to invade the area and spoil the habitat, both for the animals and the animal-watchers.

'The silent watcher.' Eric Ashby took some film shots of himself with wild badgers and foxes by remote control for Look.

In the narration to that first *Look* from the New Forest, Peter Scott aptly described Eric as 'the silent watcher'; we used it as the programme title and the phrase stuck with viewers and critics alike so that even now, 20 years later, that title is firmly linked to Eric Ashby in many people's minds. Unfortunately, the addition of Eric Ashby to the ranks of regular *Look* contributors was partly cancelled out by the temporary loss of Heinz Sielmann. We had used up most of his films on European wildlife and Heinz had lately been working on a feature documentary in Cinemascope about the Belgian Congo. Since he usually provided the highspots of our series each year, the loss of these 'bankers' was not a happy prospect for Eileen Molony who had recently joined us from London to take over the main responsibility for producing *Look*.

Heinz Sielmann's film for the cinema had been sponsored by the Fondation Nationale de la Recherche Scientifique de Belgique and the production had been completed in Brussels. There all the offcut material was stored; some of this would be used for making into educational 'shorts', but it had been agreed that some could be copied for use in a special edition of *Look* about Sielmann's work in the Congo; this programme would also include a clip from the completed Cinemascope film distributed in the United Kingdom by 20th Century Fox under the title *Lords Of The Forest* – a reference to the animal 'stars' of the picture, gorillas.

111

So I was sent on a flying visit to Brussels to view thousands of feet of film with Heinz and his colleague, George Schimanski, and select enough material to make up the main body of the television programme. For two long days we worked together, stopping only occasionally for coffee and sandwiches. For me it was a revelatory experience as it was the first time I had ever seen the raw material of a professionally made wildlife film on the grand scale. It soon became clear that, although there was much material of a totally 'wild' type and virtually all the shots had been taken on location in the Congo, many of the sequences had been filmed partly under controlled conditions: some animals must have been captured and filmed in large enclosures whilst others had been baited to approach within range of suitable camera positions. Although I was well aware that much of Sielmann's previous work could only have been achieved using such methods, I was temporarily shocked when confronted by the evidence presented by the uncut work prints. In editing wildlife film at Bristol, it was rare to find two shots showing exactly the same action; here in Brussels, looking for a shot of a palm nut vulture flying to its feeding place (in foreground) I had difficulty in choosing between 11 takes – each only marginally different from the others. It was certainly not the kind of problem with which I was familiar.

At the time the contrast was very marked between the methods used by Sielmann, the professional, and Ashby, who was basically an amateur. From now on there was to be a long, and at times uncomfortable, period of transition in which the Unit slowly moved from relying on the pure naturalist capable of operating a camera towards a more

A scene from Lords of the Forest *Heinz Sielmann's Cinemascope film shot in the Belgian Congo.*

calculated, professional approach in which no shot is considered impossible and much depends on problem-solving. The ethical issues had to be met along the way.

From 1959 on, however, the most pressing requirements were to discover new wildlife cameramen and existing natural history film. It had already proved impossible for Roger Perry to find sufficient time for the Sound Library – with its time-consuming field trips for new recordings – as well as the Film Library, and by May 1960 a new assistant, John Burton, had joined us to concentrate on film alone. The library dealt not only with the cataloguing of the Unit's output but provided an intelligence system for tracking down all kinds of wildlife film throughout the world, and efforts in this direction now had to be doubled. John scored an early success when he came across a film made by the German cameraman, Eugen Schumacher. Initial research revealed that Schumacher had a considerable amount of other wildlife footage to his credit and Desmond Hawkins immediately provided the funds for John to fly to Germany and investigate further. He discovered that Schumacher had been making films about the countryside at the outbreak of the war and Goebbels, thinking that natural history subjects would make useful complementary programme material to war documentaries, kept Schumacher hard at it for the next six years. In fact he was still working quietly away on a film about marsh and river life when the German war machine eventually collapsed around him. After the war Schumacher embarked on a mammoth global assignment to film many of the rare and endangered animal species and the acquisition of the British television rights in these films helped us through some lean times before our own production output had sufficiently increased.

New British talent behind the camera proved difficult to find but once again we eventually discovered it not far from Bristol – this time at Oxford. Gerald Thompson was lecturer in Forest Entomology at the Commonwealth Forestry Institute and illustrated some of his talks with his own colour transparencies. Most notable amongst these was a series of photographs dealing with the life cycle of the alder woodwasp and its parasites. Thompson's collaborator was a laboratory technician called Eric Skinner and it was he who first suggested that, as the subject material was essentially animal behaviour, it might be better illustrated with cine film; but at that stage nothing more came of it because the Institute had no 16 mm camera available.

Bruce Campbell saw Thompson's pictures on a visit to Oxford one day and was so impressed that he arranged for him to visit Peter Scott at Slimbridge with Eileen Molony, the producer of *Look*. They encouraged Thompson and Skinner to take up cinephotography and, as a result, Gerald used the £400 he had set aside for a new car to buy a 16 mm cine camera. That was in March 1960 but some weeks later he learned that the BBC and the Council for Nature were jointly sponsoring a Nature Film Competition; that led to the decision to go all-out and complete a film that year. The editing was finished and a print made just in time for the judging. The film not only won, but was an outstanding piece of work which was well ahead of the rest of the competition. *The Alder Woodwasp and its Insect Enemies* was not a very prepossessing title but the combination of talents involved in the film's production, from skilled

manipulation of the subject matter (which could only come from a detailed entomological knowledge) to the engineering of special equipment, provided a model for future developments in this specialised field. The film went on to win many awards and it was the first step towards the creation of Oxford Scientific Films seven years later.

An alder woodwasp lays her egg beneath the bark of an alder tree – a scene from Gerald Thompson and Eric Skinner's film which won the first BBC/Council for Nature Film Competition.

The BBC's association with the Council for Nature extended to more than the Nature Film Competition – another round of which was organised in 1963 but with less satisfactory results: for several years the BBC gave an annual grant of £5,000 to the Council in return for which it was supposed to receive help and information in the making of programmes about natural history in Britain. The Unit was certainly endeavouring to be of service to naturalists – for example, it raised the status of its quarterly radio programme *Naturalists' Notebook* to the monthly *Nature News* – but there was a growing feeling that we were not getting our money's worth out of the Council for Nature grant and that this could be spent in much better ways within the Unit.

If there were strong links between the Unit and various naturalist organisations there were even closer associations building up with the conservation movement in 1961. The conservation message had been repeatedly and unquestioningly put over at relevant times during the *Look* series but in Tanganyika (now Tanzania), in the autumn of 1961, the Arusha Conference was held at which the foundations were laid of the principal fund-raising body for conservation – the World Wildlife Fund. Because of Peter Scott's heavy involvement in this – and Bruce Campbell's support – the Unit was able to plan ahead for this event and offer a special selection of programmes for the autumn schedules, drawing attention to the importance of the conference. Armand Denis

Rhyssella curvipes *beginning to drill through the bark to lay her own egg on a woodwasp larva; one of the 'enemies' of the prizewinning film* The Alder Woodwasp and its Insect Enemies.

agreed to deliver four special programmes, the television rights to show Bernard Grzimek's film, *No Room for Wild Animals*, were acquired and it was decided to bring back a new *Look* series with an opening edition called *L for Lion*. This title came from the notion that, although an interest in wildlife was encouraged with our first alphabet book from nursery days, unless something was done the animals we took for granted would soon no longer be living in the wild. The programme, produced by Bruce Campbell and which I directed had more of a straight documentary approach than usual, containing specially shot interviews with such notable people as Frank Fraser Darling and Julian Huxley.

L for Lion took the front cover of the *Radio Times* and the publicity received for this programme and the others associated with it probably did a great deal to foster the conservation movement in this country. There were, however, drawbacks for the Unit in being seen to fly the conservation flag so openly; it may have contributed to the opinion held by a few Unit members (and, more dangerously, by some executives in London) that we, the duffle-coat and wellies brigade, were turning out worthy programmes only to an audience already committed to the subject. The monthly children's television magazine *Out of Doors*, for example, was successful in its way, having 25,000 earnest club members, but it took itself rather seriously when the trend was to make children's programmes more and more entertaining. There were indications from London that a different type of children's programme was required with a new presenter and a much wider, more entertaining brief. A number of people were invited to an audition, but there was not much doubt about the outcome: Johnny Morris got the job and in 1962 the new series was created around him. It was called *Animal Magic* and Johnny is still making a great success of it 20 years later.

In 1962 the Unit was five years old and it was experiencing growing pains. The staff had risen to about 20 but suddenly three key people decided to leave. Roger Perry's yearning for travel became too much to resist any longer and he left to write and photograph in South America; Tony Soper had been attracted by the freedom of making his own films as a freelance; and Bruce Campbell, who had never felt totally comfortable in the job, could see even less personal satisfaction ahead as the television business grew more competitive as well as technically and administratively more complex.

The long-running series Animal Magic *began in April 1962. Johnny Morris, in an early 'Keeper Morris' item, here leads Mary the camel at Bristol Zoo. Production Assistant Douglas Thomas (later the producer of the series) tows Maurice Fisher in a makeshift camera dolly.*

Johnny Morris with one of his animal guests – a young orang-utang – in the studio during rehearsals for Animal Magic.

Bruce's imminent departure raised once again the thorny problem of filling the senior post in the Unit. Desmond Hawkins was convinced that someone of good academic standing was required in order to command respect in biological circles; but finding a person who had practical experience in broadcasting, as well as a mind turned to the realities of communication at a popular level, brought the number of possible candidates down to a handful. Various zoologists who regularly broadcast in the Unit's programmes were approached but one person above all seemed ideal for the job – Dr Desmond Morris, who was in charge of the Animal Behaviour Unit at the London Zoo. Here was an academic, currently studying a subject which was always bound to be at the core of the Unit's output; he was also an ex-student of the great Niko Tinbergen, Professor of Animal Behaviour at Oxford, and had already proved himself in the popular communication business – for Desmond had for some years been writing and presenting the very successful *Zoo Time* series produced by Granada for ITV.

The question was – how could West Region possibly attract someone like Desmond Morris to Bristol to take up what was largely an administrative post? One solution might have been to forge a link with the Zoology Department of Bristol University which was just a few hundred yards down the road. Desmond Hawkins in fact began informal discussion along these lines and explored the possibility of an Honorary post there. Bristol Zoo, with whom the unit had a history of good relations, was another important consideration and that was only half a mile away in the other direction. Twenty-five miles to the north, the Wildfowl Trust already had strong links with the Unit. The notion grew that all these elements might be combined in an animal behaviour film unit based in a large house set in its own grounds a short distance from Bristol. Perhaps the entire Unit could be moved into such surroundings. These daydreams were temporarily cut short by the untimely death of the key person at Bristol University who was particularly sympathetic to the idea of a close relationship with the Natural History Unit. So the advertisement for senior producer – as the post was then still described – appeared on BBC staff notice boards and in the press and there were few ideas about who might be likely candidates.

Meanwhile I had been appointed producer, following Tony Soper's resignation, and was just about to embark on my first major overseas assignment – with Gerald and Jacquie Durrell. I had first met the Durrells when I went to Bournemouth with Tony Soper to film some of the animals obtained on a collecting expedition which were temporarily housed in Gerry's sister's back garden. This film sequence was used to introduce three programmes which Tony produced about the Durrells' visit to the Cameroons – mainly illustrated with film that Gerry had himself taken. The film coverage was inadequate but Gerry's humour and story-telling ability were attractive elements in the programmes and the Unit was sufficiently encouraged to take an option on the television rights of his next expedition. This was in Argentina and it was hoped that Gerry might be able to obtain much more comprehensive coverage in order to make a six-part series. In the event only one *Look* programme could be salvaged from the material – a disappointment which reflected the faulty judgement and lack of experience of overseas conditions on the part of BBC staff as much as failure on Gerry's part. For, as I was later to discover, running an animal collecting expedition is more than a full-time occupation in itself and even a third party with a camera represents a hindrance which is difficult to bear.

Meanwhile Gerry's popularity as a writer grew steadily but, in spite of this, he might not have appeared in front of a camera again for a long time had it not been for the enthusiasm of our newest television producer – Eileen Molony. Long ago in October 1951, Gerry had written a short letter addressed to 'Talks Department, BBC London'. 'I enclose two talks which I thought might interest you', it began. 'The first I thought might be suitable for your Travel and Adventure programme, and the second for *Woman's Hour*. I enclose a stamped and addressed envelope for the return of the MSS if you do not require them. Yours faithfully, Gerald M. Durrell'. This resulted in many short talks about his experiences on animal collecting expeditions, some of which were produced by Eileen. When she came to Bristol it was only natural that she should seek to rekindle our interest in him. Gerry, in turn, had great respect for Eileen and the help she had given him. For Gerry undoubtedly needed help, especially on television. He had tremendous energy, a passion for animals and enormous enthusiasm for communicating this, but in his anxiety his delivery suffered, and his wonderful humour, descriptive powers and personal charm all tended to be drenched in nervous sweat.

Eileen was determined to overcome these problems and set up a short series of television studio programmes which she hoped would provide a relaxed format for Gerry to tell his animal stories and show some of his favourites from the Jersey Zoo. Special display cages with glass fronts were built and the animals were flown over in a chartered plane. A small temporary zoo was set up for a few nights in various rooms near the studio. The programmes – called *Zoo Packet* – were agreeable but not an unqualified success. In the early 1960s much light was required for the television cameras and, as many of the animals were either nocturnal or used to dark forest conditions, they tended to retreat to the most inaccessible part of their cage where they stayed in the worst possible position for the cameras. Gerry was as concerned about the lack of co-operation of his animals as he was about the well-being of the animals themselves; all this on top of concern about his own performance was too much and it was surprising that he did not collapse with nervous exhaustion at the end of each show.

I was called upon to direct these programmes and so had an opportunity to get to know the real Gerry behind the polite, almost self-effacing figure I had met on previous occasions. His effectiveness as a raconteur grew with the informality of the occasion; and the generosity

Gerald Durrell brought a large number of animals to the studio from his Jersey Zoo for the Zoo Packet *series, including this great white crested cockatoo.*

which he showed to his friends was accompanied by a bawdy humour which they all loved. If Gerry started making rude remarks about you, offence could not be taken because you knew that these came out of a feeling of affection rather than hostility. As time went on I began to see the Gerry that Eileen so desperately wanted to get on the screen, but couldn't. I doubt now if anyone could at that time, for the live television studio with its glaring lights and none of the present facilities for discontinuous recording was indeed daunting for the nervous and comparatively inexperienced performer. If Gerry had something to offer television it was most likely to be on location where he would be relaxed amongst the animals and the wild places which he loved. The lessons of Argentina had been learnt, however. If there was to be a film series with Durrell overseas then a cameraman and a producer would also have to go. That, I thought in January 1962, was a very interesting prospect indeed.

Although I had got to know Gerry a little through the studio shows, I think he had been so concerned over his own problems that he had hardly noticed me – other than as someone who was part of the television machine with which he was trying to get to terms. In Jersey it was a different matter, however, for Gerry was on his home territory. In the comfort of his flat at the manor house, which is at the centre of his

Cholmondley the chimpanzee – well-known to Durrell readers and a visitor to the Bristol television studio for Zoo Packet.

zoo, we were able to drink and chat into the small hours of the night. We soon began a long and stimulating friendship and working partnership that was to last for several years.

The proposed expedition was not to be a collecting trip on this occasion but a kind of fact-finding tour of New Zealand, Australia and Malaya with conservation interests in mind. Gerry had always been motivated in this direction and, indeed, saw his zoo as being of prime importance for breeding rare species in captivity even though he had to keep some common species as well to make the zoo commercially viable. Now, with half a dozen bestsellers behind him, he hoped that he would be able to promote conservation in an entertaining way in his next book which would be based on his trip to the Antipodes. The Durrells estimated their journey would take well over six months – two months of which were sea travel since Gerry hated flying. But even four months was a very long time for a member of the small Natural History Unit to be away and if I was to go I would have to be confident of bringing back a series of at least six half-hour programmes. The distances we would have to cover appeared formidable and it was inevitable that many hours would be wasted in travel, thereby reducing the time available for filming; and if the series was to contain a satisfactory amount of wildlife film as well as travelogue material we would have to allow adequate time for periods of waiting around. Although the Durrells had never visited Australasia before, their circle of friends and correspondents extended to all parts of the globe and so, one way or another, Gerry and Jacquie were able to provide a considerable amount of information about what it might be possible to film in each country.

Armed with all this information we pressed Desmond Hawkins and Pat Beech for support. It was not too difficult to gain their confidence but Pat, who had special responsibility for television programmes for the West, had all his work cut out obtaining the go-ahead from London. Programmes with Gerry had not been particularly highly thought of and Bristol had no previous experience in mounting a long overseas filming expedition. The situation was complicated even further by the fact that, at the time of discussion, the would-be producer was officially still only a production assistant. Nevertheless Pat Beech somehow sold the idea and a contract for Gerry was prepared just in time before he sailed in late February.

The series had been costed on the basis that just two people from the BBC would accompany the Durrells – the producer and a cameraman. In response to our increasing output a second cameraman had recently been appointed at Bristol specifically for work with the Natural History Unit. He was a young West-countryman called Jim Saunders, a quiet spoken man of slight build, good-looking features and a mischievous grin. Jim and I carefully considered what equipment we should take with us: it had to be kept as light as possible as we would be carrying it around for many thousands of miles and yet we must have sufficiently long lenses to obtain the key wildlife shots. Sound was important too and although it would be impractical for us to take a heavy sound camera we hoped to use the unblimped Arriflex in outdoor situations with a long lens in order to film some scenes of Gerry speaking to camera. The recorder was the old 'midget' L2 which I had used on Fair

Isle and which was now modified to receive a synchronising pulse from the camera. In addition to the Arriflex we decided to take a Bolex – the camera on which most amateurs had shot the wildlife film which was the mainstay of *Look*. Being clockwork-driven, it was a good standby in case anything went wrong with the battery-driven Arriflex and would also serve as a second camera which I could operate if a piece of action was best filmed from two angles. So my role on the expedition was not only that of producer but also sound recordist and occasional second cameraman – a combination which would send shudders of horror through any union official today.

There was one further refinement to our equipment which Jim required and that was a special type of tripod head. This is the metal mount on which the camera is attached and which allows it to be panned and tilted. Moving the camera whilst filming requires much skill and sensitivity on the part of the cameraman but his success also depends to a large extent on the smoothness of movement of the head itself. In the early 1960s a new generation of fluid-filled heads was just becoming available and the firm which manufactured them was based in Sydney. Very few of these heads were available in Britain and so Jim decided that he would stop off en route to our first location in New Zealand and obtain one direct from the manufacturers – an arrangement which suited me well as I needed to spend a few days there myself making local contacts.

Having been promoted in the nick of time, I set off with Jim from London Airport at the end of March in a Comet IV. The modern luxury of two hops to Australia was a far-off dream in those days and there were many stops during the two-day journey across the Middle East, India, Ceylon, Thailand and Malaya until we touched down at Darwin in Northern Australia at about midnight. Jim and I had got off the plane at most stops to stretch our legs and we had only been in the Transit Lounge a few minutes when, much to my surprise, I heard my name paged on the public address system. Waiting for me at the information desk I discovered Harry Frith, Head of the Wildlife Section of the Commonwealth Scientific and Industrial Research Organisation. We had written to the CSIRO at Canberra several weeks before asking for their assistance and advice about any interesting biological research which might be relevant to the theme of our series. Harry had been visiting the Northern Territories at the time and, having discovered that my plane landed at Darwin, had taken the trouble to find me.

The unexpected meeting with Harry immediately shattered one of my preconceptions. I knew of Harry's work – we had featured his film on the life cycle of the mallee fowl, in an early edition of *Look* and he also appeared in Peter Scott's *Faraway Look*; but I had also heard that he was a difficult man who had little respect for 'Poms' and even less for broadcasters in general. A small man with brown and sun-freckled leathery skin, he spoke with a flat Australian drawl which sounded as dry as the parched mallee habitat on which he had done so much of his work. He watched me like an experienced and confident snake catcher but it was I who was on my mettle. If I got on the wrong side of this man our work in Australia might be more difficult but, after a few minutes, I could relax. Harry gave it straight and he liked it straight; airs and graces found no favour with him and as soon as I discovered we could communicate in the same language I found him interested in our project and disposed to be as helpful as he could. As Jim and I were called back to the plane, our 40-minute meeting ended with the promise of a fruitful visit to Harry's headquarters at Canberra some weeks later.

For the last leg of the journey to Sydney we flew in a cloudless sky and, as dawn broke, we looked down in amazement at the endless grey-brown landscape which scarcely gave a hint of human habitation. Here and there a faint straight line suggested a fence or a track but there did not appear to be any settlements. Never having left Europe before, I had not comprehended the immensity of Australia and was struck with the impossibility of getting to grips with even the south-east corner by road in our allotted time of five or six weeks. The BBC has an office in Sydney and the friendly staff there soon made us feel at home in what in any case seemed to be a place of good living. Within a day or two I had recovered sufficiently from jet lag to do some programme research while Jim set about finding his new tripod head. I quickly learned that Australia was best considered as a number of separate states rather than a single country and as Victoria was the most advanced state in terms of its attitude to conservation it was to Melbourne that I went for a day in order to confirm some of the tentative arrangements which we had already made with the Fisheries and Wildlife Department there.

Two days later Jim and I took off on the 1,200-mile flight across the Tasman Sea to Wellington, the capital of New Zealand, which nestles on the hilly south coast of the North Island. Gusty winds are a feature of the city and the approach to landing on the tiny airport was over an angry-looking grey sea which was gnawing away at what appeared to be the only flat land for miles around.

One of the major hazards on any overseas filming trip is Customs. Armed with the correct documentation which is recognised in the country of disembarkation, formalities can be fast and efficient, a spot-check on some of the equipment and the serial numbers of a few lenses being enough to satisfy a Customs Officer. On the other hand, the process may take many hours and in some under-developed countries may only be completed by the 'accidental' dropping of some folding paper money under the nose of an obstructive officer. I knew that such underhand behaviour would not be expected in New Zealand but there was a strong possibility that a thorough and time-consuming check of our equipment would be made. Much to my surprise, therefore, we found Customs not only expecting us but obviously determined to get all formalities over at the greatest possible speed. The reason was soon apparent when two men appeared from the Wildlife Section of the Department of Internal Affairs. The section was responsible for organising our stay in New Zealand and had already oiled the administrative wheels; they had also reacted quickly and energetically to Gerry's request for information and guidance on what places to visit in New Zealand. One of their officers, Brian Bell, had already been delegated to meet the Durrells at Auckland, while others had been given the job of whisking Jim and me through Customs, fixing a hotel, hiring a car for us to drive north to meet the Durrells, and generally looking after our well-being.

123

Wellington seemed to have a quiet charm reminiscent of West Country seaside towns which I knew so well and this contrasted with the bustling and confident Sydney that we had just left. Whereas Australia seemed to be trying hard to establish a national identity of its own, we found New Zealand bathed in nostalgia for the old home country. The fact that so much appeared to be traditionally English was rather comforting 12,000 miles from home so it was with confidence that Jim and I headed north in our hired car, laden with suitcases, camera equipment and boxes of film. We had been given a sheaf of papers by the Wildlife Section and these contained the provisional itinerary for both North and South Islands. It was a very tight schedule in terms of the huge distances to be covered and the time alloted to each location; it is one matter to visit a location and watch wildlife through binoculars for a few minutes but quite a different time-scale is involved in filming a sequence which sets the scene, establishes a presenter *and* captures close-up behaviour of wildlife. Nevertheless, I admired the efficiency of the organisation which made all these arrangements and had carefully prepared for us a map on which was the *exact* spot where we should meet Brian Bell and the Durrells the following afternoon.

The chosen rendezvous was at a roadside café near Hamilton, south of Auckland. The reason for this, we were told, was that it was close to Lake Whangope which had a large population of black swans – an Australian species introduced about a hundred years ago. As with many other introduced species, their numbers had got out of control and now they were a menace to several native ducks whose food supply was being fouled up by the swans. It was the kind of story we were to hear many times in New Zealand.

After a good night's sleep at the nearby town which, with its wooden buildings, had some of the atmosphere of the American West, Jim and I arrived at the chosen café well ahead of time. As there was no sign of the Durrells we drove down a nearby track until we had a good view of the lake. I was worried about the tight schedule and the need to get started as soon as possible. I was also anxious to see if the equipment was working properly after the long journey.

'Come on', I said to Jim. 'Let's get the gear out. If we're going to shoot a sequence on the swans we're bound to need some establishing shots of the lake and its surroundings'.

What a pity that television is only in black and white, I thought. The gently undulating hills that surrounded the lake were clothed in fresh green grass which contrasted with the vivid blue sky – the kind of sky that Englishmen notice because it is so rare at home. As I studied the distant lake I began to estimate the numbers of black spots on its surface; there were not dozens as I had at first thought – there were hundreds, no, thousands of swans there. To be amongst such numbers would surely provide a film spectacle and I was impatient to obtain real action as soon as Jim had taken some panning shots of the lake.

'Very nice, very smooth', said Jim, patting his new tripod affectionately as if it were a new member of the family.

We packed the camera away and headed back to our meeting point. On the way we saw a Land-Rover parked by the roadside and the familiar figures of Gerry and Jacquie accompanied by a stocky but

Australian black swans – graceful birds but a pest in parts of New Zealand.

muscular figure in shorts. It occurred to me that it was remarkable that I had last seen the Durrells in England when we had discussed the expedition in the most general of terms and here we were meeting up again at a lake, which none of us had previously heard of, in the middle of New Zealand exactly on schedule. Voicing such a thought seemed to amuse the Durrells no end and Jacquie's hoot of mirth temporarily stopped me from making further comments until I realised that they contributed to the kind of light banter on which the Durrells thrived. Jim, too, soon fell into the spirit of this and was uninhibited enough to volunteer the kind of personal observation or reminiscence that Gerry loved. For Gerry can see the funny side of almost anything and, through an infectious laugh and a slight change of emphasis, can turn an account of only a slightly amusing incident into sheer farce. Brian Bell was at first somewhat mystified by the almost ritualised banter that developed between the Durrells and the BBC team and which became more ribald as time went on; nevertheless, by the end of a month he too was entering into the spirit of the thing.

There was a need for serious discussion before we began shooting the first film sequence for at the time I only had the vaguest idea of the theme of our programmes and I wanted to know how the black swans fitted into the scheme of things. So we returned to the café and ordered tea and toast while Gerry told me what he had so far discovered about New Zealand's conservation problems. It seemed that they were to do with the destruction of natural habitats to make new grazing for sheep and the results of the introduction of a variety of mammals and birds

125

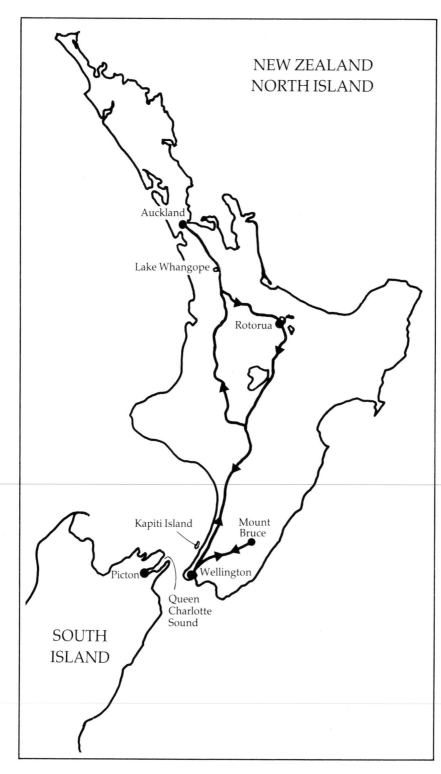

NEW ZEALAND
NORTH ISLAND

Auckland

Lake Whangope

Rotorua

Kapiti Island

Mount
Bruce

Picton

Wellington

Queen
Charlotte
Sound

SOUTH
ISLAND

The route in North Island, New Zealand. Jim Saunders and the author drove north from Wellington and met Brian Bell and the Durrells who had driven south from Auckland.

from Europe and Australia which were now competing with native species of birds. Our itinerary had been compiled so that we could see and film some of the principal trouble-spots as well as some places where the original natural forest still existed. Within this framework I hoped to film a kind of travelogue in which Gerry and Jacquie would be seen exploring the country, observing the wildlife both native and introduced, and getting involved in any relevant action for which I could find an excuse. Here, at Lake Whangope, Brian told me I could get plenty of action by merely taking a boat on to the lake.

A local warden had been assigned to meet us at the lake with a small boat fitted with an outboard motor. Normally wildlife filming is done with as little disturbance as possible but, in this case, as the swans were a pest, Brian was only too pleased to let us try and get close to the birds without taking the usual precautions. At first we approached slowly in order to get shots of the flotillas of swans undisturbed but then we accelerated towards them so that they began taking off. Then the real spectacle began. In turn, each nearby group of swans lurched forward in the water, legs and wings flailing. As they became airborne we zig-zagged across the lake causing other groups to follow and soon the sky above us was heavy with squadrons of black bodies, their white wingtips flashing, in the most spectacular natural air display I have ever seen.

Jim was in his element. In the boat he had to film everything with a hand-held camera but the birds were so close that this was no great problem. There was no need to direct Jim; he knew exactly what to do and the whirr of the camera was enough to confirm that he was enjoying it all. I had already learned that Jim never enthused greatly even when things were going particularly well but on this occasion I did notice a hint of satisfaction in his faint smile as we idled back to the shore.

Although we had filmed what would be the key shots of the sequence our work was not over for we now had to shoot the 'bread and butter shots' – the build-up action which would make the sequence edit together smoothly and work as a whole. We had already taken some establishing shots of the lake before the Durrells arrived and now we had to film them going out in the boat. They would have to take approximately the same course as Jim and me so that film of them would match the shots previously taken from the boat. Also Jim would have an opportunity to obtain additional flight shots of the swans, this time on a long lens with the camera on a tripod with the new fluid head. It was one of the easiest sequences to film on the entire trip but it was good for morale that we should have obtained such a spectacular sequence at an early stage.

Just before we set off for Rotorua, where we were to stay overnight, I checked with Jim that we had filmed everything required for the sequence. I also enquired if it had looked good through the viewfinder.

'It was all right, I suppose', said Jim non-committally. And then, perhaps feeling I needed my confidence built up, he said in a rare moment of enthusiasm 'Not bad at all, really'. His quiet West Country burr was now particularly apparent.

'In fact, quite delightful!'

Gerry and Jacquie hooted with laughter. We had made a good start.

Chapter 9

Four in the bush

We spent the next two nights in the town of Rotorua, one of New Zealand's better-known tourist spots, a thermal area dotted with geysers and bubbling mud pools. Although it lies in a beautiful setting close to a large lake of the same name, the town gave us the impression of a Hollywood Western set which is just about to be demolished; the wide main streets were bordered by low wooden shopfronts and walkways and wisps of steam rose ominously from cracks in the road or patches of waste ground. The most impressive feature of Rotorua, however, was its smell, for everywhere we went there was the stench of rotten eggs produced by the sulphurous gases issuing from the ground.

With Rotorua as our base we began filming material to support the story-line which Gerry had written. Although the programmes were to consist mainly of action sequences such as the black swans at Lake Whangope, there were other minor sequences and individual shots needed to illustrate such topics as damage to trees from the introduced deer and opossums. The large number of opossums in New Zealand was evident from the frequent occurrence of dead animals by the roadside – fatalities from impact with vehicles at night. However, even a simple eight-second shot showing the Durrells' Land-Rover passing and panning to a possum on the verge could take anything up to 10 minutes to film by the time we had stopped and set up the camera; So Brian's carefully planned schedule became even more difficult to follow and we had to compensate by starting each day earlier and earlier, endeavouring to get as much travelling as possible over before the light became ideal for filming.

After several days' concentrated work on the problems with introduced animals, over-grazing by sheep, erosion and so on, we became concerned that we had not yet been able to film many native bird species. Brian already had the answer to this in his schedule and so we hurried south to Wellington from where we set off on a one-day trip to Kapiti Island, close to the west coast. Brian drove us to a sandy shore from where we could see the long, dark shape of what appeared to be a rather uninviting island less than a mile away. Jim was silent as we started unloading the film equipment from the Land-Rover and I guessed he was not looking forward to the short sea trip. I was bound to admit it looked distinctly choppy. Jim's dislike of the sea had been worked up by Gerry – in his inimitable way – into something of a legend, ever since Jim had unwisely disclosed that he had once been seasick crossing the Rhine on a pontoon bridge. Eventually a motor launch towing a small dinghy approached and anchored close to the shore and George Fox rowed in to pick us up. George, who was warden of the Kapiti Island reserve, was a tough, stocky man with a well-weathered face like an old salt. He said very little during the short sea trip and it was Brian who spoke enthusiastically of the native bird population which we were to see; but as we walked up the path through thick vegetation to George's bungalow I could see or hear little sign of any birds. Brian must have read my thoughts for he put on a wide grin and said:

'Cheer up, Chris, don't look so gloomy, you'll have them all around you soon – they're inquisitive little beggars.'

George's wooden bungalow was on the hillside in a slight clearing in the forest and, as we reached it, his sister came out to greet us with the news that hot coffee and cakes were waiting. So we put our equipment down on the path outside and George, whose initial shyness was beginning to melt, started telling us about the birds on the island. Almost at once, I began to think that my hearing had become defective because I became conscious of a curious low, drumming noise; it seemed to come from somewhere in the undergrowth at the edge of the tiny garden. Just when I thought that I had pinpointed the exact location of the noise an identical sound was repeated from the opposite direction; soon a tiny drum conversation was going on all around us. Next a small brown head appeared, peering at us from behind a rock, followed by another a few feet away. One by one they gradually emerged, large brown rail-like birds which Brian explained were wekas. I must confess

A tui – or parson-bird – one of the tuneful visitors to George Fox's garden on Kapiti Island.

that I have never been particularly excited by the rails but these were something quite exceptional. For a start, they appeared to be ventriloquists; you could see each bird and you were sure that it was making one of those curious sounds – and yet in each case the noise seemed to come from a different place several feet away. The second fascinating thing about the wekas was their inquisitiveness; in fact, I had never seen such avian busybodies in the wild before, though I knew that New Zealand had a reputation for tame birds due to the fact that there were no mammalian predators before man came to the islands.

Contentedly munching cakes, Jim and I sat bemused by the wekas, especially when they started inspecting our equipment which was lying on the path. I suddenly realised that we were missing an amusing sequence. I need not have worried; although the birds retreated to a safe distance while we unpacked our gear, they soon returned as bold as ever walking around the camera case and pecking suspiciously at the locks and catches.

'Just like Customs officials', said Gerry with a smile, encouraging them with a piece of cake.

While we were busy with the wekas, other forest birds began flying into the garden, some of them visiting the bird table. In a short space of time, we were able to film close-ups of bell-birds, tuis and the very handsome New Zealand pigeon – a much larger and more colourful bird than the European wood pigeon. But there was still no sign of the stars of Kapiti – the parrots called kakas which Brian had assured us would present us with no difficulties. As time goes on one becomes increasingly cynical about experts who say such things as 'no trouble at all, old boy, I can absolutely guarantee they'll be there'. As this was my first expedition, however, I was still inexperienced enough to be convinced by Brian's prognostications; but I did note that he was looking a trifle concerned and having a quiet conversation with George on the side. Shortly afterwards, George went into his home and re-appeared with a handful of dates. Then, facing up into the forest behind the house, he gave full vent to a voice so powerful that it must have reached into every corner of the island.

'Come on, come on then. Henry . . . Lucy . . . come on . . . . As George started bellowing I was already recording some of the forest atmosphere around the house but, as this seemed a marvellous opportunity for a sound film shot, I hurried back with the synchronising cable to link up recorder and camera. There was no worry about camera noise this time for the level of George's voice was so high that I had to turn the recorder right down to prevent overloading.

For several minutes, nothing happened except George's repeated and, I thought, more concerned, calls. I told Jim to stop filming to conserve footage. Then George pointed to the forest behind his house and Jim had the camera running just in time to film the first kaka as it landed on the corrugated roof. At first sight, it looked like a rather ordinary large brown parrot but as it edged along the top of the roof towards us we could see that there were many subtle shades of purple and orange in its plumage and, when it opened its wings to keep balance and eventually fly down to the bird table, brilliant flashes of red showed underneath.

*'One of the kakas
forgot himself and
actually landed on
Gerry's head.'*

Within a few minutes, two other kakas appeared, once again approaching via the roof and eyeing us from every conceivable angle in the comical way that parrots do. One of them was a juvenile and spent most of its time on the roof demanding food from its parents who made frequent trips to the bird table and George Fox's hand for supplies. There was much noisy squabbling over the dates and this got so heated that one of the kakas forgot himself and actually landed on Gerry's head. Eventually all the dates were gone, the kakas appeared satisfied and flew back to the forest. George was disappointed that such a small number of birds had appeared and explained that in the 11 years he had been on the island he had trained many more to come to him and there were currently 17 birds about somewhere. 'Must be feeding on the other side of the island', he said apologetically.

'Don't worry', I told him. 'You've given us a marvellous opportunity to film beautiful close-ups and we have a fine sequence'. Indeed I was quite confident by then that we had material which would make a good ending to the first New Zealand programme.

We had planned to make the second programme entirely in South Island so, after two days taking continuity shots and filming some rare species in the Wildlife Section's experimental breeding station at Mount Bruce, we boarded the night ferry to Picton – south of Wellington on the other side of the Cook Straits. Since this passage was notorious for its rough water, Jim groaned when he heard the news and, as it turned out, he had good reason to dread the crossing. Our ferry trip was worse than expected as it was Easter and half the population of North Island appeared to be making a stampede to the south – everyone with rucksacks. The result was congestion and chaos which we managed to escape to some extent by crowding into the Durrells' 'luxury' cabin where we discussed how best to endure what was clearly going to be a nightmare. Jim's solution was to take a handful of sea-sickness pills while the rest of us drank a large bottle of Scotch.

Weary and exhausted, we were only too pleased when the stewards threw us out of our cabins soon after six the next morning and we went up on deck to see the ship glide peacefully through sheltered waters towards the pier at Picton. The misery was not over for Jim, however for, after a heavy breakfast at a waterside café, it was time to board a launch which was to take us to some of the islands in Queen Charlotte Sound, our first major location. The first stage of the trip was idyllic, however, as we travelled in the early morning sunshine through placid waters which quickly made us forget the discomfort of our previous journey. Jim and I kept camera and recorder at the ready, as Brian told us we would probably see some interesting seabirds. Within a short while we came up on the first of them – a group of fluttering shearwaters, one of the many members of the petrel family found in those parts. They allowed the boat to get quite close and, as the water was so smooth, Jim was able to take excellent shots of them – until they reluctantly fluttered away close to the surface – demonstrating perfectly the reason for their name. Then Brian shouted out from the other side of the boat and we rushed over to see that ahead of us, and just under the surface of the clear blue water, was a small feathered torpedo. Jim got his camera quickly into position but the object of our attention acceler-

A kaka. George Fox hand-tamed many of these New Zealand parrots at his home on Kapiti.

ated out of range before bobbing up to the surface a hundred yards ahead. It was a little blue penguin – the smallest of all penguins and the first I had ever seen. The boatman obligingly altered course and for a few seconds Jim had a second opportunity to film the penguin swimming underwater before it shot ahead again. We spent nearly an hour being tantalised by penguins and shearwaters and it was with some difficulty that we forced ourselves to put the camera away, having obtained more than enough shots of various birds and passing scenery to make a travel sequence.

Now we were approaching the open sea and quite suddenly the boat began to buck and the equipment slid dangerously along the deck. Hurriedly we collected everything together and crammed it into the tiny wheelhouse for protection from the spray. Jim, who until five minutes ago had almost convinced himself he wasn't such a bad sailor after all, began to look grey and unhappy. He couldn't believe that the boatman intended to head out into the angry-looking breakers ahead. Brian, grinning from ear to ear, was apparently enjoying the situation immensely. He seemed to be exhilarated by the livening-up of the elements but I also had suspicions that he was relishing the thought of putting the British party through a New Zealand toughening-up exercise.

'We shouldn't have too much trouble getting on to The Brothers', he shouted, 'but it will probably be too rough to get on to White Rocks for the king shags'.

We looked across to the swirling waters surrounding an ominous lump of grey rock, stained white with bird droppings, and I readily agreed that we should not risk losing the film equipment by attempting a landing. I realised I was no longer enjoying the trip myself as we headed out to sea. For a long time we could see nothing but the spray sloshing heavily against the wheelhouse window. Then two islands came into water-distorted view as the boat was headed towards the larger of them, on which was a lighthouse.

It was soon obvious that the island had neither a sheltered bay nor a rocky promontory to provide a landing stage. Sheer cliffs were everywhere and I could see no way of disembarking until Brian pointed out a tiny crane on the cliffs just below the lighthouse. Our skipper eased us in directly beneath the crane where the waters were less turbulent but there was still a considerable swell which caused the launch to lurch from side to side so that we had to watch our balance as well as the equipment. As the crane started to swing out over us I watched in fascination until I realised that here was a splendid piece of adventure for our programme. To Jim's dismay I asked him to get out the camera and then be first to disembark so that he could film the Durrells from a more stable position on land.

The crane hook delivered a large net on the deck into which Jim was packed together with some of the equipment. Then Brian gave a signal to the men on the cliff and with a lurch Jim shot upwards into space, twirling around as he went. Dangling like a toy on a piece of string, he was swung inland towards a flat rock where he was extricated from the net by two of the lighthousemen. I decided to go next so that I could direct Jim when the Durrells landed. I also wanted to take a few shots

LEFT
*In relaxed mood en
route from Picton
to one of the
Brothers Islands
before
encountering rough
seas are Jim
Saunders (holding
camera), Jacquie
and Gerry Durrell
and (foreground)
the author and
Brian Bell.*

RIGHT
*The Durrells endure
their turn being
winched ashore.*

OVERLEAF
*A male tuatara at
the mouth of its
burrow.*

from the net as I was hoisted aloft – this would be the Durrells' point of view in the edited sequence. I would normally have asked Jim to do this but, as it would constitute cruelty to cameramen after what he had been through, I elected to take the Bolex camera myself.

I managed to film an impressive 20-second shot as I ascended, the boat rotating and getting smaller as the net twisted round and round. With my eye fixed firmly to the viewfinder, I didn't have time to worry about the height until it dawned on me that I was neither continuing to move upwards nor swing towards land. Down below, the Durrells and Brian Bell were peering up fascinated; on the cliff, the crane operator was apparently doing nothing at all whilst Jim was putting the camera on the tripod nearby. Strange, I thought, surely the crane has not broken down, for no one seems very concerned. A minute passed and, above the noise of the waves and wind, there was nothing I could do to communicate. I looked up at the loops of rope on the crane hook from which the net was suspended; they seemed rather worn. I wondered if the BBC insurance scheme covered such unusual methods of transport. Two more minutes passed by and I began to get annoyed. I knew that Gerry was one for setting up practical jokes but surely he wouldn't have used a potentially dangerous situation like this? Or could it be that Jim was getting his own back on me for chiding him about sea-sickness? Jim had now left his camera and was nonchalantly sitting on a rock nearby. I then saw the crane operator walk towards him and after a brief conversation Jim moved his camera and tripod. Immediately the crane jerked into motion again and I realised what had happened: Jim had been in the way of the crane. After I landed I discovered that the operator assumed that Jim was filming me. It wasn't until Jim, bored with the sight of his producer swinging idly in space, sat down on a rock

135

to await developments that the crane operator realised his mistake and I was allowed to land – if that word adequately describes the action of being unceremoniously dumped on a lump of rock in a tangle of rope net.

Somewhat indignant over this treatment, it was with a touch of disappointment that I saw Gerry and Jacquie being winched up without a hitch. So to get full value out of the landing sequence I persuaded Gerry to take the freight trolley from the crane site up the last leg to the lighthouse. This he did, protesting for most of the journey up the 45-degree climb that this was not in his contract and that if the cable broke it would be the end of a great series.

The main purpose of our trip to The Brothers was to film a strange reptile called the tuatara – the Maori name for a creature known to zoologists as *Sphenodon*. It is found only on a few rocky islands in New Zealand waters and is a relic of an ancient reptilian line that goes back to the age of the dinosaurs. Many reptiles have a third, or pineal, eye on top of their head but the tuatara has a particularly well-developed one although, as this is covered in skin, it cannot be seen except in newly-hatched young. Tuataras are mainly nocturnal and, although they sometimes sun themselves at the entrance to their burrows during the day there was a danger that we would not be able to locate any in our very short visit. So Brian Bell and his colleagues in the Wildlife Section had done some organising and, in response to their radio message before we arrived, Alan Wright, the chief of the lighthouse team, had collected a couple of dozen animals the previous night and put them in a shed for safe keeping. When Gerry was shown them he could hardly believe his eyes. He had been looking forward to seeing one of these strange rare animals for weeks and now he was confronted by what appeared to be a sea of them; for once, Gerry was almost speechless.

As tuataras are not very active – yet are biologically interesting creatures, there was good reason for us to film Gerry talking about them. So we selected a prime specimen and went out to the place where Alan had collected the tuataras the previous night. The cliff top was riddled with burrows which provided homes for dozens of other tuataras but, as the sun went down at the end of a successful afternoon's filming we discovered other occupants. We became aware of a new population surreptitiously moving in from the sea around us: little blue penguins hopped up from the rocks below and delicate little petrels called fairy prions silently swept in from the ocean to land ungracefully near their nesting burrows before shuffling underground to join their mates. There they would break into an animated petrel conversation of chuckles, grunts and coos – all of which I earnestly recorded for the programme and for our sound library. Jim, using the fastest film available, photographed as much as he could in the rapidly-gathering gloom and between us we hoped we should have enough material to create an atmospheric sequence conveying the dramatic change on the island as night fell.

If we had all departed at that point, no doubt my lasting memory of The Brothers would have been quite idyllic. However, we were to stay overnight in rather cramped quarters in a small wooden hut near the lighthouse. Well-fed and snuggled down in our warm sleeping bags after a hard day's work, these arrangements would have meant no hardship – if we had not had the company of several families of little blue penguins immediately beneath the floorboards. We could not see them, of course, but the noise they made was deafening for the hut above them effectively acted as a sound box. All night long they bickered and brayed in grating tones which set our nerves on edge. After a while the cacophony would die down and we would be just on the point of dozing off when, with a grunt and a cackle, one of the penguins would begin again and this always set off a chorus of at least 20 other birds who cannot have been more than two or three feet below us. I suppose that eventually I must have been tired enough to sleep even through such a chorus but to this day I cannot look a penguin in the eye without recalling one of the noisiest nights of my life.

Most of the roads in the Sou h Island of New Zealand run down the eastern side, for to the west there is an almost impenetrable mountain barrier which comes to a scenic climax at Mount Cook in the New Zealand Alps. We took a few days to reach Dunedin, three-quarters of the way down, stopping off at various points to film a colony of fur seals, examples of erosion and over-grazing, evidence of opossum damage and so on. At Taiaroa Head, near Dunedin, we filmed some royal albatross chicks in a small, carefully protected colony and nearby some very attractive yellow-eyed penguins.

However the big story which we were hoping to make the major part of our second programme was that of the takahe – a large flightless bird of the rail family which was thought to be extinct until it was rediscovered in a remote valley near Lake Te Anau in 1948. Known to scientists as *Notornis*, the rediscovery of this bird caused a wave of excitement throughout the ornithological world and in order to restrict visitors the New Zealand government made the valley and the surrounding area out of bounds to all but a few scientists and hunters controlling deer. The Wildlife Service subsequently embarked on a captive breeding programme at their sanctuary at Mount Bruce, 80 miles from Wellington. The stock for this scheme was a number of chicks collected from the Takahe Valley and brooded during transit by specially-trained bantam hens. Fortunately, the Wildlife Service had taken some film of this curious expedition and, although the coverage was scrappy, its historic value was such that I planned to use it in our programme. To tell the story properly, however, we would have to visit the Takahe Valley to film the habitat and hopefully obtain some shots of *Notornis* in the wild.

Brian Bell had been into the valley on several occasions and knew the problems that lay ahead: the usual way in was on foot but it was a day's trek which we could ill afford on our tight schedule and in any case it would be difficult for us to carry all the necessary equipment. The only practical method for us would be to fly in a floatplane which could land on the lake in the valley. It would be only a 10 or 15-minute flight from Lake Te Anau but our problem was the unpredictability of the local weather which could send thick banks of cloud over the lakes in a short time and make flying impossible. With all this uncertainty, and our days in New Zealand rapidly coming to an end, we were all somewhat edgy and not in the best mood to enjoy fully the surroundings while we

waited for our transport at Te Anau. The lake is one of the most beautiful in the South Island and the New Zealand Tourist Board has wisely located one of their own hotels there which, much to Gerry's delight, served excellent wines and food.

'Better make the most of this', said Brian, as Gerry ordered another bottle of wine over dinner. 'It'll be a bit different tomorrow night up in the valley. Apparently there are some deer hunters working there so the hut will be a bit crowded.' Brian always took mischievous pleasure in testing our stamina for the more rugged aspects of New Zealand life but I considered that up to now we had come through everything he had arranged for us with good British bulldoggedness. Indeed, on more than one occasion we had won the day when after many hours filming and travelling – on foot or in the Land-Rover – Brian had appeared more exhausted than any of us; this was due to the fact that he was just not

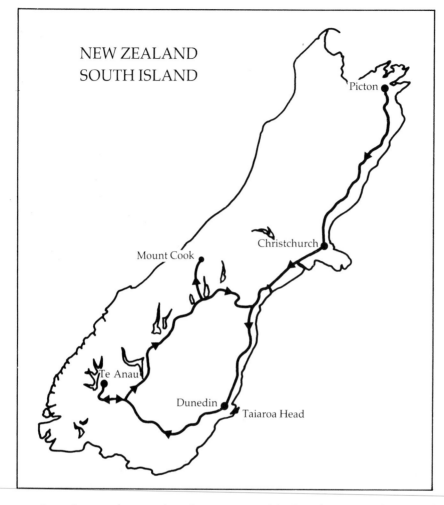

NEW ZEALAND
SOUTH ISLAND

Picton

Christchurch

Mount Cook

Te Anau

Dunedin

Taiaroa Head

*Our route in South
Island, New
Zealand.*

used to the stop/go routine that comes with the alternating bursts of
activity and inactivity during filming. During convivial dinners, such as
that at Te Anau, Gerry would get his own back on Brian, drawing
irreverent cartoons of him leading us on yet another assault course over
rugged New Zealand terrain. It is perhaps hardly necessary to add that
in the following months Gerry's cartoons of his cameraman and
producer also became increasingly irreverent.

The morning after our arrival at Te Anau the gloom which descended
on us was almost as black as the clouds over the mountains. Brian
periodically went off to telephone for a weather report and discuss the
possibilities of flying with the pilot at his base; but he always returned
shaking his head sadly. So we paced the shores of the lake and gazed
wistfully at the forest-covered mountains which rose into the low clouds
on the other side.

It was lunchtime before Brian returned with better news. There was a
chance that the clouds would lift sufficiently for the plane to take three
quick runs into the valley and we must have all the equipment ready at

the landing stage in 30 minutes. Because of the hazardous flight and the limited accommodation in the valley, Jacquie would remain behind. The short trip involved a steep climb and some tight banking within Takahe Valley to land on the short lake. This manoeuvre could only be achieved with a light loading and so there would have to be two trips with one passenger plus equipment and a final trip with two passengers. As, from all accounts the journey would make a spectacular sequence, I sent Jim in first with the most important camera gear, asking him to take as many shots as possible from the plane on the way.

By the time we had taken everything to the end of the wooden jetty, we heard the distant drone of the plane and in a minute or so picked out its tiny shape dwarfed by the mountains behind it. It skimmed down over the lake like a dragonfly and gently pierced the flat surface, sending reflections into convulsions as it coughed and spluttered its way towards the landing stage. Engine off, it drifted the last few yards, the door opened and the pilot, not wasting time, asked 'Who's first then?'. We pushed Jim forward with some boxes of equipment and in no time at all the pilot was ready for take-off again.

'What happens if it clouds over and you don't make it?' enquired Jim plaintively from his seat beside the pilot.

'Don't worry', replied Brian breezily. 'Just make for the hut and stay there. There'll be plenty of food for a few days and the deer-hunters will look after you.'

In less than half-an-hour the plane had returned and it was my turn. It was the first time that I had ever flown in a small aircraft so it was bound to be an interesting new experience, but in 20 years' flying since then I can recall no more dramatic trip than that short flight from Te Anau to Takahe Valley. After take-off we climbed relentlessly, flying up over the long lake and keeping the wooded, mountain slopes on our left. After about 10 minutes we suddenly banked to the left and, to my alarm, apparently headed straight for the mountain side, the peaks being still well above us. After a few moments, I saw where the pilot was heading – a narrow gorge. In the knowledge that the pilot had made the same trip only half-an-hour before, I convinced myself that his senses had not left him but watched with some astonishment as we flew on through the narrow slit in the mountainside, trees whizzing by only a few feet away from the wingtips. In a short time the scene changed dramatically again; the ground dropped away quickly beneath us, the steep slopes on either side broadened out and we were high again above a beautiful, deep natural amphitheatre. This was Takahe Valley. We began to lose height as we flew down the right-hand side of the valley which was a few miles long and then, when we could go no further, the pilot banked steeply to turn back the way we had come and dropped down to land on the lake. As we touched water I could see Jim filming from the lake edge. The pilot used up most of the length of the lake by the time he had stopped and then turned to taxi towards where Jim was stationed. There was no landing stage here, of course, so I had already slipped off boots and trousers to wade through the shallow water to the shore with the equipment and provisions that had been stowed behind. The water was so cold that my feet went instantly numb as they touched the surface. I waded towards Jim who was looking wet, bedraggled and unsympa-

thetic. I soon discovered why. It appeared that we had been dumped in the wettest place on earth and it did not take more than a few minutes to realise that it was unlikely we would ever feel dry again until we had left the valley. Our feet sank up to the ankles in a saturated moss; if we walked a few feet through the clumps of snow grass that were waist-high, water showered on us with every step. Even the beechwoods at the edge of the valley showed no mercy for they, too, were festooned with lichens which dripped incessantly like melting icicles.

The plane taxied back to the head of the lake and with a huge roar the pilot opened up the throttle, straining the last ounce of power for the short take-off from the lake. In a few seconds the deafening sound diminished to a drone as the plane flew up into the cleft at the entrance to the valley and soon it was gone completely. In fact, there was no sound at all. Never before had I experienced silence that was so absolute and it produced a strange feeling of loneliness.

Jim and I hauled ourselves and the equipment to slightly firmer ground and set up the recorder and camera to await the arrival of Gerry and Brian. For 10 minutes there was no sign of life whatsoever until I saw two birds about the size of crows flying purposefully across the valley. They made a deviation towards us as if coming to investigate the strange visitors from the outside world. As they got closer I recognised

the distinctive head-shape of the parrot family and with a wave of excitement I wondered if they were keas. As if in response to my thoughts they emitted a succession of eerie cries which sounded remarkably like their name and which echoed from one side of the valley to the other. I switched on the recorder quickly but, having made their protest at our intrusion, they rapidly flew to the other end of the valley and disappeared from sight. Although disappointed at their sudden departure I was encouraged by their presence in the valley as I had particularly wanted to film keas during the trip and so far had had no opportunity. There were many reports about these New Zealand alpine parrots and how inquisitive and comic they were; they were reputed to undo hikers' knapsacks and systematically search the contents and I was sure that this would be excellent material for a film sequence. In fact, my determination to film them by hook or by crook became an expedition joke, even though I protested loudly that they were an essential part of our film due to the controversy over whether or not they attacked sheep.

The clouds began to thicken again and the light faded but in the nick of time the little plane hurried into the valley once more, catching us unawares by the suddenness of its arrival. We filmed the approach and landing and Gerry and Brian clambering out of the aircraft, registering Gerry's undoubted shock as his feet touched the icy water. Then, waving to the pilot as he took off and sailed over our heads out of the valley, we trudged with all our gear to the little hut where we were to stay for two nights. Conditions in the hut were cramped to say the least and were not improved by the arrival of the deer hunters. We soon had a roaring fire going to dry our sodden clothes and a note of optimism began to creep into the conversation about what we might do and see the following day.

Brian Bell, Gerry Durrell, the author and Jim Saunders outside the hut in Takahe Valley.

When I peered out of the hut window early the next morning my heart sank for it was a total white-out – mist filled the entire valley. Nevertheless, Brian assured us that the mist would gradually burn away and after breakfast it had cleared sufficiently for us to start trudging up the valley towards the best takahe sites. Walking through the long snow grass was difficult enough in any circumstances but with a recorder and ancillary equipment as well as a camera and tripod to carry, the next two days were the most tiring and uncomfortable of the trip. To make matters worse we filmed very little apart from scenic shots for on only one occasion was a takahe briefly sighted and all Jim was able to take was a distant shot of a large dark bird disappearing into a clump of grass. I consoled myself with the thought that with the historic material of the chicks being taken out of the valley I would have just enough to tell the story, although I was disappointed that the keas had never returned to provide a bonus.

After another night in the hut we packed everything possible into knapsacks and, carrying the remainder of the equipment in our hands, started to trek out of the valley. We knew all along that we had to walk out, for the plane would have been unable to take off from the lake with our equipment and gain sufficient height to fly safely out of the valley. The path was steep and slippery but it was at least downhill most of the way, leading eventually to the edge of Lake Te Anau. We arrived at a point several miles from the hotel, but on the opposite side, and there we were picked up by a jet boat – a New Zealand invention which travels at a fast speed and seems able to cope with a water depth of only a few inches.

At the hotel Brian was eager to return to Wellington as quickly as possible so that our last few days in New Zealand could be spent there

Gerry scans the snow grass for a glimpse of Notornis *or* takahe.

filming the remaining continuity shots and the captive birds at Mount Bruce. Having now caught a fleeting glimpse of keas I was more determined than ever to film them for the series and asked Brian's advice on where we should go for the best opportunity to see them. As the conversation was conducted in the bar, my enquiry attracted advice from all quarters and after the topic had been earnestly discussed for some time the general consensus fell heavily in favour of Mount Cook.

Fortunately, we were also informed that there was another tourist hotel with a good cellar at Mount Cook and this did much to alleviate a touch of antagonism which was building up from the rest of the group over my dedication to keas. Mellowed by a good meal we set off towards the foot of Mount Cook, making specifically for a spot close to the Tasman Glacier where we were assured there was an excellent chance of seeing keas. Once again we had been told that these so-called clowns of the mountains are so inquisitive that they will appear as if by magic when you call for them loudly enough. So for half-an-hour we drove slowly and painfully up a rough boulder-strewn track which Jim assured me would shake every tiny screw out of his camera. Eventually we arrived at an excellent vantage point from which we could see the edge of the Tasman Glacier and this seemed an ideal location for Gerry to try calling the keas. We set up the filming and recording equipment and sent Gerry and Jacquie back down the track in the Land-Rover so that we could film an approach shot at the end of which Gerry was supposed to get out and summon the birds.

For some reason I had a pathetic confidence in the local advice I had been given and I was so convinced that it would really work that I decided to shoot the scene even though we had no close-ups of keas yet. For once everything looked right for us; there was good light and not a breath of wind or any other sound. We signalled Gerry and Jacquie to

approach and began filming; the Durrells arrived, turned off the engine, got out and were just about to start calling 'Kea, kea . . .', when, with a thunderous roar and a loud clanking noise, an enormous earth-moving machine appeared round the next bend of the track. For a moment I was convinced that the entire forces of nature and the devil had suddenly combined to prevent me from ever filming keas for until then there had not been sight nor sound of any human activity for miles. The Durrells, of course, saw the funny side of it immediately but as far as I was concerned it was beyond a joke. Fortunately, I had some money on me and finding a banknote I pressed it into the driver's hand with the request that he back out of the way for 20 minutes and turn off the engine. This he did, painfully slowly, and we tried the shot again. But it was to no avail; keas clearly did not like earth-moving machines.

We returned to the Mount Cook Hotel in despair and went up to our rooms just as the maid was turning down the beds. Overhearing our conversation, she said: 'Are you looking for keas, then?'

We looked blankly at her.

'If that's what you want, you'd better be up first thing tomorrow. They come to the back of the hotel every morning.'

'Right then', I said, 'that's it; everyone up before first light'. Jim groaned.

Nevertheless Jim was ready at first light, as indeed were all the party, armed on the maid's advice with quantities of bread and butter which we were assured was a great delicacy for keas. Sure enough there were the keas on the roof of one of the outbuildings at the back of the hotel. Encouraged by the bread and butter, they moved closer, strutting

Gerry would enliven our evening meals by drawing irreverent cartoons of the party on the backs of hotel menu cards; his caption to this one reads: 'What d'you mean – This is the easy way?'.

150

around like a troupe of comics arranged especially for the hotel guests. They were smaller, cheekier parrots than the kakas of Kapiti but they too had an exciting flash of orange under their wings which was revealed whenever they made a short flight from one roof to another. For about 20 minutes they performed all the tricks that keas were supposed to do: they hung upside down from the gutters, cocking their heads and looking impish, they slid down the galvanised roof like drunken skiers, and they investigated anything and everything in a businesslike way – including vehicles and an assortment of boxes and cans dumped at the back of the hotel. Every now and again there would be a little squabble between two of them and a few kea swear words were uttered in the form of raucous screams. Jim was in his element, filming roll after roll and I was able to get all the recordings I needed for the sequence, including the distinctive sound of kea feet on tin roofs. By the time that breakfast was served the keas had got tired of us and flown off but we had filmed the sequence we had so long been waiting for – and all in the space of less than half-an-hour. It was the first morning for a week that I enjoyed a good breakfast.

In the end the keas had turned out to be a bonus and, on paper at any rate, it appeared that at the end of our stay in New Zealand we had enough material for two and a half programmes instead of the proposed two. Gerry and I discussed this problem without too much anxiety on the four-day steamer trip from Wellington to Sydney – for we were now so exhausted after a month of 14-hour days that we felt only inclined to sip beer, watch the passing albatrosses and talk idly of films we wanted to make in the future. Jim, needless to say, had declined the opportunity to sail the Tasman Sea and had hurried off by plane to rest in Sydney.

Several months later, when Paul Khan edited the film, the extra New Zealand material turned out to be no problem at all; for in Australia we discovered another story about an animal returning from extinction and this, paired with the takahe, very conveniently made an additional programme for the series. The rediscovery of Leadbeater's opossum, a charming little arboreal marsupial, closely paralleled the takahe story for it too came to light again in the 1940s after having been given up as lost during the first part of the century.

The responsibility for the conservation of the Leadbeater's opossums rested with the Victoria Fisheries and Wildlife Department with whom we had already been in touch. At the time this was undoubtedly the leading state department concerned with conservation in Australia. So, with only about six weeks allocated to the whole of our stay in Australia, it was with some sense of urgency that I tried to get the party heading west to Melbourne. This was not easy for Gerry's publishers, the British Council, the local BBC office and the Australian Broadcasting Commission had all conspired to draw attention to our arrival in Sydney and this resulted in a packed schedule of press and radio interviews and receptions.

Jim had already collected the Land-Rover which had been loaned to us but when Jacquie saw it she groaned in horror. 'Mark my words', she said ominously, 'that thing is going to be a load of trouble'. It certainly looked ancient and battered, having done many years' service with a local fire brigade. And Jacquie was right. Before we reached Melbourne

the rear differential had gone and on limping into our destination after repairs Jacquie headed straight for the local agent and demanded that the vehicle be replaced. In fact, she was the unofficial expedition motor mechanic at all times, having a total fascination for the internal combustion engine in all its forms.

A reliable vehicle would certainly be required for we were to travel thousands of miles in those few weeks. Until you arrive in Australia, it is very difficult to comprehend the huge distances involved in, for example, just the south-east corner from Melbourne to Brisbane in which most of our activities would lie. A large part of this is occupied by New South Wales which alone covers the same area as most of western Europe. Although the huge amount of travelling used up valuable filming time it did have its advantages in giving us all a feel of the landscape. Quite apart from its people each country has a natural 'taste' – made up of various factors such as the quality of light, the climate, the vegetation including the scent of its commonest flowers, the colour of its soil and so on. Within two days of being in Australia, I had fallen completely in love with it and the affair has lasted ever since. The vast landscapes give me a great sense of freedom which I find intoxicating when coupled with the aesthetic pleasure I derive from images of gum trees with strips of bark dripping from bone-grey trunks, dramatic sunsets, and flamboyant wildlife which includes so many colourful cockatoos and lorakeets.

Paradoxically, in spite of a warm glow of contentment at being in Australia, our 10 days in the Melbourne area were distinctly chilly.

There was no lack of warmth in the reception which we received from the Wildlife Department but much of our work was in the hills south-east of Melbourne, not far from winter sports areas – and the Australian winter was approaching. To make matters worse, some of our first filming had to be done at night, for Leadbeater's opossum – in common with the majority of Australian marsupials – is nocturnal.

Any kind of filming at night is beset with problems, the most obvious of which, of course, is lack of light. In drama productions involving human characters, there are two courses of action open to film-makers: the first is to use large numbers of powerful lamps and, if necessary, mobile generators; and the second is to film during the hours of sunshine but achieve a moonlight effect by the use of modified exposures and blue filters. Both techniques can be used with nocturnal animals provided they can be conditioned to light over a suitable period of time. However, filming totally wild animals on location at night is a different matter.

After discussions with Bob Warnechie, the tall Australian biologist in charge of the Leadbeater project, it was decided that we would attempt to film a night-spotting sequence at the secret location in the forest where the animals had been discovered. Bob told us that he and his colleagues regularly went into the forest with powerful torches which they wore strapped to their heads and which were powered by batteries at their waist. By using the fastest film he had available, Jim calculated that the lamps were just sufficient for an exposure provided the animals were not too far away and a fast, short focal-length lens could be used. For Bob said that, fixed in the beam of a torch, the animals were often fascinated enough to remain comparatively still for several seconds at a time.

We reached our location during daylight so that we could begin filming some establishing shots of Gerry, Jacquie and Bob searching the forest. If filmed at night, none of the forest would register on film – only the flashes and beams from the torches as they caught branches of trees or one or other of the three searchers; so as many shots as possible were taken quickly in the 10 minutes or so of failing light when the surroundings still registered on film yet it was dark enough for the torches to shine brightly. For the next few hours we then plodded quietly and systematically through a large area of forest. From time to time Bob's searching torch would find a pair of glowing eyes and we concentrated our entire torch power on them so that we could identify the owner. Usually it was some other member of the opossum family such as one of the gliders who have special flaps of skin which stretch from front to back legs; when they leap from a tree they are thereby able to glide elegantly to another. Occasionally we saw one of the ground creatures such as a long-nosed bandicoot or a small marsupial mouse. After a couple of hours, I was beginning to give up hope of finding our stars when Bob suddenly froze and started scanning the leafy boughs of some young trees with his torch. As the beam finally rested we saw an attractive little animal peering back at us. It reminded me somewhat of an African bushbaby but its face was more squirrel-like. Now it is one matter to observe an animal briefly under difficult conditions but quite another matter to obtain a good picture of it. Jim was working against all

154

odds and our Leadbeater's opossum, although only seven or eight yards away, was too far away for Jim to obtain satisfactory pictures with his limited lenses. In fact, this had been the problem all evening, so that although we had plenty of shots of Gerry and Jacquie walking through the forest and shining their torches, we had only a few distant shots of the animals which were the most important ingredients of our film sequence.

Gerry was almost delirious with excitement at having seen Leadbeater's opossum in its natural habitat but I gloomily had to admit that we did not yet have a sequence of shots which could be edited together. I now had to face up to an ethical problem: I knew that there were a pair of Leadbeater's opossums in the Wildlife Department at Melbourne, for it had been considered necessary to take a pair into captivity for breeding purposes in case a bush fire should sweep through the restricted part of the forest where they lived. To tell the Leadbeater story adequately, I needed close-ups of the animals, yet to show them as captive creatures in a cage would be an undesirable anti-climax. We *had* seen them in the wild and it was only a technical problem which had prevented us from taking satisfactory pictures; it was, therefore, permissible, I argued, to film the captive animals *under similar light conditions* so that the shots could be incorporated in our night sequence. And that is exactly what we did, borrowing a small room from the Wildlife Department for the purpose. We surrounded the walls with black drapes, installed some branches of the relevant eucalyptus trees and used only a beam of light for illumination while we filmed.

We were much luckier with our second film subject in the Melbourne area although here again things started out badly. A dedicated and good-natured lady ornithologist from the Wildlife Department called Ina Watson was our guide this time and the location was a very beautiful part of Sherbrooke Forest in the Dandenong hills. The eucalyptus trees rise tall and straight there and their continuously stripping bark makes particularly untidy, yet attractive patterns. The undergrowth is not dense and there is a pleasant carpet of leafy mould underfoot; in some damp, dark areas there are groups of imposing tree ferns which give the forest a very distinctive appearance. We walked for the most part on well-established paths, for this is a favourite recreation area for people living in Melbourne. Occasionally we stopped to listen to the laughing call of the kookaburra – a large member of the kingfisher family – which was still a great novelty for us; and all the time we heard the gentle, tinkling chorus of the small green bell-birds high in the branches above.

The bird that we had come specially to film was the most famous songster of them all – or perhaps I should say mimic, for the lyrebird incorporates the calls of many other birds as he performs his display song. Sherbrooke Forest is famous for its lyrebirds but as it is such a popular tourist spot the birds have become used to intrusion and we hoped that this would make it comparatively easy for us to film the display. Ina showed us several display mounds in little circular clearings in the undergrowth – but the only activity we saw was of female lyrebirds scratching around on the forest floor for food with their large strong feet. Eventually, we found 'Spotty' – a well-known male bird who had a good reputation for performing in front of visitors but he,

155

too, seemed only interested in food. We kept close to him all afternoon but not once was he disposed to utter a single note.

The next day we resolved again to spend every available hour of daylight with cameras at the ready near Spotty's favourite display mounds, but for hours there was no sign of him at all. We were occasionally irritated to hear other lyrebirds displaying some distance away but I guessed that they would stop before we could locate them and so we decided to persevere in one location. By now Ina was getting a little embarrassed by the shortage of lyrebird activity and went off with Jacquie to make a reconnaissance in another part of the forest. Then we heard another burst of lyrebird song quite close, whereupon Jim, who could stand the suspense no longer, grabbed the small Bolex camera and strode off purposefully in the direction of the very loud and continuous song.

'Suppose Spotty comes back now?' I shouted after him. 'We won't be able to get that synch shot.'

'That's all right – it's all set up on the right lens stop; all you've got to do is press the button and Gerry can record', replied Jim gaily,

Leadbeater's opossum.

disappearing into the undergrowth. He was obviously convinced that Spotty was not going to show up so he wasn't really worried. However, I was greatly concerned in case we missed a golden opportunity, for occasions when it is possible to film a bird singing with a sound camera occur very rarely. Although we did not have a properly blimped camera (and camera noise would therefore be a limiting factor) the song of a lyrebird is so loud that, even with the limitations of our equipment, I was convinced we could approach close enough to obtain a wildlife scoop, if Spotty returned.

Within a few minutes of Jim's departure, Spotty *did* return. He approached one of his display grounds, which we had been closely watching all morning, and this time he walked on to it and burst into song. Shaking with excitement, I picked up the Arriflex camera and motioned to Gerry to turn on the recorder and move in with the microphone. Unfortunately, Spotty did not hold his tail in full display but I was so close that I could only include the head and body of the bird within the camera frame anyway. The song was almost deafening. I looked at my acting recordist with some concern hoping he was aware of the need to wind down the gain control and avoid distortion. I wasn't very confident that the recorder was working satisfactorily for Gerry is

157

one of those unfortunate people who seem to have the knack of rendering perfectly serviceable pieces of equipment useless by merely touching them. I had previously noted that at Gerry's turn of a switch, film would jam in cameras, tape would fly into a tangle in recorders, and screws would fall out of any kind of equipment. In this case, I could see with relief that the recorder spools were turning but the needle was flickering dangerously into an overload position. As neither Gerry nor I were in a position to reach it for adjustment, I signalled that he should creep in and move the microphone further away from the display ground. Two-and-a-half minutes later the film ran out of the camera but we kept the recorder going for the Sound Library until Spotty grew tired and made a nonchalant exit through the undergrowth.

I couldn't believe our luck but I wished that Jim had been there to film it. I checked exposure and focus and everything seemed all right; we also played back part of the tape and that was good too. I breathed a sigh of relief but, with little confidence in my camera-work, decided not to make much of the incident when Jim returned. He appeared about a quarter-of-an-hour later looking distinctly pleased with himself.

'Don't worry', he said, 'it's all in the bag.' Taken aback by this confident statement, Gerry and I looked at him blankly. While Jim pointedly packed the camera away, he explained what had happened. He had tracked down the bird responsible for the burst of song nearby only to find that it stopped singing when he was within camera range. But in a while another male bird approached and this caused the first male to display its tail fully and burst into song. The second bird then responded in like manner and the two faced up to each other a few feet apart, dancing and displaying aggressively over what must have been the boundary of their two territories. It was clear from Jim's description that he had filmed something quite different from Gerry and myself and so in one glorious half-hour we had turned failure into unqualified success.

We stayed in the general vicinity of Melbourne for a few days filming such activities as koala bear translocation before heading back towards Canberra to visit Harry Frith and his colleagues in the Wildlife Section of the CSIRO. We had called in on the way down to Melbourne from Sydney and had already made provisional arrangements to film what we hoped would be the most exciting event of the entire trip. The scientists were tackling the problem of how to control populations of wild kangaroos and as part of this research were endeavouring to discover as much as possible about the basic biology of the animal. There were two approaches to their work: on the one hand they had selected three areas in the wild in different types of sheep country where kangaroo movements, food and pattern of breeding were studied and compared. We visited the study area near Griffiths in what was called high class sheep country; this had a small but regular rainfall of 15 inches per year and about three sheep to an acre. To study their movements the scientists put identifiable collars around the kangaroos' necks and the catching techniques required for this gave us a spectacular and fast-moving sequence in which, for good measure, some emus inadvertently got caught up in the chase. But our greatest hopes lay in the compounds of the Research Station at Canberra where the CSIRO

Some frames from Jim Saunders' film of the birth of a kangaroo. The neonate is crawling upwards through its mother's fur towards the pouch.

was conducting a controlled breeding programme as a second line of research. Geoffrey Sharman, who was leading the research into the breeding biology of the kangaroos, had by then discovered that the gestation period was about 31–33 days. This enabled him to forecast the time of births to within a day or two and he had given us a date on which to return to Canberra for the next one.

One of Geoff's colleagues had already taken some film of a recent birth and this we had seen on our first visit to Canberra; although technically satisfactory in terms of exposure and focus, the film consisted of only a few close-up shots which would be difficult to edit together. We therefore asked if Jim could film another birth with Gerry and Jacquie present. In this way we would be able to make a major sequence with a running time of several minutes as I learned from Geoff that the female's behaviour immediately before birth was in itself interesting and worth filming. For safety, we arrived at Canberra more than a day ahead of the birth time predicted by Geoff but made use of this by filming a sequence on the echidna – the only other egg-laying mammal beside the platypus.

Having set up all our equipment in the pregnant female's compound – including lights in case the birth occurred at night – we retired to a nearby motel, keeping close to the telephone at all times like expectant fathers. On the second afternoon, Geoff rang us to say that he was now confident that the birth would occur that evening. A few hours later he called again to report that the female had begun to clean out her pouch – a sure sign that the birth was imminent. We joined Geoff in the compound within a few minutes and checked the two cameras and the recorder once more, praying that there would be no technical failure at the critical moment.

I had stationed Geoff next to Gerry with the microphone so that a running commentary could be given during the birth. This would not only provide guidance for editing but I hoped to be able to use some of it on the sound track of the completed film. Geoff had warned us that the baby was so small – no more than three-quarters-of-an-inch long – that it would be difficult to film, especially as the female would be licking herself during the birth and her head would probably get in the way of the camera's view. So Jim and I positioned ourselves at right angles to each other, Jim with the close-up lens and me taking a slighter wider shot, in order to maximise the chances of seeing the tiny neonate. We took some footage of the female cleaning out her pouch and then she began to put her head right down between her legs and lick around the uro-genital opening.

'Shouldn't be long now', said Geoff confidently, but the female got up again and shuffled around uncomfortably but without any hurry. It was a bitterly cold night so we withdrew a few yards to the cover of a small hut where Gerry produced something warming out of a bottle. A short while later, there was a call from one of Geoff's assistants and we hurried back to our action stations. This time the female had wriggled herself into a dusty depression with her back against a wooden post, tail thrust forward between her legs. We started our cameras in anticipation, but the female promptly got up again and shuffled around some more before assuming the same position. This time she licked around the uro-genital opening with more determination and suddenly Geoff said: 'There it is, I see it!'

I had the camera running but, although I knew I had focused on the right area, I could see no young. I hoped Jim was more successful. Then I heard Jim mutter softly, 'I got it. Gosh, isn't it small?' I still had seen nothing that I could recognise through the viewfinder when Geoff suddenly leapt forward with one of his assistants to grab the female. Within a few seconds, they had injected an anaesthetic into the tail and the female was already quietening down.

'Quick, get your cameras in here', Geoff said, and Jim responded quickly, putting a close-up attachment on the lens. The tiny embryonic kangaroo, bare and blind, its two feeble forelimbs with sharp claws for climbing, had just reached the lip of the pouch when Geoff had sprung into action. Deftly, but gently, he picked it up before it had time to attach itself to a teat inside the pouch and placed it on the mother's fur just above the mother's uro-genital opening. The mother was now unconscious but her minute offspring relentlessly ploughed its way back up through her fur towards the pouch again.

The camera purred away and Geoff, reading our thoughts, said, 'It is remarkable isn't it – how it knows to keep going upwards? Almost certainly the primary thing is its sense of smell. We know that because anatomically the olfactory parts of the brain are the only ones really well developed at this stage. And you can see that the external opening of the nostrils is well developed, too'. The tiny kangaroo, weighing less than a 30-thousandth part of its mother, had once more disappeared over the lip of the pouch and we left it alone to find the teat. We made sure that the female was well after she recovered from the anaesthetic and then took a few reaction shots of Gerry and Jacquie to help with the film editing. We packed away our equipment, tired but blissfully happy. That night we had very good cause to celebrate so we toasted Geoff Sharman and his fellow workers many times in good Australian wine.

Chapter 10

First steps in the jungle

Two weeks after filming the kangaroo birth in the cold night air at Canberra, Jim and I were bidding Gerry and Jacquie a temporary farewell under the warm winter sun of Queensland's Gold Coast, south of Brisbane. It had been a long drive but we had filmed many good things on the way, a visit to David Fleay's Wildlife Reserve at Burleigh Heads being particularly productive. David had been the only person to breed the duck-billed platypus in captivity and so Gerry was especially pleased to talk to him and look at his platypus exhibit.

As usual Gerry and Jacquie planned to travel by sea and this gave Jim and me an opportunity for a few days' relaxation before rejoining them in Singapore – a wise move in view of the events of the next few weeks. It was fortunate that we should film in Malaya last – rather than first – on our four-month trip, otherwise I might never have stayed the course and given up film directing for ever in a state of complete mental breakdown. Gerry had warned me that 'it takes a little longer in the tropics' and as far as I was concerned this became the understatement of the year. Things did not go well from the moment we began our drive up from Singapore to Kuala Lumpur: two breakdowns en route meant that we missed a press reception at our destination and probably lost some valuable contacts as well. Moreover, I had not yet got used to the climate and found that the hot humid weather blunted both my mental and physical alertness.

We had been booked into a comfortable, air-conditioned hotel in Kuala Lumpur and as it was rather expensive Jim and I agreed to share a twin-bedded room. While Jim checked over his cameras and lenses I did battle with local officials as best as I could and Gerry made as many contacts as possible with local European naturalists and animal-lovers. Usually this was no great problem and, indeed, for the past two and a half months we had been used to a steady stream of telephone calls from Durrell fans offering tame native animals as film subjects or potential guests at Gerry's zoo. It was no surprise, therefore, when the telephone rang one day and a gentleman with an Indian accent enquired if I was the BBC producer working with Mr Durrell. On learning that this was so, the caller then proceeded to talk excitedly about a number of semi-tame native animals which we might like to film. As some of these had names with which I was not familiar I asked the caller to hold on while I fetched Mr Durrell. There were some very odd things about the conversation and, knowing from long experience that Gerry was not averse to a little practical joke from time to time, I hurried next door hoping to catch him on the hotel telephone. When I arrived Gerry was lying on the bed, a picture of innocence, reading a scientific paper of some kind. I hurried back to my room only to find the caller had hung up. Almost immediately there were waves of laughter from the next room which confirmed my early suspicions that it was all a joke, designed no doubt to relieve the tension.

An hour or so later the telephone rang again and as I was having a shower at the time, Jim answered it. This time it was the sing-song voice of a Chinese gentleman enquiring after me. Jim, having witnessed the first incident, quickly rose to the occasion, instantly replying:

'Tellibly solly, Mister Parsons sitting on potty!' There was a strained silence at the other end, followed by a click as the caller hung up. I emerged from the bathroom as Jim said, 'Don't worry, it's only Gerry again up to his silly pranks'.

'Who was he supposed to be this time?' I enquired.

'Sounded like James Aw, Chief Game Warden or something . . .'. I stared at him, horrified.

'Are you *sure* it was Gerry?' I asked. 'I've been trying to get hold of the Chief Game Warden for days!'

I hurried into the Durrells' room and it was soon clear that on this occasion they were not the culprits. Hoping that Jim's remark had not

An albino emu with Gerald Durrell at David Fleay's Wildlife Reserve in Queensland.

A comment from Gerry after an unsuccessful attempt by Jim and the author to film seladang.

"So then he said - I'm from the B.B.C. —"

been properly understood, I telephoned Mr Aw's office to arrange an appointment. It so happened that he could see us late that afternoon but as the Durrells already had another engagement, it was up to me to get as much help as possible from this very important contact.

James Aw's residence was a considerable drive from the hotel so I insisted that Jim should accompany me; I felt he owed me something anyway for getting me into such a delicate situation. The first sight of the interior of the house was not one to raise the spirits of a film crew making a series with a conservation theme, for there were many trophies decorating the wall and floor, including a number of tiger skins. Nevertheless Mr Aw was as polite and charming as one could wish and there was no reference to the curious telephone conversation earlier in the day. Almost as soon as we arrived Mr Aw clapped his hands and his wife silently appeared from behind a screen carrying a tray on which were a full bottle of Scotch whisky and three glasses. The contents of the bottle disappeared with alarming speed while we discussed various filming possibilities, after which Mr Aw enquired if we would like some Chinese food. I thought that this might be rather a good idea to soak up some of the whisky and thinking that it would probably materialise quickly from behind the screen with another clap of Mr Aw's hands, I promptly accepted. At this point a look of horror began to spread over Jim's face for he was very conservative about his food and usually somewhat reluctant to try exotic dishes.

My acceptance having been made, Mr Aw swept out of the room, only to appear seconds later with a second bottle of whisky which he took with him as he beckoned us out of the house. We walked a short distance to the local village where there were various open-air stalls and

a Chinese restaurant to which we were led. From the food piled up on adjoining tables I could tell that this was going to be a long session. Jim's horror had now turned to near-panic and I knew that it would be up to me to keep Mr Aw engaged in convivial conversation and at the same time be seen to enjoy the Chinese food and the whisky which he so graciously had arranged for us. To make matters worse I was not used to drinking large quantities of whisky under such humid conditions and already I had begun to feel uncomfortably inebriated.

A leathery turtle digs its nest at Dungun on the east coast of Malaya.

The next two hours were a nightmare but somehow I managed to keep my senses together enough to obtain all the permissions and promises of help that we needed. Jim's abstinence on this occasion was provident for he at least was capable of the drive home while his unhappy passenger hung his head out of the window, gasping for air.

We aimed to film two programmes in Malaya but after about 10 days we had still not shot a single sequence; indeed, we had only the flimsiest outlines on paper, there being so many unknown factors. Eventually we completed all the arrangements for the filming of the giant leathery turtles nesting near Dungun on the East Coast and, borrowing an electrician and a portable generator from the Malayan Film Unit, we set off across country to rendezvous with the local Fisheries Officer. We filmed some travelogue scenes and other wildlife along the way and with the turtles as the principal sequence to my surprise I found that I had enough for one of the programmes. The other programme, which was to be about Malaya's vanishing jungle, posed much greater problems and almost every shot in the film was obtained only through an immense amount of trouble.

The theme of this programme was quite simply an account of the diversity of life in the jungle, coupled with Gerry's first impressions – for this was the first Asian jungle he had ever visited. The sting in the tail was a sequence on the large-scale felling of native forest for new plantations and the subsequent fragmentation of the jungle into pockets, many of which were not of sufficient size to maintain viable populations of some of the larger species. It is a theme that will be familiar to many viewers now but Gerry was one of the first to call attention to the problem on a popular television programme.

Having decided on the broad shape and theme of our programme we set about building up our portrait of a jungle by filming shots of the

Boarding a river boat whilst working at the National Park.

" FRANKLY, I DON'T CARE WHO YOUR FROM —"

LEFT
*Another comment
from Gerry after
filming turtles . . .*

RIGHT
*Some frames from
Jim's film of the
flying lizards; they
can extend flaps of
skin on both sides
of their bodies in
order to glide from
tree to tree.*

greatest variety of wildlife we could find. Some of the smaller species which we would probably never see in the wild, such as the charming little mouse deer, were filmed using captive animals in natural surroundings. Others, such as the flying lizard, were filmed under carefully controlled conditions in the garden of a leading naturalist, Geoffrey Allen. We obtained as much material as possible authentically at our main location which was to be at the headquarters of the largest National Park – the Teman Negara, formerly the King George V National Park.

We drove first to the town of Kuala Lipis and stayed at a Government Rest House overnight. The next morning, we assembled at a landing stage on the Jelai river where a jet-boat had been sent to pick us up. The journey was fast but also very interesting because we never knew what creature we might surprise at a river bank around the next corner. It was also a very long journey and as we were sitting in rather cramped conditions we were relieved when the boatman decided to pull in for a short while at a local town at the junction of the main river and one of its tributaries. Just before this stop Jim had lost his hat and was still bemoaning the fact to our unsympathetic ears when the boat pulled in at the landing stage. Hopping neatly out he started striding up the hill towards the nearby village.

'Where do you think you're going?' we asked in unison.

'To buy a hat', said Jim tersely. We all looked at each other and burst into laughter. Undaunted, Jim strode on, stopping to fire a last confident round while he was still within earshot.

'I'll get some drinks as well if you like.'

We gazed at him sadly as his figure disappeared amongst the little collection of primitive huts on top of the river bank. We were agreeing that three months' filming away from home was far too long for anybody's sanity when we saw the unmistakable figure of Jim jauntily

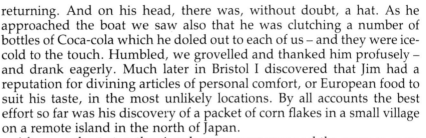

returning. And on his head, there was, without doubt, a hat. As he approached the boat we saw also that he was clutching a number of bottles of Coca-cola which he doled out to each of us – and they were ice-cold to the touch. Humbled, we grovelled and thanked him profusely – and drank eagerly. Much later in Bristol I discovered that Jim had a reputation for divining articles of personal comfort, or European food to suit his taste, in the most unlikely locations. By all accounts the best effort so far was his discovery of a packet of corn flakes in a small village on a remote island in the north of Japan.

After our short stop the river became narrower and the passage more difficult, as the frequency of rapids increased. There was a certain amount of floating weed in the river and periodically this jammed up the intake of the jet-boat so that we shuddered to a stop. Alarmingly the boatman would then leap over the side, feet first and clothed, disappear beneath the surface, and emerge 10 seconds or so later, coughing and spluttering, with a handful of weed in his hand. The frequency of this procedure increased irritatingly as we got closer to the Park Head-quarters and the last occasion when we drifted lifelessly downstream was when we were actually within sight of the landing stage. By now the clouds had gathered thickly and turned to the colour of a ripe Victorian plum and while our boatman was still groping around somewhere underneath us the first drops of tropical rain fell heavily, churning up the surface of the water into turmoil.

The accommodation at the headquarters was fairly primitive but there was electricity for Jim to charge the camera batteries and plenty of good food and beer. A party of Sikhs on a fishing trip provided entertaining company. Together we sipped our drinks and listened to the sounds of the forest slowly change as the day-shift cicadas gave way to the night-shift of tree frogs and crickets. From downstream wave after wave of fruit bats left their roosting tree, fanning out to feeding stations in the forest behind us.

I was up at dawn next morning to stand on the verandah with Gerry and record the process being reversed. The day insects began to warm up species by species but there was also a sudden chorus of haunting cries from a group of tall trees just downriver from the headquarters buildings. They were the calls of gibbons – one of the top priorities on our filming list. With powerful binoculars I could just see their gymnas-tic movements silhouetted against the sky, and one of the major problems in filming in a tropical forest was illustrated perfectly. To obtain any shots of life in the canopy we would have to find locations where we could perhaps film across a small valley or go to the expense and trouble of building a very elaborate observation tower.

After breakfast we set out on foot to explore the forest and I decided to film Gerry and Jacquie taking their first steps in the Asian jungle. We spent several hours photographing different types of vegetation, includ-ing the tall trees with their huge buttress roots, and then began taking close-ups of a great variety of invertebrates – huge longhorn beetles, giant moths, lantern bugs looking like bits of animated twig, colourful caterpillars dressed like Chinese dragons and everywhere cicadas, grasshoppers, ants and, most obnoxious of all, leeches.

I had heard about the leeches before I left England. 'Be sure to take

169

jungle boots for Malaya', the experts had said, 'it's the only thing to keep the leeches out'. They were wrong. Nothing keeps the leeches out. Jungle boots, by lacing high up around the calf, over your trousers, were supposed to present an impenetrable barrier through which the most devious of leeches could find no way. In fact, if it didn't manage to squeeze through a lacehole in your boot, any normal leech would loop determinedly all the way up a trouser leg to slide either through your flies or over the top of your trouser belt.

You never noticed the leeches when you first walked into the forest; but if you stood still just for a few seconds and looked around you there would be some of those insidious little creatures attached to the tips of nearby foliage, like slimy looper caterpillars, waving odiously around to pick up your whereabouts. Meanwhile, others would be making their way along the forest floor towards your boots, there to start their upward journey in search of blood. Gerry showed us that once you had found them, you could get rid of them either by pressing a lighted cigarette on each of them or by dropping a pinch of salt on them. Since none of us wished to smoke like a chimney all day or carry salt cellars around in our pocket we eventually resigned ourselves to the fact that inevitably there would be a mutual leech picking routine to be played

A group of siamangs calling – a chorus of these and other gibbons was often heard near the Park headquarters.

out on returning to Park Headquarters each evening. By that stage any leeches still attached would be bloated with blood and the size of large marbles.

Over a period of a week we slowly pieced together a mosaic of pictures which would give an impression of the jungle, its inhabitants and its moods. I knew it would be a rather gentle, atmospheric film with perhaps not enough action to command attention at the start of a series. So I decided that we must have an adventurous beginning to the programme which would indicate the theme of Gerry and Jacquie on the move. It then occurred to me that the last part of our trip to the headquarters had been quite exciting over the rapids and so I outlined my idea that we should shoot a sequence of just that, including an in-vision sound shot of Gerry introducing the series from the boat just on the point of entering the rapids. This idea was received without enthusiasm by the others but in spite of their reluctance to participate they could see that it might make a good opening sequence.

I knew of a piece of rapid water about a mile from the headquarters and elected to spend an entire afternoon filming there as I needed to shoot the sequence from several different angles – including inside the boat. Since our arrival at the park we had been travelling around in a long canoe-type boat with an outboard motor and I decided to use this for the sequence rather than the jet-boat as it looked much more in keeping with the surroundings.

The filming went well, the boat shipping what I considered to be a satisfactory amount of water as it shot the rapids. After we had taken three different angles of this, Gerry and Jacquie not unreasonably began to get a little bored with getting wet and in fact Jacquie went as far as to state categorically that wild horses would not drag her down that route again. Unfortunately, Gerry still had to do his sound film introduction so I sent the boatman back to the headquarters with Jacquie so that she

We spent an entire afternoon filming the opening sequence on the rapids for our first programme.

could get dry; and Jim went too so that he could fetch some more film stock and an additional wide angle lens which he needed for the shot in the boat.

Gerry and I, having been deposited on a sandbank in mid-river, were quietly discussing how the filming was going when Gerry, who had been looking idly over my shoulder, suddenly shouted 'Look out!'. Glancing behind me, I saw what I crudely described at the time as a bloody great snake swimming towards us. From the urgency in Gerry's voice I gathered it might be dangerous so, like him, leapt several yards up the sandbank at lightning speed. Our sudden movement evidently drew the snake's attention to us for the first time for it sharply raised its head well above the water surface, swerved abruptly and swam at great speed upstream, making for the opposite bank where it quickly disappeared into the undergrowth.

I watched the whole performance mesmerised until Gerry broke the spell by telling me triumphantly that we had just had a superb view of a fine king cobra – reputedly one of the most deadly snakes in Malaya. It proved a point, he claimed; all this rubbish about the jungle seething with deadly creatures who will attack you at the slightest provocation is just material that fiction writers have seen fit to perpetuate. In reality, given the chance, most large creatures that can do harm to you will take the trouble to get well out of your way. The exceptions, of course, are the multitude of invertebrates, some of which are only too pleased to make straight for your succulent skin. By watching where we walked and by inspecting the inside of our empty shoes each morning none of us came to any harm – except for a few mosquito bites and, of course, the ever-present leeches. To this day they are the only animals that I really loathe.

Chapter 11

The Major and the Prince

The four-month trip with the Durrells had virtually provided a crash course in a wide range of techniques associated with wildlife filming as well as giving me invaluable overseas experience in many different habitats. This had come at a fortunate time because the Unit now had to originate a far greater proportion of its programme output since amateur and independent sources had been used up or were not of sufficiently high quality. As my appointment had been as Film Producer for the Unit I was expected to provide single feature documentaries as well as a number of programmes for the *Look* series each year, and this requirement was the cue for four of the most crowded and exhilarating years of my career with the BBC.

The pressure was on immediately I returned from leave after filming the Durrell series which, on Jim's suggestion, was to be called *Two in the Bush*. Desmond had not been able to find a biologist to head the Unit and therefore called back Nicholas Crocker for a few years so that there would at least be a highly experienced producer in charge 'to maintain and advance the professional broadcasting standards of the Unit'. However Nicky was not able to take up his duties fully until late summer so that not only were we without a leader but also short of a pair of hands at a very busy period. The new children's series, *Animal Magic*, began while I was in New Zealand and was now running fortnightly, produced by Winwood Reade and directed in the studio by Jeffery Boswall, although he still had major responsibilities for our radio output.

Although Nicky had agreed to return for a while, Desmond had by no means given up his dream that our senior producer would have a firm academic position in his own right and he made this clear in a long paper to the Board of Management on the occasion of the Unit's fifth birthday. Desmond's report, endorsed by the Controller of West Region, Frank Gillard, was probably the most important and influential document in the Unit's history; it laid the foundations of its policy for the next 20 years and set out its principal aspirations, particularly regarding our relationship with biologists. 'The spirit of scientific enquiry must have pride of place', he wrote. 'In handling this subject we expose ourselves to the critical scrutiny of scientists, and their approval is an important endorsement. Moreover, it is their work that throws up the ideas and instances and controversies from which programmes are made. We look to them as contributors, as source material, as consul-

tants and as elite opinion on our efforts. In short, we need their goodwill.'

Many of Desmond's recommendations took a long time to realise but the fact that the Unit now had a clear and recognised role in the Corporation was substantiated by the speedy approval of extra staff for the rapidly expanding Film Library and the setting up of an annual bursary for visiting cameramen, producers and recordists in order to strengthen the Unit internationally. The need was also expressed for an additional cameraman post, although the continuing role of professionals such as Heinz Sielmann and Armand Denis, as well as semi-professionals such as Chris Mylne of the small RSPB Film Unit, was readily acknowledged. So, too, was the work of 'specialist amateurs', such as Eric Ashby, but the importance of these was perhaps not fully realised at the time, for from such talented naturalists were to develop a new breed of independent professional wildlife cameramen who today provide the cutting edge of a highly specialised industry. In the 1960s several of them were part-timers, working at holidays, weekends and in summer evenings, but it was their work which sustained us for several years and many of my own productions were only possible through the building up of very close working relationships in which we experimented, improvised and learnt from each other.

One of the key figures with whom I was involved for several years was Eric Ashby who made for *Look* further studies of his beloved badgers and foxes as well as films about hares and the behaviour of the New Forest ponies. Another to whom we owed much during the same period was Leslie Jackman, formerly presenter of the Club Room item in *Out of Doors*. Leslie had shot some short film sequences for his items in the children's programme and this fired an ambition to shoot a complete film for the *Look* series. As Leslie ran his small aquarium at Paignton during the summer months he already had the facilities and the stock for filming marine life. The tanks, pumps, filters, etc, could also be used for keeping freshwater species and with such a head start Leslie needed little persuasion from me to begin specialising in small underwater subjects. Initially his co-worker was fellow-teacher, David Halfhide, who ran the aquarium with him, but later another teacher, Ron Peggs, became his partner in an enterprising part-time film business which was responsible for a number of attractive *Look* programmes.

Before either Eric Ashby or Leslie Jackman had got into the routine of turning out at least one *Look* programme each per year, they both became involved in a feature documentary which I had begun even before setting off for New Zealand. After the success of *The Unknown Forest* it was important to offer another comparable idea as quickly as possible. I believed that one of the reasons for the success of the New Forest film was that it took something very familiar to a great many viewers – in this case a patch of forest visited, or at least seen, by many holiday-makers each year – and revealed its true nature in a surprising way.

I was considering how the same principle might be applied to a field on the outskirts of a town or a piece of coastline popular with holiday-

Leslie Jackman's subjects were available in the aquarium that he ran at Paignton: this is a hermit crab with its parasitic anemone.

'Mad March Hares'
– a scene from
another film made
by Eric Ashby for
Look.

makers, when a local newspaper article caught my eye. It dealt with a local council controversy over the felling of a tree at the centre of a village. It was a very old tree on the village green but it had become dangerous and the local authorities had declared that it must be felled. As soon as I saw the newspaper report I knew I had my story. 'The Village Tree' was a phenomenon I was familiar with, having spent most of my childhood in Devonshire. Very often there was a large tree somewhere near the centre of each village under which the local lads gathered on summer evenings and at weekends. The coach taking the local football team on away fixtures always started from this tree; on its trunk were pinned the notices of whist drives, socials and fêtes, and its branches were a testing ground for the climbing skills of the village urchins. I thought that all these activities could be used to counterpoint a wildlife film which focused on the many kinds of insects and birds that lived, fed and nested in the tree. And if I could locate another tree that had to be felled like the tree in the newspaper article, its demise would provide a poignant end to the film story of a complete annual wildlife cycle in its branches.

After consulting with my colleague, John Burton, who is an excellent entomologist, there was little doubt that the best opportunities for filming would occur if we used an oak tree as the star of the show. The problem was finding an oak tree which was due for felling at least a year ahead of the event, for it would be necessary to film it through all the seasons first. John Burton poured out endless information about oak trees from which I chose a number of bird and insect 'principal characters'; but the research material which pleased me most of all was that which John provided on jays. In the autumn these colourful

Leslie Jackman also filmed freshwater life. For some above-water scenes in a Look *film he used his two sons, Rodger and Paul. Rodger (on the left) is now a leading wildlife cameraman himself.*

members of the crow family collect ripe acorns for food, but in a good year when the acorns are plentiful the jays fly away with many of them and plant them in the ground – presumably as a winter food store. The jays don't always find their store again, however, and so the acorns germinate and eventually become young oak trees. It is believed that, in this way, jays have been largely responsible for the distribution of oak trees in Britain.

When I learned about the jays I nearly jumped for joy because it provided me with an exciting and appropriate wildlife sequence immediately before the felling which was to be the end of the film. The action of the jays showed one way in which the line of the old tree was to be perpetuated. Encouraged by the dramatic possibilities of all this I sat down and wrote a full shooting script, weaving wildlife sequences in and out of a chain of simple incidents associated with the role of the tree in village life. It looked good on paper but the problems were now building up as I still had not found a tree and not many of the wildlife sequences I had included on John's advice seemed to have been filmed before – including the jays with the acorns.

Enthusiastic help in finding a tree came from Bruce Campbell. He had many good friends in the Forestry Commission and a message eventually arrived from a contact there that a likely tree had been found in the Forest of Dean. Bruce and I hurried over to the forest to inspect it and discovered that it was next to the famous Speech House Hotel, right in the centre of the forest. It was a splendid looking tree, not as old and gnarled as I would have liked, but it did have a number of things in its favour. It was within a foot or two of the road and very close to the Speech House – so close that it was a traffic hazard because of the way it

OVERLEAF
'The Major' in all its early autumn glory.

177

obscured the view of oncoming traffic from people leaving the hotel bar; for this reason it was due to be felled. Unfortunately, there were no other houses nearby so there was no sense of a village community, but the tree did overlook a cricket field and I discovered that the Morris Men danced under its branches every Whitsuntide. These advantages, coupled with the fact that the Forestry Commission were prepared to fell the tree at my convenience in the late autumn, easily outweighed the disadvantages of its location, which I believed I could overcome by careful choice of angles and the use of juxtaposed shots taken in another village.

After several weeks' further search I could find nothing to improve on this tree so I settled for it and rewrote the script to include sequences of the Morris Men and a cricket match. A title was the next problem for I wanted to give the tree an identity and even build up affection for it in the viewers' minds during the course of the film. I then discovered that the oldest and grandest tree in an oak wood was sometimes called the major tree and this gave me the clue. The old tree in my imaginary village would be affectionately known as *The Major* – and that would be the title of my film.

The shooting script was detailed, listing individual scenes involving wildlife as well as those with human activity. It included such instructions as 'looper caterpillar moves along branch, head of blue tit comes into shot and takes caterpillar', . . . 'jay flies away from tree with acorn and buries it in nearby field'. Having written such incidents into the script I began to think seriously about how to film them. Although I would be able to use BBC cameramen and freelancers such as Bill Morris to shoot the human sequences it was obvious that the wildlife material would have to be filmed by someone who was prepared to invest a considerable amount of time experimenting and developing techniques as well as doing the actual filming. I approached the two 'part-time' cameramen who I hoped would specialise in the two main types of work involved: Eric Ashby to film the birds and small mammals; Leslie Jackman to film the insects. Both were intrigued by the idea and agreed to do their best over a period of a year or so. Leslie's subjects were so small that almost all of them would have to be filmed under controlled conditions and under artificial light in a room at his home that served as a studio. On the other hand, most of Eric's subjects were wild creatures which would be found close to his cottage in the New Forest.

The Major, in fact, was eventually filmed in four different locations by four different cameramen – and in colour, but more of that later. In each season wide-angle shots of the tree itself, together with human action sequences, were filmed by Bill Morris or staff cameraman, George Shears; additional close-up sequences on the development of the male catkins, the female flowers, oak galls, etc, were filmed on convenient oak trees in Bristol; insects were filmed in Paignton at Leslie Jackman's home, using specimens collected by John Burton near Bristol or sent to us by John's entomological friends; and finally the birds and mammals were filmed by Eric Ashby on the oak trees which grew just outside his cottage in the New Forest.

Work proceeded slowly throughout the year and although there were many failures, particularly in the difficult controlled filming, most

sequences were eventually completed. Then came the all-important autumn sequences and the collecting of acorns by the jays. This was Eric Ashby's responsibility. He was certainly the right man for the job because I knew of no one else who had the time and the patience to tackle it; moreover, he had noticed some acorn-collecting activity by jays in previous years so we knew that filming the behaviour was at least within the realms of possibility. As soon as the acorns matured Eric was indeed able to film a few brief shots in an oak tree bordering the small field at the back of his cottage. Then came a crisis. A letter from Eric arrived one day to say that there were no acorns left on the trees near his cottage, furthermore it was such a bad year for acorns that he could find no trees locally which bore any acorns at all.

I hurried down to the New Forest by car and picked up Eric to make a more extensive reconnaissance. Eric had no motor transport at the time and so could not cover large distances from his home without me or the help of local friends. After much searching we found one oak tree several miles away which had some boughs bearing acorns. Taking care not to mutilate the tree we carefully cut off some small branches and took them back to Eric's cottage. The plan was to attach them invisibly to the tree which the jays had previously visited in the hope that they would return looking for more. One of the chicken houses in the field belonging to Eric was moved into a suitable position close to the tree so that it would serve as a hide. The ruse worked; the jays did return and took the acorns. Eric then replaced the spent branches with fresh ones so that a variety of angles and close-ups could be filmed, building up a sequence of several minutes' duration.

It was only when we had completed editing the sequence that I realised how lucky we had been. Eric's skill, of course, made the sequence possible but paradoxically our luck had come with the bad acorn year. For if all the oak trees in the district near Eric's home had born many acorns it is extremely unlikely that he would have been able to pin-point any jay activity. It was because of the *shortage* of acorns that it had been possible to bait one tree with fresh supplies so that the jays kept returning.

After the film editing by Paul Khan, I asked Desmond Hawkins to write the narration and Paul Rogers to record it. Sidney Sager wrote the music, based largely on folk tunes. Between us we tried to make people so involved with 'The Major' that by the time it was felled in the final sequence, and the end credits had rolled over the cross-section of its trunk, they would feel that they had lost an old friend. As soon as we received a satisfactory print from the laboratories I invited a few colleagues and one or two contributors to visit the viewing theatre and see the film. As the final music faded there was a long silence and my heart sank; it meant, I guessed, that nobody liked it and they were too kind to say anything. There was a slightly embarrassed cough and the lights went up; then I saw that one of the secretaries was pushing her handkerchief hurriedly away and a famous naturalist was brushing a tear from the corner of his eye. No further words were necessary

The next feature documentary I co-produced with Nicky Crocker after he returned to the Unit and the idea arose out of a conversation with Desmond Morris, with whom Nicky had worked on several zoo programmes. Desmond, and his wife Ramona, were involved with books about the relationship between man and animals and on this theme it seemed that the horse would make an ideal subject for an in-depth film documentary.

The mixture of archive and specially-shot film used in our pictorial history of the man-horse relationship proved to be a very successful formula and we immediately began considering other animals which could be treated in a similar way. We eventually selected penguins as our next subject – because they are particularly fascinating birds to most people and because we already had a large amount of library film of them. Once again we asked Ramona Morris if she would provide the research but she was very much involved in another book at the time and had to decline. Desmond suggested that the work might be done by a young post-graduate who had been doing research at the London Zoo and who had helped him from time to time with his own regular television programme for Granada; his name was Dr John Sparks. John did an excellent job of work in a very short time and I was immediately impressed by his understanding of what was required for the medium and by the way in which he distilled a vast amount of information into an easily-read document. A few months later he joined the staff of the Unit as radio producer since Jeffery Boswall had by then moved

permanently to television. Due to re-organisation in the networks our radio output was an uncomfortable assortment of series which we had been running for many years, such as *The Naturalist* and some programmes inherited from London such as *Nature Parliament*. John set about rationalising this output and soon created a new series with a strong identity called *The Living World*. In one of the early editions he took the microphone into the Norfolk marshes with his contributing biologists – instead of recording the programme entirely in the studio – and this laid the foundations for a long tradition of radio nature trails with which the series has been associated ever since.

In the mid-1960s new talent behind the camera slowly began to emerge. Ronald Eastman had been a technician at a paper factory in Hampshire but, being irresistibly attracted to the film business, he also took a job as part-time projectionist at his local cinema in Whitchurch. Unable to resist getting involved in films himself he began filming first on 9.5 mm, but the limitations of this gauge soon forced him to buy a 16 mm Bell and Howell Filmo. With this he began working on a film about the wildlife of the River Test and one species in particular which fascinated him – the kingfisher. Ron became totally absorbed in his film and was determined to overcome the formidable technical problems involved in the underground nesting sequences and the fishing scenes of the kingfisher. With great ingenuity and a determination bordering on obsession, he produced a film which contained some quite outstand-

The kingfisher on the River Test – Ron Eastman's first film subject.

Ron Eastman did for kingfishers what Heinz Sielmann had done for woodpeckers – he succeeded in filming inside their nest burrow.

ing amateur material and this he sent off, not to the BBC Natural History Unit but to the Survival Unit at Anglia.

In fact, as the film was shot at 16 frames per second, it could not have been much use to either of the two units but, fortunately for the BBC, Anglia did not see a potential *Survival* programme in the kingfisher anyway and, to their great credit, they suggested to Ron Eastman that he write to us at Bristol instead. This could not have come at a better time for Jeffery Boswall, just starting a long and distinguished career as a television producer and initially having responsibility for *Look*. Jeffery, a keen and experienced ornithologist, saw at once that the material was sensational – but that it would have to be reshot at 25 frames per second before it could be used on television. This was the first step towards a full-time career in wildlife film-making for Ron Eastman and many years later he made yet another kingfisher film – this time an RSPB production in 35 mm for cinema distribution. Ron never lost his love for the big screen.

Meanwhile, at Oxford, Gerald Thompson and his collaborator, Eric Skinner, were beginning to develop some very special filming techniques in macro-photography in a basement at the Commonwealth Forestry Institute. Encouraged by the success of their alder woodwasp film they made two short films on the tiger beetle and its larvae. These were snapped up and edited into an edition of *Look* and the names of Thompson and Skinner became synonymous with amazing close-up insect photography, the like of which television had hardly seen before.

The most important factors in the excellence of the Oxford film-makers' close-up work of invertebrate behaviour were their successes in overcoming problems of vibration and excessive heat from lighting. To achieve high magnification in macro-photography intense light is

required; and with the lamps available in the 1960s a by-product of a large intensity of light was an undesirable amount of heat. The resulting temperature could be so high that not only would the insect subjects behave unnaturally, but they could actually be fried alive! So a special lighting system was designed to overcome this problem, consisting of a lamp, a flask of water (which reduced the heat slightly, but mainly acted as a condenser) and an arrangement of glass heat filters housed in a metal tube, which also helped to disperse heat by radiation. The vibration problems which occur at such high magnification were largely solved by mounting camera and specimen separately on extremely heavy metal stands on a concrete floor in a basement. Even then, at the highest magnification, filming had to stop whenever a heavy lorry passed by outside.

The work being done by Thompson and Skinner was so exciting that we were eager to adapt whatever they chose to work on – even though they were primarily making biology films for educational purposes. In fact the next subject they turned to came as a result of Gerald Thompson reading W. S. Bristowe's excellent book on spiders in the *New Naturalist* series. The feeding and courtship behaviour of the British species described in the book seemed to be an ideal subject and so Thompson

RIGHT
Gerald Thompson and Eric Skinner in their basement studio at the Commonwealth Forestry Institute.

and Skinner set to work, calling in a leading arachnologist from the Zoology Department – Dr John Cooke – for advice. Several films resulted from this co-operative venture, each quite short and each dealing with the feeding methods, and sometimes the courtship of a species of spider. There was a rich variety of behaviour involved, ranging from hunting spiders, which do not build webs, through orb web spiders and those that build complicated tunnels of silk underground, to those that construct scaffolds and trip wires to catch their prey. The courtship behaviour too was surprisingly varied and at times quite comical. As usual the close-ups were amazing.

The television value of this unique material was obvious but how best to use it posed a problem. There was far too much of it for a single edition of *Look*; but the series needed variety and therefore a group of two or three programmes on spiders would not have been welcomed. However there was now a second outlet; BBC 2 had begun transmissions and was a channel on which, amongst other things, unusual programmes were supposed to be seen. Now there was an appropriate time coming up for an unusual programme on British wildlife as National Nature Week was in April 1966. Perhaps it could only happen on British television but the idea was accepted – 50 minutes about spider behaviour at a peak viewing hour!

I knew there would have to be some attractive packaging involved; I was sure that the film would intrigue viewers – but only if we could persuade them to watch for several minutes, until they were hooked. So in the opening graphics, the narration and the music I tried to emphasise that spider behaviour was certainly fascinating but, if anything, comic rather than horrific. I therefore commissioned Alan Gibson, a well-known West Country writer and broadcaster with a nice literary style and a sense of humour, to write the narration; and Sidney Sager, who also had a good sense of humour, to write the music. As there was virtually no natural sound available there was more music than usual but this was also partly because I asked Sidney to point up various spiders' movements during courtship. In some cases these were little more than musical effects, but I believe they helped the viewer to distinguish between specific movements and postures associated with courtship, and spurious movements during the spiders' passage over delicate webs and vegetation.

As BBC 2 had such a small national coverage at the time, the viewing figures were modest but the reaction of those who saw *Walk into the Parlour* was wildly enthusiastic. In fact programmes about spiders and scorpions (as well as other 'unpopular' creatures such as snakes) have in general had a very good reception *and* large audiences ever since – an odd fact when pre-programme research has shown that these subjects are among the last that viewers think they will watch.

While the spider programme was being produced I was also involved in a special programme for National Nature Week on BBC 1. *Look* was running at the time and HRH The Duke of Edinburgh had graciously agreed to take part in a special edition. The theme of this, the second National Nature Week (the first had been held in 1963) was *Living with Nature* and the entire programme, specially extended to 45 minutes, was to be shot in London. As the *Radio Times* billing said: 'The problem of living with nature in Britain's fast-expanding urban areas is an immediate one. Nowhere is this problem more strikingly illustrated than in London, with its population of 12 million'.

Nicky had been producing some of the *Look* programmes and it was assumed without question that, as senior man in the Unit, he would be responsible for this special edition with its royal VIP. However, he asked me to direct it for him although in fact about half the programme had already been commissioned from director-cameraman John Taylor. This represented most of the wildlife sequences filmed in London for which John received much help from Stanley Cramp and the London Natural History Society as well as our own John Burton. I was to be responsible for the final shaping of the programme and all the other sequences, one of which traced the history of the development of London since pre-Roman times and the gradual disappearance of a great variety of species from lynx and wild boar to swallowtail butterflies and bearded tits. This sequence also showed how new species moved in as a result of man – from ravens and kites in the Middle Ages to the rare black redstart and a profusion of plants that were given a chance on bomb sites after the Blitz. This illustrated the resilience of nature and the fact that many species can live in a big city when given an opportunity.

This theme was to be discussed between Prince Philip and Peter Scott and, of course, the conventional method would have been to shoot this with electronic cameras in a studio. However, we wanted to keep the programme obviously in the centre of London throughout and so we

The author outlines the proposed film sequence to Prince Philip before shooting a scene for Living with Nature.

began to look for the best way of achieving this. The first clue came when we remembered that Prince Philip frequently travelled in and out of London in an RAF helicopter, landing on the extensive lawns at the back of Buckingham Palace. Because of flying restrictions over London his flight path was always to and from the Thames and then up or down river depending on his destination. As we needed aerial scenes of London to show the three principal zones defined by naturalists, this royal flying practice gave us an ideal way to feature Prince Philip. Of course, it was too much to expect that we would be able to use the Royal helicopter and instead we had to hire a machine of our own to fly up and down the Thames in order to film the royal point-of-view; but we were able to obtain shots of Prince Philip landing in the palace gardens.

The next problem was finding a location for Prince Philip's discussion with Peter Scott. We needed a quiet place but one with a good view of inner London, so I began looking at all the tallest skyscraper blocks owned by large corporations and hotels, finding out if any of them had a large room with suitable acoustics. For security reasons I was not allowed to state the name of the VIP we wished to film, although when told the subject of the programme most PR men put two and two together. Eventually I was faced with a decision between the top of the Hilton Hotel and the Vickers building at Millbank. I was sorry to have to decline the offer of a free night in the Hilton Penthouse Suite but the choice of Millbank Towers was fairly easily made as the huge picture windows of the Vickers Boardroom looked eastwards over a magnificent view of the Houses of Parliament, Big Ben, the Thames and the distant City.

All filming should be well-planned but for such an event the arrange-

The scene in the boardroom of Vickers at Millbank Towers as Prince Philip works on his script, watched by Nicholas Crocker, my assistant Sheila Fullom, the make-up supervisor and Peter Scott.

ments were, of course, checked and re-checked many times as if it was a military operation of the highest strategic importance. The senior BBC film cameraman, A. A. ('Tubby') Englander was allocated to the job and almost every piece of equipment was duplicated in case of failure; you simply don't ask Royalty to come back the next day for re-takes. I wanted two sound cameras in any case as the discussion between Prince Philip and Peter Scott was to be informal and unscripted, although the framework was agreed beforehand; the two cameras enabled me to film both participants simultaneously – rather like coverage by live cameras in a television studio except that the choice of cutting would be made in the film editor's room a few days later. In fact we filmed the discussion twice as the first take was much too long; Prince Philip was most co-operative in this respect and I soon found the occasion no different from any other involving a professional presenter. For he was very used to such work, using the teleprompting device for his long closing statement to camera with great assurance, stopping during rehearsals to make slight improvements to the script on the roller.

A few days before, I had spent a fascinating half-hour in his company at Buckingham Palace, after a script conference there, during which he gave Peter Scott, Nicky and myself a quick tour of some of the paintings. I am sure that this was mainly for the benefit of his old acquaintance Peter Scott, but Nicky and I were delighted to trail along as well. The script conference had included a viewing of the previously edited sequences of London and its wildlife and this had turned out to be somewhat farcical. We had asked for a 16 mm projector to be provided and were somewhat surprised to learn in advance that one was not available. However, when we were on the point of arranging to take one from Bristol it was discovered that there was a machine available at Clarence House and this was then borrowed for the occasion.

On arrival at the palace, Peter, Nicky and I were directed to a large room overlooking the terrace at the rear. There were many chairs arranged in rows and the room obviously served as a cinema on occasions and there was a screen at one end and at the other I could see some 35 mm projectors behind tiny projection windows.

We had brought with us the film narration which I had drafted and which Peter had re-written but not yet recorded. The plan was to run the film sequences and for Peter to read the narration aloud so that Prince Philip could see and hear how the rest of the programme appeared before he filmed his own contributions. The problem was that, although *I* knew the film inside out, Peter had only seen it once, having worked on the script from my draft. Therefore he did not know where to start and stop and so it was arranged that I should sit next to him and touch him on the arm every time a new cue came up.

I knew we were in trouble as soon as we entered the room; there was no reading light. We were still trying to figure out what to do when Prince Philip strode briskly in, exactly on time, and after a friendly greeting sat down in the centre of the room ready for the screening. An attendant drew the heavy curtains and the lights went down. Optimistically, Peter held up his script hoping that enough light would bounce back off the screen for him to read it, but it was hopeless. I put my hand into the projector beam and through the window signalled to the projectionist to rewind and start again. The lights came up and we apologised and explained the problem. Someone was sent to look for a torch but the palace is a large building and in any case I shouldn't think there is much requirement for torches; minutes ticked by and no torch appeared.

I suggested to Peter that if we went over to one of the windows I could hold back a curtain just a fraction – enough to give a chink of light to illuminate the script, but not enough to cast light on the screen and spoil Prince Philip's viewing. We decided to give it a try and arranged ourselves in a ridiculous and uncomfortable position, holding the curtain around us and almost enveloping Peter's head. I called across to Nicky, who was sitting next to Prince Philip, and he cued the projectionist. For nearly half an hour we remained locked in position at the window while I repeatedly dug Peter in the ribs with my elbow as each cue came up. I suspect Peter was sore at the end of it all but he was certainly also very hoarse; for the room was large and Peter had to raise his voice to communicate clearly to Prince Philip many yards away in the centre.

This Royal *Look*, one of a number of occasions in which Prince Philip took part in Natural History Unit programmes, came at the end of a four-year period in which I had made many films about British wildlife; but because many of them required minimal supervision while cameramen such as Ashby and Jackman had got on with the good work, I had, at the same time, been able to undertake two major overseas projects. And both of them involved Gerald Durrell.

The first was a 50-minute feature documentary about the Camargue, in particular the story of one of the wild black bulls that graze in the marshes. These bulls are used in the Course Libre – a bull game rather than a bull fight, for the animals are not killed but are matched against a number of *razeteurs* who try to snatch prizes attached to the bull's horns. These events are conducted in village and town arenas in the neighbourhood of the Camargue in Provence and some of the bulls achieve much fame after a few years because of the way in which they hold on to their prizes – and in spectacular fashion chase the *razeteurs* out of the ring. Some *razeteurs* become famous as well as the bulls and our story featured a currently successful man by the name of Soler. Much of the film was about the work on a typical Camargue *manade* – a ranch in the marshes used to raise the bulls as well as the famous white Camargue horses – and this enabled us to film the local wildlife as well.

The idea for the film had come originally from Gerry's brother, Lawrence Durrell, and Gerry had first talked about it with me on the four-day sea trip from Wellington to Sydney on our *Two in the Bush* expedition. I was very attracted by the idea and, after our return to England, went down to the Camargue with the Durrells for two weeks to make a detailed reconnaissance. Gerry subsequently wrote the script which I filmed with Jim Saunders in three seasonal visits over the next 18 months.*

The other project with Gerry was an expedition to West Africa. We

* The story of this film is told in *A Bull Called Marius* by Christopher Parsons, BBC Publications, 1971.

began talking in earnest about a series to follow *Two in the Bush* after the formation of the Jersey Wildlife Preservation Trust in 1963, when Gerry agreed that the notion of some programmes based on a collecting trip for the Trust would be worth considering. I had greatly enjoyed reading about Gerry's collecting trips in the Cameroons and thought that the day-to-day upkeep of a collection as well as the adventures in trapping animals would provide good television material. At first we considered going to British Guiana but we had difficulty in selling the idea to the Chief of Programmes at BBC 1 and the right time for an expedition to the area then passed. It was not until the end of 1964 that it was finally accepted by the new BBC 1 Controller, Michael Peacock, but by that time Gerry had got interested in Sierra Leone where he had his eye on such things as pygmy hippos and some of the leaf monkeys which were being harassed because of their nuisance in local cocoa plantations. Final arrangements were made in a great hurry and Gerry set sail for Freetown on January 15 1965 with his young assistant, John Hartley. Jacquie had declined to go but instead John was to take a large share in looking after the animals so that Gerry would have more time available for filming. I was to join them several weeks later, after they had established a base camp, and with me would go a new young camera-man, Ewart Needham. This time, a film recordist, Howard Smith, would go too, for techniques were more sophisticated than those used in *Two in the Bush* and a large proportion of our series would be filmed with synchronised sound. On this trip that extra pair of hands would be very welcome for I anticipated having to help a great deal with the animals. I also looked forward with relief to being based in one place without having to drive hundreds of miles each day to the next location. But had I known the problems of a different kind that were in store for us, I should have perhaps been a little less light-hearted as we boarded the Sierra Leone Airways 1–11 at London Heathrow.

Chapter 12

Catch me a Colobus

In the cabin of our Land-Rover, the three of us, Ewart, Howard and myself, whistled happily in unison as we sped eastward out of Freetown. It was early and the morning still cool, the road was good – much better than we had expected – and in fact things had gone well ever since we touched down at the airport a few days ago. Although the sights, sounds and smells of Africa had been new to us, most of our business had been with Europeans and almost everything – from checking through Customs on arrival, to picking up the Land-Rover – had been done through a network of contacts which Gerry had apparently set up with the utmost efficiency. Obviously the old Durrell charm had been at work again.

The key to Gerry's success had been the contacts he had been given with Diamond Corporation personnel before he left England and a chance meeting with a District Commissioner on the boat. This resulted in a warm reception for the BBC team and for a few days we stayed insulated from Africa by the air-conditioning of our modern hotel and the hospitality of expatriates in a block of luxury flats on the outskirts of town. Now at last we were on our way to a very different style of life, perhaps three months under canvas and no sight of another white man for weeks on end. Long before we left Bristol, I had told Ewart and Howard that this was going to be a collecting expedition for real: no staying at a convenient hotel and turning up at nine o'clock to start filming – we would be part of the expedition and as far as possible filming everything as it happened. Gerry and I had discussed it many times: it would not be a glamorous account of a collecting trip. Certainly it would include the excitement of catching and trapping animals but it would also show the day-to-day routine of cleaning out cages, dealing with sickness, buying food from the local villages and so on. Far from being boring I hoped that the realism of these day-to-day routines would give the series an authentic quality. I even planned to have Gerry's commentary in the form of a diary. Ewart and Howard had not been discouraged by the threat of tough conditions ahead and we were all sufficiently enthusiastic about the programme opportunities to be in excellent spirits.

We had been informed that Gerry had set up camp in the ruins of an old chrome mine a few miles east of Kenema and about 200 miles inland from Freetown. Far though that was, we might just be able to drive there in one day so we started out immediately after an early breakfast. We soon left behind the untidy but charming muddle of old weather-board houses and new concrete office blocks in Freetown. Now there were attractive rural settlements including round, grass-roofed huts which looked like the little missionary boxes that they gave out at church before the war. Then, after travelling about 90 miles, we saw a red dust cloud ahead and our initial curiosity turned to concern when we realised that our road led right into it. With a thud and a clatter as our equipment suddenly re-arranged itself, we left the tarmac behind and hit our first conventional African road. The dust cloud in front had been no more than the wake of a heavy lorry preceding us. In a few seconds it filled the cabin and every surface had a thin powdery coating of laterite. Too late, we slid the windows tight and battened down the ventilators, but now the vehicle started vibrating as if one of the wheels was coming loose. We had hit our first set of corrugations – rows of tiny furrows lying at right angles to the road which are caused by the action of the wind and rain on the laterite. I had heard about corrugations from well-seasoned African travellers but only now did I understand what effect they had. After 10 minutes' driving we were forced to stop, re-pack the equipment, and bring some of the more delicate pieces into the cabin so that they could be cushioned on the passengers' laps. Then, after passing what we knew was the last village with a petrol pump for miles, we felt a new kind of vibration – we had a flat tyre. That was no surprise in the circumstances and so without concern we stopped to change the wheel. Howard undid the tool box.

Our base for Catch me a Colobus *was at a chrome mine near Kenema in Sierra Leone.*

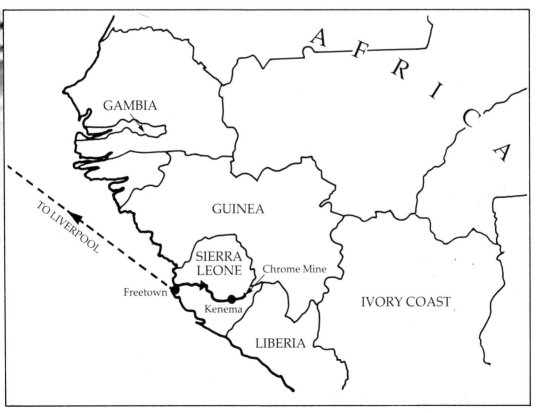

'What have you done with the tools?' he asked in a matter-of-fact tone. Ewart and I looked at each other quizzically. I had an odd feeling in the pit of my stomach. None of us had moved the tools yet last night when we had taken delivery of the Land-Rover the box had been full. Another lesson learnt: check everything before you leave *on the day of departure*. We drew lots and the loser, who was Ewart, started walking back to get help from the last village we had passed through. Our mistake took hours to rectify and prevented us from reaching Kenema that day. Slightly ashamed – and our enthusiasm dampened – we found a rest house for the night at the next town.

The next day's drive was mainly spent in testing three separate

Gerald Durrell and his assistant John Hartley in Sierra Leone.

theories on the best speed to drive over corrugations. The results were inconclusive and we eventually resigned ourselves to the fact that we, and the equipment, were in for a three-month shake-up. It was with great relief that we reached the smooth tarmac on the outskirts of Kenema. It was a bustling little market town with a few shops including a cold store in which the small expatriate population could buy endless supplies of cold beer and such delicacies as smoked salmon. Near the open market was an area which served as a kind of bus station for the local transport system – an assortment of lorries known as 'mammy wagons' on which were written such slogans as 'Look for Timber Jack', 'Save me, O God', and 'Love me a little but long'. John Hartley was waiting nearby with his huge Land-Rover – a high wheelbase vehicle of a type I had not seen before. On the doors of the cabin were painted in smart lettering 'Jersey Wildlife Preservation Trust'. John shone a broad smile from the top of his beanstalk figure. In answer to my question, his reply was guarded: 'Well, as Gerry warned you, it's pretty tough out here but we're making the best of it'. I noticed, however, that there was a twinkle in his eye.

John led the way and we drove six miles the other side of town until we reached the village of Bambawo. Here a track led off to the left through the village and then wound up a steep hill to the forest at the edge of the broad valley in which we had been travelling. As we climbed it became noticeably cooler; there were several hairpin bends and the surface was so bad that it resembled a dried-up river bed. Heaps of abandoned and rusty machinery could be seen at the roadside and soon we were driving up through a small settlement of decaying single-storey houses, set among the trees – one of which I was pleased to note was an avocado, dripping with fruit. At the highest point in the settlement – which appeared completely deserted – we turned into the back yard of one of the less deteriorated houses and, from the back of it, emerged Gerry beaming with arms wide open in welcome. The air was cool and still, carrying only the gentle accompaniment of insects in the forest behind us; the dust and discomfort of the long journey vanished in a few seconds.

'I thought this was supposed to be a tough trip!' I said, glancing at the cookhouse from which some delicious smells were wafting.

'Ah, you wait until we start collecting and have to camp in the bush', Gerry replied. 'Things will be different then! But I must say this is the most luxurious base camp I've ever had. It's marvellous to come back to after a long day down there in the heat.'

'We had a little surprise worked out for you', piped up John. 'Gerry was going to leave directions for you at Kenema and we planned to set up a sort of Customs Post at the bottom of the hill – but we couldn't get it organised in time.'

'Anyhow, what you need is a large beer, so come on out to the verandah and see the view.' Gerry took us through the large living room with its red-painted concrete floor stacked with crates of nets, tools and medical supplies. A glass door led out to the verandah where there were several comfortable chairs and a table on which glasses were promptly placed by Sadu the cook, whom Gerry had taken on in Freetown. Sadu was a small man with a smiling, wrinkled face and with him was his

Ewart and Howard at the chrome mine.

assistant, named Lamin; he was a fresh-faced boy, even smaller than Sadu. The beer arrived and I was surprised to find it ice-cold. I looked at Gerry whose eyes were twinkling with amusement.

'How come?' I asked, nodding at the glass.

'Straight from the 'fridge', said Gerry, then, anticipating my next question, 'We've actually managed to get the old generator working. Some of the people down in the village used to work up here at the mines – including someone laughingly called "the electroshitty man".'

The cool drink had at last cut through the dust in my throat and I looked again at the view from the verandah. It was magnificent. Far below we could make out the rooftops of the village of Bambawo, near the main road. Beyond that the broad valley stretched away into the blue-green haze towards distant hills and the Liberian border a few hundred miles away.

'There are more surprises to come', said John. 'We'll take you for a walk after you've seen your house and show you something *very* interesting.'

Gerry had hired two local lads to help with the housework and the animal collection and these two, Amadu and El Mamin, now unloaded our Land-Rover and installed us in the next house down the hill. The rooms were bare but at least they provided a piece of personal territory for each of us as well as a large communal room in which to sort out and test all the equipment after the long bumpy journey from Freetown. This would take most of the following day so we spent the one remaining hour of daylight exploring our immediate neighbourhood before dinner. Although the mine had been occupied until only a year or so ago, it was amazing how quickly the jungle was taking over again. In the house next to ours, a sunbird had built its nest on the end of an electric light flex and particularly evil-looking social wasps were tending their nests which hung from the ceiling and such unlikely places as the bath taps. Vines curled through open windows in a menacing fashion and the long clay tunnels of termites stretched everywhere.

Led by Gerry and John, we picked our way through the vegetation, stumbling over hidden rails and occasionally finding dumps of ore wagons and other machinery. Eventually we arrived at a clearing near the edge of the forest and there in front of us, but difficult to believe, was a large swimming pool! True, its concrete sides were crumbling a little but, nevertheless, it was a deliciously cool, welcoming pool. We were staring open-mouthed at this when there was a loud splash and Gerry's form could be seen swimming underwater towards the far end. He surfaced and spluttered: 'Come on you chaps, what are you waiting for?'

Two hours later we were on the verandah again, refreshed and dust-free and watching Sadu prepare the supper table accompanied now by the night sounds of the forest behind the house. Sadu had cooked one of his special curries for our arrival and the table was first arranged with dozens of little containers each with a different kind of nut or vegetable or fruit – the 'small-small tings' to go with the curry. A great variety of moths and other insects were attracted by the light and landed on the white wall behind the table, providing a non-stop but rather disorderly

Filming at the chrome mine; Lamin and Sadu are at the far left.

cabaret during the meal. It was absolutely delicious and quite the best curry I had eaten for a very long time.

I woke early the following morning as the first grey light began to seep into the Chrome Mine. Ewart and Howard were still sound asleep so I dressed quietly and strolled on up the slope to Gerry's house to sit on the verandah and take in the dawn scene. Gerry was already there, dressed in a blue dressing-gown, relaxing with a cigarette and a cup of tea.

'Ah, I'm glad you've had the sense to get up and enjoy the best part of the day', he said. He called into the house for Lamin to bring another cup, and continued: 'If you sit quietly there and wait a while you'll see a sight you won't forget'. We looked out over the lowlands which were covered in a milky sea of mist; here and there the tallest trees left blue-grey dabs of water-colour on the scene which seemed to extend to infinity.

'Any minute now. Just watch', said Gerry. On the horizon a fiery line suddenly appeared, pushing upwards into a crescent and in no time at all developing into a gigantic sun.

'Just like a frosted blood orange', murmured Gerry softly.

I turned to him. 'It's a good line for the narration', I said, 'especially as we're still shooting in black-and-white'. Colour television was only a year or two away and it was tragic that money could not be found for us to film the series in colour.

John arrived, shuffling and bleary-eyed, and folded himself into a chair.

'Hartleypools, what *have* you been doing with yourself all night? You look like a seasick giraffe.' John merely grunted and sipped his tea noisily. John was rarely addressed simply by his Christian name and if he was referred to it was usually as 'Long John' or 'Hartleypools'. By now I was resigned to the fact that I would usually be 'Wellington' to the Durrells (on account of the nose) and so when the mood took me I addressed Gerry as 'Napoleon'.

'And what are those two layabouts doing down there?' enquired Gerry, nodding in the direction of the BBC house.

'Probably building up their strength for the hard work ahead', I replied. 'All that equipment is going to get very heavy after a long day in the bush in this climate.' But today Ewart and Howard would first have to unpack and clean everything and this would give me an opportunity to plan the series with Gerry in the light of his experience so far.

We strolled round the side of the house to see the animals as we talked, for already there was the nucleus of a collection housed in a line of recently constructed wooden cages. The animals had been acquired in a variety of ways. Some had been brought in by Africans after Gerry had passed the word around the local villages and some had come from Europeans who wanted to find a good home for orphaned animals which they had found or saved from hunters. The collection, so far, included a young and very friendly chimpanzee called Jimmy, a charming little putty-nosed monkey, a potto, two young hornbills, some forest squirrels and a pangolin. As John started getting down to work to clean out the cages and prepare the animals' food, Gerry led me back to the verandah.

'All those are fine', he said. 'They'll be useful to give some variety back at the zoo and they'll be good for the film – but what we really need are colobus monkeys, and believe it or not, they actually came to that tree down there the other day.' He pointed to the nearest tall tree down the slope from the house about 200 yards away. It was a vivid green tree from which hung long pink seed pods and it was on the edge of the forest.

'They were the red-and-black colobus – a magnificent sight, their fur gleaming in the morning sun. Pity you weren't here, but they may come back one morning so you'd better have the camera ready for them.'

Gerry had learned that between two and three thousand monkeys were killed locally each year in monkey drives. These were held to flush the monkeys out of the cocoa plantations where they do a great deal of damage to a crop important in Sierra Leone's economy. The locals were paid a bounty for each monkey head and no one was fussy about what species of monkey was killed. So the two kinds of colobus, red-and-black and black-and-white, although protected in theory, were frequently rounded up and killed with common species such as putty-nosed and Diana monkeys. Gerry was convinced that if this was allowed to go on the colobus would eventually be seriously endangered, so he wanted to capture enough of each species to start a breeding colony in Jersey. It was for just that kind of work that the Wildlife Preservation Trust had been formed.

The monkeys would not be easy to capture, that was certain, but that in itself would help to make it a high spot in the series. However, catching them in the tree near the Chrome Mine was apparently out of the question. It could only be done close to the cocoa plantations where the monkey drives were normally held. The first problem, therefore, would be persuading the Africans that we wanted the monkeys alive; and the only way to catch them alive would be to drive them into a tall tree and quickly cut down the surrounding trees and other vegetation so that they could not leap to safety. This was possible only in an area already set aside for felling.

As Gerry outlined his scheme it sounded as if it would require military-like planning for weeks ahead and I wondered how on earth our little team would be able to cope with it. As Gerry pointed out, we had to try for the colobus weeks before departure for even after capture the most difficult part of the exercise still lay ahead. Colobus monkeys eat leaves – vast quantities of them – and they have specially large stomachs to digest this food. The main problem would be gradually getting them off their usual diet and coaxing them on to a different one – consisting of such leaves, vegetable and fruit as would be available at the camp and on the boat travelling back to England.

This was the kind of subject which I saw as being the very essence of the series. For, apart from the colobus capture – and a few other trapping sequences – there would not be very much exciting action to film. The series would have to survive principally on the day-to-day

Gerry with Jimmy the chimpanzee.

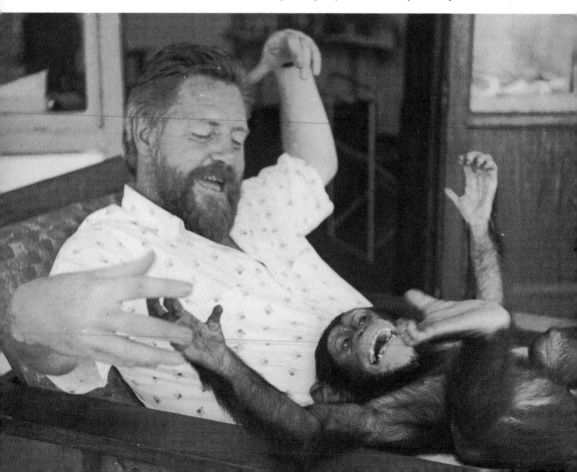

incidents and problems involved in establishing, managing and trans-
porting a collection of animals from Africa to Jersey. Some of these
activities might appear mundane at first but they would take us to a
wide variety of locations and involve an interesting range of characters –
the people in the market, the local chief and the carpenter, the hunters
and, of course, Sadu and Lamin. So the series would also be a kind of
travelogue but with a very definite story line. By filming the collection as
it grew, we would be able to develop animal 'characters' while the series
progressed. Jimmy the chimp was already useful in this respect.

I was convinced that one of the secrets of success was good film
sound. The day-to-day activities and encounters would hold interest
only if they were filmed in such a way that viewers could feel that they
were privileged onlookers; and that meant filming almost everything
with synchronised sound. This was going to be a tremendous challenge,
particularly for Ewart and Howard. A few years later it would have been
so easy with light self-blimped cameras, radio microphones so small that
they can be pinned under a safari shirt lapel and crystal-controlled
operation enabling camera and recorder to work synchronously but
independently without connecting wires. But we were working in 1965
and the noisy camera had to be encased in an unwieldy glass fibre
blimp. This made it very unsuitable for hand-holding – a major
disadvantage in view of the fact that so much of the action would be
unpredictable. True, the Sennhesier gun microphone was available so
that speech no longer had to be recorded with a microphone held a foot
or two in front of the speaker, but even then the recordist had to work
close to the action and risk getting into the cameraman's shot. For the
next three months, therefore, I would be setting Ewart and Howard a
hard task, but at least their hours of work would be considerably less
than mine. From now on, my day would begin at dawn with a planning
meeting over the early morning cup of tea. Apart from our own
breakfast, it would then be cleaning out and feeding time for the animals
(and, of course, this became more of a task as the collection grew) and
this I would sometimes help with, not only because it interested me but
because it was a time-consuming job which had to be done before we
could start filming. During the day, I would have to act as my own
production assistant, marking the clapper board, noting the action
details in the shot list. In the evening, after supper, I would then write
down the editing instructions, for this was best done while it was fresh
in my mind as each day's work was inevitably a jumble of separate
sequences, some which were moving the story forward as well as some
which were reconstructing past incidents for the first programmes.

For a few days we worked mainly at the Chrome Mine where Gerry
had held up some developments until we arrived to film them. These
included erecting the long line of trestles for the cages, putting up a
tarpaulin to protect them from the rain, unpacking medical equipment
and so on. And in order to recreate the arrival scene, we even had to
move the furniture acquired from neighbouring houses well out of sight
and generally make the place look unkempt and dirty again.

Soon after our arrival, I learnt that there were two special animals
temporarily being kept in an outhouse which had once served as a
lavatory; the reason for this unusual accommodation was that the

"Now, what I want you to do ----------"

animals needed large, strong cages which were still being constructed. They were two charming leopard cubs, named Gerda and Lokai. The word cub hardly did justice to either of them for they were both heavy and strong as I discovered to my cost a short time later. Howard and Ewart were none too keen on these two young leopards for they were kept only a short distance from the back of our house. They had been brought to Gerry by a young American admirer who was currently working as a member of the Peace Corps in Kenema. His name was Joe Sharp and he had reared the leopards for a few months since acquiring them from a hunter who had shot their mother. They had now got rather out of hand and, in any case, Joe was due to return to the United States quite soon. Hearing that Gerry was in the district collecting animals for the Trust, Joe immediately saw a solution to his problem which would also be in the interests of conservation. Naturally Gerry was overjoyed to acquire such fine potential breeding stock but it was an arrival that he had not bargained for. Hence the temporary accommodation in the lavatory.

"Now remember — this time the expression is one of ecstacy — tinged with a weeny bit of sadness — *then* you speak —"

In fact, Howard and Ewart's reservations were throroughly justified for within a few hours of finding out about our interesting neighbours, Howard walked past the lavatory and saw to his horror that the two leopards were on the roof, having forced and squeezed through the boarding that had been nailed against the window. For Howard, who was already expressing strong reservations about the invertebrate life around him, this was the last straw and, yelling to Ewart and me in the house as he went, he pounded up the hill to inform Gerry.

I hurried outside only to discover that one of the leopards had already jumped down from the roof and was trotting downhill through the bushes. I set off in hot pursuit telling Ewart to stand guard over the other cub. However the first leopard had disappeared as if by magic. There was a sudden crashing noise in the bushes behind me but it was only Gerry carrying a long rope; he had left John to deal with the leopard on the roof. Soon Gerry, with his practised eye, saw the missing leopard lying under a tree and murmuring sweet words of affection walked cautiously towards it. It was Lokai, the male cub, who purred a little and allowed Gerry to slip the rope through his collar. To my dismay, I was then asked to hold the rope while Gerry returned to help John. My instructions quite simply were to hang on at all costs and go wherever the leopard wanted to go. I realised I should have asked Gerry how he expected to locate me after being dragged 20 miles away into the depths of the forest, but he was already halfway up the hill.

For some time, Lokai watched me without any apparent emotion and I began to think that there was no problem after all. I would be content to sit the situation out for hours, if necessary. Then Lokai yawned, lazily rose to his feet and began to look around. I followed Gerry's example and spoke quietly to the leopard, wooing him with comforting facts about the meal that would be on its way soon and how he would be

reunited with his beloved sister any minute now. All this seemed to wash right over Lokai and he began to get more restless, trying to decide which direction to explore including, to my concern, *upwards*. With an effortless bound, he reached the first branch of the tree above him, jerking the slack out of the rope. I was determined not to let go and had wound several coils around my arm but I did not relish the prospect of being hauled up into the tree by a bad-tempered leopard. So, ignoring Gerry's instructions, I began to pull gently but firmly on the rope – an action which caused Lokai to express displeasure with a little snarl and an angry patting motion of his paw. After a while, I think that Lokai realised that my weight on the end of the rope was more than enough to stop further progress upwards and so he settled down in a more comfortable position draped over the low bough. Fortunately, Gerry returned before Lokai became bored again and with more gentle words and tugs persuaded him to descend. Slowly he was coaxed back to his temporary home where John was soothing the recently reinstated Gerda. During the past hour all thoughts of television had gone out of our minds but as soon as the leopards were safely locked up I remembered that this was just the kind of incident which we should be filming for the series.

'Don't worry', said Gerry, when I ventured this thought to him over a beer. 'There'll be plenty more excitement when we try to get them into their permanent cages as soon as the carpenter has finished.'

The author with Lokai after the two young leopards had been recaptured.

Before that we had to film the arrival of the leopards at the Chrome Mine and Joe Sharp was sent for so that he could re-enact the occasion. This was accomplished without difficulty, for the cubs remembered Joe and were easily handled by him; but Joe had left and it was dark before the cages were complete so that filming the cubs being installed in their new homes had to take place under bright lights. This gave an extra edge to an already tense situation but the cubs were successfully transferred with only a few scratches suffered by Gerry and John. However, it has to be said that they were both in a state of nervous exhaustion at the end and for a while I suspected that they bitterly regretted ever agreeing to a television crew filming their more difficult moments.

The combination of one of Sadu's curries and a good night's sleep usually dulled the memory of bad experiences and after the night of the leopards I deliberately chose to film a gentle sequence at the Chrome Mine to calm everyone's nerves even further. The pangolin, or scaly ant-eater, had to be fed a special mixture of raw egg, milk and mincemeat each day – a diet that Gerry had successfully used on previous collecting trips. On this expedition, however, he was also adding a drop or two of formic acid in the belief that this would give the mixture a kind of tang similar to the pangolin's natural diet of ants. This bizarre mixture of ingredients gave Gerry the idea of filming a sequence showing the preparation of the pangolin's food as if it was being done by Philip Harbin for one of his television cookery lessons.

Lamin and Sadu, as well as the two local recruits, Amadu and El Mamin, soon lost interest in our strange antics with camera and recorder and within a few days were quite used to being filmed. In the local villages, however, our presence aroused a lot of curiosity and we had to resort to all kinds of tricks to pretend that we were not filming even when we were. One day we went down to the village of Bambawo to film a re-enactment of Gerry's first meeting with the Chief. He duly appeared in his best clothes, wearing a highly polished pair of black squeaky shoes and carrying a brand-new brief case. I am sure that there were no papers in it but he clearly regarded it as his badge of office and nothing would part him from it whilst in front of the camera.

A few weeks later, we drove to a village near some cocoa plantations where there was supposed to be plenty of colobus monkey activity. Gerry wanted to start making arrangements for a monkey drive with the Paramount Chief and I planned to film this meeting unrehearsed. However, Gerry advised me that as it was the Paramount Chief and as it was in a comparatively remote area where people were not used to cameras he would prefer to go ahead and ask permission first. I kept the crew in the background with the equipment well concealed and Gerry eventually emerged to report that the Paramount Chief would allow us to film what we liked. We got the equipment out of the Land-Rover and hurried over to find about 20 elders assembling in two lines, the front line seated, the rear line standing. Having taken up these positions they froze; not a single hand moved, not an eyelid flickered. They remained completely immobile, gazing at us impassively as we assembled the equipment. They knew about photography but their only experience had been of a kind of Victorian family portraiture. Under the circum-

ABOVE LEFT
A possible hollow tree is inspected prior to the smoking-out sequence.

ABOVE
Gerry examines the rope ladder before the tree climber ascends.

stances, there was only one thing for us to do: pretend to take a picture. After that they unfroze and we were able to film them without difficulty.

The weeks went by and slowly the collection grew until there was quite an impressive line of cages arranged alongside Gerry's house. In pidgin English the animals were referred to as 'beef' and so the Chrome Mine gradually became known as the Beef Mine. This gave Gerry the idea of a title for a calypso which could be used at the beginning and end of each programme and he immediately began composing verses which we hoped to record at the Sierra Leone Broadcasting Service studios on our return to Freetown. Our filming of the collection – showing feeding problems and medical attention – was interspersed with short collecting trips and although these had produced a variety of animals including a potto and a monitor lizard, I was not satisfied that we had yet shown a very interesting range of trapping techniques.

'What we need is a hollow tree', said Gerry with great confidence as if this would immediately solve all my problems. 'Some of those giant hollow trees are like blocks of flats – they've got animals living in them at all levels. You smoke them out and it can be one of the most successful of all collecting techniques – you could get as many as 50 animals out of one tree. . . .' This sounded more like it. '. . . on the other hand', he added ominously, 'you could work at 50 trees and not catch a single animal.'

Nevertheless, it seemed to be worth trying and I asked Gerry to outline the method. Apparently a giant hollow tree can have many holes in it and the first part of the operation is to get an expert climber to scale the tree and fasten nets over all the openings. The bottom of the tree is then surrounded with a large net and a small fire is lit in the hollow base. Green leaves are added once the fire is well established and this produces dense smoke which filters up through the tree and, in theory, drives out the occupants at various levels into the nets. It was an interesting technique which ought to make a good film sequence so we agreed to organise it at the earliest opportunity. John detailed some men from our village to hunt for hollow trees and, in a few days, we heard that an ideal tree had been found.

Things did not augur well when we arrived at the village to pick up the ace tree climber. He turned out to be a strange fellow with an unsteady gait and a slight look of madness about him – or so I thought until Gerry quietly said: 'He's been at the palm wine by the look of it!' Perhaps we should have abandoned the project there and then but there was an air of expectation around and several hangers-on were eager for action. So we made our way to the pre-selected tree, which was very tall and, as far as I could see, devoid of branches low enough to make climbing possible. Gerry seemed undismayed, however, and started the preparations with rope ladders, nets and tins of kerosene.

All this took an incredibly long time; to make matters worse it was unbearably hot and the insects were particularly irritating. One of the helpers was trying to throw a rope over the lowest of the branches – which was at a considerable height – and failing every time. A local lad who had been commissioned to find the tree was shouting hysterically at everyone and everything and Gerry was endeavouring to get him to shut up so that he could take control. It was just the right kind of situation for tempers to get frayed and I'm ashamed to relate that I lost mine twice in quick succession; as I lose my temper on average once every three years this was quite an achievement and perhaps a measure of how fraught things were at the time. It was Howard who received the first blast: like all recordists he would start the day by carefully checking the recorder, making a test with his own voice and identifying the roll number, programme, sequence and so on. Unfortunately, Howard occasionally got carried away with the microphone in his hand and he would keep going for minutes on end, chuntering away to himself about the state of the weather or what breakfast he had had that morning while he watched the needle flicker on the meter registering the sound level. In this way it was possible for him to use up most of a tape while making tests. On this particular day this is exactly what must have happened for we had hardly started filming the long complicated procedure for smoking out the tree when Howard announced that he had run out of tape. This was at a particularly critical juncture, just as our intrepid climber arrived with a net at the first hole in the tree, for by now the team had succeeded in getting a rope ladder over the first branch.

When filming collecting sequences before, we had always concentrated on getting the final stages of the capture first and had then 'built up' the sequence afterwards by filming approach shots, 'cutaways' of the hunters and other details so that it would be possible for the film editor to reconstruct the story. With the hollow tree, however, I decided to film everything from the beginning as it would probably be impossible to repeat anything once the smoking operation had taken place. So I instructed Ewart to stay glued to his viewfinder and film every move that our inebriated climber made in the tree above us. But I did not realise at the time what uncomfortable conditions he was working under: he was pointing the camera upwards at an angle of about 60

209

degrees, he was perspiring heavily and this made the insects bother him even more than usual and to make matters even worse the eyepiece of his viewfinder kept misting up. It was through dealing with one or other of these difficulties that he missed a crucial piece of action and this caused me to lose my cool the second time, hurling the clapperboard into the bushes. El Mamin, who was sitting on a log watching everyone else as usual, narrowly missed receiving this missile on his left foot, whereupon he shot into the air and began helping the others to fix the main net around the base of the tree with a degree of application that we had never seen before.

What had happened aloft was that our climber had begun throwing out bits of debris from a hole in the tree without realising that these were parts of a tree ants' nest. In no time at all he had ants swarming all over him and was madly scratching at every part of his anatomy with one hand whilst holding on to his perilous position with the other. Eventually, he could stand it no longer and disappeared from view behind the trunk of the tree, only to re-appear a minute later minus his trousers but still clad in a grimy pair of short underpants.

After the nets had been fastened over all the exit holes in the tree, Gerry started lighting a fire in the base, some of the rotten wood having been chopped out to provide a small chamber. As soon as the tinder had caught, a few green branches of leaves were placed on top of the fire and clouds of white smoke began rising into the hollow trunk. The base of the tree was now completely surrounded by a net with helpers stationed every few feet around its circumference. We waited expectantly, gazing up at the nets on the upper trunk, but nothing happened. Eventually a wisp of smoke trickled out of the first hole but nothing more. We suspected that the tree was not as hollow as we had been given to believe and were just about to abandon the entire sequence, when loud shrieks of excitement came from the helpers holding the net at the far side of the tree. A tiny forest squirrel had appeared from somewhere and shot into the net where it was quickly grabbed and popped into one of Gerry's small collecting bags.

'Well, that's how it goes', Gerry said philosophically. 'As I told you, some you win and some you lose.' Nevertheless, in spite of the anti-climax, I felt we had a sequence that at least showed a new method of trapping. The irony of it was that the squirrel was of a species that was common and constantly being brought in by hunters at the Beef Mine.

By now it was early April and the collection lacked only the most important element – good numbers of colobus monkeys. We had a few young monkeys brought in by the locals but we did not yet have the nucleus of a breeding group which Gerry hoped to take back to Jersey. The red-and-black colobus had tantalised us by visiting their feeding tree within sight of Gerry's house a couple of times and this at least had given us an opportunity to film good shots of them feeding and jumping through trees. But we also needed to film the black-and-white colobus and so we moved to a different area for a few days where we would be more likely to see them and where it might also be possible to arrange monkey drives. So, leaving John behind to look after the collection, Gerry, Ewart, Howard, Sadu and I set off for the Kpuwabu Cocoa and Development Station which was several hours' drive away. A small rest

house had been made available for us in the middle of the plantation
and as soon as we arrived we could see that it was a good area for
filming monkeys. There was a large clearing immediately in front of the
rest house, and even as we unpacked our equipment we could see the
branches of the trees at the edge of the clearing moving under the
weight of feeding monkeys. They were mainly spot-nosed and Diana
monkeys but, after lunch when we started to explore the area, we found
a troupe of black-and-white colobus without much difficulty. They were
making their way through the tops of the trees and by anticipating their

route we were able to get into good positions to film spectacular shots of them leaping from tree to tree.

The next day Gerry managed to get the arrangements made for a monkey drive two days hence. The hunters insisted that, as it would be a long and difficult day's work, we should have to start very early. However experience had shown us that in the forested areas we did not have sufficient light for filming until about nine o'clock. This was a disappointment as I wanted to film all the steps in the operation but I was finally persuaded that we should have to start our film sequence at an intermediate stage when the monkeys were already cornered in a selected part of the forest.

The big day arrived and we set off well-provisioned with the large Land-Rover full of brand-new empty cages. We were met at the roadside by our guide who had also helped to organise the drive; he was a young man who had obviously had a good education for he spoke excellent English, albeit in a loud, shrill voice. In fact, most of his communications were shouted, not only at his fellow Africans, but also at us and it was so infectious that we became hoarse through shouting back at him.

Koromo, as he was called, led us along a track through a plantation until we reached a section of forest in which grew many tall trees as well as smaller trees, bushes, palms and other undergrowth. From this came shouts, yells, crashes and above all the sound of dozens of choppers hacking away: in fact, pandemonium. We found ourselves in the middle of this frenzy but because the undergrowth was so dense it was difficult to make out any order or purpose in the whole endeavour. Koromo then led us to a particularly tall tree in which we could just see a group of monkeys in the uppermost branches. After an hour, the small trees and undergrowth surrounding the monkeys began to diminish visibly under the onslaught of the choppers and we could begin to discern some kind of purpose in the activity. There was a tremendous sense of urgency, constantly whipped up to greater heights by Koromo who was running about like a madman shrieking orders at everyone. Suddenly he reached a point near hysteria and the reason was easy to see. As the circle began to close around the monkeys, they began leaping across the ever-increasing gap, legs out, tails waving to balance them as they sailed into space to land with a crash in saplings a hundred feet away. Gerry began to worry that all the monkeys might be lost in this way but the hunters began chopping with renewed vigour and by the time that the remaining escape routes had been cut there were still a few black-and-white and red-and-black colobus in the tree, although it was impossible to tell exactly how many.

We had been filming for nearly three hours and all we had to show for it were a few distant shots of monkeys leaping and an incredible amount of undergrowth being cleared – accompanied of course by a very noisy sound track. For once Howard didn't have to worry about inadequate recording levels. By mid-day there was a lull in the proceedings and the Africans took a break, many of them cutting a type of vine to get at the water inside and chattering away in little groups as they rested. There was evidently no great hurry now as the monkeys were isolated in their tall tree and for them to leap out of it while we were there would seem unlikely, if not suicidal because of the height. After we had all taken a

Gerry with some of the hunters involved in catching the colobus monkeys.

rest and some refreshment Gerry asked Koromo what the next step was for it was difficult to imagine how we were to get the monkeys out of the tree.

'We are going to build a coop, sir', squeaked Koromo, now hoarse, we were delighted to hear.

'A coop?' asked Gerry.

'Yes sir, a coop. You will see.'

Gerry shrugged his shoulders and looked helplessly at me. He had not come across this term before in West Africa and I had the suspicion that he was not very confident about the capabilities of Koromo and his gang. However, they were supposed to have caught monkeys before, so it seemed best to let them get on with it for the time being. Koromo chivvied some of his men into action again and this time they started collecting some of the small branches they had already cut, building them into a great mound under the tree. A large net was then arranged around the coop. Some of the men cut long forked sticks, the purpose of which was not clear. As things seemed to be reaching a climax – although we still couldn't see how the monkeys would be forced out of the tree – Gerry gave instructions for the cages to be moved in closer.

It was now about 2:30 and very hot. Most of the Africans were sitting down again having made the final preparations – for what we were not sure – but two men then appeared with a very long cross-cut saw. This was rusty and obviously very blunt for it took a long time to cut even a few inches into the base of the tree. By four o'clock the men at the saw were still only half-way through the trunk when there was a sudden movement in the tree and one of the monkeys scampered down a little way. Immediately there were yells from the onlookers but instead of

213

Gerry waits as the first wisps of smoke rise towards the monkeys.

RIGHT
Ewart's film shows clearly the use of the tail as a monkey leaps.

going upwards again the monkey launched itself into space and landed in cut undergrowth some distance from the base of the tree and yards outside the coop. Fearful that the rest of the monkeys would follow Gerry yelled to Koromo to get his men organised, and Koromo, who had now regained full control of his vocal faculties, shrieked venomously at his workers to take their stations.

The men with the saw, sweat glistening on their bodies, plodded doggedly on but it was another 20 minutes before there came a resounding crack and the tree began to sway. But the monkeys did not come down as planned. They were far too cunning. They hung tenaciously on to the branches as the tree toppled over and when it was accelerating towards the ground and at an angle of about 30 degrees from the horizontal they leaped clear and bounded away into the undergrowth. The height of the tree was such that it took the monkeys well clear of the carefully prepared coop and, in a few seconds, the entire day's work had been wasted. Gerry was furious. Even Koromo was silent for once.

'Next time . . .' said Gerry grimly, 'we'll finish it my way if you don't mind.'

A few days later, we witnessed the same long process again although we did not bother to film the early stages. All I was interested in now was the final capture – if it could ever be achieved. By early afternoon we had once more succeeded in getting a group of colobus into one tall tree. This time, however, extra special precautions were made to surround the large coop with a net and a man was stationed at every few feet around it. Instead of cutting the tree down, Gerry lit a fire, carefully regulating the ascending smoke so that it would be irritating to the

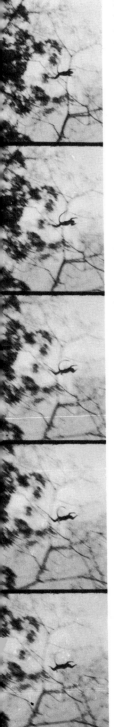

monkeys above but not so thick that it would envelop and asphyxiate them. As the first wisps reached the upper branches the monkeys began to get restless and soon one was working its way agitatedly down the top part of the trunk. Suddenly it leapt – right into the middle of the coop which was piled high to break the fall like a trapeze artist's safety net. For a few moments the monkey completely disappeared in the foliage and then when we thought we had lost it, it shot out like a cannonball straight into the net where it was quickly enmeshed and pinned down by the men with forked sticks. After being carefully disentangled, it was bundled into a cage. Gerry was now shouting to the others to get back to their stations as the other monkeys were beginning to jump. For a few minutes there was utter chaos with monkeys jumping out of the tree and rushing into the net in all directions, whilst others leapt clear of the net and escaped in the general confusion. But, within an hour – and just in time before the light fell – we had some of each species of colobus and were heading back towards the Beef Mine.

We now had only a few weeks left before the long drive to Freetown to catch the boat for Liverpool. Everything depended therefore on Gerry's and John's success in getting the colobus to feed in captivity, converting them to a diet on which they could be sustained on the journey back to Jersey. The state of the various colobus and what they were eating became almost the sole topic of conversation and it completely dictated the mood of the party each day. After great difficulty, the black-and-white colobus settled down and indeed became quite tame, taking from our hands a variety of greenstuff which had been bought at the local market. The red-and-black colobus were of a completely different disposition, however, and none of the tricks of the trade that Gerry had up his sleeve would make them take alternative foods. They became sullen and lost weight and sadly Gerry had to let them go for fear they would not survive.

For the last few days before leaving camp, we filmed all the remaining odds and ends of continuity shots and we were beginning to feel quite light-hearted when disaster struck. We had been filming at the bottom of the hill near the Beef Mine when Gerry decided to sit on the tail-board of the small Land-Rover for the short ride home. On the way back we hit a large stone in the track and the vehicle lurched so violently that Gerry was thrown upwards, landing heavily on the base of his spine. There was an anguished cry from him and we stopped the vehicle to find that he was in great pain from a bruised spine and a blow in the ribs. We discovered later that he had, in fact, broken two ribs.

Gerry stoically tried to keep going as usual but it was obvious that he would not be able to take part in all the usual activities involved in the upkeep of the animals. It would also be impossible for John to manage on his own. Fortunately Jacquie was due back in Jersey from Argentina by then, so a cable was sent asking if she could come out on the *Accra* which was sailing from Liverpool in a day or two. Although Jacquie would be able to help on the boat journey from Freetown, we still had the problem of getting all the animals out of the Beef Mine and the equipment packed ready for the long road journey. Then Joe Sharp, the young Peace Corps man who had brought the leopards, came to the rescue. He not only gave a hand with the packing but also offered to

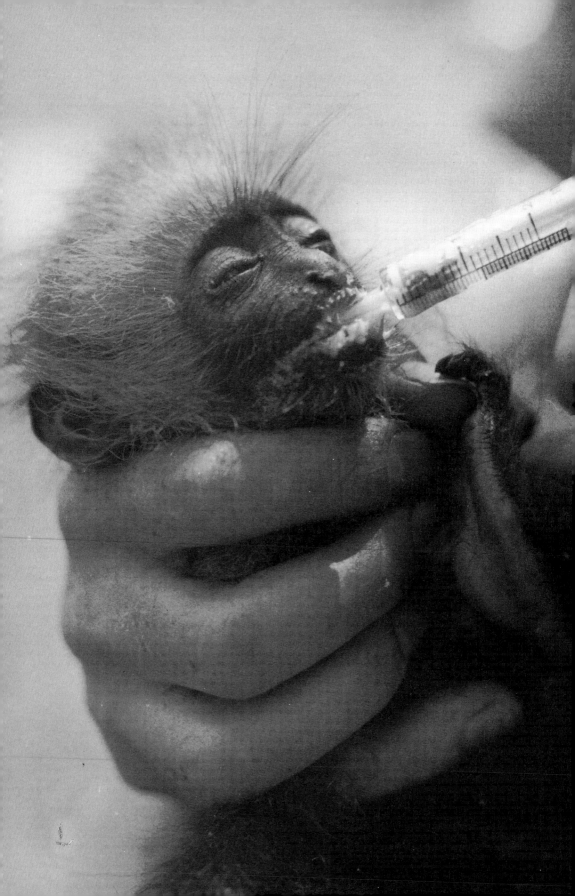

Feeding one of the baby black and white colobus monkeys.

drive Gerry in his own Land-Rover which he would suitably furnish with an assortment of cushions and rugs to make the journey as comfortable as possible. They would travel by day and Gerry would take with him a number of small and delicate animals, leaving the rest of us with the main collection in three hired lorries to travel through the cool of the night.

Even during the last two days at the Mine there was some filming to be done. The Chief at Bambawo had invited us to a farewell dance and this seemed a good opportunity to film Gerry's last contact with the villagers who had played a significant part in the events of the past three months. Unfortunately, Gerry's accident prevented him from entering into the spirit of the occasion in his usual style but John more than made up for it by dancing every number with wild enthusiasm – much to the delight of the village maidens. But we had to excuse ourselves before the festivities ended as there was a long hard day ahead packing up all the expedition equipment. This, as well as the loading of the vehicles, we also filmed of course, which no doubt added to the general difficulties. The three hired lorries were carefully padded with hay in order to cushion the cages against vibration from the rough road. Then great care had to be taken in arranging the cages when loaded – the front of one could not be close to the front of another for fear of a monkey sticking his hand into an unfriendly neighbour's cage and getting it bitten. Most of this work fell on John for Gerry had already departed with Joe Sharp carrying all the baby animals in the collection. Nevertheless, by the end of the final afternoon, John had achieved a miracle and had supervised the loading of all the lorries without losing his temper once and without any serious mishap.

There is nothing more boring than endless film of lorries going by – especially at night when little or none of the surrounding countryside can be seen; nevertheless, I needed to convey something of the long night drive to Freetown so it was necessary to film at least a few shots. Ewart, Howard and I therefore had to drive ahead of the main convoy on occasions, first down to Bambawo in order to film the convoy leaving the district, and later at one or two suitable passing places. John periodically checked that all was well with the animals and we also filmed one of these routine stops. We had left the Beef Mine at about five o'clock in the afternoon and we saw the sun come up again before we reached Freetown; in fact, it was after seven in the morning when we hurried on in front of the main convoy in order to film the arrival at the Dicor flats where Gerry was anxiously waiting. The Diamond Corporation had not only lent Gerry a flat again but had allowed him to house the collection temporarily in two large garages there.

The next few days involved some filming yet they seemed like a holiday to us. We had lived in comparatively comfortable conditions in the mine yet it was only on reaching our European-style hotel that we could finally rid ourselves of the laterite which had blown and vibrated into every corner and crevice of our equipment and every fibre of our clothing. Now there were only a few straightforward scenes to film in Freetown, depicting Gerry and John's arrival nearly four months before. There was also one last important recording session – with an *ad hoc* group of singers and musicians arranged by courtesy of John Akar, the

217

Director of Sierra Leone Broadcasting. At the studios we found one male singer whose English was good enough to sing the verses of Gerry's calypso – different ones for each episode in the series. We then had to teach the remaining singers and musicians the chorus – Gerry had also composed a tune. This had not been written down so for the first half-hour Gerry hummed it again and again until the musicians learnt it. Eventually, after great difficulty, we obtained a rendering that was both intelligible and at the speed we required. We had recorded the music for two programmes when there was animated discussion amongst the chorus and two female members strode off. This was rather disconcerting just as we were beginning to get into the swing of things so I demanded to know why we could not continue. It turned out to be a call of nature – but of a rather unusual kind. The two ladies concerned had young babies and the time had come for them to breast-feed them. We resumed recording again in half-an-hour.

At last the day came for the collection to be transported down to the *Accra* which had just docked. The Sierra Leone Army, which had a base not far from the Dicor flats, laid on transport for us and the move was conducted with great efficiency. We filmed the lorries arriving at the quayside as well as the cranes lifting all the cages on board. The Elder Dempster Line does not normally allow animals on its passenger ships but had made a special concession for Gerry, allowing him to house the collection in the hold right at the bow of the ship. Jacquie had arrived to help with the animals and on seeing Gerry's delicate state had hurriedly cabled for his secretary, Anne Peters, to fly out and join the party so that she too could help with the cleaning and feeding on the voyage. This extra effort was crucial because not only did it free Gerry and John for filming on the way back, but it turned out to be a very time-consuming business sitting in front of the cages persuading the colobus monkeys to try the new foods on which they now had to survive. The journey home – starting from the Beef Mine – formed most of the sixth and final programme in the series and Gerry wanted to illustrate all the aspects of that part of the expedition which most people would not have considered: the necessity of arranging special meat supplies from the ship's butcher, getting on friendly terms with the 'chippy' in case of running repairs – and, of course, making sure that the Captain is sympathetic to the unusual requirements of a cargo of animals. And, in addition, we filmed scenes of Gerry and John re-enacting the *outward* voyage for Programme One.

The voyage to Liverpool took 10 days and on the fourth day we made a welcome call at Las Palmas in the Canary Islands where we were able to make a quick sortie to the market to buy fresh greenstuff and other vegetables for the animals. Most of them were doing well, some eating better than ever because of the sea air although Anne and Jacquie were having special problems with one or two of the colobus including a bad-tempered male who was quickly named The Sod. What with the animals and the filming, it was hard work for everybody and both the Durrells and I were concerned about the strain of the last difficult leg of the journey – from Liverpool by road to Weymouth and then the ferry across to Jersey. Gerry was still in considerable pain and needed medical attention and rest as soon as possible. Jacquie and I discussed the

*Loading the animal
collection on the
Accra at Freetown.*

situation and decided that the only sensible thing to do would be to
charter a plane to fly the collection direct from Liverpool to Jersey the
same day that we docked. The Trust had originally considered this to be
an extravagance they could ill-afford but I offered to cover half the cost
from the BBC programme budget and immediately put in a radio
telephone call to Bristol. Fortunately, my assistant, Sheila Fullom, was
in my office and I gave her all the necessary details including a request to
arrange a cameraman at Jersey to film the arrival of the plane; I would
then be able to release Ewart and Howard so that they could travel
straight back to Bristol from Liverpool.

We arrived at Liverpool on the morning of May 10 in good spirits. The animals were doing well and even The Sod had succumbed to Anne's guile and was contentedly taking food acquired at Las Palmas. In just a few hours, we assured ourselves we would have achieved the first object of the exercise and all the animals would be in their new homes at Jersey. Unfortunately, fate had two more cruel tricks to play. First of all there was a problem with permits; the papers for the leopards, which should have been at Liverpool waiting for us, had in fact only arrived at Jersey that morning and no copies had been sent to the docks. Endless telephone calls took place. Gerry nearly burst a blood vessel in his rage, and only after several hours' delay were the bureaucrats satisfied. By early afternoon we had at last got the cages to Liverpool Airport by lorry and loaded on to a Bristol freighter. We strapped ourselves in the seats at the back of the aircraft and the engines spluttered into life. The Captain seemed to spend a long time revving up the engines but at long last we were relieved to find ourselves taxiing to the end of the runway. A couple of hours or so and we'd be in Jersey.

Red and black colobus monkey.

With a tremendous roar and a vibration that threatened to shake every rivet out of the plane we lurched down the runway, gaining speed at first but then, instead of taking off we heard the Captain throttle down and we slowed and turned off to the side. More roaring of engines followed, more coughing and spluttering, and then the Captain came back to apologise that there was a fault and we would have to go back to the hangar. After attempts to correct the performance of the engine that was failing the Captain admitted there was no hope of take-off that night. Indeed, there was nothing definite that could be said about departure tomorrow as a spare part had to be flown in. The airline had no other plane available in the vicinity so there was nothing for it but to unload all the animals again and install them in one of the hangars, making them as warm and comfortable as possible and setting up an emergency feeding station for them. I think that if I had been Gerry at this point I would have wept in desperation, for the situation was akin to removing water from a man dying of thirst when his fingertips were just about to touch the glass. But there was no weeping, just a particularly rich assortment of Durrell curses, most of which were directed at a certain air charter company. The same company was told in no uncertain terms that it was now responsible for the health and safety of a very valuable collection and it therefore did not argue with the suggestion that it should immediately sub-contract the transport to another charter company.

The following day the animals were loaded once more, this time into a larger and more convenient DC4, and the flight went without a hitch. At Jersey Airport, my old friend Bill Morris was there to film the arrival and the unloading of the animals. Gerry thought that they had had quite enough disturbance for one day so they were taken to the zoo but left in their travelling cages for the night. The next day we filmed a few of the animals being released into their permanent homes, including, of course, the colobus monkeys for whom a tall, spacious cage had just been built. One by one they went in, looking surprisingly fit and now quite used to human contact. Even The Sod looked down at us quite benevolently; for all the concern he showed, he might have been in Jersey since birth.

Chapter 13

A dream in full colour

I first started watching wildlife programmes regularly on television during 1954 when I was on National Service with the Royal Air Force. I was stationed at a large Radio School in Wiltshire and fortunately the Officer's Mess had a television set on which I was able to see Peter Scott introducing Heinz Sielmann's woodpecker film – possibly the most significant half-hour of my life. Sielmann's film was exceptional and at least a decade ahead of its time but the monthly programmes which Peter Scott introduced (and which were the forerunners of *Look*) were all important events as far as I was concerned; and they made it possible at last for me to decide what I really wanted to do when I left the RAF. I became so fascinated with the potential of natural history on television that I actually used to dream about seeing wildlife on the screen – always in colour. This phenomenon continued long after I started work at the BBC and each time it was a dream in full colour – so vivid that I could hardly believe colour television had not yet arrived and, on one occasion after waking up, I recall wandering in a daze to the nearest receiver to check it out.

Filled with such an obsession it was only natural that I should be agitating for the Natural History Unit to make its first colour production as soon as we knew that the advent of colour television was just years away, rather than decades. The start of such a service would be delayed until well after the introduction of the 625-line high definition system which brought BBC 2 first into the homes of London and Birmingham in 1964; but most of the output of the Natural History Unit was on film, which could be transmitted on *any* standard, and there were good arguments for stockpiling material and gaining experience in colour as soon as possible. Unfortunately, there was also a strong argument *against* shooting in colour, namely lack of money. However, a small colour development fund became available in London in the early 1960s and, as soon as we had a suitable programme project already agreed in monochrome, Pat Beech set about tapping this fund. The programme in question was *The Major*, the film which I had proposed immediately after the success of *The Unknown Forest*. Pat quickly seized the opportunity and with the same terrier-like determination that had achieved so much for the development of television at Bristol, he succeeded in extracting a few hundred pounds from the central fund to cover the difference between monochrome and colour film costs. In those days it was not a particularly small sum of money.

There was a further complication, however. When we began filming in 1961, the BBC engineers had not made key decisions about the colour system and the equipment to be used. Nor would anyone give me an official statement on what type of colour film would be likely to come into general use, although all the indications were that it would be reversal rather than negative stock. At the time, 16 mm film producers mainly shot on Ektachrome Reversal which was then used as a master for making colour prints. I asked Eric Ashby to shoot some test rolls on this stock and when these had been printed we took them, together with some rolls of Eric's own Anscochrome and Kodachrome, to Lime Grove Studios in London. In the telecine suite there the engineers had built an experimental colour machine on which we ran our first rolls of natural history film. It was, of course, a thrilling moment and, although the quality was poor compared with today's standards, the experiment confirmed what we already knew – that natural history on television would make an even greater impact as soon as colour arrived. The engineers in charge of the colour telecine machine were eager to get their hands on all kinds of film to experiment with so they gladly ran our test rolls a second time. And so, while they examined their waveforms and noted the characteristics of the different film stocks, Eric and I sat back and for just half-an-hour saw a dream coming true.

The outcome was daunting: if we were to shoot *The Major* in colour it would have to be on Ektachrome, a film stock balanced for artificial light with a speed of 25 ASA. In daylight, using a conversion filter, the effective speed would be only 16 ASA – a horrifying prospect for any wildlife cameraman used to working frequently in marginal light conditions. Nevertheless, both Eric Ashby and Leslie Jackman accepted that challenge. But for Eric, working out of doors and often in the shade of trees, the number of filming hours per day was immediately reduced and he would suffer the frustration of seeing behaviour required for the film without being able to shoot it for lack of light. For Les, working in his backroom studio at Paignton, the heating and lighting problems with controlled filming would be compounded. Even BBC cameraman, George Shears, who filmed the felling sequence in the autumn, had to order a pantechnicon full of powerful lights to be sure that he could cover the event on an overcast day.

When it was finally decided to adopt the PAL colour system in this country, the most suitable film stock after all turned out to be Eastmancolour negative so we later discovered that we had backed the wrong horse. But the mistake was not serious, for the experience in working in colour proved valuable and showed that, film stock apart, the differences in production costs between monochrome and colour were not as marked as some people had feared. When completed, *The Major* was first shown in monochrome and indeed was twice repeated in monochrome before colour finally arrived. Then it enjoyed further transmissions and, in fact, became one of the most repeated of the Unit's programmes – overtaken a few years later only by another early colour film – Jeffery Boswall's production of *The Private Life of the Kingfisher*, filmed by Ron Eastman and shown on television no less than eight times.

Having been given extra funds for colour so early in the 1960s, we perhaps became over-optimistic about our chances of further subsidies;

but other BBC departments were also on the hunt and, in spite of our protests, films such as *A Bull Called Marius* had to be shot in monochrome, ignoring the obvious attractions of the rainbow colours of bee-eaters and skeins of salmon-pink flamingos against an indigo sky. The main problem here was that this was a BBC 1 production and the colourisation of that channel would follow much later. Nevertheless by the mid-1960s there was a slight relaxation of the rules and it was somewhat reluctantly agreed that we could shoot about half of a new BBC 1 series, called *Animal People*, in colour. Each programme was about a well-known figure who was involved in some way or other with animals, and the five subjects chosen were H. G. Hurrell, the Devon naturalist; Frank Sawyer, a riverkeeper on the Avon in Wiltshire; Len Williams, who kept a woolly monkey colony at his home in Cornwall; Gerald Durrell, Honorary Director of the Jersey Wildlife Preservation Trust; and Peter Scott, Honorary Director of the Wildfowl Trust at Slimbridge. Most of the subjects were at some time in the public eye through television appearances but the idea of these programmes was to show a more personal account of each man's interest in animals, supported by any biographical material available which would illustrate the development of this interest.

Due to other commitments, I was able to produce only three of these programmes but to my delight all three were to be made in colour. The Eastmancolor negative available then, although not as fast as today's Eastmancolor stock, did at least have great advantages in speed and adaptability over the Ektachrome we had used for *The Major* and, therefore, gave considerably more scope for filming. I was immediately pleased with the fidelity with which it captured the subtle pastel colours of a variety of birds on H. G. Hurrell's bird table, when we began working on his programme. HG had recently been investigating the intelligence of the blue and great tits that visited his bird table and had constructed several tests made of perspex and wood. To obtain the reward of a nut, the birds had to pull out a number of matchsticks in a certain order from a perspex panel. After they had learnt what was required, the birds' task was made even more difficult by using a greater number of matchsticks, and in some cases even a little matchbox drawer. As all this was observed from the Hurrells' kitchen, it was a very agreeable way to film bird behaviour.

As usual, HG had a number of tame creatures which he was either nursing back to health after an accident or using for intelligence investigations. Atlanta the seal was still going strong and so a major sequence was devoted to her, for she had many new accomplishments since I had last filmed her in monochrome. There was also an engaging raven called Black Rod who did some interesting 'tricks', including pulling a trolley up a slope for a food reward. But the most remarkable thing about Black Rod was its ability to talk. It could not only speak several phrases but did so in a voice which was quite clearly an impersonation of HG himself. It was so accurate that the first time I heard it say 'Come on, Black Rod!' I was convinced that it was HG talking until, to my amazement, I saw him walking towards me a hundred yards away.

As each of the *Animal People* programmes attempted not only to

explore the subject's attitude to animals but also to tell viewers something about his way of life, we spent many days filming in homes for there was much to discover about the personality of the individual from scenes showing the decor and details of books, pictures and other bric-a-brac about the house. For years I had known and been affectionately amused by the charming disorder of the Hurrell household with its wildlife paintings (many by HG himself), files of books and journals and naturalists' paraphernalia – nets, binoculars, coats, rubber boots, film cans, cameras and so on. So I had to find an excuse to film at least part of the action of the film against this delightful jumble; and the entire Hurrell family, as friendly and co-operative as ever, naturally obliged.

The contrast with the setting of the next film in the series could not have been more marked. Since the early days of *Look* I had regularly visited Peter Scott's studio at Slimbridge for programme discussion and film viewings and had always enjoyed the mellow, relaxing atmosphere of a room which was tastefully appointed yet at the same time so comfortably casual. As you went through the door, an easel was on the left in an area set aside for painting and there was always an interesting collection of Scott's pictures lying there. At the far end of the room there was a desk close to a wall completely covered in bookshelves; and there was also a draughtsman's stand where Peter could work on watercolours for books or the pen and ink drawings we sometimes needed for his television programmes. In the middle section of the room was a spacious area with deep, comfortable chairs and a sofa; the fireplace was on the right and an enormous picture window on the left which looked out on to the pond in the Rushy Pen. Here you could see a great variety of ducks, geese and swans, some just a foot or two away the other side of the window. Memories of sitting quietly in the studio with a glass of sherry in my hand whilst watching the sun go down are among the precious recollections of 20 years ago.

When Peter agreed to be the subject of one of the programmes in the *Animal People* series, it gave me great personal as well as professional pleasure, for I looked forward to the experience of working in that delightful studio at Slimbridge again. Although Peter was well-known to viewers as a presenter of natural history programmes, and a great authority on ducks and geese in particular, I was sure that few would know about his early life when he had become interested in the sport of wildfowling and, whilst living in an old lighthouse in Norfolk, had achieved international recognition as a painter of wildfowl. Before I joined the BBC, I had seen a programme produced by Desmond Hawkins in which Peter had painted a picture and had chatted to viewers at the same time. I thought this would be an excellent technique to use in my film so that Peter could talk about his life in the 1930s but on this occasion it would be even more attractive as the painting would be seen in its true colours.

The subject of the painting was not difficult to select. In the 1960s the great excitement at Slimbridge was the new work being done on Bewick's swans. For a long time, a small number of these swans from Arctic Russia had occasionally visited wintering grounds some distance from Slimbridge but wild birds only began flying in to the Trust grounds after they had been attracted by captive birds of the same species resident in the collection. By encouraging them with food, and by making the Rushy Pen area out of bounds to the public during the winter, Peter was able to increase steadily the number of visiting wild Bewick's swans each year. And by watching them literally just outside his studio window he was able to distinguish family groups and identify individuals by differences in the patterns of the yellow and black

markings on their bills. The fact that these markings varied from swan to swan had been known for many years but it was Peter Scott who was first able to draw and paint each new individual and identify it with a name. Once that had been done the door was open for a fascinating long-term research project on these graceful winter visitors.

There was little doubt, therefore, that for the film a painting of Bewick's swans it had to be. And what more appropriate than a painting of the swans swimming on – and flying over – the pond just outside the studio window – 'my magic window', as Peter called it. By filming in mid-winter when the number of swans was at a peak we would have a wonderful opportunity to observe Peter painting from real life subjects. So for three days we were installed in the studio, beginning with an empty canvas on the easel, and ending with the artist adding his signature to the completed painting. I chose a number of key stages in the painting and over each one Peter talked about an important period of his life; in the edited film these led to sequences which we filmed at a number of other locations, particularly in East Anglia and including the old lighthouse where he once lived. After each session in the studio, we left Peter to take the painting on to the next key stage while we went outside to film flight shots of the Bewick's swans or other material in the Trust grounds. The climax came on the third day when the painting was nearing completion during late afternoon. Just outside the studio, Peter had installed floodlights to illuminate the pond in the evenings and as the daylight began to fade these were turned on about the same time as grain was scattered for the swans. Many of the swans went out to the

LEFT
The Scotts watch the Bewick's swans during a break in filming . . .

. . . while the author studies drawings of the bill patterns of the swans which enable each individual to be identified.

Swan Lake in 1967 – the pond outside Peter Scott's studio in Rushy Pen.

salt marshes on the banks of the Severn during the day, but as the sun set on the short winter days, the swans would fly in to Rushy Pen again for their free meal. On that third day we were fortunate enough to have fine weather and a good evening sky and the plaintive calls of the birds as the little family groups flew in against the western horizon gave a touch of enchantment to an already beautiful scene. Finally, the daylight gone completely, we were left with a quite astonishing scene to close the programme; Peter and his wife, Philippa, relaxing in the evening while just outside could be seen graceful flotillas of wild swans on an inky-black pool. It was indeed a magic window.

During the course of filming the programme, I discovered that Peter usually had the record-player on whilst painting, for he had a great love of classical music. I made a note of some of his favourite works and, after discussing these with the film editor, John Merritt, made a short list from which to choose a piece to accompany the final sequence of the film. This sequence, in which the painting was completed and the swans flew in to the Rushy Pen at sunset, seemed to embody all that Peter had tried to communicate through the words he spoke earlier in the programme: his scientific interest in the birds, the aesthetic joy they gave him, his professionalism and skill as a painter, and the way all these blended so well together in the setting at Slimbridge. I was confident that I had filmed all the shots required to make the sequence

RIGHT
Peter Scott at work on the painting he made especially for the Animal People *programme.*

228

work; but I was not yet sure exactly how they would all cut together. In such a situation, if you have complete confidence in your film editor as I did with John Merritt, i. is best to go away and let the editor have his head, having first told him what you would like the sequence to convey. So I left Bristol for a few days to make a reconnaissance for another film. What John showed me on my return exceeded my highest expectations. He had first roughly assembled the sequence and had then selected the piece of music that he thought was most apt – a section from the Brahms Violin Concerto. He had then finely edited it, matching most carefully the phrasing of the music with the visual shape of the images and the rhythm of the sequence. As I watched it in the cutting room I felt a tingle of emotion in my spine – a sure sign that a piece of good film editing is doing its job. I could see why it was working so well: the mood of the music was just right to bring together all the elements I had described to John but he had seen something else in this particular piece. The soloists' bow, sensuously drawing a phrase from the violin, matched perfectly the close-ups of Peter's brush sensitively touching the line of a swan's neck in flight; in their way, sound and image were both describing a beautiful moment and the combination of the two crafts produced an exquisite result. With moist eyes at the end of the viewing all I could do was to thank John – and order him not to change a single frame.

The third film in the series posed a new set of problems and was completely different in style and character – reflecting the contrasting personality of Gerald Durrell. As we had already filmed Gerry overseas on a collecting expedition we decided at the outset to make this programme at his home in Jersey, where he lives in the manor house at the very centre of the zoo. His living quarters were on the first and second floors of the central part of the manor, the ground floor being mainly offices used for the administration of the Jersey Wildlife Preservation Trust. Accommodation for some of the keepers was in the two wings on either side. In such a situation it was inevitable that the Durrells' lives were inextricably linked to the routines of the zoo from breakfast to supper, sometimes in the middle of the night as well. So, as Gerry said to me, what better way to show what life is like than to portray a typical day at the Trust Headquarters from dawn to dusk? This would certainly include a great variety of animals, the staff concerned with the cleaning and feeding routines at the zoo, and, of course, Gerry's own involvement, for he was frequently consulted during the day and often visited animals in the collection. Now with modern lightweight equipment and fast film stocks, together with the simultaneous use of two crews, it would be possible to shoot such a film in one actual day. But in 1967, with comparatively bulky equipment, the need for lights in many of the indoor situations, and only one crew available, it was inevitable that we would have to build up an impression of a typical day by filming over a period of nearly two weeks. Gerry suggested that the film could be made almost entirely with natural sound and very little narration, making most of the essential points of information through 'overheard' conversations at meetings and meals.

Filming went splendidly for the first week and the time came for us to shoot an evening sequence in the Durrells' living room. I knew from personal experience that this was an extremely enjoyable part of the day: the zoo routines were over and occasionally a member of staff would come up to the Durrells' flat to discuss a problem over a drink in company with other visitors from England or overseas house guests. Frequently I had been a guest myself and had always looked forward to the moment when the animals had the floor – literally. Firstly, there was Keeper, an amiable boxer who loafed around the Durrells' flat most of the day. Then there were the squirrels which lived in cages in the corner of the living room. Gerry had brought back some charming forest squirrels from Sierra Leone but undoubtedly the squirrel with the most attractive personality of all was Timothy, an African ground squirrel. In the evening, when the traffic in and out of the Durrells' flat had died down and the living room door could be kept shut, Timothy's cage was opened. This usually signalled the start of an hour's entertainment which was better than any night-club cabaret that I had seen. For it seems that African ground squirrels are nature's comics – at least Timothy was – and his routine and thorough inspection of the room and its occupants was conducted with such mischievous showmanship and perfect timing that every little action brought ripples of laughter from any of Gerry's guests who were quietly watching proceedings from the sofa. Whatever Timothy was doing, his actions after release from his cage would be punctuated by little bursts of scratching and grooming. Keeper, meanwhile, would usually be stretched out in front of the fire, pretending to ignore this distasteful exhibition but in reality maintaining at least one jaundiced eye on the proceedings – provided this did not actually require him to move his head from its comfortable position on the rug. Timothy, taking Keeper as part of the fittings, would sometimes stop and groom whilst on top of the dog – a liberty at which Keeper drew the line if he happened to be on his side and Timothy stopped in a position which threatened his masculinity.

It was such amusing antics that I hoped to include in the final evening sequence of Gerry's film, but it is one thing to sit quietly as a guest and witness them with the lights down low, and another thing to film them with bright lights and a roomful of technicians. George Shears, the cameraman, keep the lighting down to a minimum and sent everyone not essential to the filming out of the room, but even then it took several evenings before we had begun to obtain shots of Timothy in anything like his true colours, in spite of the cajoling that went on with a variety of nuts. In fact, we were in danger of spending a disproportionate amount of time on Timothy and Keeper and this gave an opportunity for Gerry to practise his prankish humour on his old antagonist Frank Sherratt, the Programme Executive at Bristol. I use the word 'antagonist' but it must be said that negotiations were usually conducted in a friendly way even if Frank was considered by some to be an obdurate man. He took his responsibilities for not throwing away public money very seriously and, although a few of the more experienced professionals were occasionally irritated by Frank's obstinacy, most accepted his final offer which often came with the message that they would 'have to take the rough with the smooth'. Gerry, on this occasion, had thought Frank's offer of a facilities fee to the Trust was none too generous, but had finally accepted on the basis that exposure on the screen would be good for the

OVERLEAF
The swans under floodlights, seen through the studio window at night.

231

Trust in any case. Nevertheless, the time spent in filming Timothy and Keeper gave Gerry an opportunity to have a playful dig at Frank. After the filming had been completed he wrote as follows:

The Durrells at home with Keeper and Timothy the squirrel.

Dear Mr Sherratt,

After our previous correspondence I am, as I am sure you will appreciate, extremely diffident in writing this letter to you. However, I would beg you to realise that it is not of my wish that this is written, but it is my duty as an agent to do so.

As you know, for the past three weeks, Mr Christopher Parsons, together with the BBC Natural History Unit, has been making a film here. During the course of the filming, one or two minor items emerged which I feel I should bring to your attention.

To begin with, in signing the initial contracts, I was not informed by either Mr Parsons or yourself that the presence of my wife's squirrel, Timothy Testicle, or that of my dog, Keeper of the Keys, would be required. However, it transpired from Mr Parsons, during the course of the chaos that he was creating in a hitherto calm and reasonable establishment, that it was necessary for these two animals to appear: as I say, I have been appointed agent for both of them.

As their appearance was not mentioned in the original contract, I feel that it is necessary for me to now negotiate terms with you on behalf of my clients and, knowing you to be a fair-minded (one might almost say generous) individual, I feel sure that you will not consider the following proposals excessive.

Timothy Testicle was required to have his own private room infested by a vast series of lights, combined with an array of ham-handed and apparently inebriated technicians and was then expected to go through, at the drop of a hat, a routine that would have made even Bertram Mills' wife think. He was expected to do a Bolshoi ballet across the carpet; to lie supine upon a large and potentially savage carnivore, to wit a dog; to stand on his hind legs with his nose wiffling (looking not unlike a young BBC producer who is wondering whether he is going to get something other than *Look* to do) and then undergo the ignominious experience of lying upside down in my wife's hands, displaying an astonishing proportion of his more intimate anatomy, while giggling hysterically.

In my private conversations with him, he has given me to understand that he would not have minded subjugating himself to these indignities quite so much if it had not been for the constant clouds of beer-laden breath which were wafted to him from the direction of the cameraman and the producer. I think you will agree, my dear Mr Sherratt, that as he so willingly took part in something for which he had not signed a contract, it is up to the Corporation to show a certain amount of generosity. I am, therefore, empowered on his behalf to request the Corporation for the following fee:

> 1 cwt bag of hazel nuts
> 300 copies of the *Radio Times* (for bed-making)
> 2 bottles of Chanel No 5
> A year's supply of Smith's potato crisps
> 1 female ground squirrel, approximately 3 years old and
>   of an uninhibited disposition

My client also wishes me to point out that, should the shots of him lying on his back reveal what he thinks they reveal, he would not wish to have a credit in the film.

We now turn to my other client, Mr Keeper of the Keys. The circumstances here were slightly different, since in spite of his Kennel Club pedigree (which he constantly showed to the producer) he was forced to place himself in the most degrading and ignominious situations and was on more than one occasion pulled by his hind legs across the floor in order to get him into shot. He also, at one point, sustained a slight – but powerful – wound from my first-mentioned client, in a portion of his anatomy which I shall leave to your imagination, when they were both endeavouring to obey the producer's somewhat bibulous and incoherent instructions. Again, no contract was signed, but I feel sure my client would settle for the following:

> One boxer bitch, preferably in season, of suitable
>   aristocratic lineage
> 4 tons 'Good Boy' chocolate drops
> Oriental-type back scratcher
> A yearly visit from the lady at Tring whom I believe
> has made a life work of collecting fleas

In conclusion, might I say that neither of my clients wish to appear unnecessarily harsh, but they would like to point out that, during the intrusion into the peace of their home, by what appeared to be a lot of drunken Irish plough boys, they found several personal items missing – to wit:

> One rubber bone smelling of chocolate and labelled
>   'With love from Lassie'
> 14 chocolate drops
> 1 celluloid Father Christmas
> 3 sheets of the *News of the World*

In closing, may I say that both my clients feel that both the producer and crew behaved in a manner unbefitting their station which they take to be St Pancreas.

We do hope to hear from you in the near future and hope that this matter can be settled amicably.

With kindest regards,

Yours sincerely,
Gerald Durrell
Agent

Frank has never received a letter quite like this before but I persuaded him to reply in similar vein and the correspondence ended with a curt note from Gerry that in view of Frank's tone 'I am being forced to put the whole matter in the hands of my two clients' solicitors, Messrs V. D. Jaguar and Savage of Lincolns Inn Fields'.

Chapter 14

Island interlude

Although virtually all my work was now in colour, making programmes for BBC 1 was the exception rather than the rule; the second channel, having begun on 625 lines in 1964, was due to go into colour in 1967, and from 1966 onwards most of my efforts were concentrated in making programmes for BBC 2 under its new controller, David Attenborough. Until then the Natural History Unit had contributed little to BBC 2, although a handful of the best *Look* programmes had been repeated under the rather obvious title of *Look Again*. But in 1965 after Attenborough's appointment – when Michael Peacock moved to BBC 1 – things began to look up for us. We were given a brand-new fortnightly series called *Life*, presented by Dr Desmond Morris, and this began in November – just two months after Bristol began receiving BBC 2 pictures from the UHF transmitter at Wenvoe in South Wales.

The producer was Ron Webster, a Bristol-based man who had been responsible for a wide variety of programmes ranging from the Regional Television Magazine to outside broadcasts and a number of documentary films. An old colleague of Nicky Crocker's, Ron had already been involved with some of the Unit's output having suggested various ideas for *Look* and he had also previously worked with Desmond Morris on zoo programmes. Ron had no academic background in biology but he had a lively and enquiring mind into things natural which enabled him to establish a good working relationship with Desmond, based on healthy mutual respect. *Life* was a studio-based magazine and Ron was not afraid to gather together leading biologists to talk about subjects at a level not possible in the mainstream *Look* on BBC 1. The tenor was set by the *Radio Times* billing for the first edition on November 12 – 'A fortnightly challenge to our ideas and understanding of life in the animal world'. The programme ran on Sunday evenings, alternating with *Horizon*, which at that time also had a magazine format.

Ron Webster's attachment to the Unit was very valuable, for he assembled a small production team of comparatively new recruits, which he managed with characteristic bluntness, and to whom he gave the benefit of his considerable experience. It is not surprising that several of them later became distinguished producers in the Unit – John Sparks, Richard Brock, Barry Paine and Peter Crawford. I regretted not having had the opportunity of working with Ron in the *Life* team but at the time I was enjoying an extremely active life almost entirely on location – including one of my old haunts from boyhood days in Devon, the Exe Estuary.

The series Life *was the Unit's first regular contribution to BBC 2. Its presenter was Dr Desmond Morris, seen here with sculptor Jonathan Kenworthy, who was then just making a name for himself. Nearly ten years later he was the subject of an edition of* The World About Us *entitled* Kenworthy's Kenya.

For several years I had usually managed to get approval for a general documentary film about the relationships between man and animals in addition to the conventional natural history programmes that I contributed to regular series. And so, following in the tradition of *The Major* and *A Bull Called Marius*, I had proposed making a film about the Exe Estuary, which seemed to have all the ingredients with which I enjoyed working. Because it was a 'round-the-year' programme, work on it had to be fitted in with other projects and the most ambitious of these in 1966 was undoubtedly a film I made in Corfu with Gerald Durrell, entitled *The Garden of the Gods*. A great deal of interest in Corfu had been raised ever since publication of Gerry's first book about his early family life there, *My Family and Other Animals*, and when Gerry cabled me the previous summer suggesting that I fly over to discuss a possible film script, Desmond Hawkins obligingly found my air fare from one of his reserve funds. In the mid-1960s very little of Corfu had been developed for tourism and I immediately fell under the spell of the island's charm, becoming more and more besotted with the place as Gerry took me to one location after another which had been featured in his book. It was an ideal place for a colour documentary but initially I had a more ambitious idea.

One of the attractions of BBC 2 was that the Controller was sometimes able to clear the schedules and make an entire evening available for a major project, be it an opera or an important outside broadcast event. What better, I thought, than to take viewers to Corfu for an entire evening's entertainment, the basic framework of which would be an adaptation of *My Family and Other Animals*; but in it would be incorporated elements of both travel and natural history programmes. Even though I anticipated that a drama director would be required for much of this strange project, David Attenborough quite reasonably pointed out that we had no drama experience in the Natural History Unit and therefore asked us to think again. Nothing daunted, Gerry came up with a more straightforward documentary approach in which he would reveal the wonders of Corfu to his town-bred godson visiting the island for the first time. The film would be a kind of relaxed travelogue in which Gerry would revisit all his boyhood haunts for the benefit of his godson but there was an additional ingredient which made it even more attractive: Gerry had persuaded one of the characters in his book, Dr Theodore Stephanides, who was now living in London, to return to the island for the film. This was particularly significant because Theodore had been Gerry's mentor and had taught and encouraged him in all his natural history pursuits.

I had a good picture of Theodore in my mind as a result of reading Gerry's book; on meeting him it was therefore a delight to discover that he was exactly as I had imagined – a remarkable thing indeed, not just because of the accuracy of Gerry's portrait but because Theodore had apparently not changed in 30 years. He had the posture and carriage not of an old man but of a soldier; indeed, he had served during the war and had written a fine book about his experiences entitled *Climax in Crete*. But his grey-white hair and long beard belied his age; early photographs of Victorian naturalists immediately came to mind. He seemed to be a man out of his time for he spoke, thought and acted exactly how I had always assumed the great Victorian naturalists did. He had an insatiable curiosity about the natural world but his interest – and his knowledge – extended to history, archaeology, anthropology and many more subjects. He was a poet: he even had a crater on the moon named after him. The respect and affection that Gerry bore for him was not surprising; to be taught by Theodore during a boyhood spent on Corfu made Gerry a very lucky person indeed.

The production team which went to Corfu was the largest I had ever taken overseas, for the film was quite complex in that it involved several types of shooting. Large parts of the programme would involve sound filming so for a start there was a basic three-man crew consisting of George Shears, the cameraman; Maurice Fisher, the assistant cameraman (later to become senior cameraman on *Life on Earth*); and Robin Drake, the recordist (later a senior producer responsible for programmes such as *The Antiques Roadshow*). As some of our filming would be indoors, film lighting had to be taken too; and since some of the locations were in remote areas where no electricity was available, this also meant taking a generator which was built into a special Land-Rover. So, 'Dusty' Miller, the electrician and Maurice Fisher, drove through Europe and down Italy to the Brindisi-Corfu ferry while the rest of the team caught a direct plane to the island. With us were two specialist cameramen: Douglas Steen, an underwater cameraman from Australia who was on attachment to the Unit; and Andrew Neal, a young man just starting to take up wildlife photography.

Doug Steen's availability was a bonus, as the budget would not normally have stretched to an additional cameraman for underwater work alone. He was with the Unit on a Bursary to learn about filming

techniques in general and his experience underwater could at the same time be put to good use during the few days we were scheduled to film in the sea. Doug subsequently returned to Australia where he made wildlife films on a part-time basis for many years, but he was tragically killed in a crash when piloting his own light aircraft on a trial flight.

Andrew Neal, son of the famous naturalist and badger-expert, Dr Ernest Neal, came along to concentrate on details of insect and other invertebrate life which would intercut with the sequences the main unit would be filming with Gerry, Theodore and the boy. The boy was Andreas Damaschinos – the curly-haired and mischievous teenage son of a Greek friend of Gerry's.

As there was a large amount of sound filming and the work was complex, I also took my assistant, Sheila Fullom, so all in all there were eight of us, not including the artists. At the time Gerry had a flat in Corfu town, so he was already in residence when we arrived; so was Theodore who was staying with his sister who lived next door, but Gerry had found a pleasant hotel, just a few miles outside town, which could accommodate the BBC team and which was conveniently situated for many of the film locations.

The actual timing of the filming, which stretched over a month, was chosen to coincide with the great annual procession through Corfu town on August 11 when a miracle performed by Saint Spiridion is commemorated. Gerry was particularly insistent on this point as he stressed that Saint Spiridion was the most important person on the island; indeed a very high proportion of the male children on Corfu are named Spiro in his honour. His embalmed body lies in a silver coffin in the church but on a few occasions – including August 11 – it is removed and carried round the town in a special casket as a part of a grand procession of church dignitaries led by the town band. This particular occasion celebrates the miracle Saint Spiridion performed when he was seen to come out of the sky with a host of angels whilst the Turks were besieging Corfu; this was accompanied by a tempest which wrecked the Turks' camp and allowed the Corfiots to counter-attack and drive them off.

Each day there was a constant stream of people calling in at the church to light a candle for Saint Spiridion. Some were on their way to work, some were returning from work perhaps after a night's fishing, others had come in from the surrounding countryside for market day. Whatever their standing or age, to each of them Saint Spiridion seemed to be the most important thing in their lives, so naturally we requested permission to film in the church. Aided no doubt by the reputation that the Durrell family has in Corfu, we were granted permission to film a sequence in which Gerry and his young godson paid their respects to the saint. I offer it only as an interesting fact, but it was curious that before this filming was done, our work was difficult and fraught with problems, whilst afterwards everything went comparatively smoothly.

The Garden of the Gods was a particularly enjoyable film to make because it involved such a delightful mixture of topics. There was a little of the history of Corfu, something of its music and dance, beautiful scenery, and running through it all, a series of incidents concerning wildlife – usually linked to memories of Gerry's childhood experiences or lessons with Theodore.

Gerry and Andreas light a candle in the church of St Spiridion.

'Ah yes, that's *very* interesting', Theodore would say after Gerry had handed him a giant water bug. 'Yes, it's, er, *Bilostoma niloticum*. You know your brother Lawrence was the first to find one of these here at

Kalami in October 1936 – I looked it up in my notes only the other day. And you found two of them in Kondokali in 1937.'

Wherever we went and whatever we looked at, Theodore had a story. We were filming some scenes one day in what Gerry used to call 'the fields' when he was a boy – in reality a low-lying area that once contained the old Venetian salt-pans. We stopped to take a close-up of a beautiful swallow-tail butterfly on a chaste tree. I asked Theodore why it was so called.

'Well, um, it's called the chaste tree because from ancient times an infusion of seeds was supposed to promote chastity, and it was even known in the Middle Ages in England as "Monk's Pepper". The Crusaders, before going off to the Crusades, generally arranged that their wives should be given their little daily dose.' He paused, and then added with a mischievous smile, 'History doesn't say if they themselves took a daily dose in Palestine or wherever they were!'

Unfortunately, although Theodore felt comfortable enough walking about with Gerry and Andreas in front of the silent camera, he was somewhat nervous and camera-conscious whenever we attempted to shoot with sound, so these delightful asides were hard to capture on film; but I did manage to get some of them recorded later, after the camera had been put away, so that his voice could be used on the soundtrack. In fact, Theodore would probably have been much happier to stand well out of shot and quietly observe the process of film-making, with which he became greatly intrigued.

Theodore also expressed keen interest in the editing stages of the film

so, in due course, I invited him down to Bristol to see the cutting rooms
and to watch the soundtrack being mixed. The post-production stage of
The Garden of the Gods came several months after filming, however, for
as soon as I returned from Corfu I flew to Jamaica on another assignment. This trip later proved to be far more important than I realised at
the time for it represented a crucial stage in the formation of what is
surely the most technically advanced biological film unit in the world –
Oxford Scientific Films.

The visit to Jamaica arose out of a conversation I had with Gerald
Thompson at Oxford earlier in 1967. By then the Thompson and Skinner
team had significantly improved their equipment as well as their
techniques and filming had become an increasingly important part of
their lives. Gerald's young son, David, had become involved in the
business, too, and since 1964 had acted as assistant. Their work attracted
a good deal of attention in the university itself as well as through
occasional television exposure and, one day, Gerald Thompson was
approached by a young zoologist who had attended one of his lectures.
It was Peter Parks, a junior member of the Zoology Department just
down the road and a part-time demonstrator who was also an excellent
freelance biological illustrator. Although Peter shared Gerald's interest
in overcoming the problems of obtaining close-ups at high magnification, he was primarily interested in a rather different type of subject
matter. Whilst Gerald concentrated on detailed studies of insect and
spider behaviour, Peter was fascinated by the microscopic world of life
in ponds – much of it single-cell forms which could only normally be

observed under a microscope. He was particularly interested in the technique of dark-ground photography for filming such subjects, an arrangement whereby the tiny translucent creatures can be illuminated from behind but are seen against a dark background. Parks designed and built an optical bench for this, arranging for the camera to be locked firmly at one end whilst the position of the subject – in a tiny perspex cell – could be finely adjusted and brought into focus by a set of controls operating in three different planes. Having camera and subject on the same heavy and rigid bench helped to avoid vibration problems at high magnification and the precision engineering involved in the construction of the bench effectively enabled the camera to 'follow' smoothly the movements of the subject on a microscopic scale – although of course it was the controlled movement of the miniature aquarium in front of the locked camera that achieved this. Parks had the benefit of a camera which already belonged to the Zoology Department, but with no other room available so his equipment had to be housed under the stairs.

When Gerald Thompson introduced me to Peter Parks and his work, my eyes were opened to a new world. Whereas I had been only slightly interested in peering down microscopes and looking *at* a community of water fleas and diatoms and paramecium, now Parks' photography suddenly pulled me *into* this unknown world which I began to see properly for the first time. There were real dimensions to these strange

RIGHT
*Peter Parks'
photography
opened up a new
microscopic world
for television. This
is a single-cell
organism,*
Paramecium.

BELOW RIGHT
*The first BBC
sequence shot by
Parks', Paling's and
Morris' Oxford
Biological Films
was on the rabbit
flea, for* Life.

BELOW
*Peter Parks' first
optical bench
under the stairs at
the Zoology
Department,
Oxford University.*

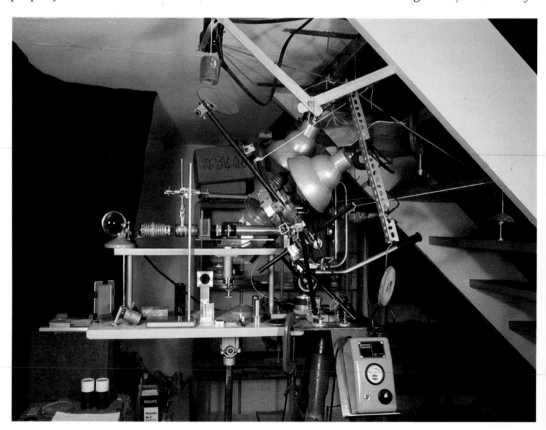

organisms, yet you could see into them and, they also displayed a range of striking colours which was aesthetically pleasing.

Through sharing common interests in solving the technical problems of close-up biological cinephotography, it is not surprising that the acquaintanceship of Thompson and Skinner at the Forestry Institute with Parks at the Zoology Department should strengthen into real co-operation and friendship. Parks was not the only person in the Zoology Department who had the filming bug, however. Dr John Paling, a young demonstrator specialising in fish, was also making short films and an undergraduate named Sean Morris was involved too. They had combined forces within the department, calling themselves Oxford Biological Films, and indeed had already shot some short sequences for *Life* at the instigation of Barry Paine. By 1967 the notion had already grown that the two groups might combine into one biological film unit for the purpose of making educational films. There was some interest in this idea from the university authorities and it was suggested that it might even be possible to operate on university premises, although the films made would require much wider distribution than Oxford if the group was to be viable on a full-time basis. The next crucial stage was to see if they could all work together satisfactorily, and the long summer vacation would be an ideal time to put this to the test.

The group had been offered laboratory facilities and accommodation on the campus of the University of the West Indies at Kingston, Jamaica. Although air fares to Kingston were high, the running costs there would be minimal and the great variety of subjects available ideal. The university had a marine laboratory and boat facilities nearby and a short distance inland behind the campus there was plenty of tropical forest, rich in invertebrate and bird life. The marine facilities provided opportunities for John Paling's fish studies but they were also important for Peter Parks because he now had a chance to try out his dark-ground techniques on minute marine forms. The combined talents of the group – which would include Dr John Cooke, the spider expert, to act as a kind of scout – seemed ideal for tackling a fairly comprehensive project on the wildlife of Jamaica and it was with that in mind that Gerald Thompson approached me. If the BBC would buy the television rights in their film, this would go some way to underwriting the cost of the expedition, which included a considerable sum of money for film stock. The problem was that no one really knew for certain what species they would be able to film and so it was impossible to write a storyline. Furthermore, to raise enough money from television rights at least three 50-minute programmes would have to be produced and that was asking a lot of a group with so little experience. Nevertheless, it was one of those occasions when, knowing the quality of Thompson's and Parks' work, one felt obliged to take a chance, and fortunately the Controller, David Attenborough, agreed to our recommendations.

The main condition I put on the exercise was that the group must be available for two weeks near the end of their assignment to film such additional material as might be required under my direction. I sensed that, although much stunning close-up work would be taken, it would be in short sequences of unrelated material which I would have trouble in linking together. The only solution to this problem was to structure the programmes as a straightforward account of the adventures of a number of biologist-photographers, each following his own special interest. The Oxford group would regularly send back material to England for processing and that would give me an opportunity to view it before I left so that I could work on some ideas on how to link it all together. On returning from Corfu, therefore, I had a large amount of viewing to do before heading towards the Caribbean.

Predictably, the 'rushes' were an attractive mixture of short sequences on a variety of insects, spiders, birds, reptiles, amphibians and fish, but the most amazing material of all was that filmed on Peter Parks' optical bench. He had installed his equipment in a small building on the harbourside at Port Royal and had been busily filming all the planktonic creatures that he could collect by trawling in the waters nearby. Delicate and beautiful forms abounded and every new roll brought some amazing semi-transparent creature unlike anything I had ever seen before. Many of the images might have come from space-age fiction. There were also more familiar freshwater forms, including developing tadpoles filmed in such huge close-up that the capillary blood-flow could be seen within their tissues. The rushes were indeed a succession of shattering images but could they be made into three programmes?

Several of the group met me at the airport at Kingston and whisked me in a Mini Moke up to the university campus where they were installed in a pleasant house belonging to the Professor of Zoology. The cameramen had found many suitable subjects within the garden itself and it was not long before I, too, was relaxing with a cold drink in my hand and watching anolis lizards on the trunks of nearby trees and various birds such as ground doves, saffron finches and the occasional yellow-billed parrot. But most exciting of all were the humming-birds which were competing with the bees for the garden flowers' nectar. The tiniest were the vervain humming-birds, just seven centimetres long and one of the smallest bird species in the world.

The next day Sean Morris took me up the twisting road leading to the Blue Mountains where many of the specimens for controlled film work in the laboratory had been collected. It had been very hot in Kingston but, as we drove higher, the temperature dropped and by the time we reached the settlement of Newcastle it was relatively cool and comfortable. Here the road passed through an army camp where there had once been an acclimatisation centre for British troops new to Jamaica. We drove on up to the top of the mountain and parked by the roadside at a spot where Gerald Thompson had been filming the nesting habits of some charming little birds called todies. Although they're about wren-size they are more related to the kingfisher family and dig out a room for their nest at the end of a tunnel in a bank. The surrounding forest was shrouded in mist and everything was extremely moist. Many of the trees were covered in vines and creepers and their mossy boughs bore several types of bromeliad – plants which grow on the trees but are not parasitic. The hollow in the centre of the larger varieties becomes filled with water and in these miniature arboreal ponds there lives a strange and often specialised animal community. Sean climbed up one of the trees like a monkey and brought down a bromeliad for me to see, tipping out the contents into a small dish. There were mosquito larvae, beetle larvae and even tadpoles – for there are some species of frog which rely entirely on these tiny ponds for breeding purposes. From amongst the leaves of the bromeliad there were crickets, millipedes and beetles and Sean told me that they had even found a species of crab which spends its entire life there. It has a very flat shape so that it can move easily between the leaves.

The following day Peter Parks and John Paling drove me to Port Royal where they had the use of the small university motor launch, *Pelagia*; from this Peter was able to make daily plankton hauls. Port Royal was originally a city in itself but most of it vanished beneath the sea in a great earthquake in 1692. Supposedly lost at the time was a huge quantity of pirate gold, looted by the notorious Henry Morgan, to whom there is a memorial tablet at the naval cemetery; for he became respectable in the end, having bought a knighthood and risen to the heights of Deputy Governor.

The Oxford zoologists saw other things of interest in the derelict cemetery which gave them subjects for their film: a nightjar's nest had been located and the sandy soil was riddled with the little circular pits dug by ant-lions. Gerald Thompson had quickly seized on these as an ideal subject for one of his close-up studies. An ant-lion is the larval stage of a type of neuropterous insect and it obtains its food by digging a trap into which other small insects – particularly ants – may stumble. If the ant does not immediately tumble to the bottom of the pit its efforts to get out are thwarted by the ant-lion which throws sand at it. Once at the bottom, the ant is seized by the ant-lion's jaws and dragged under the surface to be consumed at leisure.

Within two days I had been able to see most of the locations at which

Peter Parks sent back amazing close-ups of marine planktonic forms from Jamaican waters – such as this starfish larva.

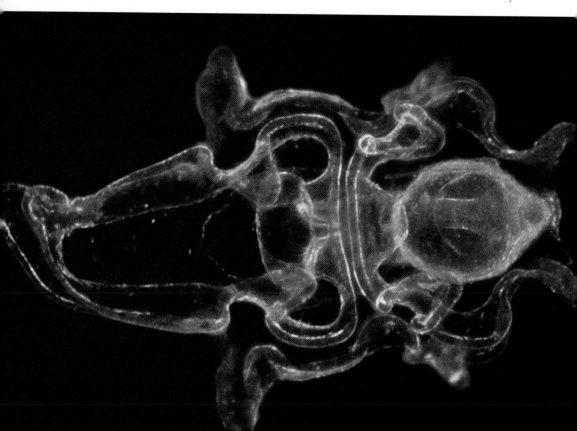

the zoologists had filmed and collected specimens so I could prepare a shooting script of establishing shots and linking sequences to tell the story of the expedition and the methods used in filming. I then started working with David Thompson, using him as cameraman to film his colleagues in as many different locations as possible so as to build up an impression of Jamaica's scenery. One of the most difficult problems was to find a way of linking all the marine material on molluscs, crustaceans and fish which John Paling had been filming. This contained some remarkable sequences – including an account of a strange fish named *Fierasfer* which spends most of its life inside sea-cucumbers. Unfortunately, these close-up studies were filmed under controlled conditions and gave little impression of the sea. However, most of the specimens had been collected at an offshore island and a return visit there seemed to be an ideal way of weaving in some film of a more adventurous kind as well as taking some genuine underwater establishing scenes.

John Cooke, John Paling, Sean Morris and Peter Parks were the marine enthusiasts, so early one morning I travelled out on the motor launch to be with them for a couple of days on their island location. The trip was quite short but a group of bottle-nosed dolphins soon entertained us by swimming close to the bows. When we reached the island, which was only a few hundred yards long, we were greeted by frigate birds soaring overhead and the piercing calls of roseate terns which had a nesting colony there. Small it might be, but the island certainly had much to offer: just off-shore there were reefs which provided a profusion of colourful invertebrates and fish, whilst on land there were the seabirds and swarms of little hermit crabs; there was even a convenient patch of mangroves.

Peter Parks' plans for the periscope which he took to Jamaica.

The shallow waters around the roots provided an excellent opportunity for Peter to use his periscope which he had built in Oxford and which had been shipped out with his optical bench. This apparatus could be suspended from a camera tripod and enabled Peter to obtain underwater shots just a few inches deep. Peter used this to great effect with the fascinating jellyfishes called *Cassiopeia*, which are commonly found in the shallow waters of mangrove swamps. A creamy-grey colour, they were a few inches in diameter and, although they could swim perfectly well when disturbed, they spent most of their time lying 'on their backs' on the bottom, tentacles up and feeding on the plankton in the water. They have symbiotic algae living in them which produce oxygen as a by-product and this enables the specialised jellyfish to live in the poorly-oxygenated waters. Peter's invention, although somewhat difficult to operate, was an excellent device for filming in shallow water and the results on the screen were infinitely better and more convincing than anything that could have been achieved by reproducing the habitat in an aquarium. It was another example of how Peter's unique combination of talents as draughtsman, engineer, photographer and biologist enabled him to find an elegant and aesthetically pleasing solution to a photographic problem.

Although the Oxford group was working extremely hard – for their entire future as a professional film unit depended on the success of the expedition – there was, nevertheless, something of a happy holiday atmosphere present, and it was no more marked than on that short island trip. There is, of course, something very special about islands, particularly if you are the only inhabitants, but as the evening approached and we prepared supper at the camp our island had a haunting Caribbean magic of its own. Against the setting sun we could see the pelicans taking their last reckless dives of the day, while at our feet the ubiquitous hermit crabs continued to ransack the camp for tiny morsels of food. Accompanied by a chorus of shrill screams from the terns we collected driftwood and started a bonfire just as the last pelicans settled down for the night in their trees amongst the mangroves. After supper, Sean got out his guitar and Peter a pair of bongo drums; together they played and sang long into the evening.

Sean and Peter were accomplished performers and a few weeks later, when I was screening the film taken on that memorable evening, I realised that their music would be an important ingredient in recreating the island magic. I invited them to Bristol so that we could record them in a studio for the sound track. By complementing the zoologists' close-up photography with such sequences, two very agreeable 50-minute films eventually emerged from the cutting rooms. However the third programme posed rather different problems. A high proportion of the total film shot by the Oxford group had come from Peter Parks' camera on the optical bench and Peter had expressed the hope that a complete programme might be made from his footage on marine plankton. From the biologists' point of view it was indeed remarkable material – easily

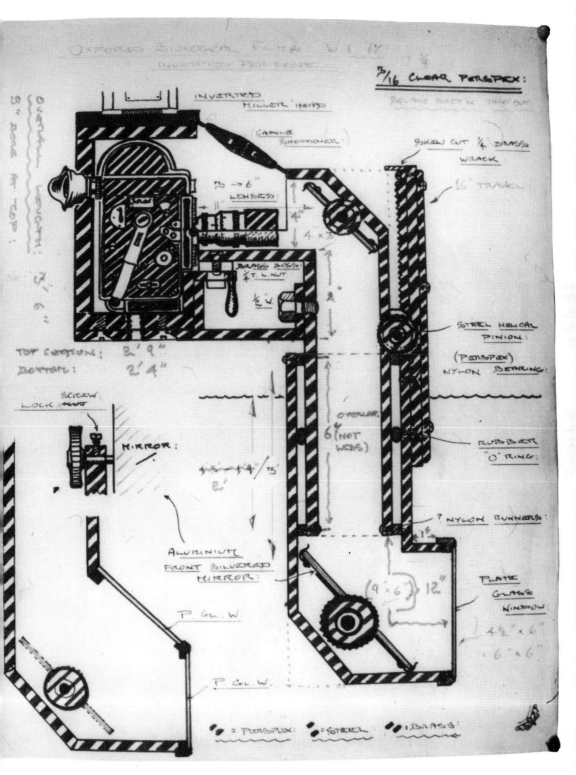

A pearl fish (Fierasfer) about to enter its sea-cucumber host.

the best of its kind I had ever seen. The aesthetic value of the images, and the bizarre nature of many of the forms, also made it appealing to the general public, or so I believed, but not necessarily at 50-minutes' length. To make a feature documentary on plankton for television was certainly a challenge but, sensational as they were, the unusual images could not be expected to hold the screen unaided and uninterrupted. True, many of Peter's subjects were larval forms and some visual relief could be found by showing their development into a variety of marine invertebrates – crustaceans, molluscs, worms and echinoderms. But I know this would not be enough so I began looking for new angles on the subject of marine plankton. On Peter's advice I started with Professor Sir Alister Hardy's excellent book *The Open Sea: The World of Plankton*. Soon, a fascinating historical theme began to emerge, beginning with J. Vaughan Thompson, an army surgeon in the early 19th century who made the first description of the larval stages of crabs, and ending with Sir Alister Hardy himself who had devoted a lifetime to the study of plankton. All this involved some extra filming in Britain and, together with some material on the importance of plankton in food chains compiled from our Film Library, it was eventually edited into a 45-minute film for which a special music score was written by Sidney Sager.

BELOW LEFT
The periscope was particularly useful for filming creatures in shallow water – such as this jellyfish Cassiopeia *which spends most of its time upside-down feeding on the bottom.*

When the film was eventually shown in colour on BBC 2 in June 1968, it astounded viewers, most of whom had no idea that such life forms existed. The programme was not shown in isolation but as part of a newly-established series which was beginning to make a name for itself by bringing the colourful wonders of nature into viewers' living rooms. The series had been set up by someone who had never worked as a member of the Natural History Unit, but nevertheless was later to have numerous links with the Unit's output – David Attenborough. It was he who thought of the name for the new series: *The World About Us*.

Chapter 15

The World About Us

During the autumn of 1967 the BBC was preparing for the opening of a full colour service on BBC 2. A few transmissions were already being made in colour but for several months there was only one fully-equipped studio and the output was low. The retail trade was restless; the sale of receivers was sluggish for, as yet, there were not enough colour programmes on the screen to tempt customers into the dealers' shops. David Attenborough knew that he had some good cards to play if he opened a full service in time for Christmas but resources would be stretched to the limit. There were some good drama productions, feature films and light entertainment – including an ace card in the *Black and White Minstrel Show* – but little in the way of new BBC programmes on travel and natural history – subjects which Attenborough knew would make a strong impact in colour. He had already commissioned colour films from both the Travel and Exploration Unit and the Natural History Unit but most of these would not be ready until the following spring. There was a possible solution, however; both Units usually purchased a proportion of their output from independent producers and some of the material in this category already transmitted had originally been filmed in colour. Furthermore, both Units had extremely good intelligence systems for tracking down film from all over the world and they would therefore know of any suitable colour films available but not yet transmitted. So telephone calls were made to Nicholas Crocker at Bristol and Brian Branston, editor of the Travel and Exploration Unit in London, to see what they could offer to fill a possible 50-minute programme slot. The answers were encouraging; between them they could sustain a series for at least three months, possibly more.

Having seen the subjects available, Attenborough chose an umbrella title for these films and decided to place the series at the start of his first full colour evening, immediately before the *Black and White Minstrel Show*. So, on Sunday, December 3, the first edition of *The World About Us* was billed at 7:25 – 'A series of films from all over the world about our astonishing planet and the creatures that live on it'. Attenborough himself took on responsibility as editor of the series and opened with Haroun Tazieff's *Volcano*. Clearly he was concerned that BBC 2 in colour should begin, not with a whimper, but with a bang.

The Natural History Unit's first contribution was an edited version of a film made in Trinidad by the Swedish wildlife film-maker, Jan Lindblad. Entitled *Forest and Firebird* it contained several sequences which must have pleased the television retail trade, including spectacu-

Scarlet ibis – the 'firebirds' which featured in the Unit's first contribution to the new BBC 2 colour series The World About Us.

lar shots of a colony of 'firebirds' – Scarlet Ibis. For many weeks the series was kept going from London and Bristol with re-dubbed versions of purchased programmes, including a high proportion of National Geographic Society Specials. Later on the underwater films of Jacques Cousteau and an occasional production from the RSPB Film Unit were valuable contributions. The series began in such a hurry that there were few staff available to service it but fortunately a comparatively new recruit, Suzanne Gibbs, was able to step into the breach and supervise the presentation of these programmes under the general guidance of Nicholas Crocker. It soon became clear, however, that the series was working so well that it would be extended as long as possible; and so a young assistant producer, Richard Brock, was moved from the *Life* production team to work on specially shot programmes. In fact, *Life* was coming to an end after more than a two years run as its original presenter, Dr Desmond Morris, had become such a successful author that he had gone to live in the Mediterranean. Although the last few editions of *Life* were produced in colour from a London studio – the series was running out of steam and the Unit was content to take advantage of the unexpected opportunity provided by *The World About Us*.

Enough existing programmes were available to keep the new series going through the spring of 1968 and into early summer, but the pile

was diminishing rapidly and we were transmitting faster than either the London or Bristol Units could find new material. Fortunately, specially shot programmes began to emerge from the BBC cutting rooms – including the five films I had been working on the previous year and which were now hungrily snapped up and fed into the series. By then it looked as if *The World About Us* was there to stay as the subject matter was ideal for promoting colour and, indeed, some branches of the trade began including a reference to the title in advertisements for colour receivers. All this meant that new films had to be commissioned quickly and from then on all my own efforts were to be concentrated entirely on making programmes for the series. Similar redeployment of staff was undertaken in the Travel and Exploration Unit and both Units prepared to provide equal numbers of programmes in the following year with David Attenborough continuing to act as the series editor. He also commissioned some films from a young wildlife cameraman from Kenya who had worked with Bernard Grzimek but who was now beginning to make a name for himself – Alan Root.

David had first met Alan when he stopped off in Nairobi on the way to Madagascar in 1960. Alan had since been making very successful films for *Survival* but he had been unhappy about the presentation of some of his material with regard to the style of narration and music; he was therefore interested to learn of any possibilities of working for the BBC. After he completed his last *Survival* programme in the Galapagos, Alan met David again in London; by then David was Controller, BBC 2, and very much in a position to commission new work. Unfortunately, the BBC could not afford to underwrite the total cost of Alan's films but a modest sum was available for United Kingdom television rights, the rest of the world being retained by Alan for exploitation in the future. What Alan wanted above all was the freedom to conceive an idea, direct and film it and be closely involved in the post-production. In other words he wanted it done *his* way, and fortunately David Attenborough liked the sound of Alan's way. Although the Natural History Unit was to have final editorial control the assemblies which Alan Root eventually delivered to Bristol were perfect for *The World About Us* and were valuable in adding to its prestige in the early years. The irony of it is that the two films, *Baobab* and *Mzima*, were eventually distributed as *Survival* productions in the USA on Alan's return to Anglia. The reason was that Alan set himself the highest possible standards which could only be attained by his unique talents combined with personal application over a very long period of time. The heavy financial investment therefore required in his productions was made possible only through Survival Anglia's network sales in the USA. Against this the BBC never had a chance in spite of a previous good working relationship and strong mutual respect.

Providing more films equal to Alan Root's standard, but with the modest budgets available, was an almost impossible task; but some judicious recycling of material went on which filled a few programme slots. In due course Heinz Sielmann's half-hour programmes which had been shot in Australia and the Galapagos were re-edited and came up looking fresh and strong. There was also the odd windfall. One of these was a programme originally destined for *Look* but which had outgrown itself. It was a film about gull behaviour, made jointly by Professor Niko Tinbergen of Oxford University – one of the most famous names in the study of animal behaviour – and Hugh Falkus.

Hugh Falkus is a remarkable man with a special talent for writing film scripts and I was to use him on many occasions for adapting the purchased films and voicing narrations. Later on he also directed a number of his own films for the series. Hugh had an extraordinarily rich and varied background for he had been at one time or another an actor, playwright, broadcaster, fisherman, amateur cricketer and film producer. Before the war he was acting on television from Alexandra Palace; during the war he became a fighter pilot but was shot down and held in a German prisoner-of-war camp. After his return to England, he went on tours as an actor, he had his own plays running in the West End, and he began making films for the cinema. It was whilst making a documentary film about basking sharks off the coast of Ireland that a tragic accident occurred in which Hugh's wife was drowned. It was a shattering blow and Hugh withdrew to a small cottage in Eskdale where he found solace in a very beautiful valley by pursuing his interests as a naturalist and all-round sportsman. It was fishing in particular in which he was to find fulfilment, for the Esk is a superb river for sea-trout and Hugh has become a leading authority on the subject, writing what is regarded as the classic book on the subject called *Sea Trout Fishing*.

Hugh Falkus came back into the business of film-making through a coincidence: close to his home lies the coastal town of Ravenglass, in which vicinity lies one of the study areas used by Professor Niko

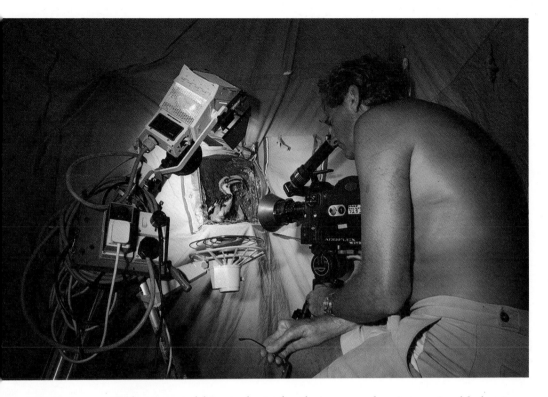

Alan Root filming hornbills inside their nest in a baobab tree.

Tinbergen and his students for their researches into animal behaviour. Hugh and Niko met at an opportune time. On the one hand it was just the moment for Hugh to be lured back into film-making through the respect and fascination he developed for Niko's work; and on the other hand Niko was eager for someone to help him over the difficulties of film-making. Niko was already using a film camera satisfactorily as a research tool; but he wished to use film to disseminate his ideas and discoveries about animal behaviour as widely as possible. To communicate effectively with the general public a greater degree of sophistication in production would be required and this was outside Niko's experience. Hugh had that experience and the two men began a long and fruitful partnership which was to find an outlet in the production of a number of classic films for the Natural History Unit. Hugh's greatest talent was in storytelling – the careful and logical presentation of Niko's interpretation of animal behaviour. Often the camerawork was no more than adequate, but the clarity of thought behind the structure of the films – and the care with which Hugh chiselled away at the narration so that every word was just right – gave a special quality to what at first might appear to be a rather simplistic presentation.

Hugh and Niko co-operated on two films for the *Look* series and had shot most of their third when it became clear to them that they had far too much material for a half-hour programme. Their subject was a study of behaviour and communication in a lesser black-backed gull colony. One day, after *The World About Us* had been running for several months, Nicky Crocker called me into his office and told me he had a problem.

259

The gull film had been commissioned by Jeffery Boswall for *Look* but Hugh was insistent that he could not adequately reflect Niko's work in a single 30-minute programme. Would I have a look at the film and see if it might run at 50 minutes for *The World About Us*? At the time we were so desperate for material that I was tempted to say 'yes' immediately and be grateful, but on reflection it did seem that asking viewers to look at nothing but gulls for nearly an hour might be stretching things a little too far.

So I saw the film, which had already been roughly assembled, while Hugh outlined the story and the interpretation of the action. On the face of it there was little visual variety, although there were shots of some gull behaviour which I had not seen before; if the rushes had been seen by a programme editor with no knowledge of biology at all, and without any guidance on the meaning of the behaviour, he could be excused for dismissing the entire project as being worth no more than a magazine item of a few minutes. In fact the film was a masterly exposition of animal communication through a detailed analysis of the language of one species of gull; and by language I mean communication by posture as well as voice. Fascinating though the material was, I had no illusions about the difficulty of holding viewers' interest for 50 minutes, but I had enough faith in Hugh's talents to take on the project willingly. I had already worked with him several times, for he had written and narrated the *Animal People* films and I knew that we generally saw eye to eye.

The film had been almost entirely shot by Niko but under Hugh's

Lesser black-backed gulls – a pulling fight between neighbouring males in Signals for Survival.

careful guidance; he had shown Niko the necessity of obtaining a variety of camera angles and had made sure that no shots essential to the construction of a careful exposition were missing. Sound was of paramount importance, for much of Niko's work was concerned with distinguishing various gull calls and interpreting their meaning. Fortunately, it had been part of the original arrangements that John Burton should spend a few weeks at the gull colony to obtain good quality recordings of the entire gull vocabulary. The best of these were then transferred to magnetic film and in the autumn Hugh and I met to work on the final stages of production at Bristol with the film editor, David Aliband. Then followed one of the most careful and detailed pieces of post-synchronisation yet undertaken on a wildlife film at Bristol, for we knew that the success of the programme depended largely on the accuracy of the sound track – not only for scientific purposes but also in order to create a sense of realism, of actually being *in* the gull colony. Today, of course, no one in their right mind would embark on such a film without the use of a sound camera in the first place, but for many reasons that was out of the question when Hugh and Niko first started on their project. So David, Hugh and I spent many days working long into the evenings and over weekends, before we were finally satisfied that we had recreated the sounds of the gull colony and had matched every call and wing-beat to the action in every film shot. Sometimes a scene showed several birds calling at once and so a separate track had to be laid down for each bird. As the tracks developed Hugh occasionally had to adapt and modify his narration to fit between the loud calls of the birds, but eventually everything was ready for the final recording of the commentary and the mixing of the tracks. We completed this just in time for the transmission in December 1968 – almost exactly a year after *The World About Us* series had first begun.

BBC 2 transmitter coverage then was still very limited, and the audience was probably no more than two-thirds of a million, but those who saw the programme, entitled *Signals for Survival*, were fascinated by the revelation of an apparently familiar subject in a new light. The programme also received great critical acclaim and, in case the television departmental heads in London had been misled by the simplicity of presentation, David Attenborough was reported as having addressed the Television Programme Review Board the following Wednesday on how good it was, and why. Next year the programme became the official BBC entry in the television documentary category of the Italia Prize – one of the most coveted awards in European television. Personally I did not seriously think it stood much of a chance and I was therefore surprised when I was contacted a day or two before the awards ceremony, which that year was at Mantua, and told to stand by as there was a good chance the BBC would win. Unfortunately, a previous engagement prevented Hugh from attending but at a few hours notice Niko Tinbergen and I boarded a plane for Milan and it was with great pride that I walked on to the platform with him at the presentation to receive the inscribed certificate.

There was great relief about the success of *The World About Us* in the Unit for on BBC 1 we were having serious problems; in recent years there had been growing doubts about the continuation of the *Look* series. After its inception in August 1955, it had been for many years the Unit's most important programme on television. However its style of presentation had not greatly changed, although it had moved out of the original set representing Peter Scott's studio and was now a series of complete films usually narrated by Peter Scott but by no means always involving him in vision. The series had begun when the BBC had the only television channel and the audience was distinctly middle-class; now ITV coverage was virtually nationwide with an audience profile bulging into the great masses of viewers now available in the industrial areas of the Midlands and the north. BBC 1 was taking a hammering as a result and the traditions and the style of *Look* and its presenter did not ideally suit the new competitive scene. Previous controllers had at times been uneasy about the future of *Look* but it was Paul Fox who took the final decision to terminate it. Sadly, it also brought to an end the close working relationship between the Unit and Peter Scott, for although he was retained in a consultative capacity for a while he was understandably attracted by the offer of a greater amount of programme involvement with *Survival*. Anglia had tailored the presentation of their programmes to the widest possible general audience and this had led to Colin Willock and his team adopting a style of narration and music that some producers at Bristol considered to be decidedly jazzy. The success of the formula was undeniable in terms of viewing figures and this was the cause of some envy at Bristol, although it was clear that we neither wished to compete in the same style nor was it prudent to do so for fear of endangering the respect and co-operation we enjoyed with many noted naturalists and zoologists. Paradoxically, I suspect it was because Anglia needed a touch more scientific respectability that Peter Scott was so valuable to them at a time when he was considered by the BBC 1 Controller to have just the wrong image.

There were other factors in Anglia's success with *Survival* and the most important was that at the outset they were able to employ a small team of full-time professional wildlife cameramen so that there was a steady flow of high-quality animal behaviour film guaranteed. That this was commercially viable was due to a regular national outlet, backed by a growing world market for natural history material which Anglia were quick to exploit. The BBC, on the other hand, had got caught in a vicious circle: in general, programme controllers still considered that wildlife programmes could depend largely on dedicated amateur naturalists and therefore the programmes should be cheap. Low budgets meant that producers were rarely able to commission any high quality filming and if an independent cameraman did decide to embark on an ambitious project in collaboration with the BBC we could usually only afford to take United Kingdom rights; this in turn meant that the most attractive programmes were not available for international sales. Not until the late 1970s when at last controllers were able to take a more realistic view of budgets for the Natural History Unit – and BBC Enterprises were organised on a more commercially aggressive basis – was it possible to utilise completely and effectively the considerable experience and specialised knowledge of the Unit's producers.

In 1969, however, there was still a long uphill battle for us all to obtain

A celebration after The Private Life of the Kingfisher won a silver medal at the Moscow Film Festival in 1967. Nicholas Crocker, Desmond Hawkins (then Controller, BBC South and West), Rose Eastman, film editor Tom Poore, Ron Eastman and producer of Look, Jeffery Boswall.

Maurice Tibbles (seen here with a young cuckoo) left his job as a Daily Mirror *photographer to become a wildlife cameraman and work on the* Private Lives *series.*

even adequate budgets and no one had a greater problem than Jeffery Boswall who now had to create a new series which *would* be acceptable to Controller, BBC 1. At the time the decision was made to end *Look*, there were some 33 projects on hand at various stages of production. It was possible that some could be moved sideways to the other channel – as happened with *Signals for Survival* – whilst others, in an early stage, would just have to be written off. There were a number of single-species studies under way, however, and this gave Jeffery the notion of building on the success of Ron Eastman's *The Private Life of the Kingfisher* and offering a complete series of *Private Lives*. This idea was accepted and it enabled Jeffery to commission a number of films from Ron Eastman, and later, Maurice Tibbles, setting them both on the first stages of their professional careers.

Private Lives turned out to be a first-rate series but his liberation from the treadmill of *Look* programmes also gave Jeffery an opportunity to make a name for himself as a television personality as well as a producer. He had made a major contribution to an edition of *Life* through a film on baboon behaviour which he had made as director-cameraman in Ethiopia. Desmond Hawkins had also been impressed with Jeffery's studio performance as a guest ornithologist in another edition of *Life*. Later Jeffery put up a proposal for a series of six programmes for BBC 1 to be filmed in Ethiopia with the author and traveller, Alan Moorhead. Although the idea was accepted in principle, Moorhead was unable to accept the invitation at the last minute and Desmond Hawkins immediately suggested that Jeffery should take his place. Jeffery contacted a very experienced freelance cameraman, Douglas Fisher, to work with him and together they made *Wildlife Safari to Ethiopia* which arguably is one of the best series of its genre ever

made. Its success led to further expeditions to Argentina, Mexico and Thailand.

If it was Jeffery's turn to get the interesting locations overseas now, it was only fair that I should spend more time at Bristol organising material for *The World About Us*. When *Look* ended, it at least provided the opportunity to divert some of the camera effort formerly used on it towards the new BBC 2 series, and this I quickly did by setting up projects for Eric Ashby and Leslie Jackman in the New Forest and Torbay respectively. Ron Eastman too was attracted by the prospect of working for the series; having a strong interest in films in the widest sense, he found pure behavioural studies somewhat restricting and favoured more generalised documentaries with a wildlife theme – a formula well suited to the 50-minute length. So Ron was given a contract to make three films for *The World About Us*, the first of which was to be about his beloved River Test. Working with him would be his wife, Rose, acting as his assistant and also making sound recordings. Before they became too involved with such long-term projects, however, I thought they might benefit from the discipline of shooting a film in a limited time to a tight brief. I began looking for a suitable subject at an overseas location at which we would work together; the maximum time I could be away from base was about two months and this fitted in well

Jeffery Boswall made a number of Wildlife Safari *series including one in Argentina where he filmed this hairy armadillo.*

with the requirements for Ron and Rose so that they would not be held up on their British projects. I had on a number of occasions seen films from American cameramen about the birds to be found on the National Wildlife Refuges run by the US Fish and Wildlife Service. Duck and goose hunting is an important and widespread sport in North America, the number of hunters being estimated at 15 million; as a consequence, there is throughout the USA a large network of refuges which are staging posts and wintering grounds for vast numbers of migrating wildfowl. Many of them also provide feeding and breeding grounds for species that are not hunted but the location of the refuges is determined largely by their position on one of four main migratory routes for wildfowl, known as flyways. Because of the spectacular concentration of birds on some of these refuges during the autumn migration, it would be comparatively easy to make a film about the refuge system, the way they are run and why, and the birds that frequent them.

Luther Goldman and Cornelius Wallace at Blackwater Refuge, where corn is planted especially for the migrating geese.

I travelled ahead of the Eastmans to make the final arrangements. The Fish and Wildlife Service were very helpful in planning the film and provided their resident biologist-photographer, Luther Goldman, to travel with us as a guide and adviser. His subsidiary task was to obtain

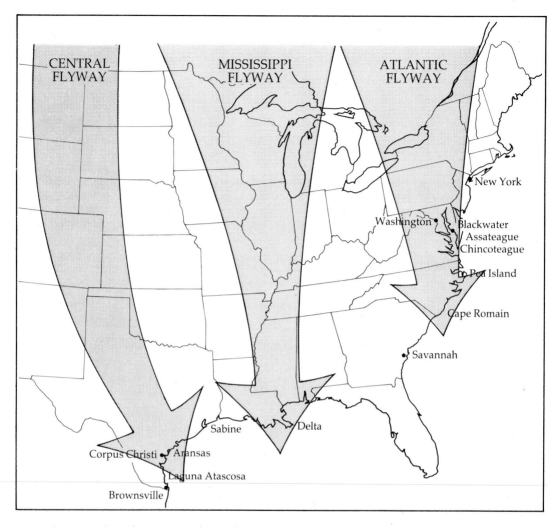

CENTRAL
FLYWAY

MISSISSIPPI
FLYWAY

ATLANTIC
FLYWAY

New York

Washington Blackwater
Assateague
Chincoteague

Pea Island

Cape Romain

Savannah

Sabine   Delta

Corpus Christi Aransas

Laguna Atascosa

Brownsville

new photographs of various refuges for the service's own information
department. Although one normally travels long distances in the USA
by air for convenience and speed, we decided to tackle the entire
expedition by road as many of the refuges were in remote areas and far
from the main airports. So I hired a large station wagon, which would
easily accommodate the four of us and all our film equipment, and drove
it to Dulles International Airport to meet the Eastmans.

Some of the national wildlife refuges visited during filming for The World About Us – Flyway

For a few days we stayed in Washington whilst the film equipment
was checked and the Eastmans recovered from their jet-lag. This was
also a good opportunity to do some local filming, for the Wildlife Section
ran a research station at Patuxent nearby where they were attempting to
breed whooping cranes in captivity. The few wild whooping cranes left
in the world breed in a remote part of Northern Alberta in Canada and
not until 1954 was the exact nesting location discovered. Each October
the birds migrate southwards for 2,500 miles and winter at Aransas on
the coast of Texas. There some of them stay in a National Wildlife

Refuge – which we would be visiting on our trip – and some in an adjacent refuge run by the Audubon Society. The American and Canadian authorities were co-operating in a captive breeding pro-gramme and in the last two years before our visit single eggs had been removed from nests in the wild and flown in incubators to Patuxent. In the wild the cranes usually successfully raise only one of their two chicks, so the young birds at Patuxent could be regarded as a bonus and possibly a key to the future breeding in captivity; we therefore filmed them to complement the footage which we hoped to obtain in a few weeks' time in Texas.

The expedition got going properly when we finally left Washington and set out eastwards for Blackwater Refuge in Maryland, 10 miles south of Cambridge. The manager at Blackwater, Cornelius Wallace, was an old friend of Luther's and had been there for 27 years. During this time he had increased the wintering population of Canada geese – once the most important species for hunting – from 5,000 to nearly 100,000 birds. One of the reasons for this increase was the planting of special food crops for the geese and Cornelius took us to a plot of about 900 acres where crops of clover, soya beans, millet, wheat and maize were grown. There we found no shortage of geese to film. Their numbers were absolutely staggering and the noise they made was almost deafening.

One of the remarkable things about Blackwater and most of the refuges we visited was the quality of the road systems. Although hunting was forbidden at all seasons within the refuges, the public were encouraged to use the roads for bird-watching and recreation so there were many picnic sites and parking facilities, often close to the birds' feeding grounds; this enabled us to use our vehicle as a mobile hide. Birds quickly become accustomed to road traffic and will tolerate vehicles very close to them provided that the occupants do not get out. We therefore developed a novel way of filming in which Ron would arrange himself at the back of our station wagon, the tail window open, and the camera mounted on a short tripod. Ron was seated in a kind of rear gunner position and the only disadvantage with the arrangement was that Ron could not see where he was going. So within the refuge, where traffic was restricted, we travelled mainly in reverse; and I did most of the driving, carefully manoeuvring Ron into the best filming position. I must have driven hundreds of miles like this but it was an extremely successful method of operation and enabled us to work very quickly, as it was seldom necessary to erect special hides.

We gradually made our way southwards, travelling down the eastern seaboard and calling for a few days at various refuges to film their specialities – such as the wintering greater snow geese at Assateague on the Atlantic Ocean. By the time we had reached South Carolina the geese were thinning out, although there were plenty of wintering duck. Each new refuge offered a different management story and when we started moving west to take in the Mississippi flyway in Louisiana we found yet another series of wildlife spectacles. Sabine Refuge had been created in 1937 and is a gigantic area of 140,000 acres; an oil company had retained the mineral rights so that everywhere we looked there was the curious combination of natural gas installations with flocks of

OVERLEAF

LEFT
Canada geese in the cornfields at Blackwater Refuge.

RIGHT
Blue geese at Sabine Refuge.

BOTTOM
Whooping cranes on their wintering grounds at Aransas. The bird on the left with a coloured leg band is an immature.

feeding duck. The *pièce de résistance* at Sabine was undoubtedly the blue geese for whom the refuge had mainly been created. Blue geese are the same species as lesser snow geese but have a different colour phase and we were able to film them in rather unusual circumstances which gave Ron a fine opportunity for slow-motion photography. The geese have to take on a certain amount of grit from time to time which they use for grinding the food they get from the marshes. Some years ago, the authorities hit on the idea of establishing an area of sand close to the refuge headquarters just to provide grit for the geese. Over a period of years the birds caught on to this and by the time of our visit the geese visiting this site provided one of the finest wildfowl spectacles in Louisiana.

Our next stop was at Aransas, a fine refuge near Corpus Christi, with 24 miles of good roads. The weather was warm and sunny and everywhere we looked there were birds to be filmed; out on the lagoons, skimmers, with their long curious lower mandibles, flew inches above the water scooping up surface plankton; under the shade of the trees little groups of wild turkeys, the sexes segregated for the winter, scratched around for food; occasionally, we saw visitors from further south – vermilion flycatchers adding a few dabs of vivid colour to the scene. The birds which dominated the refuge, however, were the cranes. About 5,000 sandhill cranes were wintering there, having come south from the northern states and Canada. Elegant, grey birds with a patch of red on their foreheads, they were over three feet tall and could be seen everywhere feeding in groups on the open parts of the refuge. They made beautiful flight shots and had distinctive rattling trumpet calls, a chorus of which I think is one of the most haunting sounds of nature. However, the real ornithological gems of Aransas were the larger whooping cranes. The birds being so rare there were strict regulations about photographing them but the refuge manager, Gordon Hansen, had been given authority from Washington to help us as much as possible.

The week we arrived it was estimated that there were 47 whooping cranes in the area – the same total as the previous year's record. As there was still time for a few late arrivals there was great excitement locally to see if a new record would be set up. The count was made weekly from a Cessna plane piloted by a warden who once flew with the American Air Force; as this provided a marvellous opportunity for us to get aerial scenes of the refuge, as well as shots of the cranes, we asked if we could take part. Joe, the pilot, knew where to look for most of the birds as they had well-defined territories and known pairs – with or without young – tended to be in the same general areas each week. We had nearly finished the survey and had reached the previous record of 47 when there was one last section of the marsh to search. To our delight we found another pair there, making a new record of 49. And after we left Aransas we learned that a final straggler had arrived to make a round 50.

The final leg of our trip took us to the south-east corner of Texas at Brownsville, close to the Mexican border. For Luther this was a nostalgic return to former haunts as he had once been manager of the two refuges nearby. One was the Santa Ana Refuge, comprising a very small area of unspoiled wooded country in the lower Rio Grande valley full of attractive small birds. Its tree-enclosed ponds also provided a last staging post for three species of teal on their way down to Central and South America for the winter. Luther's greatest pride was in the work he had done to develop and improve the Laguna Atascosa Refuge 40 miles away on the Texas coast. Here were 45,000 acres of marsh and salt flats as well as coastal prairies and scrubland. Various kinds of cactus grew there and tortoises browsed at the sides of the tracks in the warm winter sunshine; mocking birds scolded at us from the tops of bushes and yuccas. In the lagoons, avocets and egrets fed in shallow waters which Luther had created for them many years ago. He told us how, when he first took over the refuge, he would rush out to see which direction the water ran during heavy storms. Then, when he eventually got the money to undertake major earth-moving, he knew exactly where he should build impoundments and put in dykes. It was the kind of big-thinking and intelligent forward-planning in which the Americans seemed to excel and which was so evident in the refuges we had already filmed.

The Laguna Atascosa Refuge takes its name from the largest lagoon in the area and this holds one of the most spectacular concentrations of ducks in the United States. They are redheads – handsome diving ducks which breed in the north-western United States and in Canada – and practically the entire population winters on Laguna Atascosa. At times they may total nearly a quarter of a million birds and, although the redheads were not present in those numbers during our visit, they were nevertheless extremely impressive. They would spend most of the day on the lagoon but towards late afternoon they became restless and started to take off for the sea. This was our opportunity to film marvellous flight shots against the evening sky and Ron was almost delirious with excitement during his work on this. His only regret, I think, was that he was not shooting for the big screen in Cinemascope.

If the footage we took back to Bristol was a little weak on story, it did not matter too much at that early stage of *The World About Us* when colourful wildlife footage of good quality was the first essential. Another important factor was the speed – and therefore the low cost – at which we were able to shoot the film. Leaving Bristol only for a few weeks at a time was an important consideration for me and opportunities for worthwhile programmes which could be filmed in such a short period were rare. However, the New Zealand Wildlife Service, with whom we had worked on the Durrells' expedition, came up trumps again and provided research and field help to the extent that I was able to shoot a 50-minute film about the service's work in conserving rare species in two and a half weeks flat. On the way back I was invited to visit the embryonic Natural History Unit of the Australian Broadcasting Commission at Melbourne and this led to a long period of close co-operation which has been helpful to both Units ever since. One of their senior producers, Ken Taylor, subsequently came to Bristol for a few months and, as a direct result of that visit, two remarkable films eventually found their way into *The World About Us*.

Ken mentioned one day in Bristol that a personal friend of his in Melbourne had recently told him of a cousin who had been making underwater films of whales and sea-lions at the Valdez peninsula in

OVERLEAF
*Wild turkeys at
Aransas Refuge.*

273

Patagonia. He was there with his wife and another young couple who had invested all their savings in an attempt to break into the wildlife documentary film business. His name was Krov Menuhin and he was the son of the violinist, Yehudi Menuhin. Now we took some pride in running what we considered to be an efficient intelligence system about wildlife film-makers on an international scale, mainly through the dedication and efficiency of Mike Kendall, our film librarian. Mike had to admit that he had not heard of Krov and so we set about trying to track him down. Ken Taylor was able to trace the telephone number of Krov's mother who was living in Switzerland and a call to her revealed that Krov and his wife Ann had joined Ann's parents on their boat, cruising through the rivers and canals of Europe. As they occasionally telephoned Krov's mother, we left a message requesting they then get in touch with us in Bristol.

A few weeks later, Krov and Ann arrived, somewhat breathless, and clutching some rolls of film – a short six-minute presentation piece about their expedition and 20 minutes of assorted rushes. They were indeed a good-looking couple and one immediately thought perhaps a new husband-and-wife underwater team had arrived in the footsteps of Hans and Lotte Hass. Krov, in his early 30s, was strongly built, had good features and spoke with a mid-Atlantic accent, whilst Ann, several years younger and American, was blonde, had a model figure and a beautiful, calm personality.

We took their film down to the viewing room and watched hopefully. The six-minute presentation was shown first, clearly styled to catch the

Filming with Ron and Rose Eastman at Laguna Atascosa.

RIGHT
Luther, at his old refuge, finds a tortoise.

276

attention of a potential American sponsor or distributor but containing some truly astounding underwater footage of Ann swimming alongside huge right whales in the bay at Valdez as well as good material on penguins and sea-lions. One scene showed the graceful, but delicate figure of Ann underwater being caught by a movement of a whale's enormous fluke. It was the shot of a decade. Eagerly we looked at the 20-minute roll of rushes. Our hearts sank a little; the material was extremely variable, some quite well photographed, other parts waste-fully shot with bad camera movements and much duplication, but there was excellent material amongst it all. Krov told us that he had about 50,000 feet altogether – about three times the amount from which we normally edited a *World About Us* film. Surely, we thought, there must be a 50-minute film there somewhere?

Krov told us that he had sold almost everything he owned in order to finance the expedition and to make this his first attempt at a complete film; even then funds had kept running out so that they had had to dive for scallops which they sold to local restaurants. At present all the master film was with a New York company who had taken an option on

A mass of redheads at Laguna Atascosa.

the rights and was supposed to be trying to achieve some kind of deal with a television network. Krov was not confident about their ability to do this. I knew that we did not have the budget to take over the entire production but I was able to offer Krov a modest sum for United Kingdom television rights plus the post-production facilities to lick the material into shape. Krov was attracted by the idea, for he had a high regard for BBC productions and thought that at least he would then have a complete film which he could market internationally, but first he had to extricate himself from the American film company.

A few months later, Krov was able to get his film out of New York and arrived with piles of cans in Bristol ready to start work. With such a large amount of material, we knew that it would take at least twice as long as a normal production to edit. Fortunately, a talented freelance director and editor named Noel Chanan had recently set up a cutting room in Bristol and as all our own facilities were fully occupied we contracted Noel to look after the project. Krov and Noel together made order out of chaos and shaped an extremely attractive film with four main acts, a prologue and an epilogue – the classic shape of an American television special and

279

one that would hopefully enable Krov to market the film as widely as possible. This is not a procedure I would normally encourage, for productions have to be made primarily to suit BBC requirements for UK transmission; but in this case the four-act shape provided the most useful template against which to shape a story-line which would bind much unrelated, but visually spectacular, material together. Helped by some specially written music by Edwin Roxburgh, and by carefully recorded voice-overs from Krov and Ann themselves, the formula did indeed work. When the material was shown to *Radio Times* editorial staff they saw that the combination of the attractive man-and-wife team with some very unusual film sequences was highly promotable and it was therefore decided to give the Menuhins a front cover. Krov and Ann have been making successful films ever since, most of which have been seen on BBC television.

The second *World About Us* that Ken Taylor of the Australian Natural History Unit had a hand in was specially shot in Australia. Just before Ken returned to Melbourne, we received news through him of extraordinary scenes in the Simpson Desert in Australia as a result of the highest rainfall for many years. Apparently there were carpets of vegetation where no one had seen many plants before and large tracts of what was usually parched desert were now in bloom. It sounded like a once-in-a-lifetime opportunity and ideal for a co-production between the two Natural History Units. As it happened, I had a young producer working with me on the series who was fast making a name for himself and who had just completed his last production. His name was Barry Paine. A hurried conference took place and Ken scurried back to Melbourne to start making local arrangements. Barry always took a little time to warm up on a new production but on this one I knew we had to act very quickly so I booked him on a plane to Melbourne a week or so later. It was taking a big chance but I had great faith in Barry and I guessed that, if there was any kind of story at all in the Simpson Desert, then Barry would know how to deal with it. A year later, *The Year of the Green Centre* appeared on television and turned out to be an outstandingly beautiful and unusual film. Barry subsequently wrote a book about his adventures in making it with the ABC team.

The series brought the work of several new wildlife cameramen to the screen but it is with special satisfaction that I remember my first viewing of some film sent by David Hughes. Now if there is anything that sets up a chorus of groans in the viewing theatre it is film of turtles laying eggs. I had filmed such a sequence myself with Jim Saunders in Malaya in 1962 and I guess about every well-travelled wildlife cameraman has photographed it at one time or another. Given the right conditions, the right place and the right time, it is a very easy sequence to shoot once a turtle has started laying; the amount of film that has passed through cameras whilst turtle eggs have been plopping like soft ping-pong balls into the sand must total thousands upon thousands of feet. It was without enthusiasm therefore that I followed Mike Kendall down to the viewing room one day to see some new turtle film that he had just acquired for audition purposes. Mike would not call me unless it was something special but I couldn't quite imagine what could be new about turtles.

The film turned out to be on Pacific Ridley turtles and their nesting behaviour at a remote beach in Costa Rica. These turtles, too, lay their eggs in the sand but in a spectacular manner, for they arrive on the beach in extremely large numbers – an event locally known as an *arribada*. So there was already a new angle to the story, but there was more to come; the huge concentration of eggs means that when it is hatching time several weeks later there is a multitude of young which have to make their way down the beach to the sea. Inevitably this attracts many predators – all kinds of birds and most bizarre of all, hundreds of sand crabs which intercept the baby turtles before they reach the water. There is yet another twist to the story because the *arribadas* take place at intervals roughly corresponding to the incubation time of the eggs; this means that a new wave of females coming up the beach to lay their eggs sometimes meet the young of the previous laying and occasionally the young turtles get steam-rollered into the sand by the tank-like adults. All this action was on Hughes' film and it would have been exciting enough even if adequately covered. In this case, the photography was outstanding for the composition of the scenes and the careful choice of camera angle – often at sandtop level – showed that the film had been taken by a true artist. David Hughes, whoever he was, in my opinion had all the makings of one of the world's outstanding wildlife film-makers.

Mike had shown me the film not only because of the standard of the photography but also because he knew that we were planning to make a television survey of turtle behaviour, conservation and captive breeding on a worldwide basis. The producer in charge of this project was Ned Kelly, a comparatively new recruit from the local ITV station, and a very experienced traveller and mountaineer who had won an award with one of his recent climbing films. Ned learned that David Hughes' work in Costa Rica had been sponsored by the National Geographic Society for whom he was to write an article and supply photographs of the Ridley turtles' *arribada*. Ned also discovered that David Hughes was a biologist who was distinctly interested in pursuing a career as a wildlife film-maker.

The film, although truly remarkable, did not do full justice to the Ridley turtles' behaviour and the dramatic predation on the beach so Ned got David to agree to return to Costa Rica with his wife and daughter to film the entire story again in a more detailed way. Ned planned to feature the Hughes' sojourn there as part of *The World About Us* film, shooting the remainder of the programme with a BBC crew. As luck would have it, David was not able to film an *arribada* of the size he had originally witnessed but his camera technique improved enormously and easily came up to our expectations.

David Hughes was now on the threshold of a new and potentially brilliant career and the next questions were – could he be given the responsibility of a complete film of his own and, if so, how could it be financed? With the budget I held for eight purchased films each year, I could only afford a small sum of money for UK television rights which would just about pay for David's stock and processing. If he was to film at all he wanted to study one area intensively and, if necessary, stay there for a year or 18 months. It was the kind of approach which Alan

Root favoured and it involved the same financial problems. Although BBC Enterprises were not yet able to make an investment in such a project I did have a faint hope; I telephoned an independent film producer of wildlife films, Mike Rosenberg.

I had met Mike several months before when I had bought from him a film he had made about wildlife in Israel. He had mentioned at the time that his newly-formed wildlife production company, Partridge Films, was interested in any joint ventures I might propose – particularly with regard to investing in new talent. David Hughes was the ideal man and so I arranged an introduction. The outcome was that Partridge Films would underwrite the cost of the production provided I agreed to a pre-purchase for *The World About Us*, the UK version being produced in Bristol. The resulting film, made in the Okavango swamp, was not the best we have ever shown in the series by a long way, but it was very attractively photographed and gave David valuable experience. Its shortcomings were largely in its structure and were probably due to the involvement of too many people. So when the opportunity came again to invest in a second Hughes film, in which David would take a greater responsibility for the biological storyline, I willingly agreed. David wanted to make a film in the Namib desert and this news was received without much enthusiasm from some of my colleagues. *Survival* had produced some unusual footage from the Namib and there were also several desert films on offer from other parts of the world. Nevertheless, ignoring advice from around me, I agreed to go ahead with the project with David and Partridge Films because I had a hunch that the subject material was something which David would cover particularly well, bearing in mind the imagination he had shown in tackling the beach scenes in Costa Rica. It was a hunch that paid off for *Strange Creatures of the Skeleton Coast*, as the film was titled, was an outstanding contribution to *The World About Us* and, in my opinion, one of the six best wildlife films made in the last 20 years.

Chapter 16

The Man Who Loves Giants

With a commitment to fill 20 programme slots each year (another 20 being provided by the Travel and Exploration Unit in London) and an increasing amount of time being spent in setting up deals with various cameramen and independent producers, it was inevitable that I should get even further removed from direct involvement in programme-making. Occasionally, however, the opportunity arose to direct a film on a subject which could be shot in a few weeks and I was always on the lookout for something of that kind which would interest me. One day an assistant cameraman called Mike Aldrich called into my office to say that he had recently been working on a magazine item at the home of the wildlife painter David Shepherd. During a break in filming, Mike had heard about David's other great love for steam locomotives – and the fact that he actually owned two; Mike had also learned about David's early painting career, when he had done much work with the armed services, and his most recent concern for conservation which had caused him to donate many paintings to raise money for anti-poaching measures in Africa. Mike had been so struck by David's effervescent personality and his eventful life that he was convinced he had found a good subject for a film in *The World About Us* series.

I liked the sound of the idea and was certainly familiar with David Shepherd's work; indeed, it was difficult to find someone who had *not* seen his elephant paintings at one time or another. I set off as soon as possible for David Shepherd's home and studio in Surrey and it must have taken me all of 10 minutes after I arrived to agree with Mike Aldrich's suggestion. Everything about David Shepherd fitted into a film director's dream – including the beautiful Elizabethan farmhouse set in delightful gardens, the high timbered studio, and even an entire room devoted to a model railway layout which, of course, reflected his infatuation with railways. His two massive steam locomotives, *The Green Knight* and *Black Prince*, were some distance away in Hampshire, parked on tracks belonging to the Army, but at the slightest excuse it was obvious that David would get them into steam. *The Green Knight* had been salvaged from the locomotive graveyard at Barry in South Wales – another location which was superb for photography. David's early artistic career had been closely linked with the armed services, particularly the RAF, and this had involved flying on flight refuelling exercises and other activities ideal for film-making. Lastly and most importantly, there were his regular visits to Africa to sketch elephants and other animals in the wild, followed by the detailed painting at his studio in Surrey.

David is the most energetic and enthusiastic person I know and, far from having any difficulty in persuading him to be the subject of a film, it was a case of telling him we couldn't actually start tomorrow. He talks as fast as he lives and although this enabled me to get all the information I required from him in a very short time, it did leave me somewhat exhausted. So it was with some relief that I saw Avril, his tall blonde wife, bring in refreshments. Avril complements David beautifully for she is one of the most radiant and calm people I know as well as the mother of four charming daughters, whose ages at the time of our film ranged from six to twelve.

It was obvious that a major sequence in the film would feature David painting one of his elephant pictures, for this above all was how he had made his name. It so happened that quite soon David would be starting work on a large canvas which would be auctioned later in the year in the USA to raise funds for conservation; this would go towards the sum necessary to purchase a helicopter for anti-poaching activities in Zambia, one of David's favourite places in Africa. This immediately suggested part of the framework for the film and I hurried back to Bristol full of ideas and immediately wrote a script to incorporate them. The script was unusually detailed and, because it involved a large number of predictable human sequences as well as wildlife, I was able to plan the filming very carefully and arrange an extremely tight schedule both in

David Shepherd with his two giant locomotives Black Prince *and* The Green Knight.

this country and in Africa. In the event, it turned out to be a once-in-a-lifetime production, for almost everything worked as planned and David's infectious enthusiasm set the tone for the happiest atmosphere I have ever known on a production.

Most of the shooting was concentrated into two weeks in England and three weeks in Africa but we had to begin with a few days' isolated work whilst David put up a blank canvas in the studio and started the preliminary stages of his new elephant painting. Ten days later we returned to continue filming the painting, alternating with other sequences around the house and garden – in a similar routine to that I had used at Peter Scott's studio. As it had been Mike Aldrich's original idea, I arranged for him to be the assistant cameraman on the production, working under my old friend, Jim Saunders, with whom I had not filmed for several years.

I knew that there was a wonderful family atmosphere in the Shepherd household, which I wanted to capture on film, and so we tried to make everyone at ease in the hope that the camera would be soon forgotten. Avril gallantly offered to put everyone up in the farmhouse and, as a result, an extraordinarily friendly relationship developed between crew and subjects. Each day would begin with us all having breakfast in the large farm kitchen, various members of the team helping to run the children to school or wash up before filming began.

In two very entertaining weeks, we filmed with childish delight David's two giant locomotives in steam, recreated the restoration of one of them at Barry, and took part in an aerial refuelling training exercise with Victor bombers over the North Sea. Then we all boarded a plane for

David Shepherd sketching at the locomotive graveyard at Barry.

At work on the
jumbo painting
featured in the film
for The World
About Us.

Johannesburg. The quest there was not for wildlife but for steam
locomotives again, this time at Germiston Sheds just outside the city.
David had first visited Germiston on the very day that British Rail ran
their last steam special and he had been returning there at the slightest
excuse ever since. It is indeed a mecca for steam enthusiasts, who have
been known to charter a special plane to visit it. David was in near
ecstasy, rushing around with a sketch pad so that our main problem was
tying him down in one place long enough to do justice to the atmospheric scenes which surrounded us. The only other major problem was
finding a toilet for my assistant, Pam Jackson – apparently the only
female ever seen in Germiston Sheds.

Our main wildlife sequences were to be in the Luangwa Valley in
Zambia and, on arrival in Lusaka, we were met by two of David's
friends who were to accompany us as guides and organise our expedition. Johnnie Uys was Chief Game Warden – a small, tough man who
was born and bred in Africa and looked as if he had spent all his life out
of doors; Rolf Rohwer was a tall, handsome American who was a
professional hunter with a safari firm. Rolf seemed rather surprised by
the fact that the film crew consisted only of three and there was only one
producer and his assistant. He had just finished an assignment with an
American film crew working on a network television programme and
had been involved in arrangements for over 20 people.

We flew to the Luangwa Valley where we were met by Solomon
Kalulu, a cabinet minister, who escorted us to the Park Headquarters

287

where there was a comfortable guest house set alongside a small lake. I could easily see why David had kept returning to this park, which he regarded as one of the loveliest in Africa; it certainly had a special magic of its own and was quite unlike the vast open spaces of the East African parks. It was October and the end of the dry season so that the long grass was burnt yellow by the sun and the tangled branches of trees washed down by last year's floods were bleached after shedding their bark. There were plenty of trees to give shade though and, where the river had snaked back on itself to produce an ox-bow lake, there were watering places for buffalo and feeding places for birds. The colours and textures I had already seen in many of David's paintings and I began to appreciate much more the craft of his work. I had heard his paintings criticised as being so representational as to be photographic, but no photograph ever captured the textures of the African landscape in the way that David's brushwork could. We filmed him at work in temperatures of 120 degrees, sketching such details as the tracery of a dead tree or elephant droppings on the ground which would some day be incorporated in one of his paintings.

There was one favourite spot on the river to which we returned each day at 4:30 and where David was painting a scene in the evening light. There carmine bee-eaters flew in and out of their nesting holes in the bank while others arranged themselves like jewels on the branches of a

Germiston Sheds, Johannesburg. A South African Railways official poses with David Shepherd and the BBC team – Cliff Voice, Pam Jackson, the author, Jim Saunders and Mike Aldrich.

bush; as their colours deepened in the sunset there was usually an additional attraction a few hundred yards down river. At that time the elephants, which had spent the day in the safety of the park, came to the river to drink and then cross it to spend the night in the bush on the other side. It was a thrilling sight which we could only just film in the diminishing light but it was made all the more interesting by the fact that the river banks were high so that there was much pushing and scrambling as the herd left the river – providing marvellous material for David's sketchpad.

The key sequences we had planned in the valley involved much closer contact with elephants. One of the specialities of the Luangwa Valley is that, with rangers at close hand to keep an eye on you, you can explore on foot. So by careful approach work downwind it was possible to get very close to wild elephants – which was what David wanted to do in order to paint his subjects in the wild. It was an activity not without risks and this was the reason David particularly wanted the company of his old friends, Johnnie Uys and Rolf Rowher, whom he trusted implicitly. With them was an African Ranger called Nelson who worked in Rolf's safari firm and who was also a crack shot, should there be an emergency.

Carmine bee-eaters nested in the river bank where David painted each evening.

The evening before we attempted to film this strange sequence, we set out on a trial run without cameras. We found a group of elephants without difficulty – spotting them from some distance away and then deliberately giving them a wide berth in our truck so that we could eventually park downwind and approach on foot. There was much ominous loading of rifles before we left the vehicles – the ultimate precaution – in case of emergency. Then Johnnie and Rolf gave us our instructions: David and I, with the crew, were to keep just behind them and do everything they did; when they stopped, we were to stop; when they stayed perfectly still, we were to do the same. This final instruction was repeated; if an elephant started towards us as if charging, we were not to move if Johnnie, Rolf and Nelson remained stationary, but, at the same time, look out for the nearest climbable tree!

Thus prepared, we set off in the direction of the elephants, taking care not to tread on dead twigs or rustle the bushes and keeping a sharp eye for signs from Johnnie or Rolf. After about half a mile we suddenly saw the elephants only 60 yards ahead. Johnnie signalled us to stop and we studied them for a few minutes. They were completely unaware of us for elephants have poor eyesight; however, they do have acute hearing and sense of smell so we now closed in very cautiously indeed. I looked around me for the trees within easy reach.

Still the elephants were oblivious of us and by now we must have been no more than 30 yards or so from them. Suddenly, the largest male elephant turned towards us, putting up its trunk to test the air. We froze. The huge ears were brought forward, directed at us like two parabolic reflectors. My eyes turned towards Jim without turning my head; he looked as if he had stopped breathing. Then the elephant took a few quick steps towards us as if starting to charge. We must have been well briefed and very confident of Johnnie and Rolf for I'm glad to say that, to a man, we stood rooted to the spot. Fortunately, the elephant did exactly as had been predicted. Its sudden movement was bluff and it stopped dead, facing us but still looking very aggressive. I'm still not sure how long we stayed motionless, the elephant and our group looking towards each other; it seemed like half an hour but I suspect it was just a few minutes. Eventually, the elephant began slowly backing away, facing us all the time. Its companions were already receding into the trees behind and our elephant finally turned as it reached cover and lumbered away. Slowly and soundlessly we now backed away ourselves, only daring to speak when we had retreated about 50 yards.

'Wasn't that absolutely marvellous?' gasped David, his face wreathed in smiles. 'Now that's what we've got to do tomorrow, chaps, only I shall have to carry my easel and paints and you'll have to carry all the film gear!'

I looked at Jim, who was wearing a sphinx-like expression. I thought he was going to say something about camera insurance; instead he said. 'What I can't understand is why you can't paint them at London Zoo!' David looked at him quizzically and then realised it was a typical tongue-in-cheek Jim remark.

The next day we went through the same procedure again, but this time Avril was with us and David had his easel and paints. All the film equipment had to be carried too, of course, and spare rolls of film and tapes were distributed all round. Johnnie had found a solitary elephant feeding not far from a dried-up river bed, and this gave us an ideal approach route. Rolf and Johnnie led the strange procession, followed by David carrying the easel with its legs already extended so that it could quickly be set up. Next came Jim with the camera and Cliff Voice with the recorder and a gun microphone; then me and the assistant cameraman followed by Avril and Pam with Nelson behind to guard the rear. Eventually we reached a point in the river bed which was opposite the elephant and this we made our base camp, leaving all but essential equipment in the charge of Nelson and the ladies whilst the rest of us made the last careful approach towards the elephant. This time we had to *film* the approach but, as speech was out of the question, sign language was used whenever I wanted to take any shots. Use of the clapper board was also impossible, of course, so we devised a system of signs for cueing the camera and recorder; a short burst of tone, activated by Jim when he started the camera, would later enable the film editor to synchronise each take. Jim was using the Arriflex BL – a self-blimped camera which emitted only a gentle purr whilst running. Even so, the elephant might detect this if we approached too close or the wind changed direction so we were always on the alert for any change in the elephant's behaviour while we were filming. We manoeuvred into a position 30 yards away, which Rolf and Johnnie indicated was as close as we could go with safety, and David put down his easel and started to work. The elephant browsed contentedly on, oblivious to the strange human circus a short distance away – David painting at an easel stuck up in the middle of the bush, surrounded by guards with loaded rifles and a film crew creeping around them making curious signs to one another.

After our return from Africa, there was only one remaining sequence to film – the auction of five pictures donated to conservation by David including the large one of 'jumbos' which we had filmed him painting in his studio. The auction was to be held at the annual conference of the Mzuri Safari Club, an American hunter-conservation organisation, at a large hotel in Lake Tahoe on the California-Nevada border. David knew several officials in that organisation, and one of them in particular, Bill Stremmel, was a close friend who had been instrumental in arranging many previous art donations to conservation.

I wished to film the auction of only the large jumbo painting but it was a very important sequence as I planned that the first bids would open the programme and the completion of the auction would lead to the climax of the film. I could neither justify nor afford taking my Bristol film crew to the USA for such a short sequence so I hired a freelance crew from San Francisco, which by American standards of distance was very close. The conference lasted about three days and I arrived the day before the auction to make sure there were no sound or lighting problems. David and Avril were already there and they introduced me to Bill Stremmel, a large jovial man who ran a motor distribution business. Although I will never shoot game myself, Bill proves the point that there *is* such a thing as a hunter-conservationist, for he clearly enjoys his sport yet is someone with a real concern for endangered species and prepared to work hard to do something about conservation.

Bill was the auctioneer and very good at it. There were more than 20 paintings by various artists but David's jumbos proved to be the highspot of the evening. The cameraman and I used the sale of his other paintings to obtain establishing shots of the crowd and details of would-be bidders and then started the sound recording as soon as Bill gave me a pre-arranged sign.

'This is the climactic painting of the Mzuri Safari Club – the proceeds go to the World Wildlife Fund – most of the proceeds are for Zambia – David Shepherd, the English artist has drawn this one and donated it to the Mzuri Safari Club – we've all watched it for the last three days, we're now going to put it up for auction – do I hear ten thousand dollars . . .?'

The bidding was fairly brisk up to $12,500 and then slowed down around $17,000. I think David was hoping to reach the magic 20 but, after getting up to $17,500, Bill could not move it any more and sold it at that price. It was, nevertheless, a huge sum of money for a painting by a contemporary artist and, together with the sale of the other four paintings, served well to indicate the degree to which David was contributing funds towards conservation.

In England, David had mentioned that he was a good friend of the film star, James Stewart, whom he had originally met in Africa and who shared his deep love for that country's wildlife. Stewart was therefore an obvious choice as narrator and so the Shepherds and I flew on to Los Angeles after the conference had ended to talk to him about the film and see if he would take part. We met Mrs Stewart at the family home, a gracious residence on one of the tree-lined lower roads in Beverly Hills and not at all the ostentatious and extravagant mansion that one might expect to be the home of one of the world's superstars. After coffee Mrs Stewart drove us to the studios where her husband was filming interior scenes for his next picture, *The Dynamite Man from Glory Jail*, directed by Andrew McLaglen.

The studio was empty apart from a wheel-less, but otherwise complete, railway carriage and the star's dressing room which had been erected a few yards away. There he welcomed us warmly before briefly

David sketches hurriedly while the crew film quietly.

discussing David's film, although from the first moment there seemed to be no doubt that he would gladly take part. So the conversation gravitated quickly, as it usually does with David, to steam locomotives as James Stewart had recently returned from location in Virginia where he had been filming action sequences on and around a steam-hauled train. He had many photographs of this but our enjoyment of them was cut short by a call for the star to prepare for the next scene; he was already made-up but the character he was playing had a glass eye and the necessary dummy shield could only be inserted immediately before each scene for medical reasons. While this was being done the Shepherds and I were escorted into the railway carriage where we were invited to sit down to watch the scene being played. It was the first time I had seen Hollywood in action and it was by no means as I had imagined it. One is so conditioned to the Hollywood image on the grand scale – with sets occupying several acres, enormous camera cranes, casts of thousands and temperamental film stars – that it comes as a shock to the system to find a modest-sized film crew operating on a small set with equipment that is instantly recognisable, including a hand-held camera and a quarter-inch tape recorder. Moreover, the director, crew and actors were all friendly people going about their business in a well-organised and unflustered way; there was a deceptive calmness about it all but every person was on his toes and master of his job.

A few months later I returned to Hollywood to record the great man's narration at a film sound studio, having made sure that everything was impeccably prepared for him. Well in advance of the recording session I sent James Stewart a print of the edited film together with a pre-mix of the effects and music and a copy of the script which I had checked very carefully to ensure that it was timed to suit what I thought would be a fairly slow delivery.

'I like the movie very much', Stewart said when he arrived promptly at the recording time. 'It's kinda different – fresh, I guess.' This was an encouraging start so we went to the narrator's cubicle without delay and made him comfortable. All the film narrations I had previously produced had been recorded to picture, the narrator sitting in front of a screen or a television monitor and reading from a script whilst the film is projected. The start of each paragraph is cued by a green light placed near the narrator and, although he cannot really watch the film and the script at the same time, there is usually much value in the narrator being able to get the 'feel' of the production as well as the producer being able to check that the words really do fit the pictures. I had assumed I would record Stewart in this manner and so I did not bother to explain the procedure. I did wonder, however, why he looked so puzzled when I asked for the cue light to be checked. We started running the film and I gave the first cue. Nothing happened, so I flicked the cue light again. This time Stewart started reading. He was now running very late but nothing daunted we ran the film straight on to the next cue and I flicked the light again. There was another delayed start and this time he spoke a few words, stopped, cleared his throat and began again. I told the projectionist to stop and hurried into the cubicle to see what was wrong. The problem was soon discovered. James Stewart had not understood about recording to picture and thought he would be doing it 'wild', section by section. In fact, he had done very little straight film narration at all.

'You see', he explained carefully to me in his slow characteristic drawl, 'the fact is I've never been very good at reading lines!' I'm still not quite sure if he was serious or not but either way it was typical of the modest but direct approach of one of the most genial men with whom I have worked.

The Man Who Loves Giants, as we called David's film, had such a rich and varied mixture of ingredients that success was assured even if the wildlife content was less than usual. In fact it was a film which could have reached the screen by other production pathways apart from the Natural History Unit. *The World About Us*, once it was a well established series, also proved to be a very useful seeding ground for programme ideas which might have been very difficult to sell to controllers on a one-off basis. In television jargon, a regular series placing in the schedules is known as a 'strand' and, remembering the famous television commercial, there is an expression in the business – 'You're never alone with a Strand!' I was glad of that on more than one occasion during the 7½ years that I was responsible for filling the Bristol quota of this series, which we continued to share with the Travel and Exploration Unit in London.

Chapter 17

The Insect Man and other naturalists

During the mid-1970s, I began to feel that we had become so involved with sophisticated photographic techniques that we had lost sight of some of the very simple methods of presentation which nevertheless work well on television. For example, we had lost a sense of immediacy in programmes as the number of live broadcasts had been reduced. Moreover, our advanced filming techniques gave viewers a marvellous account of the behaviour of animals but mainly strange creatures in faraway places; I felt there was a place again for *live* broadcasts with expert naturalists, this time direct from the British countryside – low-key programmes in which marvellous photographic detail would not be expected but which would bring informed comment and, above all, a sense of occasion. One of the producers who shared this opinion was my old friend Peter Bale, who was now on the staff of the Unit. Our ideas for a series of countryside outside broadcasts were hampered by the considerable size of the cameras and supporting equipment and, in any case, the controllers showed little interest. So that matter was shelved until the summer of 1975 when I suddenly had to postpone a programme a few weeks before it was due to go on the air. As I did not wish to bring forward a strong programme which was ready for the start of the autumn season, I began looking for a quick substitute. It then occurred to me that we might be able to do some of the things Peter and I had discussed but on film, using film cameras in the continuous manner of television cameras, and editing the material so quickly that it could be on the air just a few days later whilst still seasonally topical.

The essence of the idea was a kind of nature trail – similar to those developed in radio so successfully by Dilys Breese in *The Living World*. However, there were important differences; somehow we must hold the viewers' interest for no less than 50 minutes and, of course, the technical problems were much more formidable. At least a three-man sound film crew would be involved and there would be organisational difficulties in filming a country walk completely unrehearsed. For example, we could not afford to run film through the camera continuously for several hours and yet how could we know when to start and stop if our speakers reacted spontaneously to the natural events around them?

The location also required careful consideration. To give viewers a sense of direction, I felt that a visible and defined route would be necessary as opposed to a random wander through the countryside. To sustain visual interest for 50 minutes there would have to be not only high scenic value in the chosen location but also a good chance of seeing a wide range of species – both plants and animals. Peter and I considered several locations without finding the ideal place for our experiment; then I remembered my summer visits to the Cotswolds for badger watching during my days in the RAF. The area I frequented was near Sapperton, close to a beautiful valley and a disused canal. When I revisited the area, I knew at once that we were in business; the old canal's tow-path was now a public right-of-way and it passed through both fields and woodlands; there were several access points, there was still water in some places including a large feeder pond; and there were old locks and even a canal tunnel for historical interest. At one point, where a road crossed the canal, there was also a convenient pub.

Now everything fell into place and all the problems of structure could be solved. For our day out, we would use two pairs of naturalists walking towards each other, starting from two points on the canal a few miles apart, and we would arrange for them to meet at the end of a day's exploration near the pub. An additional ingredient, which would provide the close-up interest difficult to obtain during the walking, would be a wildlife cameraman stationed beside the pond all day, filming and commenting on anything that visited the pond. We selected Malcolm Coe, an ecologist, to walk with Peter Fowler, an archaeologist; John Gooders, an ornithologist, to walk with Richard Mabey, a botanist; and the wildlife cameraman was Maurice Tibbles. We planned to shoot the entire programme in a single day about nine days before transmission. As there were two walking teams there would have to be two film crews as well as an additional recordist to work with Maurice Tibbles. To preserve the spontaneity of the occasion, we chose to keep the location a close secret from the participants until the evening before the filming, when we would all assemble at a hotel about five miles away, ready to make an early start at 7:00 am.

Although the final location would be a secret, we did need to rehearse what was, in fact, a completely new approach for the directors, camera crew and artists. So 10 days before the programme was to be filmed, we assembled on the Mendip Hills and spent a day rehearsing, not always running film through the camera but establishing a production style of filming and methods of communication – deciding whether or not the camera team would always walk in front of the speakers, working out methods of signalling from the speakers when they were about to comment in response to an observation and so on. It was soon clear that instantaneous starting would be needed and so each 'take' would have to be identified at the *end* of shots, rather than at the beginning as normal. The sound coverage was achieved by using radio microphones so that there was no restriction at all on where the speakers walked, although they were instructed to keep as close together as possible in order to assist the cameraman. The most profound change in style had to be learnt and practised by the cameramen, Maurice Fisher and Martin Saunders; not only did they have to hand-hold their cameras all day but also act as if they were 'live' and on the air. Having established the rudiments of the new game we began shooting some trial sequences on the Mendips and these were processed and edited in time for projection at our hotel in the Cotswolds the night before the real event. There, after a splendid dinner in which the crew and the artists continued to get to know one another, we discussed, analysed and re-ran our trial film until we were sure we had learnt everything possible from our mistakes. Only then did we go to bed for a good night's rest in preparation for the long day ahead.

The day itself produced perfect weather and things began to go well from the outset. Peter Bale and his crew with Malcolm Coe and Peter Fowler arrived at Sapperton to begin their walk from the east just as the local hunt was setting off to go cub hunting, adding a nice touch of local colour. I was with the other crew walking with John Gooders and Richard Mabey and quite early in the day John spotted a rare bird – a hobby – which Maurice Fisher managed to film by quickly switching to a telephoto lens. Later on we even found a young fox lying up in the bushes beside the tow-path but most of our material came from the plants and insects we found along the way and the stories that the walkers had to tell about them. We had arranged for an assistant to bring a lunch hamper to suitable points half-way along the routes of both groups (not forgetting Maurice Tibbles beside his pond) and even the lunch siesta was shown in the film. At the end of the day the weather was still fine and warm enough for us to shoot the closing scenes for the credits outside the pub, with the tired walkers downing a pint or two.

The fact that we had episodes from two teams of walkers (one invariably filmed from left to right and the other from right to left to enable the viewers to achieve a sense of direction) as well as Maurice's

In Deepest Britain was filmed in a single day in the Cotswolds. One team consisted of Richard Mabey and John Gooders – accompanied by Lyndon ('Dickie') Bird, Maurice Fisher, Paul Morris, Judy Copeland and the author.

Maurice Tibbles filmed at a pond all day, accompanied by recordist Alistair Crocker and assistant producer Suzanne Gibbs.

RIGHT
The second mobile team – Peter Fowler and Malcolm Coe – with producer Peter Bale, Martin Saunders and Jerry Gould and, in the background, Diana Richards and Roger Long.

report from the pondside, enabled us to regulate the gentle pacing of the programme during the editing, switching scenes frequently enough to maintain interest but allowing the lazy atmosphere of a hot summer's day to come through. *In Deepest Britain*, as Peter had cleverly called it, aroused so much interest when transmitted that we were flooded with letters of appreciation and enquiries asking for the location of this most beautiful part of the countryside. Others didn't need to ask; they worked it out for themselves and for the next few weeks I'm afraid that that part of the Cotswolds was inundated with tourists. At least the innkeeper did some good trade – although one viewer wrote to complain that we had ruined a beautiful programme by closing it with scenes of beer-drinking, thereby doing untold harm to the morals of young viewers. Nevertheless the formula had worked and as a result of that single programme, Controller BBC 2 later accepted a new series of 30-minute country walks under the same title.

Fabre's house at Serignan, now a museum.

Possibly the most adventurous, but not the most successful, programme which I presented in *The World About Us* was a film about the great French entomologist, Jean Henri Fabre (who died in October 1915) which was called *The Insect Man*. Although I had long known of Fabre's popular books about insect behaviour, I had never really appreciated the man and his works until Gerry Durrell took me to Serignan in Provence to see his home which is now preserved as a museum; we were making *A Bull Called Marius* at the time.

Fabre was born into a humble peasant family at St Leons in the Department of Aveyron in the south of France and, at a very early age, showed an innate curiosity for all the living things around him, insects in particular. The family wandered about the south of France as the boy grew up – his father never seemed to make a great success of anything – but at Avignon Jean Henri won a bursary to the Ecole Normale Primaire. From then on he rose to become a Professor of Physics and Chemistry, but his academic life was spent in poverty and he retired prematurely to a house at Serignan. Eventually his studies of insect behaviour – and his writing – gave him lasting happiness. He went out into the countryside each day watching the activities of insects such as solitary wasps, mason bees, processionary caterpillars and so on, and he kept many of his subjects in captivity in the laboratory at the side of his house. This has been preserved and is now on show to the public – complete with collecting jars and other entomological equipment.

Over the years, Gerry and I talked frequently about Fabre and at one time I tried to get a BBC controller interested in a full dramatisation of his life complete with insect behaviour sequences. To my knowledge, nothing like it had been done before, it was extremely ambitious and – the final nail in the coffin – very, very expensive. Eventually I aban-

Bembex – *one of the sand wasps studied by Fabre and specially filmed by Gerald Thompson.*

doned the idea of a full dramatisation but there was such good programme material in Fabre's writings that I continued to look for a style of presentation which would be less expensive but still do justice to the great entomologist. Then it occurred to me Fabre was such a great communicator that he would have made an ideal television naturalist had he been born a hundred years later. The next step was to imagine what kind of programme we might have made with him had he been still alive – perhaps visiting him at his home at Serignan, interviewing him in and around his house and laboratory and filming him as he showed us insects at various study areas in the surrounding country-side.

I discussed this notion with my old friend and collaborator, Alan Gibson, who was especially interested in the great naturalist figures of the 19th century, and together we devised a format in which an actor would be used to play Fabre, the structure of the programme alternating between straight documentary sequences about Fabre's entomological work and 'interviews' in front of camera; even his reactions with the BBC crew would be included. Although unusual, I felt that this would be the best device to explore the true character of the man in an informal situation.

The film was bound to contain a rich vein of insect behaviour to justify inclusion in *The World About Us* and the integration of this with the scenes involving the actor would be the most difficult problem. To some extent the small size of the insect subjects were a help for any shot able to include insect and man would generally be a close-up – perhaps showing Fabre's hand or fingers; in a long shot a tiny insect would not even be seen. This suggested that we should make the film over two years – shooting the key insect behaviour sequences first. Fabre carried out many field experiments, sometimes digging out the nesting chambers of solitary wasps or other insects to examine the larvae underground. In the first year, such experiments were carefully recreated as Fabre described them, using close copies of his instruments from the museum. If necessary the cameraman used his own fingers in shot and afterwards we edited each sequence and carefully analysed the hand movements which would have to be reproduced by the actor playing Fabre in the second year's work on the same locations.

The insect sequences were ideally suited to the talents of Gerald Thompson of Oxford Scientific Films and Gerald was delighted with the opportunity to spend a couple of months in the Provençal sun literally following in Fabre's footsteps. He succeeded in filming most of the important behaviour sequences and experiments and such omissions as were unavoidable could be accommodated by minor changes in the script; we were also able to take account of a few lucky breaks that Gerald had in filming species for which there was no high priority in his original brief but which nevertheless Fabre described. The following spring we cast Ralph Michael as Fabre and Joan Wakefield, the wardrobe supervisor at Bristol, kitted him out after studying photographs of the man himself. So Ralph Michael, Grisell Lindsay, our make-up supervisor, my assistant producer, producer's assistant and the film crew and I set off in convoy for Provence in June 1972.

It was at this point that Gerry Durrell began appearing in my life

Ralph Michael as J. H. Fabre in his study at Serignan.

again. Having discussed the Fabre film with him originally, I very much regretted that he could not be involved in the preparation of the script but the programme had moved so far from the original concept that I did not feel it was appropriate. Nevertheless, I half expected to hear from him on location for I knew that he was currently staying at his house near Nîmes. I was not disappointed. The first evening at the hotel the manager, his face wreathed in smiles, arrived with a bottle of champagne. He explained that this came with the compliments of Mr Durrell who had intimated that it 'might enable Mr Parsons to overcome his shyness'. My wife, Liz, and I had been married the year before and she was with me to have a holiday and sunbathe while I worked on the film. The Durrell joke was largely for her benefit, for further interrogation of the manager revealed that Gerry had told him we were on our honeymoon.

The filming proceeded smoothly and we kept to schedule in spite of some delays due to jet aircraft from a local French Air Force station. Then on the third day we arrived back at the hotel to find a message that a Professor of Zoology from Toulouse had been trying to get in touch with regard to insect specimens for the Fabre film. This seemed rather odd as we had no contact with such a professor. As he did not leave his telephone number I did nothing. A few days later another message awaited my return from filming. This time the tone was indignant because I had not been in touch with the professor. I began to have suspicions about the source of these messages. After a few more days we were having dinner one night when there was a telephone call for me; I picked up the receiver only to hear a torrent of French from an agitated lady who claimed that she was the secretary of the professor. It appeared that the professor was enraged by my lack of communication and that the reputation of the BBC was destroyed for ever. For a few moments I did actually wonder if I had misinterpreted the previous telephone calls. Then we remembered that Gerry's new secretary was fluent in French and there seemed to be a marked similarity to her voice. No more was heard of the professor for the remainder of the filming but I was convinced by then that Gerry was behind it all and that it was time he was taught a lesson. I discussed the problem with a new member of the team who had just arrived for one particular sequence in the film – Michael John Harris from the BBC Special Effects Department in London. We had to call in Michael to recreate a famous experiment by Fabre in which he fired the local ceremonial cannon near his house in order to determine whether or not cicadas in the plane trees could actually hear sound. Now there are strict regulations about the use of firearms or explosives in film work and so the sequence could only be filmed with the aid of an expert.

RIGHT
George Shears and camera operator Bernard Hedges filming on the slopes of Mount Ventoux.

BELOW
Ralph Michael re-enacted some of Fabre's field experiments in the same locations as Gerald Thompson had filmed close-up insect behaviour the previous year.

Michael John Harris flew out to Marseilles, picked up some gun-powder from a local supplier, and drove up to Serignan. He was a jolly character who obviously enjoyed his work enormously and was delighted with the opportunity to make another explosion. The village 'cannon' was in fact a small mortar, used for saluting the patron saint on his day and other great occasions. I would have been quite happy with a puff of smoke and a modest bang which I could have amplified if necessary during the sound mix, but Michael insisted on doing the job properly and nearly deafened the entire crew – not to mention cracking the odd window. It occurred to me that he was just the fellow to help me deal with Gerry Durrell.

I knew that negotiations were currently taking place over the film rights on one of Gerry's books and that they were in a fairly critical stage. This seemed to be a fertile area to explore but if there was to be a hoax we had to ensure that I was not suspected. After the filming had ended, my wife and I were to spend a few days with the Durrells at Nîmes and this seemed a good time to perpetrate something from England when I would not be suspected. Michael agreed to co-operate and when he left Serignan he took with him a carefully written message which he promised to send as a telegram to Gerry while I was at Nîmes.

A few weeks later I was sitting on the Durrells' patio when a lad from the Post Office arrived with a telegram. Gerry was in the shower but his secretary opened the envelope. From outside the house I could hear shrieks of excitement and animated conversation. I knew exactly what was in the telegram which Michael John had sent. It read: FILM DEAL NOW IMMINENT STOP IMPERATIVE YOU FLY NEW YORK IMMEDIATELY, and it was signed in the name of Gerry's agent. I could now hear the secretary starting to telephone airlines and travel agents and things seemed to have gone far enough. I went inside the house and saw the telegram lying on a table; everyone else was in the next room. I just had time to scrawl 'Touché' on it before returning to the garden again. A few minutes later, Gerry appeared looking decidedly sheepish and holding the telegram. 'Did you write this?' he asked, pointing to the scribbled word. I nodded. Gerry went back into the house with hardly a flicker of expression on his face. Half an hour later we were enjoying a drink together on the patio; the matter was closed – or so I thought.

The next day we were all due to drive north to a party at the lovely old Provençal farmhouse of Elizabeth Frinck, the sculptress. Various local friends of Gerry's were also to be there including the film actress and director, Mai Zetterling, and her husband, the writer, David Hughes. On the morning of the party Gerry heard from Mai that she and David would not be able to come as David had a deadline with some writing. Gerry was unaccountably angry at receiving this news.

The party was very enjoyable and included a delicious meal of octopus washed down with liberal quantities of local wine. After the meal, when everyone was in a jovial mood, Elizabeth's husband, Ted, brought out a curious package addressed to me which he said had been left by an eminent zoologist who had heard I was in the area. I opened it suspiciously, finding inside six objects resembling the cocoons of emperor moths – one of the subjects we had been filming at Serignan. Although plausible imitations, they were not good enough to fool me

The cannon is fired!

and the onlookers quickly realised that the game was up. The reason behind Gerry's disappointment with David Hughes' absence was now revealed; *he* was the person chosen by Gerry to impersonate the Zoology Professor who had supposedly been trying to contact me and who should have descended on me in fury as soon as I arrived at Elizabeth Frinck's house. So Gerry's retaliation had misfired. Curious to see how the cocoons had been made I started unpicking one of them, for I could feel something rattling inside. I discovered a small piece of paper, tightly rolled. Unravelling it I saw it bore a message – it was something extremely rude about the BBC. Once more Durrell had somehow managed to have the last word.

Chapter 18

Life on Earth

When Kenneth Clark's *Civilisation* reached the television screens in 1969, producers in the Natural History Unit knew that sooner or later a major television part-work on the world of nature must be produced in Bristol. Unfortunately, this was not as blindingly clear to the Television Management in London as it was to us and several other major projects were produced from the metropolis before the Natural History Unit at Bristol was in a position to launch its first 'megaseries' after many years of lobbying.

In truth the Unit was not ready to take on a major project in the very early 1970s for it had not acquired enough experience in colour or in the production of 50-minute programmes by then; but because of the time it takes to get a major series agreed, financed and staffed it was not inappropriate that I and some of my colleagues should be agitating for action at that time. For some years, unfortunately, there was a commonly held belief in senior BBC circles that the Natural History Unit was staffed with regional producers who must be considered in a lower category and not equal to the high standards of a prestige series. It was to be a long hard battle to eradicate such misconceptions and get our aspirations taken seriously but I found myself in a position to fire one of the opening shots early in 1970.

At that time I was particularly restless, not just to launch a major series, but because I felt that my career was no longer progressing in the way I would wish. *The World About Us* was already well established and offered good opportunities for programme-making but I am most happy when breaking new ground and I was concerned lest I should be confined to the routines of a long-running series, however successful. One of the few disadvantages of working in Bristol was certainly a lack of contact with other departments and I thought that experience outside the Unit might be valuable if occasionally I was to develop new methods of presentation within the Unit, such as dramatisation. Furthermore, some London experience might be advantageous politically when the right time came to press for a prestige series. I talked over my concern with Nicky Crocker and he arranged for me to have an interview with the Director of Programmes, Television – David Attenborough.

Attenborough was the kind of person you could relax with whatever the level of post he held, be it Producer, Executive Producer, Controller or Director of Programmes. He saw immediately what I needed and soon made it possible for me to have a rewarding attachment to Arts Features, during which time I worked with Fred Burnley on a filmed

A drink to celebrate The World About Us winning the Radio Industries Club award for the outstanding television programme of the year. Back row, left to right: Keith Hopkins, Mick Rhodes (then Editor, Natural History Unit), Peter Bale, Mike Salisbury, Peter Crawford; front row: Suzanne Gibbs, the author and Ned Kelly.

dramatisation of the life of Modigliani. Whilst I was talking with David Attenborough in his comfortable office on the sixth floor of the Television Centre I was able to voice my ambitions for the Unit's mammoth series. He readily agreed that, sooner or later, it would be done. The problem in my mind was that there was only one presenter in the running for the series and that was Attenborough himself. He was obviously not available while he occupied his present chair, although he was still occasionally voicing narrations and had an arrangement with the BBC that enabled him to take a few months off at a time to make films. I ventured the thought that he might like to consider presenting such a series as the Unit envisaged some time in the future if he should, by any chance, become available. The suggestion was not as inappropriate as might appear for there were rumours that Attenborough would probably not remain within the BBC for many years and that he was already itching to get back permanently into writing and presenting programmes. He expressed unqualified enthusiasm for my suggestion, appeared even flattered by it, but was stone-faced about the future. He

wasn't giving any clues as to if and when he might be available – but I thought I noticed a gleam in his eye.

Involvement with *The World About Us* series prevented me from thinking more about the special project until early summer 1972 when I sensed that, because our films were doing so well in *The World About Us* – and because there was evidence of considerable co-production finance being available for the right project – it might be timely to begin lobbying at the Television Centre again. So I reached for an old file and re-typed some of the ideas in it for a definitive natural history series – the television equivalent of all the glossy Time-Life nature books and other noted coffee-table volumes rolled into 20 programmes. The first half of the series would deal with a survey of life on a phylogenetic basis, starting with single-cell forms and working up through invertebrate life to vertebrates, including man. Each major group would have its own programme – fish, amphibians, reptiles, and so on. The second part of the series would deal with important biological concepts such as symbiosis and commensalism, convergence and so on. I wrote a paragraph on each and searched in my mind for a snappy title to put on the first page. I could not think of anything totally satisfactory so in desperation I wrote down the one phrase that at least seemed to include everything – *Life on Earth*.

By now there had been a major re-organisation of the non-metropolitan parts of the BBC with the result that the old regional status of Bristol had disappeared and it was known as a Network Production Centre; two similar centres were at Birmingham and Manchester. The Head of our centre was Stuart Wyton, previously the head of the News Department at Bristol, and he gave me a good deal of encouragement with the *Life on Earth* proposal in the absence of Nicky Crocker, who was ill at the time. It so happened that he met Robin Scott, Controller BBC 2, within a few days of the completion of the outline proposal and mentioned it in passing. Scott appeared interested and so I sent the outline to him without delay asking for some reaction before the Unit made any informal approaches to would-be co-producers. We also reminded David Attenborough of our long-term plan when he visited Bristol shortly afterwards.

Meanwhile, my colleague John Sparks had also been busy. He, too, was convinced that the time was ripe for the Unit to mount a major series but because of the popularity of wildlife programmes he felt that it should be offered to BBC 1. His approach was somewhat different from mine but covered much of the same ground in terms of natural history subject material. Neither idea could progress further until other important matters were resolved, for Nicky Crocker was now retiring and a new Unit editor had to be found. This time I had sufficiently strong views about the future policy of the Unit to wish to be considered seriously and, as I had acted as Nicky's deputy on many occasions, I had sufficient knowledge of the job to realise what it entailed. So, although I was competing against some of my colleagues, I considered that I had at least a fighting chance at the appointment board. That was to be my next meeting with David Attenborough, for he was the senior member of the board. To the surprise of many, no one from Bristol was appointed and the successful candidate was Mick Rhodes, a *Horizon* producer in the

Science and Features Department from London. Mick had produced a number of programmes on biological subjects for that series, including a prize-winning account of the work of Oxford Scientific Films – *The Making of a Natural History Film*. I was personally disappointed at my failure at the time but completely unaware of the future series of events which would turn failure into one of the most fortunate incidents in my career. Those events began a short time later when David Attenborough announced that he would be resigning his post in the BBC.

In fact, the Unit needed an outsider as its new chief, for it had undoubtedly become too inbred, even too introverted. The continuity of its staff had some advantages, including the development of specialisation in production methods, but the time was ripe for new ideas as many of the staff had been doing the same things in the same way for far too long; if there was to be a shake-up it could in many ways be best done by an outsider. With a forthright style which sent ripples of indignation through the frailer members of the Unit, Mick took a long hard look at everything the Unit was doing and began questioning and re-organising. Some of my colleagues found it more destructive than constructive and there was the smell of anarchy in the corridors; others, including myself, found the net effect rather refreshing and saw it as a necessary phase in the Unit's history. There were other advantages too; we now had an editor of considerable vitality who had several years' experience in London. That experience, coupled perhaps with a consequent increased faith by the controllers in our ability to deliver a quality product, might just provide the extra muscle we required to achieve the coveted prestige series.

Even before David Attenborough resigned it had already been agreed that he would take three months off from his administration duties to work on a six-part BBC 1 series produced by the Unit. The man in charge was to be Richard Brock and the series would be filmed in Sumatra and Borneo and later billed as *Eastwards with Attenborough*. When David came down to Bristol in January 1973 to plan the series, it provided an opportunity to take the *Life on Earth* notion a little further and, following our discussions, John Sparks immediately drafted a modified proposal. This approximately followed the progression outlined in the early part of my own proposal but also took into account John's more functional approach. David said that he had recently mentioned the series idea to Michael Peacock, currently Executive Vice President of Network Television at Warner Bros; they were old acquaintances, having both joined the BBC as producers on the same day in 1953.

As Peacock was in England at the time, Mick quickly arranged a meeting in London at which it was established that Warners were, in principle, *very* interested in co-production. At long last it looked as if things were coming to the boil but the series was bound to be a major drain on BBC resources, staff and finance and, although still actively encouraged by Robin Scott, Controller BBC 2, there could be no formal acceptance of the project for some time. Nevertheless, more meetings were held to discuss the format of the series later that year and there was an air of optimism around.

Then, in the spring of 1974, when it seemed only a matter of time before we would receive the green light, disaster struck – at least as far

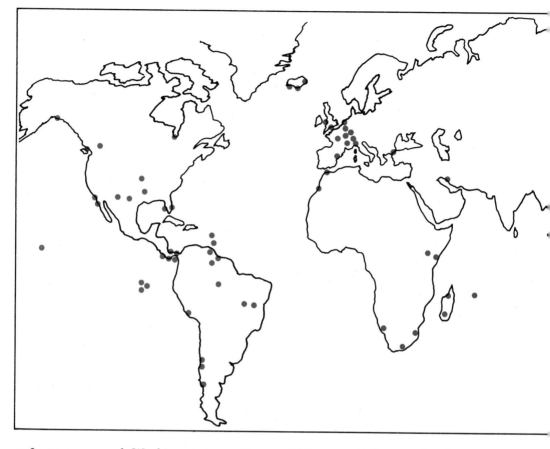

Principal locations for Life on Earth *1976–1978*

as I was concerned. Working at renovating an old house which my wife and I had recently bought, I slipped a disc in my back. In agony and unable to move, I was admitted to hospital 'for a few days'; still in some pain and limping, I emerged 12 weeks later! Two more months' convalescence were required before I was able to take up full duties again. During my absence, and unknown to me at the time, there were earnest high-level discussions about our series. The appointment of Aubrey Singer to succeed Robin Scott as Controller BBC 2 had put new life into the proposal, as one might have hoped bearing in mind that Singer had been head of the Features Group from which most of the previous blockbusters had been produced. At the same time, Singer also asked searching and sometimes awkward questions. Did the series really need a presenter at all? Should it be produced as part of the Natural History Unit's output?

Meanwhile Mick Rhodes had himself been wrestling with the problem of whether it was wise to commit 12 people – including a substantial proportion of the Natural History Unit staff at the time – to a project which would take three years. It was a high investment and there was no guarantee of success. The Bronowski series, *The Ascent of Man*, had acquired tremendous prestige but not all other big projects had been so well received and the failure of the British Empire series was fresh in people's minds. Nevertheless, after discussions with the production teams involved on such projects, Mick became much more confident and did not, therefore, have any sympathy at all for Aubrey Singer's suggestion that the series might be better produced from outside the Unit. Tom Salmon, normally in charge of the BBC at Plymouth, was acting head of the Bristol Network Production Centre at the time and took the full force of Mick's anger. Mick took the view that the Unit had been pushing the idea for years and that only the Unit's staff, with its acquired expertise, would be capable of delivering high quality programmes in such a specialised subject. He hinted darkly that if London management was to persist in such views they would be soon looking for a new editor. Tom Salmon passed the gist of this on to London, using his well-known tact and adding that if the series were to be produced outside the Unit he was fearful of the effect it would have on morale at Bristol. He noted that the third producer was yet to be nominated but the selection of this person and the remainder of the team should wait until Parsons had made a full recovery. He also tentatively suggested September 1975 for the commencement of shooting.

In fact it was autumn 1975 before the long build-up to *Life on Earth* drew to a close. The third producer had been an obvious choice: Richard Brock was by then experienced at working with a wide range of wildlife subjects in many parts of the world and had also struck up such a successful working relationship with his presenter on the series *Eastwards with Attenborough* that he seemed to have produced David at his best on location. The BBC had at last committed themselves to form a production team during spring 1976; and, encouraged by the enthusiastic Singer, Warner Bros were happy to co-produce, having in the meantime backed a shorter anthropological series with David called *The Tribal Eye*.

David has now written an outline of the *Life on Earth* series, drawing on previous proposals and several discussions, but adding many ideas of his own and, most important of all, his superb skill as a communicator. Although the series was not to be about evolution as such, David saw the advantage of maintaining a strong evolutionary thread running through the programmes and the simple terms in which he was able to tell this basic story was one of the major factors in the series' success.

Now the most pressing requirement was to set a budget for the series and a predicted cash-flow over the three-year production period. This was not easy with only a two-page outline of each programme and Mick and I pondered over this problem at length. Mick suggested that previous series such as *The Ascent of Man* could provide guidelines, not only in terms of budgeting but also on method of production, but I was never confident that the comparisons would be reliable. Certainly both series involved locations all over the world but our overseas filming would be largely influenced by seasonal considerations, restricting work in many countries to particular seasons. Furthermore, the variability of the seasons would make long-term planning especially difficult in some parts of the world. Against those factors we did have considerable experience in such matters and would be able to make reasonably

313

accurate estimates of the time necessary to film animal behaviour sequences.

For the purpose of budgeting, Mick and I decided to take two guiding principles; firstly that David would be required to appear in at least six different locations all over the world in each programme; secondly that we should aim for a standard of wildlife photography very much higher than that currently enjoyed on the screen – this meant that any previous thoughts about the use of library material could effectively be forgotten. Even then, with no detailed storyboard available, calculations were liberally laced with guesswork; we elected to embark independently on two methods of estimating costs and see if there was any agreement between the two totals. Given that we were allowed three years for the entire project only a certain amount of time could be spent filming on location; Mick therefore costed out blocks of work in Africa, Indonesia, Australia, South America and other areas of operation. Meanwhile, I attempted to write a more detailed script for one programme and determine the cost of filming it as accurately as possible – multiplying the final figure by 13 but making due allowance for concurrent shooting for more than one programme whilst cameramen were working in various geographical areas. To our surprise and delight the figures that we arrived at independently differed by only 8 per cent. As this indicated we were on the right lines we added a reasonable amount for contingencies and sent the estimates to London. The total was about three quarters of a million pounds – excluding staff costs – and when corrections for inflation were subsequently built in the total budget came close to a round million.

By April 1976, Mike Andrews had arrived from London to take over my duties as the Bristol series editor of *The World About Us* and I was free at last to concentrate on *Life on Earth*. In the intervening months two assistant producers, Mike Salisbury and Neil Cleminson, had been appointed to work with John, Richard and myself, as well as a number of producers' assistants and secretaries, and, extremely important to the project, a team organiser, Derek Anderson. Controller BBC 2 had been most insistent that the team should include an organiser to monitor finance closely and control resources but his duties would include being the central co-ordinating point for all communications and travel on a world-wide basis.

From the outset we agreed that for most purposes we would have to regard the 13-part series as one huge programme; if David Attenborough was required in Western Australia for Programme One, for example, it would be desirable to film at the same time any sequences involving him for other programmes that had to be shot in the same area. This situation would occur in many different countries. On the other hand, it also seemed desirable for Richard, John and me to have responsibilities as producers for complete programmes within the series so that we could specialise in our research and gain maximum professional satisfaction from the work. The two general principles were contradictory but a sensible compromise was that whilst on location in any part of the world we would have to be prepared to direct sequences for each others' programmes.

Filming could not begin for many months, until the first draft scripts

Filming a sound sequence for Life on Earth, *David Attenborough talks about the origins of life at a thermal area in Yellowstone Park, USA.*

had been completed and detailed research undertaken on at least some of the programmes. David had been delayed with the scripts due to a late schedule on his *The Tribal Eye* book but as he completed each programme draft it was snapped up by whichever producer was nominated for that programme. Then began a long period of detailed research in which every part of the script was checked and, if necessary, modified. This was done by going straight to the leading experts in each subject area; sometimes this was done by correspondence, sometimes by telephone but more often than not by visiting the expert concerned wherever he or she was. This involved a large amount of foreign travel, visiting universities and other scientific institutions in the Americas, Australasia, the Far East, Africa and Europe. At the same time key locations such as fossil sites were checked, as well as the availability of the world's finest fossils in various museums.

In his first draft scripts, David suggested animal and plant species with which he was personally familiar, to serve as illustrations for his storyline; he fully expected that research would sometimes lead to far better and less well-known examples and, indeed, this was often the case. Sometimes after research the script had to be modified in the light of recent work not as yet published. As a result of all these endeavours, scripts were continually being modified during the first year and in some cases fundamental structural changes were required, moving material from one programme to another. On occasions there were heated arguments between producers and presenter about biological content and the academic level of the series but the compromise which inevitably resulted usually enhanced the programmes rather than weakened them. If there was intellectual tension running during the first year of production there was also too much mutual respect between

Cameraman Maurice Fisher walks backwards as David Attenborough strolls through a shallow river in Alaska where salmon were spawning – and dying – in their thousands.

us all for this to have any long-term damaging effect and the team spirit was never less good – and frequently infectiously light-hearted.

By the end of 1976, we had established a worldwide network of advisers and helpers on each subject who were to prove invaluable as we tackled the formidable filming problems which lay ahead. For example, Richard Brock was in touch with just about every zoologist in the world working on frog reproduction and bat behaviour; John Sparks had a corresponding selection of scientists whom he consulted on reptile physiology and marsupial reproduction; and I had visited or corresponded with some of the leading workers on microfossils and the evolution of photosynthesis.

It was always clear that there would be two separate approaches to filming: on the one hand there would be sound filming with David at between 80 to 100 different locations all over the world. David would appear only when it was necessary to convey information or discuss a concept which could not be readily illustrated by animal behaviour footage. These in-vision sequences would be at important fossil sites or close to wild animals on the few occasions this was possible. The filming of such sequences would be arranged in four to eight week blocks in various geographical areas of the world and, with some breaks, we estimated that this work alone would take David and a sound film crew over 18 months, each producer and assistant producer taking turns to direct. A three-man sound film crew was appointed – Maurice Fisher as cameraman, Paul Morris as assistant cameraman and Lyndon 'Dickie' Bird as sound recordist; Martin Saunders and Hugh Maynard provided a back-up camera team with recordist Roger Long.

Although Maurice Fisher would be able to film some animals on his assignments with David Attenborough, most of the wildlife filming would be done by a team of cameramen each specialising in some aspect of the work, be it underwater, macrophotography or field activities using telephoto lenses. The cameramen who provided the backbone of the effort on the series were old friends from previous productions –

RIGHT
Preparing to film the closing of programme six at the salmon river in Alaska.

Rodger Jackman (son of Leslie), Ron Eastman, Maurice Tibbles, Peter Parks and David Thompson of Oxford Scientific Films, and Hugh Miles. We also established a studio base in Australia, using a newly-discovered and talented pair in Sydney – Jim Frazier and Densey Clyne who specialised mainly in invertebrate work. David Parer of the ABC Natural History Unit in Melbourne was co-opted to film for us while in Papua, New Guinea, on another assignment. There were also other cameramen contracted for short sequences in various parts of the world so that at the height of filming there were sometimes a dozen cameramen simultaneously working on individual projects for *Life on Earth*.

By the autumn of 1976 the scripts were advanced enough for us to begin work on many of the pure natural history sequences. David had written on the basis that nothing was impossible so his pages were liberally dotted with references to such ambitious items as 'platypus with egg in burrow', 'coelacanth swimming', 'yucca moth pollinating yucca flower', or 'millipedes mating'. As research progressed, the production team added to these a few of their own daydreams. To our knowledge many of them had never before been filmed.

By early 1977 the sound filming with David Attenborough had begun and, with the wildlife work well advanced, there was now a steady traffic of producers and cameramen passing in and out of London Heathrow every week; and almost daily there would be film arriving at the BBC Shipping Office from all over the world. The film was sent direct to Rank Laboratories for overnight processing and viewed early the next morning by our laboratory co-ordinator, Ken Clack, who would immediately telephone a report to the production office. By the afternoon, the rushes could be viewed at Bristol and a report cabled to the cameraman in the field. At the centre of all this activity our organiser, Derek Anderson, lived in a world of international telephone calls, telexes, customs and shipping procedures while his bible was the international air timetable, constantly in use on his desk.

There were also quantities of livestock coming into London Airport for us from time to time. Much invertebrate and small vertebrate behaviour can best be studied under carefully controlled conditions in a reconstructed environment so specimens were flown into the country for Rodger Jackman and the cameramen of Oxford Scientific Films to work on in their studios. For example, Rodger Jackman was supplied with a batch of Darwin's frogs, *Rhinoderma darwinii*, from South America. The sixth programme in the series was about amphibians and included a long section on the methods of reproduction of a variety of frogs. In the scientific literature, Darwin's frogs had been recorded as having a particularly fascinating method of reproduction: after spawning has taken place the males guard the little blobs of gelatinous eggs on the forest floor and then take them through their mouths into their vocal sacs. There the tadpoles develop into froglets and are eventually 'born' out of their fathers' mouths. At least, so said the literature.

Richard Brock, the producer of the amphibian programme, was determined to film this extraordinary behaviour and therefore arranged for a batch of the inch-long frogs to be sent to England in their breeding season when they were carrying young. The 'birth' sequence was entrusted to Rodger Jackman at his studio in Paignton. Rodger's main problem was that nobody knew exactly when the birth would take place or, indeed, what behaviour was exhibited by the frogs when the event was imminent. He was therefore forced to keep a close and constant watch on the frogs every day for any signs of abnormal behaviour which might indicate that the time had come. After several days he inspected the frogs early one morning and discovered that the froglets had arrived during the previous night, and so another batch of frogs was arranged. This, as far as Richard was concerned, had to be Rodger's last chance. Determined to succeed this time, Rodger hired an assistant to help keep a day and night watch. He moved his bed into the studio so that, if woken, he would instantly be ready for action. After 14 days' continuous watching, Rodger and his assistant noted increased restlessness amongst some of the frogs, presumably due to the movement of the froglets inside. Rodger was on the alert and ready with his finger on the camera button but he only managed to obtain one shot of a froglet appearing out of its parent's mouth. Nevertheless it was a unique shot. The actual 'birth' lasted only a second – it was so fast that in the final programme the film had to be optically stretched so that viewers could appreciate the extraordinary behaviour.

Another long vigil – or more accurately a series of vigils – was undertaken by Densey Clyne and Jim Frazier in their studio at Sydney. John Sparks produced the ninth programme, which was mainly about marsupials, and he had set his heart on another first – filming the birth of a small marsupial. Many years before I had discovered that filming the birth of a kangaroo was not easy – because of the thumb-top size of the neonate – so it could be assumed that there would be formidable problems coping with the minute young of a marsupial eight or nine inches long. As with so much of our work on *Life on Earth*, success would undoubtedly depend on the co-operation of any biologists already working on the subject. In this case it was Dr Heather Aslin of Adelaide who was studying the reproductive biology of a small marsupial called a kowari. These animals were being bred in captivity and as the gestation period was roughly known it was possible to predict the time when a pregnant female would give birth to within two or three days. John therefore arranged for a pregnant female to be sent from Adelaide to Jim and Densey's studio at Sydney. Then the problems really began.

The fact that the animal was small was a bad enough start. The next difficulty was that nobody had yet witnessed a birth – not even the biologist at Adelaide. Finally, for good measure the kowari was a burrowing animal which normally gave birth to its young underground. Jim and Densey, far from being despondent about the odds against them, took on the assignment with determination and Jim began using his already proven ingenuity to overcome this unusual combination of problems. Constructing an underground home in which the animal could be conditioned to light was not an exceptional problem in his business. The main technical difficulties were in obtaining a clear view of the birth which was presumably in a crouching or hunched position – difficulties compounded by the fact that the young would be minute and difficult to get in focus. Jim reasoned that the only way he would have a clear view at all would be to look almost vertically upwards during the moment of birth. This being the case he built his underground set on a glass floor and mounted it on an old gramophone turntable mechanism so that he could rotate the entire set above his upward-pointing camera, thereby accommodating any position the kowari might assume.

The first pregnant kowari was delivered to its new home and Jim and Densey started their long vigil at the appropriate time. After many hours the birth took place, but it was a disaster for the film-makers. Before the arrival of the neonates a quantity of mucous fluid was released from the uro-genital opening of the female and dropped on to the glass floor – immediately obscuring the camera view. Jim and Densey were powerless to do anything and, although they had not seen the birth, they inspected the kowari's pouch soon afterwards and found several neonates already attached to the mother's nipples – each neonate no larger than a grain of rice.

Jim and Densey now knew something about the behaviour of the kowari when giving birth and decided that the camera should be pointed *diagonally* upwards on the next attempt – so that if another discharge of fluid occurred it would fall to one side of the camera lens. Jim and Densey began an all-night vigil with the second female, and although the camera was in a better position, again nothing of the birth could be seen. The film-makers were also concerned that some of the neonates were being wasted – spilling out on to the glass floor of the burrow. Were these a natural wastage – supernumerary neonates that did not necessarily make it into the pouch – or was it abnormal behaviour due to stress caused by the filming lights?

Three more attempts were made, all were unsuccessful and, by the autumn of 1978, time was running out as Programme Nine was already being edited. Nevertheless, Jim and Densey were determined to have

Darwin's frog. Rodger Jackman spent two weeks watching the males before he was able to film a 'birth'.

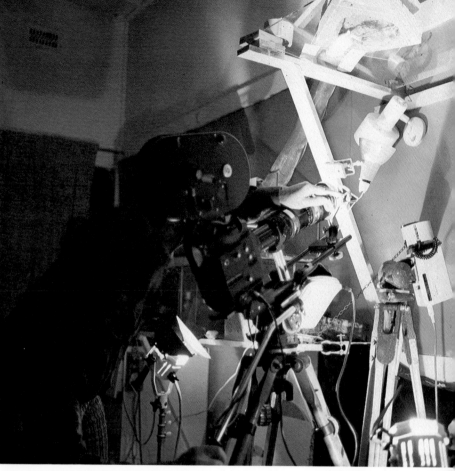

*Jim Frazier's
equipment for
filming the birth of
the kowaris. The
glass-bottomed
chamber is at the
top of the picture.*

*The female kowari
a few minutes after
having given birth.*

one more attempt. John Sparks was in Africa at the time but Jim telephoned me from Sydney to report that this final attempt was apparently unsuccessful as he had not been able to see anything through the camera viewfinder, although he had been running the camera when the birth had supposedly taken place. The vigil had lasted from Sunday night until Thursday morning. Jim and Densey later confessed that, completely exhausted, they had finally collapsed in tears when they realised they had failed again. The exposed film was nevertheless sent to the local laboratory and viewed as a matter of routine a week later. Immediately afterwards Jim telephoned me again and his excited voice indicated that there was something interesting on the film after all. He explained that the first time they had projected it nothing was noticed, although there had been a suspicion of a movement amongst the mother's fur at one brief point. The film was next inspected frame by frame and only then was it possible to distinguish briefly three of the neonates immediately after emergence from the birth canal. Within a few frames of film they had all slipped through the mother's fur and into the pouch. Now we knew why Jim had not been able to film the birth before; unlike the kangaroo birth, the entire action was over in three seconds. Ron Martin, the film editor, instructed the laboratories to stop print the small film section and a circle was superimposed to draw viewers' eyes to one of the tiny kowaris at the moment of birth – an event that had never been seen before, but which took no less than 300 hours of observation before filming was successful.

In the broadest terms our three-year *Life on Earth* project was in three phases: the first 12 months was mainly research and some filming; in the second year research continued but filming was at a peak whilst the first film assemblies were made in the cutting room; and the start of the final year saw filming still in progress but very soon all efforts were concentrated on editing work. With executive responsibilities for the entire series, I knew I could never leave Bristol for long during phases one and three. So I elected to produce the early programmes in the series; these included much close up work on single-cell forms and invertebrates, most of which would be filmed under control in the studio and therefore did not require my supervision overseas. However, there were many sound sequences with David Attenborough including a particularly large number in Programme One since this dealt with so many basic biological ideas and concepts. The locations were mostly in the USA and Australia and I arranged to shoot these during the second phase of production.

David's overseas sound filming trips were usually between four and eight weeks long and concentrated in one country or geographical area of the world. One of our two producers' assistants, Pam Jackson or Jane Trethowan, would accompany the team to act as a kind of road manager, dealing with continuity, shot lists, hotel and travel arrangements and generally keeping everyone in order. The producers' assistant concerned would plan the trip with organiser Derek Anderson, with the help of his international airline timetable. Careful consideration of the route taken, the length of the trip and sometimes the dove-tailing of arrangements with two directors leap-frogging from location to location made this type of scheduling one of the most complex aspects of planning in the series; an intelligent advance re-arrangement of the order of locations could save hundreds of pounds in air travel and days of valuable effort. Much depended on the producer's correct estimation of the time required to film a sequence – with due regard for weather problems – but from then on it was the accuracy and effectiveness of arrangements made weeks and sometimes months in advance for locations many thousands of miles away which were the secret of success. The following is an abbreviated schedule for the first two weeks of a 43-day trip to the USA during 1977. It went almost exactly as planned and illustrates well the degree of forward planning required for just one of a dozen such trips. It begins with our journey to Delaware Bay to film the horseshoe crabs:

Day 1 (Monday, May 30)
Chris Parsons and Pam Jackson depart London Heathrow at 11:00 hours on Flight TW753 for Philadelphia, arriving 15:19. Collect hire car, drive to Cape May Court House, New Jersey.

Day 2
Maurice Fisher (cameraman), Dickie Bird (recordist) and David Attenborough depart from London Heathrow at 11:00 hours on Flight TW753, arriving Philadelphia at 15:19.
Meanwhile: Paul Morris (assistant camerman), having finished another assignment with cameraman, Martin Saunders, and Neil Cleminson in Florida, departs from Tampa at 09:30 hours on Flight DL340, arriving Philadelphia at 11:43. There he checks film equipment previously freighted out from London and confirms arrangements for hire car and station wagon for film crew. Then meets Fisher, Bird and Attenborough off plane.
Meanwhile: Parsons and Jackson rendezvous with Dr Carl Shuster, horseshoe crab expert, and inspect beach location for following day's filming. Also check arrangements for collection and packing of crab eggs with local Marine Laboratory. In the evening all rendezvous at hotel at Cape May Court House. (Neil Cleminson remains in Florida making reconnaisance for his next film location.)

Day 3
Pam Jackson spends morning in administrative matters, checking forward bookings for planes, hotels and freelance cameraman. The crew sleep off jet-lag, check and prepare equipment for filming. At 18:00 hours everyone assembles at pre-arranged access point to beach. Meet Dr Carl Shuster, and a hired electrician who has travelled from Washington. The filming proceeds to about 22:00 hours (for Programme Two).

OVERLEAF
The operations map (simplified!) originally in the organiser's office at Bristol for filming in the USA from May 31 to July 11 1977 inclusive.

Day 4
Nominated as a reserve filming day in case the crab sequence is unsuccessful the previous evening. If all well, plan A goes into operation: Parsons, Jackson, Fisher and Morris set off by road for Washington in the station wagon, having returned one car to a local hire car agent. Attenborough and Bird drive to Philadelphia to catch Flight DL263 at 11:35 hours to Tampa where they will meet Neil Cleminson and Martin Saunders. There they will shoot a sound

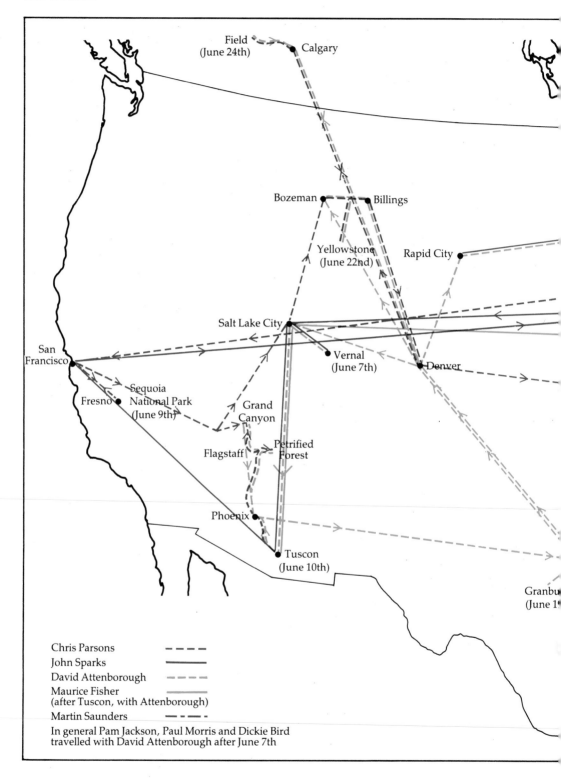

Chris Parsons
John Sparks
David Attenborough
Maurice Fisher
(after Tuscon, with Attenborough)
Martin Saunders

In general Pam Jackson, Paul Morris and Dickie Bird
travelled with David Attenborough after June 7th

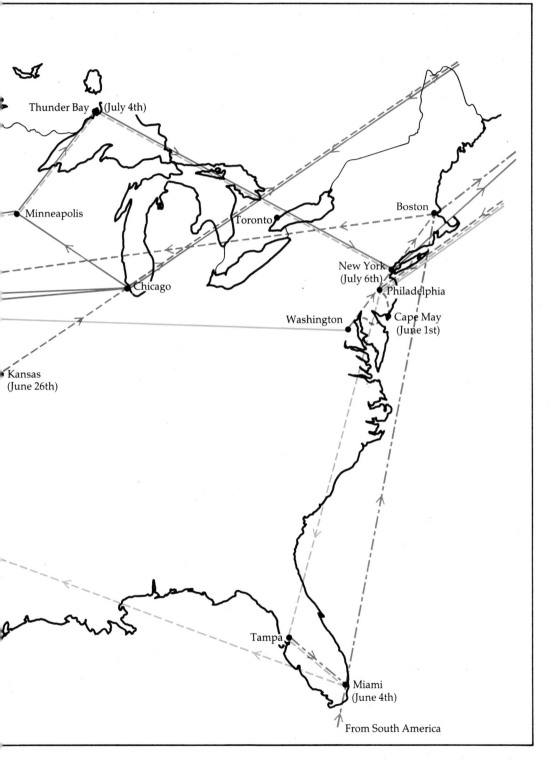

Thunder Bay (July 4th)

Minneapolis

Toronto

Boston

New York
(July 6th)

Philadelphia

Chicago

Washington

Cape May
(June 1st)

Kansas
(June 26th)

Tampa

Miami
(June 4th)

From South America

sequence for Programme Six that evening. At Washington, Fisher and his crew book into their hotel while Chris Parsons and Pam Jackson drive to Dulles International Airport and despatch package of horse-shoe crab eggs to London. They telephone Derek Anderson at Bristol with flight details.

Day 5

Parsons and crew arrive at Smithsonian Institution, Washington, for filming various fossils for Programmes Two and Three. Arrange-ments have been previously made with Dr Fred Collier, the collec-tions manager, and a hired electrician has also been arranged.

Meanwhile: Attenborough, Saunders and Bird depart with Neil Cleminson from Tampa on Flight UA559 at 11:35, arriving at Miami at 12:23. In the afternoon they film experiments with dolphins at Miami Seaquarium for Programme Ten.

Day 6

Fisher, Morris, Jackson are given a day off in Washington.

Meanwhile: Chris Parsons flies to Boston at 10:00 on Flight AA312 and proceeds to Boston Aquarium where he meets officials to make final arrangements for underwater filming of shark locomotion in large circular tank. In Florida, Saunders, Bird, Attenborough and Clemin-son carry on filming at Seaquarium. Saunders leaves in time to catch 17:45 Flight DL276 to Boston, meeting Chris Parsons at hotel.

Day 7

Parsons and Saunders go to Boston Aquarium to film close-ups of certain fish species using a local assistant and electrician. At the same time they meet underwater cameraman, Stan Waterman, and his son, acting as assistant. Waterman has to work with underwater lights in the circular shark tank and this involves complicated feeding of cables from above as Waterman swims in anti-clockwise direction with sharks. Close-up studies of shark movement are for Programme Five.

Meanwhile: John Sparks departs Heathrow at 12:30 hours on Flight TW771 for Chicago. After changing there early afternoon he arrives at Salt Lake City at 17:59, four minutes after Fisher, Morris and Jackson have flown in from Washington. At 19:08 they take a plane for Vernal, Colorado, arriving at 19:46. Accommodation – a local hotel whilst filming at Dinosaur National Monument close by.

During the day Attenborough has been in Florida with Cleminson and Bird.

Day 8

Parsons and Saunders have stayed overnight in Boston but are working today at Harvard University, a few miles away at Cam-bridge. There they visit the Biological Laboratories and spend the day with Professor Elso Barghoorn, authority on micro-fossils. A local hired assistant works with them. They film a sequence on how Gunflint Chert from the shores of Lake Ontario was prepared for detection of micro-fossils (Programme One). While Fisher and Sparks make a lighting reconnaissance with electrician to plot the filming at Dinosaur National Monument, Attenborough and Bird depart from Miami at 11:00 hours and, after changing planes at Denver and Salt Lake City, arrive at Vernal at 19:46.

Professor Elso Barghoorn of Harvard University, authority on microfossils. He, and over 500 scientists all over the world, advised and helped with the series.

LEFT
*Giant metasequoia
in California.*

Day 9

Attenborough, Sparks and the crew are now all at Vernal and a complicated lighting rig is set up to shoot the scenes of Attenborough with the dinosaur bones (Programme Seven).

Meanwhile: Parsons with Saunders and his assistant have stayed the night at Cambridge ready for another day's filming at Harvard. This time they work in the Museum of Comparative Zoology with Professor Frank Carpenter, a leading authority on fossil insects. He provides some fine specimens in rock and amber which Martin films in close-up (Programme Three).

Day 10

In Vernal, this is a reserve day for filming at Dinosaur National Monument. Sparks decided to fly on to his next location in Tucson whilst the crew pack up equipment and prepare a batch of film for despatch to England. On the east coast, Parsons and Saunders have completed their work at Harvard and Saunders now sets off for England. (He has been away for several weeks, having worked on wildlife sequences in South America before travelling north to film in Florida with Cleminson and in Boston with Parsons.) Parsons moves to the west coast taking Flight UA095 at 10:00 from Boston to San Francisco. A change of plane takes him to Fresno in California by 14:11. He collects a hired car and drives up to a lodge in the Sequoia National Park.

Day 11

Parsons visits Superintendent Stanley Albright at the Headquarters of the Sequoia National Park and obtains advice for his reconnaissance.

BELOW
*The author at Grand
Canyon.*

He is looking for best locations to film the giant Metasequoia trees.

Meanwhile: Attenborough and Fisher's crew leave Vernal at 09:06 on Flight FL633, and after changing at Salt Lake City arrive at Tucson on

Flight RW14 at 12:00. They meet Sparks and make reconnaissance at Senora Desert Museum.
Day 12
At 10:30, Parsons meets freelance cameraman, Bryan Anderson, at Sequoia National Park HQ. They film sequences of giant trees for Programme Three. Drive to Fresno and catch 19:20 Flight to San Francisco. Parsons changes to NA44 to Las Vegas – the first stage of journey to Grand Canyon. Arrives at hotel at 23:00.
Meanwhile: Attenborough, Sparks and Fisher crew have been filming at Tucson, notably the closing sequences of Programme Seven with a rattlesnake a few feet from David.
Day 13
At Las Vegas, Parsons catches 08:00 Flight YR103 in a light aircraft to Grand Canyon South. This will provide good opportunity to make aerial reconnaissance of canyon relevant to filming in few days' time. After arrival at Grand Canyon at 09:15 he collects hired car and drives to the National Park Headquarters to meet Merle Stitt of the HQ staff. This is to make final arrangements for filming on one of the trails down the canyon.
   Parsons drives south to Flagstaff to contact Dr Bill Breed, Curator of Geology at the Museum of Northern Arizona. Breed will accompany the crew whilst filming in the canyon and advise on filming of fossils at the museum.
Meanwhile: In Tucson, Sparks, Attenborough and crew complete filming. Attenborough and crew start driving north towards Petrified Forest in Arizona, staying the night en route.
Day 14
Parsons makes a reconnaissance of best locations in Petrified Forest with help from HQ staff. David and the crew arrive early and all meet at Park Museum entrance. Filming proceeds for Programme Three. Everyone stays overnight at nearest town of Holbrook.
Meanwhile: Sparks has taken Flight AA71 from Tucson to San Francisco, ready for work at Steinhart Aquarium the next day.
Day 15
Sparks meets Dr John McCosker at the Steinhart Aquarium and makes necessary arrangements for filming the following day. Parsons, Attenborough and Fisher's crew drive to Flagstaff to film fossils at the Museum of Northern Arizona with the help of Dr Breed. Afterwards they all drive north to Grand Canyon and book in at one of the Park Lodges. Scott Ransome, a hired cameraman, is also there for some special work the following day.

If the above gives some impression of the general pattern and organisation of one filming trip, it may be helpful now to focus in greater detail on one scheduled stop in the itinerary – our few days at Grand Canyon. We had come to film a sequence which would illustrate the geological succession and the immensity of the geological timescale. This was important introductory material in the first programme but it was a difficult concept to convey visually without resorting to graphics and animation, which we wished to avoid whenever possible throughout the series. Although life originated on earth more than 3,500 million years ago, the major part of our story was concerned with the last 600 million years during which time practically all life, apart from single cell forms, evolved. At Grand Canyon, rocks representing the last 225 million years were missing, but it was possible to walk downwards in time to the river at the bottom and cover the previous period of nearly 350 million years. Moreover, there were a number of fossils *in situ* in various strata which could be used to illustrate the level to which life had evolved in different geological ages.

I had made a reconnaissance of the Grand Canyon in the summer of 1976 and had met geologists at the National Park Headquarters as well as Dr Breed at Flagstaff. A number of trails zig-zagged down the canyon and my task was to choose the most appropriate one for scenic effect and for any fossils *in situ* which could be filmed along the way; for it was the visual scale of the canyon which must help to convey the geological scale of our story. Using wide-screen techniques in the cinema this would not have been difficult, but squeezing one of the grandest panoramic scenes in the world into a tiny television tube seemed, on the face of it, quite impossible. I had contemplated this problem at some length during my reconnaissance as I sat one evening at a look-out point on the South Rim. To do this, especially after the daily parade of coaches and cars had ceased, is an awesome experience. Nowhere have I found a place in the world which demonstrates so dramatically one's insignificance and inadequacy. As I watched the shadows lengthen on the canyon walls, one of the little planes that takes tourists on aerial tours of the canyon swept by, disappearing into space like an insect. It gave me a clue; with the plane for reference, one could begin to grasp the scale of the place. Taking David down one of the trails, perhaps on muleback, would be fine for the geological concept and for the fossils he found on the way but, for it to be really effective, we somehow had to relate him to other objects of recognisable size within the canyon panorama.

My reflections were interrupted that evening by the arrival of a large car bearing a Texas number plate. Two large men wearing stetsons got out and walked to the look-out wall, close to where I was sitting. They contemplated the scene and were strangely silent. Eventually one of them said: 'Well, I guess that is a mighty big hole!' The other man didn't answer for a few seconds, then tipping his hat back a little and shaking his head he replied, 'Yeah, and I'd sure like the contract for fillin' it in!' Despairing of the human race, I drove sadly back to the lodge.

The next morning I went early to one of the other look-out points where there was a good view of the Kaibab Trail – the one which seemed most appropriate for our film sequence. Near the rim of the canyon, the trail zig-zagged tightly down the near-vertical face, its pale dusty surface showing up well from a distance. With binoculars I could see the early morning walkers striding down the trail and the first of the mule-trains bearing the less hardy tourists on the start of the seven-mile journey which would take them a vertical mile down to the river. At one point the trail turned sharply round a promontory, silhouetting mules and walkers against the distant landscape. Further down, the trail stretched across a small plateau before descending out of sight again; here, too, it was possible to distinguish riders and walkers with the aid of powerful glasses. These were obviously the key points for film shots which would

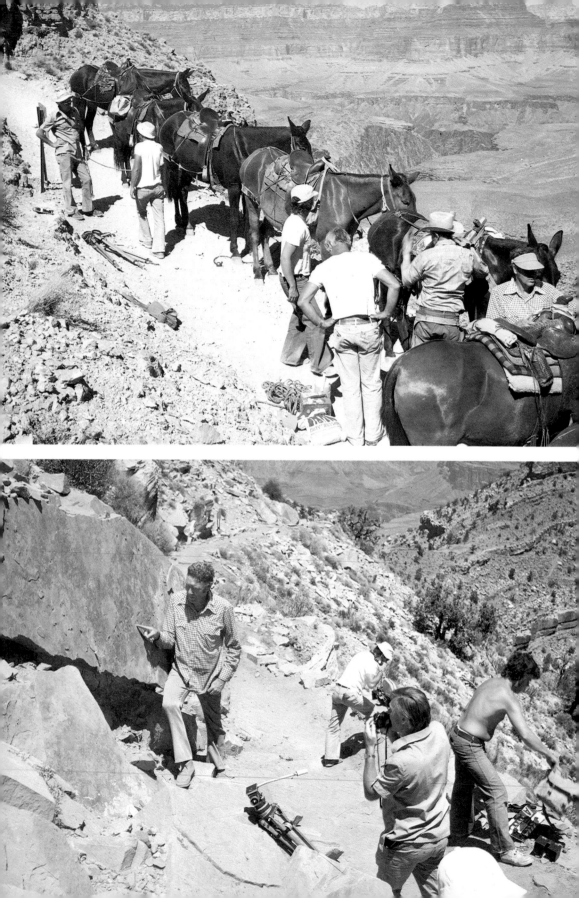

LEFT
The mule train assembles for our journey down the canyon.

LEFT
The mule train assembles for our journey down the canyon.

RIGHT
The last part of the journey: the inner canyon.

LEFT
Dr Breed finds, and David Attenborough photographs, some fossilised reptile tracks on the Kaibab Trail down the canyon.

provide viewers with a human reference scale. For this sequence, however, I would need two cameramen – one to travel down the canyon with David and one to stay at the South Rim to take those key scale shots. A 20:1 zoom lens would be needed in order to 'find' the tiny figures on the trail below; and if I could arrange for a light plane to be in such a shot as well, that would work even better. I looked at the shadows on the cliff face near the top of the trail; the sun was only just reaching the best place to film David. Obviously timing was critical and the first scene could not be taken from the South Rim until about 10 am.

So a year later Maurice, Pam and I met the concessionaire responsible for mule trains to make our arrangements for the following day. The plan was for the crew, David and me to go down the trail on mule back with additional animals to carry our equipment and provisions supplied by the concessionaire. Stationed at the vantage point on the South Rim would be Pam and Scott Ransome, the American cameraman who had been assigned to take the shots with the 20:1 zoom. Pam and I would both have radio telephones so that we could communicate throughout the day, particularly when setting up the key shots from the Rim. Our next task was to clarify arrangements with the pilot of a small plane from Grand Canyon airport who was to take a specified flight path at the exact time we would be passing a certain point on the trail. This was the moment when Scott would take an establishing wide-angle shot including the plane and then zoom slowly into the mule train rounding the promontory. There was a major communication problem here; although we could arrange for all these events to happen on the dot of 10 am it would be necessary to inform the pilot if a re-take was required. Fortunately there was a public telephone near Scott's vantage point so Pam could use this to contact the airport flight controller who could then radio the pilot on our behalf.

The next morning we all drove to the top of the Kaibab Trail where we found our guide waiting with the mule train. After loading and securing the equipment not immediately required we tested the radio telephones and the team mounted their mules. I was still suffering from intermittent back problems and at the last minute decided that I would be better off walking; other members of the team came to the same conclusion later in the day. We had asked the guide how long it would take to reach our first filming point but I allowed an extra 30 minutes for safety, as not only did I need a matching shot from Maurice at the same spot, but the crew and I would then have to find somewhere to hide so as not to be in Scott's view; for as far as the film sequence was concerned the mule train would consist only of the animals ridden by the guide and David together with some pack mules. In the event it took some time for Pam and Scott to locate us at the promontory, even using the map I had marked for them and listening to instructions on the radio-telephone; for with his 20:1 zoom fully extended Scott found that the mule train could only just be seen in the viewfinder.

A minute before ten o'clock we heard the drone of a small plane and saw our pilot flying out over the canyon before turning for his run on the route we had drawn for him. It all worked like clockwork, Pam cueing me on the radio-telephone when Scott was zooming in to the mule train so that I, in turn, could cue the guide to move forward into the most exposed part of the trail at precisely the right moment. Meanwhile, the rest of the crew and I were hiding behind some nearby rocks out of camera view. We had arranged for the pilot to make two runs so that we could repeat the operation for safety. After the second run, Scott radioed that he was satisfied and we set off down the trail to film the first fossil site – some reptile tracks in a rock face.

Scott and Pam remained on duty at the South Rim for there were two more points on the trail which I hoped Scott would cover on telephoto shots and we did not expect to reach them for several hours. As we descended the canyon the temperature rose alarmingly for at one stage the trail passes across a desert plateau; after that it drops steeply by another series of zig-zags into the Inner Canyon and down to the Colorado river. In effect the Grand Canyon is one canyon inside another; by the time we reached the rim of the Inner Canyon we were out of visual contact with Scott and Pam and I had struck two serious problems. The first was lack of water; the previous day we had understood that the mule train concessionaire would provide everything we needed for the trip, including food and water. The food had appeared, but too late we discovered there was no water. Fortunately, knowing that it was extremely hot in the canyon, and that Maurice in particular needed a lot of liquid in such conditions, we had brought our own extra supplies. Now we had to rely entirely on these (except for the guide, who had brought his own water bottle), conserving as much as possible for our cameraman. By the end of the trail when we reached the river, Maurice was almost in a state of collapse and was only just able to make the last part of the journey to our overnight cabin accommodation.

In any case, we had to abandon our last two film locations on account of a second problem; David had developed a very swollen right eye. We were not sure at the time if it was an insect bite or some kind of allergy but by early afternoon it was extremely swollen and anything but distant shots of David were out of the question. On the basis that it would take longer to climb out of the canyon than it would to go down, we had reserved the following day for travel only; but it was now clear that the final part of the film sequence depicting David's journey *down* would have to be filmed the following morning coming *up* – reversing the direction of the mule train every time we wished to film.

The next day the swelling around David's eye had gone down considerably but it was still puffy and red; at least he could see out of it, which was an improvement on the previous afternoon. All of us had been glad of a good night's rest in comfortable tree-shaded cabins in a little side valley at the base of the canyon. Refreshed and well fed, we filled up as many water bottles as we could carry and set off to face the problems of yesterday's unfinished work. The two important sound sequences with David both involved comparatively long speeches to camera. The first of these – in fact the last part of the film sequence as David arrived at the base of the canyon – was beside the river and because of the duration of the piece and the information it had to carry I would normally have filmed most of it in close-up. With David's eye still swollen this was out of the question and so Maurice composed the most visually interesting scenic shot he could with David framed against the ancient rocks he was describing.

Further up the trail the problem returned again, this time more acutely for David was required to sit on a rock, the face of which bore the fossilised imprints of the tracks of worms – some of the oldest invertebrate fossils in the canyon. For this I needed David close to camera, otherwise the fossils would not have registered in the same scene. The problem was solved by shooting the scene so that part of David's face, including his right eye, was in shadow during his speech to camera. Every time the film is shown I can see the swollen eye quite clearly and yet not one viewer has ever commented on it. But at the time, Maurice's clever photography won the day and enabled us to get back on schedule.

Chapter 19

Pictures of perseverance

Reaching other important fossil sites for *Life on Earth* provided a variety of interesting organisational problems as the locations were often comparatively inaccessible. That is not uncommon with wildlife photography, of course, but for the fossils, sound filming with David was essential and so a full crew and its equipment always had to be transported. One of the key locations for Programme Two was on a remote mountain slope near the Great Divide in the Canadian Rockies. It was there that an American geologist, Dr Charles Walcott, had stumbled upon a unique fossil site at the beginning of the century. In crumbling shale he found traces of invertebrate animals which lived about 550 million years ago, and from that site at Mount Wapta has since come a marvellous collection of worms, trilobites, crustaceans, molluscs, brachiopods and other strange forms that have no modern parallel. Only rarely are soft-bodied animals preserved as fossils but due to unusual anaerobic conditions at the time the animals died, these creatures in the Burgess Shales can be seen in exquisite detail, even the soft parts being almost photographically represented on the rock as a dark carboniferous film. Maurice Fisher had filmed many of these superb fossils at the Smithsonian Institution in Washington and the Sedgwick Museum in Cambridge but the sequence could only be completed by filming David on location where he would explain the significance of the collection and how the fossils were formed.

The Cambridge geologists were familiar with the site and were able to brief me on the methods of reaching it. Originally the only way in had been on foot or on horseback; this entailed a day's journey each way and the need to set up a camp – thereby increasing the amount of equipment to be carried. Nowadays the quickest and easiest method is by helicopter, for there is a convenient flat piece of ground to land on not more than half a mile from the fossil slopes. In due course we were able to obtain the necessary clearances from the National Park authorities in Canada, in whose domain the site lay. The small helicopter could take only three passengers, or two passengers and some equipment, on each run but as it was only a ten-minute flight it was practicable to airlift the six of us and our equipment in quite a short time.

'Airlift' is an appropriate word for the short flight from the baseball ground outside the small town of Field; for our flight was a long climb straight up the mountain-side followed by a short sweep through a pass into an adjoining range. It might seem a costly operation for such a short film sequence but, compared with the alternative of hiking and camp-

After a helicopter airlift, we film David Attenborough talking about the Burgess Shales fossils on the slopes of Moun Wapta.

ing, it was less expensive in time and wages, and certainly a lot less tiring.

Several hundred miles north of Adelaide in the Flinders Range of South Australia there is an area in which even older animal fossils have been found. Most of this Ediacaran fauna, as it is known, had been discovered on dry open scrub which we visited and where, indeed, we ourselves found fragments of worm and jellyfish fossils. On a previous visit to Adelaide I had learned from geologist Dr Richard Jenkins of locations in the mountains where it was possible to find complete fossils of jellyfish, and their relatives the sea-pens, *in situ* on the rock face. The Ediacaran fossils are exciting enough to any palaeontologist and we derived much pleasure from filming unique specimens in close-up at the museum and university in Adelaide, but to film David with such fossils *in situ* was the kind of scoop we needed in the first programme – although it could be argued that only the scientific members of our audience would really appreciate it. I asked Dr Jenkins if he would guide us to the site and he agreed to do so on condition that we did not ever disclose the exact location – for Ediacaran fossils are very valuable and there are disreputable collectors who would not hesitate to hack the fossils out of the rock. As the site was hundreds of miles from the nearest helicopter base and in any case there was no suitable landing area, this was one location requiring a long climb. We were able to find accommodation 30 miles away but had to make a very early start as Richard Jenkins informed us that the best fossils were on a rock only exposed to the sun before ten in the morning. After driving as close as possible to the site we had a tiring, two-hour scramble carrying the equipment mostly in haversacks on our backs but it was well worth the effort. For to be able to film David with his fingers on the impression of a marine organism which lived 650 million years ago, long before there was life on land and indeed before there was any creature with a backbone, was for me one of the most magical moments of the entire three-year project.

Those fossils were to be used as part of the evidence for the first true multi-celled creatures on our planet, the jellyfish and their relatives, which featured in the closing stages of the first programme. Work on modern forms of jellyfish was being undertaken by Peter Parks of Oxford Scientific Films – most of it on Lizard Island, a continental island on the edge of the Great Barrier Reef. I had selected Peter to film most of the close-up work for the first two programmes as I knew that his optical bench photography of small organisms and planktonic life was second to none. In this case it was not practicable to fly marine specimens from afar to the OSF studios in England and so it was necessary to set up Peter's equipment at a suitable location. I gave him a long checklist of species and behaviour for both programmes and he suggested that two locations would be necessary over a five-month period – one on the Great Barrier Reef and one in Bermuda, where there would be a greater opportunity to find some of the oceanic forms required.

When Peter Parks travels with his special equipment he does it in grand style. The full range of optical benches, periscopes, underwater camera housings, collecting jars, aquaria, tools, pumps, lights and so on is secured in dozens of stout wooden crates – robust containers as so much of the equipment is extremely delicate. Unfortunately it is also very heavy and something of the order of 2 tons of gear had to be shipped round the world for Peter's specialised work. Now throughout the 18-month peak period of filming for *Life on Earth*, crews were arriving and departing almost weekly but only on one other occasion did a consignment of equipment go so badly astray that Derek Anderson personally had to track it down in a Dutch freight shed and then accompany it all the way to South America – the cost of which was later reimbursed by the airline at fault. Peter Parks' numerous crates of equipment, however, turned out to be something else and produced trouble all the way.

With the comparatively modest amount of equipment carried by a standard film crew, it is often best to fly it as excess baggage although it may apparently be more expensive than separate conveyance as freight. The knowledge that camera equipment is on the same aircraft, can be personally checked through customs, and used immediately after arrival, more than makes up for the financial disadvantages. Parks' equipment was very heavy and bulky and it had to be freighted; it was therefore packed in good time so that it would be well on its way when Peter himself caught a plane for Australia. When he arrived, he discovered to his surprise and annoyance that there was no sign of his crates of equipment. A telephone call to Bristol sent Derek Anderson on the trail. At first he was assured by the agent that the equipment had been sent on the flight originally designated. However, closer investigation revealed that the consignment had been delayed by a strike of cargo handlers at London Heathrow and the crates had subsequently been put on a different carrier flying to Hong Kong, presumably for onward shipment. Unfortunately, at this stage the consignment was loaded on to more than one aircraft and it took several days of frantic telephoning before Derek was confident that everything had reached Australia; at one stage some of the crates had reached Sydney, some were in Manila, and yet others remained in Hong Kong.

It was with some trepidation, therefore, that we awaited the outcome of Peter's move to Bermuda after he had completed his work on the Great Barrier Reef. Moving the crates across the Pacific, then across the USA to New York, and finally the last leg to Bermuda, gave the airlines plenty of scope for confusion. Derek was able to check that the consignment had arrived on the American West Coast, but by then it had come within the range of the BBC Shipping Manager at our New York office. The next stage to New York also went without a hitch but then it got stuck, and once more Peter arrived at his location before his equipment. I was to meet Peter at Bermuda soon after his arrival so that we could assess the work so far and agree on priorities for future filming. I had flown to New York on the way and was in the BBC office while efforts were being made to extricate Peter's crates. Apparently there was a problem in that some of the crates were too large for the doorway of the aircraft originally destined to take them to Bermuda; so there was a delay until a suitable aircraft with wider freight doors was scheduled to fly to the island.

One result of this was that instead of Peter having his studio already fully set up for my arrival, most of the equipment was still in crates at the airport; my first task was therefore to give him a hand to get it installed. Peter had worked in Bermuda before and had always centred his operations in an old house on the tiny island of Nonsuch, formerly belonging to Dr William Beebe, the famous American naturalist. Nonsuch Island is only a few hundred yards long and is situated close to one end of the main airport runway, but separated from it by a channel. It is now Bermuda National Trust property and maintained as a reserve, the house being available to visiting naturalists and scientists for research work.

When Peter met me at the airport he had with him a friend from England, Ron Swinden, who was spending his holiday assisting Peter on diving and collecting trips. At a landing stage near the airport Ron and Peter had loaded most of the crates on a large raft supported by a series of oil drums, and this was to be towed behind a motorboat which Peter had borrowed for the occasion. It was only a short journey of a couple of miles across the bay, but there was difficulty in starting the engine. Eventually Ron and Peter got it going and began towing the raft away from the landing stage. I was on the raft, ready to help steer it out of trouble should it drift too near the jetty as we manoeuvred out into the bay. A few yards out the motor coughed, spluttered and finally died. Frantic efforts to start it again were to no avail and by now a light wind was taking the raft slowly and relentlessly towards a nearby bridge. With the weight carried by the raft there was no hope of breaking the impact and with a sickening crunch of wood it lodged against the stone arch of the bridge. One corner of the raft was ominously low and I

suspected that one of the drums had been punctured. Some of the crates were in danger of slipping and water was lapping around the base of one of them. We managed to throw a rope up on to the bridge where it was secured while Ron started the motor again; but the damage had been done and the raft was so off-balance that we had no choice but to haul it back to the jetty and unload. As the wind was still rising the transport of the crates was abandoned for the day and we set off for Nonsuch in the motorboat without them. Once more it seemed that Peter's equipment was fated.

The following day was calm and all the remaining crates were taken to the island in two journeys without mishap. Peter worked long into the night unpacking his gear and setting it up in a laboratory used by visiting scientists. By the next morning it looked like a room at the Oxford Scientific Films headquarters at Long Hanborough. Before I left Bristol I had seen all Peter's film from the Great Barrier Reef so together we could now check it off against the 'shopping list' I had originally given Peter, and discuss where the priorities lay for the remaining period at Bermuda. Something I was most anxious to obtain was film of the sessile and motile forms of certain kinds of jellyfish. One of the most common species grows in the form of a small polyp attached to rock or seaweed. At certain times of the year a horizontal division occurs, and a saucer-like depression forms at the top of the polyp; other divisions occur underneath so that the effect is rather like a stack of saucers. Eventually the top one splits off completely and swims away – a tiny larval jellyfish which will eventually grow into the large familiar form. Such jellyfish then reproduce sexually, and the resulting larvae settle on a suitable substrate to form more polyps and start the cycle all over again. This alternation of generations between sessile and motile forms was an important sequence in the first programme and our studio work in England had so far failed to provide a satisfactory sequence. I therefore told Peter that this was highest of all on the priority list, for time was running out.

That day an incredible piece of luck had already occurred. In the morning Peter had gone out in his rubber boat to make a plankton haul from the sea. Peter knew that the open sea to the south of Nonsuch Island was a rewarding area for collecting as many types of oceanic creatures occasionally drifted in and bits of sargasso weed frequently turned up bearing strange fauna. This morning had been no exception; Peter had collected several fragments of sargasso weed from the surface of the sea and on examination under the microscope he had found them to be covered with Hydrozoan polyps – members of a class of animals closely related to the true jellyfish we had been trying to film in England. Close inspection showed that the delicate branches of some polyps also bore tiny transparent vessels shaped rather like a Grecian urn; inside each were several medusae – miniature jellyfish almost ready for release into the sea.

When Peter told me this I rushed into the laboratory to inspect the specimens immediately. Although quite different from the species we had previously been filming in England, they were nevertheless just as good to illustrate the transition between sessile and motile forms. As I

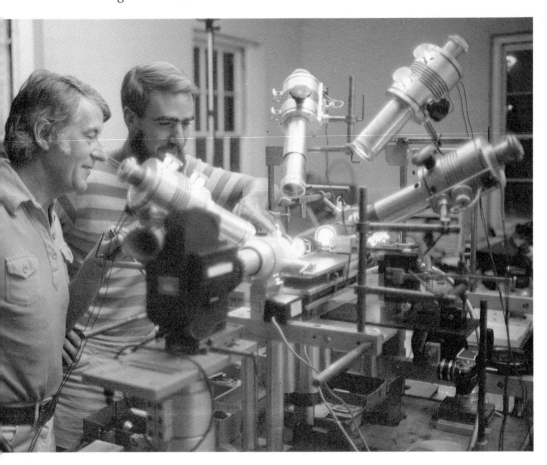

watched the delicate little vessel a medusa inside twitched suddenly as if trying to free itself. It was difficult to imagine how it could possibly squeeze out of the narrow opening at the top. Elsewhere under the microscope I could see free medusae swimming through the tracery of the polyp stems indicating that other vessels had already discharged, so perhaps the 'birth' of presently-enclosed subjects was imminent.

Peter transferred the fragment of weed bearing the polyps to a miniature aquarium measuring a few centimetres; he placed it on his optical bench, adjusting the lighting until he could obtain a perfect view of the medusae in their vessel. And then he made himself comfortable for a long wait. We stayed talking long into the evening but nothing happened. I was still suffering slightly from jet-lag so Peter insisted that I retire to bed while he waited up for a few more hours. In the morning I rose before Peter, anxiously awaiting his news. When he appeared he looked tired and his expressionless face gave nothing away.

'Do you want the bad news or the good news first?', he enquired.

'Bad news first', I replied impatiently.

'Well, I stuck it out, staring at that thing until half past 11. And then I couldn't wait any longer – I had to go and have a pee! When I got back the damn things had gone – swum away!' I was stunned. To have been so close to success and then failed was heartbreaking. 'And then I had another look in the dish', Peter went on, 'and I found another vessel full of medusae. So I focused on that and about three this morning it all happened. It should all be in there.' He tapped the yellow square box containing a hundred-foot roll of film.

If we had had a bottle of champagne we would have opened it there and then, even though I had not yet seen the results on the screen. But celebrations would have been premature for that precious roll of film very nearly had a disastrous end. I had to fly to New York for some meetings a few days later before returning to England, so I arranged to take with me the batch of film for processing – including our little jellyfish sequence. On the morning of my departure there was a strong wind blowing across the bay and the waves were so high that Peter expressed doubt as to whether or not I would be able to leave the island. However, it was important that I should reach New York that day and so, after further consideration, Ron agreed to get me to the airport, although it was quite clear that I was going to get extremely wet in the process. Peter had spare waterproofs so I put these on over an old pair of trousers and a sweater, packing the rest of my clothes into a suitcase. The precious rolls of film were put into a sealed polythene bag, which was then surrounded by a towel and placed in the middle of my packed clothes. Whatever happened I was determined that the film would get through dry and intact. The suitcase was wedged into the bow of the rubber boat and I sat as far forward as possible to prevent the boat flipping over, for we were heading straight into the face of the wind.

At first we appeared to make hardly any progress at all. Ron eventually managed to steer towards a more sheltered area but we were shipping water at an alarming rate and soon the level inside was much the same as the level outside. Only furious bailing prevented us from becoming completely waterlogged and immobile. The suitcase was sitting in six inches of water by the time we slipped alongside the jetty near the airport buildings half-an-hour later and it had been severely damaged by a battering against a fuel tank. I opened up the case and seawater poured out of it; every inch of clothing was saturated, but inside the towel the polythene bag was tightly sealed and the film perfectly dry. I was so relieved that it took me a few minutes to realise that I was in no state to travel on an aircraft. Fortunately we had left Nonsuch in good time, fearing a misadventure, and I now had half an hour to spare before the check-in time. I secured a taxi from the airport forecourt and asked the driver to take me to Georgetown, a few miles away. There I bought the only large suitcase available in the local stores together with a shirt and a pair of trousers two sizes too large. I changed in a nearby toilet and, much to the taxi driver's amazement, placed the two suitcases on the pavement and wrung the sea out of my clothes before transferring them. So, still dripping water and smelling of the sea, I made my way by plane and taxi to my Manhattan hotel, under the suspicious eyes of airline officials, customs officers, taxi drivers and finally the hotel receptionist who, for a moment, looked as if she was going to call the manager.

In my hotel room I quickly ran the bath full of water, extracted the precious package of film from the suitcase – and emptied the rest of the contents straight into the bath. I only hoped the hotel had a good laundry and valet service. The final good fortune with the jellyfish was one small incident in the broad filming pattern of 'some you win, some you lose'. In general, however, we usually won – although the variability of seasons all over the world gave us plenty of headaches. The yucca pollination story was a case in point.

Yucca plants are common in Central America and in the southern areas of the United States, and in the spring they send up tall spikes bearing a profusion of cream-coloured flowers. There are many kinds, each pollinated by its own special moth. The story of how the yucca moth goes about this is a classic one, appearing frequently in the scientific literature but not, to my knowledge, on film. The relationship between the yucca and the moth is binding and, in a manner of speaking, has taken both plant and insect up an evolutionary cul-de-sac, since if either should become extinct the other would probably suffer a similar fate. The yucca can only be pollinated by the moth, and the moth needs the yucca for food for its larvae. The relationship begins when the female moth collects pollen from the flower's anthers and makes a little ball of it. She then proceeds to a flower which is ready for pollination and wriggles down inside the flower, using her ovipositor to penetrate the side of an ovary wall. She lays her eggs inside the ovary and then climbs up to the green-tipped stigma and smears some of the pollen from the ball she is carrying on to the receptive part. The procedure is then repeated with other ovaries. So the flower gains from having an efficient pollinating agent; and the moth gains by ensuring that her larvae, after hatching, will have a rich source of food to hand. The whole arrangement is kept in balance for the larvae do not eat all the seeds and there are plenty of seed-pods left to develop to ensure the next generation of the plant.

When faced with the problems of filming this sequence, my first thoughts were, as usual, to find any botanists or entomologists who had

OVERLEAF

LEFT
A fragment of weed bearing many hydrozoan polyps.

TOP RIGHT
A tiny vessel (gonetheca) *containing several medusae.*

BOTTOM RIGHT
Medusae after 'birth'.

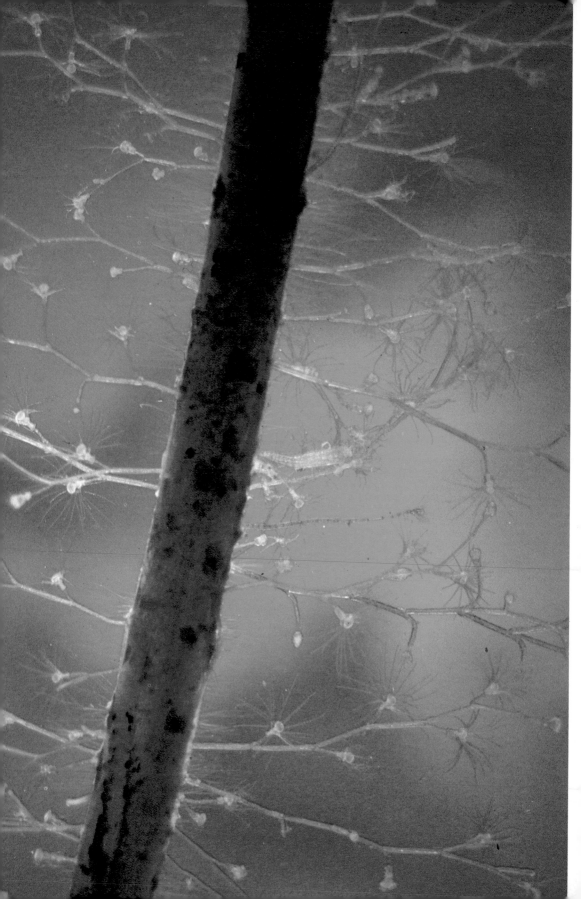

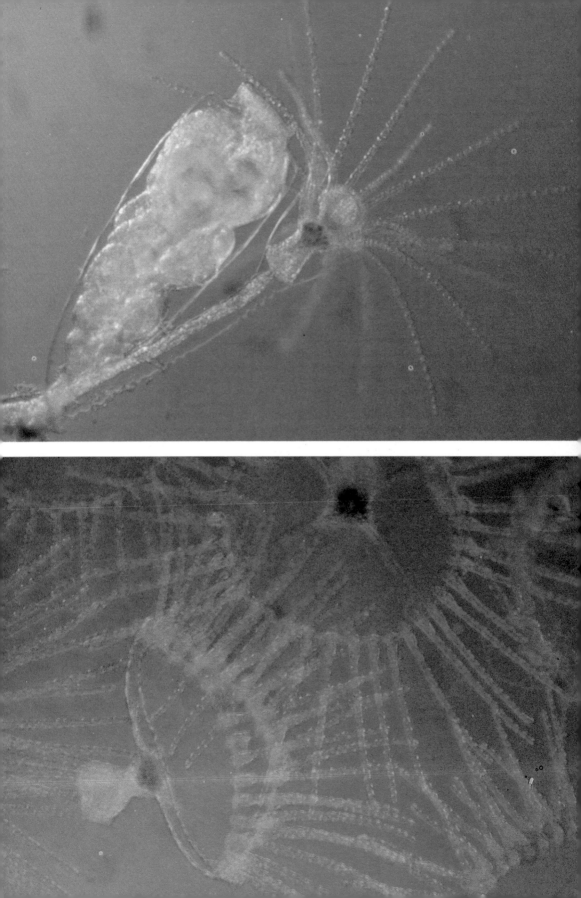

recently been working on yucca pollination; and then to ask them to co-operate with one of the cameramen from Oxford Scientific Films. Correspondence with the experts suggested that there were two courses of action open to us: one was to choose a yucca species which is normally pollinated at night, in which the flowers were fairly open and observation is therefore easy; the second course of action was to work with another species in which pollination occurs during the afternoon, but here the snag was that the flowers do not open widely and therefore filming the action of the moth would be extremely difficult.

David Thompson of Oxford Scientific Films was scheduled to work in Central America on social insects during the spring of 1978 and, if the seasons in California were on time it appeared that David would be able to tackle the yucca story at the end of his assignment in Costa Rica. So during his work there we carefully monitored the progress of the season in California through one of our consultants at San Diego, only to find that it was running very late. It was almost certain that the peak of the yucca moth activity would fall out of the period when Thompson was available. Derek Anderson studied his chart and informed me that Densey Clyne and Jim Frazier would be completing an assignment in Indonesia just prior to the predicted yucca moth period, so we arranged to fly them across the Pacific, transferring responsibility for the sequence to them.

The timing was perfect. They contacted our local adviser who showed them the areas where yuccas were most common and where observations on pollination had been previously made. Jim decided to work on a species which was pollinated by day – one which did not grow so tall that it was out of camera range. However, he discovered that the moths moved fast and unpredictably from flower to flower so he systematically cut observation windows in the petals of dozens of flowers on one stalk before he began work. As a bonus, however, this particular species of moth was black. It therefore showed up well against the creamy white petals. Within three days Jim had successfully filmed everything I required and he and Densey were soon heading back to Sydney to have another attempt at the kowaris.

In the end, filming of the yucca moth was only possible because we had a budget which could cover the cost of flying Densey and Jim across the Pacific at a few days' notice. Their actual time on location was minimal and this was true for much of the filming for the series. The money was used where we knew we could get value from it; and *that* depended on intensive research. We were using some of the best wildlife camera teams in the world; but much of the success with individual sequences was due to the fact that for once the Unit had a large enough budget to exploit fully the level of research and production expertise which had been built up over the years.

All over the world biologists seemed to be eager to help us. For example, in Lawrence, Kansas, entomologists at the university kept a colony of tiny eusocial bees active through the winter under controlled conditions so that we could film their behaviour at a time which fitted in with one of our complex itineraries; in New Caledonia, Dr Peter Ward, a palaentologist from Columbus, Ohio, got in touch as soon as he had collected specimens of nautilus for us to film; and in Ruanda Dr Diane

Fossey led David Attenborough and John Sparks' camera team up into the forest to meet the mountain gorillas which she had been studying for so long. When John returned from Africa he was delighted with the success in filming David with wild gorillas but was concerned about the tameness of the animals.

'No one is ever going to believe they're wild!' he moaned, as we watched the rushes in the viewing theatre. Then on to the screen came scenes of David lying in the undergrowth with young gorillas playing around him and one actually sitting on top of him. They were sensational. John was almost embarrassed by them.

'Those were taken when we'd virtually finished work, everything was getting out of hand then.' At that point a young gorilla walked right up to Martin Saunders' camera, peered in from a few inches away and stuck a finger on the glass. 'See what I mean?' John said. 'We can't possibly use any of this stuff.' However the shots of David submerged beneath gorillas *did* go in eventually and the public *did* believe they were wild animals. Indeed many viewers rated those scenes as among the most memorable of the entire series.

During the last 18 months the power house of the production moved to Ron Martin's cutting room and Alec Brown's assembly room next door. We had decided to edit two programmes one year ahead of transmission – Richard's Programme Six on amphibians and John's Programme Seven on reptiles; this was to see, at the earliest possible stage, how such a variety of material, filmed by so many different cameramen in so many parts of the world, would come together when edited according to the script. To be of any value in this respect the programmes had to be taken right through to the last stages of production – composition of music by Edward Williams, writing of the narration by David and the mixing of the sound tracks. Only then would we be able to judge if the format was working. For example, was it annoying to the viewer that David should begin a sentence in South America and end it in Australia? Were the programmes paced at the right speed? Was the level of narration correct? Was there too much music?

To answer these questions and many more we arranged a number of special screenings to a variety of invited audiences: a party of office cleaners from the BBC, a sixth form of a local grammar school, a Parent-Teacher Association, and so on. At the end of each screening viewers were asked to fill in a simple questionnaire of the multiple-choice question type. The results of the questionnaires were carefully analysed and proved very encouraging. One thing was quite clear; the majority of viewers found the photography quite stunning. The answers to some questions revealed that a few important pieces of information were not going home. We looked at the sequences concerned very carefully, and then re-edited them, in one case adding extra graphics to clarify a difficult evolutionary point. This luxury of having a second chance would not be available on the other 11 programmes but our experience with the two pilot films gave us no excuse for not getting the very best out of our material.

From the spring of 1978 onwards Ron Martin worked at the final editing of the assemblies, which had been slowly building up over the

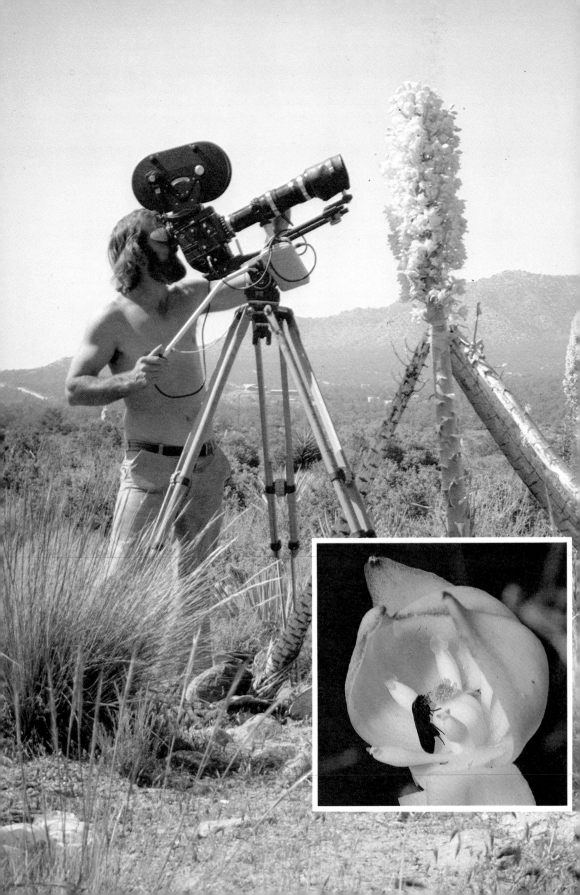

previous months. Now he began at Programme One and brought them off the production line every month, ready for Edward Williams to write his music and David Attenborough to write his narration; meanwhile, Alec Brown and his two assistants, Peter Simpkin and David Barrett, began laying down the effects tracks. The last two programmes were still in the cutting rooms when the first went on the air on Tuesday, January 16 1979. We were in an optimistic mood, having given a preview to the national press a few weeks before at the British Academy of Film and Television Arts. The response had been good and a few television correspondents were heralding the series as something special. Our main worry was: would viewers be put off by the opening programme? The most serious disadvantages of the series' structure lay in that programme which included such things as the origin of life, bacteria, blue-green algae, protozoa, microfossils and corals – not to mention such important but difficult concepts as DNA, photosynthesis, and the geological succession. With such material how could we expect to hold the large audience we hoped for later in the series? Apart from the overall high production standards which we had set ourselves, my hopes were pinned on two factors: the outstanding photography of Peter Parks; and David Attenborough's charisma.

The morning after the first programme had been transmitted David telephoned me as soon as I reached the office. 'I think we've done it!' he exclaimed. I, too, had seen the reviews and was able to agree with him. Furthermore, David had received a warm response from people in the street as he went to collect the papers. If the audience reacted favourably to bacteria and corals, what would their reaction be to Richard's colourful amphibians and John's amazing reptiles?

The answers were provided by the viewing figures and audience reactions as the weeks went by. BBC 2 was running the series twice weekly – on Tuesdays at 8:10 and Sundays at 7:15, and the total audience for the first programme was about nine million, an exceptionally high figure for a documentary on that channel. By the end of the series, total weekly audiences for the two transmissions were reaching the 15 million mark. The Reaction Index, a measure of the audience's appreciation of the programme, broke records too, RIs, as they are known, tend to be higher than average for wildlife programmes, but we are usually well satisfied when programmes achieve figures of 80 or more. The first *Life on Earth* clocked 83 (85 for the repeat) and by the end of the series the RI had twice climbed into the 90s, breaking the Unit's previous record of 89 (for a Sielmann and an Ashby film many years before).

Perhaps the most deeply satisfying result from the Unit's point of view came from the response of the scientific community. To achieve high praise from the viewing public and television critics alike was heart-warming indeed, but to receive bouquets from biologists made the project especially worthwhile. For we had striven from the outset to produce a series which would not only have the widest public appeal but also have enough scientific integrity to make it a valuable teaching aid. Several hundred biologists had willingly helped us over the three years; it was only right that they and their colleagues should get something back from their investment.

Chapter 20

Towards 2000

In December 1979, the Natural History Unit received a Christmas present; at the Unit party Philip Daly, head of the Network Production Centre at Bristol, stopped the festivities for a few moments to make a short announcement. Alisdair Milne, managing director, BBC Television, had authorised that the Unit should now be given departmental status, with the consequent re-designation of the senior post as head – rather than editor. It was a proud moment for us all and an emotional one for me as I was the only person in the room who had remained with the Unit since it had been established 22 years before. Furthermore, I was now the holder of the post which was being re-designated, for Mick Rhodes had left England to take up an executive position with a Public Broadcasting Station in Boston, Massachusetts, during the summer of 1978, and I had been appointed in his place.

Angela Rippon and Phil Drabble – two of the regular presenters of In the Country *in recent years.*

For some years the Unit had really been too large for its name as, within the BBC, 'Unit' usually denotes a modest sized production group associated with a regular series *within* a department. It is therefore somewhat misleading to apply the word 'Unit' to a staff of 70 people annually producing over 200 natural history programmes for the BBC's radio and television services, not to mention its Sound and Film Libraries and the specialised service which it provides to other departments such as Schools, Open University, Science and Features, and so on. Nevertheless, when Phil Daly consulted me before the announcement was made I agreed that, even if we were given departmental status for internal administrative reasons, we should still continue to be known to the general public – and the scientific world – as The BBC Natural History *Unit*; and that is what we will always be – even if we grow to twice our present size.

Alisdair Milne's gesture was, I am sure, one of confidence – made not only in the light of *Life on Earth* but because the controllers were now able to look to the Unit for a regular and significant contribution to programme schedules. Indeed, the Unit now has a wide spectrum of output on radio and television to suit all tastes and ages and the most popular programmes regularly attract very large audiences indeed. For example, in one series of six *Wildlife on One* films, four of them were in the JICTAR Top Ten audience figures for the week and one of them represented the largest BBC tv audience from any department that week. Viewers make a point of turning the set on – or the channel switch over – for such programmes; a single special edition of *Wildlife on One* about urban foxes was transmitted in the summer of 1981 and seven million *additional* viewers switched on compared to the programme before – and that was at a time when audiences were generally at a low ebb.

The question we all ask ourselves is – can it go on? The answer, of course, is that it must; television is itself stimulating even greater public interest in natural history and the increase in leisure time will provide more potential. To maintain our high audience appreciation, however, we must raise production standards continually and find fresh ways of presenting our material. Our first faltering steps in dramatisation with *The Insect Man* have already been overshadowed by John Sparks' series *The Discovery of Animal Behaviour* in which key field research and experimental work by leading ethologists is re-enacted. Much of our future progress will inevitably depend on new technology; and, surprisingly for a Unit which has relied so heavily on film during its first 25 years, the key word for the 1980s may well be *video*.

Apart from magazine programmes which are regularly presented from the main television studio at Bristol, the Natural History Unit had on only a few occasions used electronic cameras for wildlife broadcasting in the field. Then in 1975, just as I was preparing to begin work on *Life on Earth*, Peter Bale took on an interesting new project for *The World About Us* covering the research of Dr David McDonald on wild foxes in Oxfordshire. Much of this work took place at night, so it raised once again the vexed question of how to photograph animal behaviour in the dark. In this case, the option of conditioning captive or semi-captive animals to light was not available as the observation and trapping of wild foxes was involved. If working on film, the only method available would be the use of image intensifiers – only viable at dusk or on a bright moonlit night. Peter, although an experienced film producer, had much of his early training with electronic cameras and his mind immediately began thinking of the possibilities resulting from the sensitivity of these cameras – particularly in respect of the infra-red part of the spectrum.

Peter had enough experience with his engineering colleagues to know that when you have an enormous technical problem it is best to take the 'I am right in thinking, am I not, that it is absolutely impossible to . . .' approach. It worked. John Noakes, from the BBC's Technical Investigations Department at the Acton outside broadcast headquarters and his Bristol colleague, Paul Townsend, immediately made an extensive study of invisible light sources. From ex-government stock and equipment found lying around in various places in the BBC they constructed four 'infra-red' lamps which gave just enough 'black' illumination to produce a good quality monochrome picture on a silicon diode vidicon tube. The camera chassis was a redundant one left over from the old Bristol news studio and all the other ancillary equipment was built or 'discovered' by Townsend and his colleagues.

So on a dark July night in 1975 the equipment was taken to the edge of a field on an Oxfordshire farm and set up near a baited fox-trap used by zoologist, Dr McDonald. A quarter of a mile away the remote control equipment was operated from a parked caravan and there, using panning, tilting and zooming mechanisms, the Bristol team picked up

Badgerwatch.
The interior of the caravan, parked a few hundred yards away, from which cameras and infra-red lights were controlled. Peter Bale, producer, is in the left foreground.

their first wild fox. The dog fox actually walked between the legs of the camera tripod, past the infra-red light stands and towards the baited trap. The fox hungrily consumed the tin of dog food which had been placed outside the trap but did not fall for the dead chicken inside the trap; so McDonald did not on that occasion get the specimen he required for his radio telemetry experiments.

However, the early success, achieved within an hour of first switching on the equipment, inspired Bale and Townsend to greater things and the next step was to install the camera – and larger, improved lights – at a disused tennis court in McDonald's study area where he planned to observe the behaviour of a pair of foxes in a controlled area. Several hours of behaviour were eventually recorded on tape and provided a valuable ingredient in the programme which Peter Bale made for *The World About Us*, called *The Night of the Fox*.

The next logical, but daring, step was to consider the possibilities of using such equipment 'live'. Wild foxes' nocturnal habits are so wide-ranging that they would not have provided a good subject for such a venture but a broadcast from a badger sett in May or early June when there is regular family activity at the sett above ground seemed promising. During 1976 a second camera was developed and in the early spring of 1977 elaborate preparations were made at a badger sett in the Cotswolds for a series of late-night outside broadcasts during one week in May. One of the cameras was mounted on a high rostrum and the

FACING PAGE
More dramatised scenes from The Discovery of Animal Behaviour.

BELOW LEFT
Niko Tinbergen observes the response of his sticklebacks to the red colour of a Dutch Post Office van (late 1930s).

LEFT
John Sparks on location in Wyoming filming Lewis Henry Morgan who studied beavers in 1865.

BELOW
A remote-controlled camera and infra-red lamp in position for Badgerwatch.

other in a 200-year-old beech tree overlooking the sett. The equipment was in operation two weeks before the live broadcasts and a number of recordings were made as an insurance against badgers failing to turn up on the five transmission nights. In fact the badgers obliged, and for the first time in television history live pictures of wild badgers were brought into the homes of the viewers all over the country – although some of the recorded material was also used to hold interest when things went quiet.

The next use of the remote control camera equipment and infra-red lighting was not for a live broadcast but as a facility for recording the behaviour of urban foxes in Bristol. A long-term research project by Dr Stephen Harris was the starting point of a *Wildlife on One* project produced by Mike Beynon, and the night sequences were shot partly with film cameras using image intensifiers and partly with a one-camera mobile adaptation of the 'Watch' equipment – in this case, however, using available street lighting. The equipment was to prove most valuable when it came to recording the behaviour of a fox family in its 'earth'. In Bristol, foxes frequently give birth to their cubs under garden sheds or in the basements of large Victorian houses – perhaps gaining access through some dislodged stonework or an air vent. Since it would be impracticable to move in the bulky electronic equipment after a wild fox had given birth, Dr Harris suggested that the remote-control camera should be used to study the behaviour of a pair of semi-tame animals enclosed within a restricted area. It so happened that the BBC had recently acquired a derelict house on its Whiteladies Road site but would not be able to start renovations for some months. It had a cellar which

was ideal for reproducing the exact conditions of a number of local fox earths, and so a large window was installed in it through which two cameras could view the foxes using infra-red illumination. The remote controls were conveniently situated in a small room close to the news studio. A high fence was built surrounding the house and its adjoining garden, and the property placed out of bounds, except to Dr Harris and a few engineers. The foxes were introduced to their new home in the autumn of 1978 and everyone waited hopefully.

Foxes mate in the early part of the year, and although there was some interaction with other foxes in the neighbourhood and plenty of evidence of vocalisation, no one ever saw the BBC pair mating. There was some dismay, therefore, in the spring when we passed the period in which it was expected that the vixen might give birth. True, Dr Harris thought that she had put on some weight but there came a point when it appeared that the experiment had completely failed. The cameras were turned on all the time now and the output sent around the 'ring main' – the closed circuit system which takes broadcast channels and local studio output into various production offices. The vixen remained asleep for much of the day, curled in a corner of the cellar on which the camera was trained. She had excavated a deep depression so that unfortunately the lower part of her body was hidden from view and it was unlikely we would be able to record the birth even if she was pregnant. Then, close to a few days of abandoning the enterprise, some strange new sounds were heard from the earth one lunchtime. A secretary had the monitor turned on in Peter Bale's office at the time and thought that she saw a tiny head appear for a brief moment. Within a few hours we knew for sure that there were four cubs and recordings were being made.

The electronic cameras see into the darkness and millions of viewers watch a live transmission of wild badgers.

LEFT AND RIGHT
Scenes from Foxwatch, *including (right) the vixen with her newborn cubs.*

Rolf Harris, Tony Soper and Sir Peter Scott in the hide for Birdwatch *from Slimbridge.*

RIGHT
During one Sunday, viewers were able to see wild geese and these wild Bewick's swans 'live' from Slimbridge.

Although very little happened in the earth for hours on end the pictures on our office monitors had a strange hypnotic effect, and it proved to be a great temptation not to sit and stare. There was a fascination in being a voyeur, for the foxes were unaware of the cameras in the darkness of their 'earth' whilst we could see the most intimate family behaviour in well-defined pictures. If *we* were fascinated by it all then perhaps the general public would appreciate the foxes too. We sent the pictures up the line to the Television Centre and asked Brian Wenham, Controller BBC 2, if he would like to run a series of late night programmes – *Foxwatch*. He accepted the offer and the first broadcast was on Tuesday, May 8 1979; over a period of two months nine broadcasts were transmitted so that viewers would be able to see the development of the cubs. Like *Badgerwatch* before it, *Foxwatch* became a great talking point in pubs and in the morning commuter buses and trains, and so much interesting behaviour was recorded both on and off the air that a special edition of *Wildlife on One* was compiled from the recordings shortly afterwards. It was not until two years later that the complete programme, *Twentieth Century Fox*, which Mike Beynon started filming in September 1978, was finally transmitted; but by then such outstanding material on foxes in the streets of Bristol had been filmed that the infra-red material from the earth only justified a minor sequence.

RIGHT
Electronic cameras will have an increasingly important role in the future. Here one is being used to look at the head of a bulldog ant on Jim Frazier's optical bench in Sydney.

I found these electronic developments within the Natural History Unit very rewarding and the 'live' broadcasts seemed to rekindle some of the old excitement of the television medium. The number of topics available

New wildlife recordings are now made in stereo whenever possible; John Burton with recording engineer Dave Toombs.

at night is strictly limited; there are, however, other possibilities for live coverage of wild animal life in Britain during the day – particularly with birds. The notion arose that, by visiting a well-chosen site, we might offer viewers a new bird-watching experience by making a number of outside broadcasts throughout a single day. This idea was put to Bill Cotton, then Controller BBC 1, and much to my delight he agreed to the experiment. The first set of *Birdwatch* programmes was transmitted from the Wildfowl Trust at Slimbridge in February 1980. That particular location was chosen because a large number of wild geese and wild Bewick's Swans could be almost guaranteed, but having made the format work, the 1981 location was more adventurous – the Royal Society for the Protection of Birds Reserve at Minsmere in Suffolk. There the 'bankers' were the avocets which breed close to the RSPB observation hides but the BBC engineers mounted a complex operation with six cameras which on the day of transmission brought no less than 25 wild bird species into viewers' living rooms. This type of broadcast has brought a sense of occasion back into some of the Unit's output and I am sure that it is here to stay and will develop into even more adventurous forms as new lightweight electronic equipment becomes available.

For the electronic revolution which has been made possible by the development of micro-chips will undoubtedly have a profound effect on wildlife television as well as the rest of the industry. The number of live outside broadcasts it is possible and sensible to undertake will not be large in any given year but the portable electronic camera and recorder will have many advantages over the film camera. Of prime importance is the facility for continuous recording, wiping the tape if nothing happens. Also possible is remote control operation underwater or underground – the pictures monitored by an operator some distance away. Furthermore the Unit's extensive and fast-growing film and tape library will be computer-filed and cross-indexed, making retrieval for the production of video books and video discs more speedy and efficient. In the 1980s, the Natural History Unit will undoubtedly be communicating with its public in many more ways than through existing broadcast channels; soon bird-watchers may use a video disc to call up pictures of a species they wish to identify and, if they have a receiver capable of showing Teletext, they may also use this disc to obtain pages of written data about the same species.

If the last 25 years have seen the establishment and development of a new specialised branch of the industry through a subject – natural history – which seems to have suited television so well, then I am confident that the next 10 years will see its true fulfilment through all these new opportunities. For it was opportunity, not chance, which brought the Natural History Unit to Bristol; an opportunity seen first by Frank Gillard after he was appointed West Regional Programme Director in 1945. He began a policy of specialisation at Bristol – choosing in particular agriculture and horticulture, country life and country sports, archaeology and natural history – and in the autumn of 1945 he brought in an old friend of his, Desmond Hawkins, to be Features producer with responsibility for developing natural history output. Frank Gillard regards that recruitment as the best thing he ever did for the BBC.

And, as a member of the Natural History Unit, I cannot argue with *that*!

Glossary of film and television terms

Answer print The first print produced by the laboratories after the negative has been cut.

Atmosphere track A specially recorded sound tape to convey the general background noises of a scene.

Blimp Ideally a sound-proof case for a film camera to prevent noise from the camera reaching the microphone (and in natural history work, from shy animals).

Camera dolly A trolley, often running on specially laid rails, on which the camera is mounted to provide smooth travelling shots.

Clapperboard The hinged board on which is chalked details of a take and which is clapped together to provide a guide for synchronising sound and picture in the case of a sound take.

Crab To move the camera sideways.

Cutaway A different shot from the main action which enables the film editor to condense the action.

Cutting copy The film editor's working print, assembled from the rushes.

Cutting ratio The relationship between the film exposed and the film used after completion of the editing process.

Cutting room The room in which the film editor and his or her assistant works.

Dissolve See **Mix.**

Dub To blend speech, effects and music into a pleasing and artistic mixture.

Dubbing mixer The technician responsible for operating the control console on which all the sound tracks are mixed in a dubbing theatre.

Dubbing theatre A special studio in which there are a number of sound bays to reproduce sound tracks which can be mixed together artistically whilst the film is projected. There are also facilities for recording special effects and narration.

Dupe neg A duplicate negative produced from a specially made fine-grain print or from a colour positive.

Edge numbers See **Key numbers.**

Editor Often short for *film editor*; also the person in overall charge of a documentary series.

Establishing shot Usually the first wide-angle shot in a sequence which identifies the general view, principal characters, etc.

Extension tube A cylindrical attachment between camera and lens which alters the effective focal length of the lens for filming small forms of life.

Film speed A measure of the sensitivity to light of a film stock usually on the ASA scale; the higher the ASA number is, the greater the sensitivity.

Freeze frame A single frame of film which is optically repeated many times by the laboratories so that a split second of action may be studied for several seconds. This may also be achieved electronically in the case of video.

Gallery The production control room of a studio.

Hand-held Sequences in which the camera is not on a tripod but carried by the cameraman.

Image intensifier A special adaptor used between lens and film camera involving fibre optics and electronic amplification; it permits filming in very low levels of light such as bright moonlight.

Joiner See **Splicer.**

Key numbers Consecutive numbers which appear at regular intervals along the side of the negative; as they are printed on to the rushes they allow fast and accurate matching of the negative to the cutting copy when neg cutting takes place.

Labs The laboratories for developing and printing film and making special optical effects.

Lay With film sound to arrange various tracks in the cutting room so that when mixed together in a dubbing theatre they can be blended artistically and remain synchronised with the picture.

Macrophotography Extreme close-up photography of small subjects (such as tiny insects) usually with the aid of extension tubes and often on an optical bench.

Magazine The lightproof case which contains the film stock and clips on to the camera.

Matching shots The pictures from two or more cameras in which the size of the subject is the same.

MCR Mobile Control Room for an outside broadcast.

Mix To change slowly between two images or sound tracks. (Also used to denote the period in a dubbing theatre during which the sound tracks are blended.)

Monitor A high quality television receiver used in a studio, control room, etc.

Montage A sequence of usually short film shots edited together in a dramatic way.

Mute Film without sound.

Neg cutting The process of finding the negative to match the cutting copy and joining it up accordingly.

OB Outside broadcast.

Off cuts Unwanted sections of film taken out by the film editor.

Optical bench In natural history work a precision device which allows the camera to film extremely small subjects; this calls for great stability and the means to move the subject accurately and smoothly on three axes in front of the camera.

Out of vision (OOV) Refers to dialogue spoken when the speaker is not appearing in front of camera.

PAL Phase Alternate Line. The colour television transmission system adopted by Britain and most of Western Europe.

Parabolic reflector A concave dish of paraboloid shape which may be placed on the ground or on a tripod and directed towards a distant subject in order to concentrate sounds on a microphone placed at its focal point.

Post production The processes of film-making which take place after shooting has been completed, ie, editing, dubbing, etc.

Rushes The sequences of film processed overnight by the laboratories in order that the previous day's work may be quickly assessed. In natural history work in remote locations this may only be possible at intervals of a week or longer, but the same term is used.

Scanner The MCR of an outside broadcast.

Self-blimped A film camera in which the normal housing damps the mechanical noise to such an extent that a separate blimp is not needed.

Show print The carefully graded print made for transmission.

Splicer A device for joining film shots in the cutting room. Formerly done by overlapping the film and using film cement; cutting copies are now normally joined with a device that butt-joins the shots and connects them with a strip of transparent adhesive tape.

Sprocket holes The perforations at regular intervals down the sides of film which engage in the sprocket wheels of cameras and editing equipment.

Take An attempt at a film shot which may be repeated under the same number, ie, take 2, take 3.

Take board See **Clapperboard**.

Telecine A machine which electronically scans film and converts the visual information into a television signal.

Telephoto lens A lens of long focal length for filming distant subjects and frequently used in natural history work.

Time lapse filming Exposing a single frame of film at regular intervals with the camera in a fixed position; when projected the film will show the action many times faster (eg, flowers opening).

Track To move the camera following a moving subject; hence *tracking shot*.

Trims Short pieces of film cut out in the last stages of editing.

Wild track Sound recorded without the camera running.

Zoom lens A lens with continuously adjustable focal length which allows the subject to be brought effectively closer (or taken further away) during filming.

Glossary of biological terms

Anaerobic Living in the absence of free oxygen.

Anther The tip of the stamen of a flower that contains pollen.

Blue-green algae Primitive organisms capable of photosynthesis but more closely related to bacteria than true algae.

Brachiopods A group of animals with two-valved shells superficially resembling molluscs but not closely related. They were much more common in prehistoric times.

Carapace The dorsal part of the external skeleton of animals such as crabs; also applied to the 'shell' of tortoises and turtles.

Cephalapods The group of molluscs with well-developed heads which includes octopus, squids, cuttlefish, etc.

Commensalism Describes animals living in close association but with little mutual influence (eg, two creatures sharing the same burrow).

Convergence Process of evolution which produces close similarity in some characteristics between animals originally very different in form (eg, dolphins, although mammals, have evolved into a fish-like form).

Crustaceans Large group of animals which includes crabs, lobsters, shrimps, etc.

Diatoms Single-celled algae common in marine and freshwater plankton. The cell walls contain silica and often appear beautifully sculptured under the microscope.

DNA Deoxyribonucleic acid; what genes are made of, the material of inheritance.

Entomology The study of insects.

Eusocial Term used for primitively social insects.

Invertebrates Animals without backbones.

Mandible In insects, one of the pair of mouthparts which does most of the crushing of food; in mammals, the lower jaw.

Marsupials A group of mammals whose young are born in a very undeveloped state and are then reared in a pouch.

Medusa A free-swimming and umbrella-shaped jellyfish.

Molluscs Large, and mainly aquatic, group of animals without backbones, often with a hard shell; includes mussels, snails, cephalapods, etc.

Neonate Newly-born animal.

Neuropterous Of the order of endopterygote insects including alderflies, lacewings, etc.

Olfactory Of sense of smell.

Ornithology The study of birds.

Ovipositor An organ at the hind end of the abdomen of female insects through which eggs are laid. Often very long and capable of piercing hard ground or tree bark.

Palaentology The study of fossils.

Paramecium A genus of ciliated Protozoa – single-celled animals.

Phylogenetic Based on closeness of evolutionary descent.

Pineal eye Part of the brain thought to be sensitive to light. In some primitive reptiles it lies near the skin surface and since it functions as a photoreceptor organ it is sometimes known as the third eye.

Plankton Small forms of life in seas or lakes which float and drift, mostly near the surface.

Polyp A sedentary form of a coelenterate (one of a large group of animals containing hydroids, jellyfish, sea anemones, corals, etc). Of a cylindrical form, it has a mouth surrounded by tentacles.

Protozoa Group of animals differing from all others in consisting of only one cell (but differing from bacteria and blue-green algae in having a well-defined nucleus).

Radio-telemetry The means by which information about a wild animal may be continuously monitored by a remote observer through radio; necessitates capturing the animal first and attaching a miniature radio transmitter.

Stigma That portion of a flower which receives the pollen during pollination.

Symbiosis An association of two different types of organism to their mutual advantage.

Trilobites Once-abundant group of marine animals (now extinct) superficially resembling crustaceans.

Natural History programmes from Bristol

The following is intended to give a broad view of the output of the BBC Natural History Unit and the West Region Features group which preceded it. It is by no means comprehensive although most of the major series are listed as well as some single features. Only the first year of transmission of a series is noted. Also included are some programmes which have historic interest and national changes in broadcasting which affected the Unit. **S** denotes a series of programmes.

1946	*The Naturalist* **S**	Home Service
1947	*Bird Song of the Month* **S**	Home Service
1948	*Out of Doors* **S**	Light Programme
1951	*Birds in Britain* **S**	Home Service
1953	*Severn Wildfowl* (First OB from Slimbridge, May)	Television
	Wild Geese (First of a series of monthly programmes introduced by Peter Scott, December)	Television
1954	*Look* (A single programme introduced by Maxwell Knight, August)	Television
	Also presented from London this year: *Filming Wild Animals* with Armand & Michaela Denis; and *Zoo Quest*.	
1955	*Woodpeckers* (Sielmann's film; this and all earlier studio-based programmes transmitted from Lime Grove studios)	Television
	Look: Foxes (The first of the series, August)	Television
	Also presented from London this year: *Diving to Adventure* with Hans & Lotte Hass.	

ITV begins transmissions September 22

1956	*Naturalists' Notebook* **S** (Quarterly)	Home service
1957	*A Visit to Hagenbeck's Zoo* (Eurovision OB)	Television

Natural History Unit formerly established

	Faraway Look **S**	Television
	Naturalists' Notebook **S** (Now monthly)	Network 3
1958	*Out of Doors* **S** (for children)	Television

	Travellers' Tales **S** (*On Safari* with Armand & Michaela Denis)	Television
	The Undersea World of Adventure **S** (with Hans & Lotte Hass)	Television
1959	*News from the Zoos* **S**	Television
	The Return of the Osprey	Television
1960	*Nature News* **S**	Home Service
	BBC/Council for Nature Film Competition announced	
1961	*The Unknown Forest*	Television
	World Zoos **S**	Television
	Zoo Packet **S**	Television
	Discovery **S**	Television
1962	*Animal Magic* **S**	Television
1963	*Two in the Bush* **S**	Television
	Birds of the Air **S** (Replaces *Birds in Britain*)	Home Service
	The Major	Television
	Look No 100 (with HRH The Duke of Edinburgh)	Television

1964	**BBC 2 begins transmission in April**	
	Look Again **S**	BBC 2
	Horse	BBC 1
	In September regular radio series such as *The Naturalist*, *Birds of the Air* and *Country Questions* (also produced in Bristol but not in the NHU) all move from the traditional 1.10 pm Sunday placing to about 4.45 pm on Sunday.	Home Service
1965	*Nature Parliament* **S** (Transferred from London)	Home Service
	Zoo Challenge **S**	BBC 1
	Life **S**	BBC 2
1966	*Catch me a Colobus* **S**	BBC 1
	Look – Living with Nature (with HRH The Duke of Edinburgh)	BBC 1
	Walk into the Parlour	BBC 2
	The Living World **S** (Monthly)	Home Service
	Wildlife Review **S** (Monthly)	Home Service
	Country Parliament **S** (Monthly)	Home Service
	(*Countryside Today* also produced at Bristol but outside the NHU)	Home Service
	A Bull called Marius	BBC 1
1967	*The Silent Watcher* (Compilation of Ashby films)	BBC 2

	In October: National radio re-organisation into Radios 1–4	
	Animal People **S**	BBC 1
	Life, No 45 (First edition in colour using a London studio October 3)	BBC 2

BBC 2 opens full colour service, December 3:

	The World About Us begins	
	The Private Life of the Kingfisher (First colour transmission)	BBC 2
	Forest and Firebird (First NHU contribution to *The World About Us*, December 17)	BBC 2
1968	*Wild New World* **S**	BBC 1
	The Living World **S** (Becomes weekly, September 12)	Radio 4
1969	*Wild World* **S** (for children)	BBC 1
	Great Zoos **S** (for children)	BBC 1

BBC 1 goes into colour, November 15

1970	*Private Lives* **S**	BBC 1
	Wildlife Safari to Ethiopia **S**	BBC 1
	In July the BBC Regional system is re-organised and Bristol becomes a Network Production Centre.	
1971	*Sounds Natural* **S**	Radio 4
	The Countryman **S**	BBC 2
	Soper at Large **S**	BBC 1
1972	*Great Parks of the World* **S**	BBC 1
	Wildlife Safari to Argentina **S**	BBC 1
	Animal Design **S** (for Further Education)	BBC 1
	Animal Stars **S**	BBC 1
	Around the World in Eighty Minutes (Christmas spectacular)	BBC 1
1973	*Their World* **S**	BBC 2
	Web of Life **S**	BBC 1
	The Animal Game **S**	BBC 1
	Eastwards with Attenborough **S**	BBC 1
	Natural Break **S**	BBC 2
1974	*What on Earth are we doing?* **S**	BBC 2
	Wilderness **S**	BBC 1
1975	*Wildlife* **S**	Radio 4
	Animal Marvels **S**	BBC 1
	Spectacular Britain (for Christmas)	BBC 1
1976	*Barnyard Safari*	BBC 1
	Boswall's Wildlife Safari to Mexico **S**	BBC 1
	The Great Alliance **S**	BBC 1
	The Flying Prince of Wildlife (Prince Bernhard)	BBC 1
	The Country Game **S**	BBC 2
	In Deepest Britain **S**	BBC 2
	Through my Window **S**	Radio 4
1977	*Badgerwatch* **S**	BBC 1
	Wildlife on One **S**	BBC 1
1978	*Wildtrack* **S** (for children)	BBC 1
1979	*Bird of the Week* **S**	Radio 4
	Life on Earth **S**	BBC 2
	Boswall's Wildlife Safari to Thailand **S**	BBC 1

	Foxwatch **S**	BBC 1
	In the Country **S**	BBC 2
	It's a Dog's Life **S**	BBC 2

The Natural History Unit is given Departmental status in December

1980	*Birdwatch*	BBC 1
	Bird Spot **S**	BBC 2
	Animal Olympians	BBC 1
	Symphony of the Oceans	Radio 4
	Natural Selection **S**	Radio 4
	Catch me a Butterfly	Radio 4
	The Truth behind the Turkey	BBC 1
1981	*To Fly where the Sun Never Sets* (Stereo feature)	Radio 4
	Zoo Talk **S**	Radio 4
	David Attenborough's Videobook of British Garden Birds	BBC Home-Video
	Serengeti (Stereo feature)	Radio 4
1982	*The Flight of the Condor* **S**	BBC 2
	Animal Language **S**	Radio 4
	Back in Ten Minutes **S**	Radio 4
	The Discovery of Animal Behaviour	BBC 2

Acknowledgements

Although this has been a personal, and therefore a selective, account of 25 years with the BBC Natural History Unit, I have attempted to sketch in some of the most important aspects of the Unit's history, particularly in the period immediately before and after its establishment. This would have been very difficult without the help of David Attenborough, Bruce Campbell, Nicholas Crocker, Desmond Hawkins, Sir Peter Scott and Tony Soper; I am indebted to them all for their time and wholehearted co-operation. Many others have made valuable suggestions, in particular Eric Ashby, Peter Bale, Patrick Beech, Jeffery Boswall, John Burton, Philip Daly, Frank Gillard, Leslie Jackman, Mike Kendall, Barry Paine, Peter Parks, Winwood Reade, Mick Rhodes, John Sparks, Gerald Thompson and Stuart Wyton. In addition, Gerald Durrell kindly allowed me to reproduce some of his cartoons.

Sheila Fullom and Pamela Jackson were very helpful in tracing historic documents for me and, in addition to my enthusiastic and encouraging editor, Carole Drummond, both Eileen Todd and Vi Hicks gave good advice on the text. To meet the completion deadline my secretary, Helen McCullough, gave up many lunch-breaks and weekends to type the manuscript, helped on occasions by Wendy Dickson and Kate Tiffin.

I am grateful to the BBC for permission to quote from documents held in Registry and to reproduce official photographs. However, I must add that views expressed in this book are my own and are not necessarily shared by the BBC or any of the above contributors.

Picture credits

Armand Denis Productions: 71 *top*; **Eric Ashby:** 106, 107, 111, 176; **David Attenborough:** title page, 18, 19 *top*, 45, 47; **G. Baker:** 198, 207, 211; **BBC:** 21, 22, 26, 28, 29, 38, 39, 42, 43, 52, 53, 54, 71, 73, 74, 76, 87, 91, 92, 116, 117, 119, 161, 164, 169, 177, 189, 190, 215, 226, 227, 229, 238, 260, 261, 264, 265, 297, 298, 299, 309, 322, 350, 353, 355, 356, 357, 358, 360; *Bristol Evening Post:* 120; **Bruce Coleman Ltd:** 79, (David Hughes) front endpaper, (M. P. Kahl) 84, (D. Plage) 170, (Jane Burton) 166, 183, (Alain Compost) 171, (Peter Jackson) 221; **R. Eastman:** 184, 185, 186, 267, 277; **D. Fisher:** 266; **L. Golman:** 270, 271, 274-5, 276, 278; **D. Haylock:** 341; **E. Hosking:** 64; **David Hughes:** half title page; **Mantis Wildlife Films:** back cover, 321, 348, 359 *bottom*; **D. Miller:** 241; **P. Morris:** 315, 337; **W. Morris:** 178-9, 181; **C. Mylne:** 78, 93, 94; **E. Needham:** 216; **New Zealand Wildlife Service:** 129, 132, 136-7, 140, 141, 145, 148, 149, 153; **Oxford Scientific Films:** 125, 245 *bottom*, 249, 252 *top and bottom*, (Dr J. A. L. Cooke) rear endpaper, (Peter Parks) 19 *bottom*, 20, 244, 245 *top*, 248, 251, 344; **B. Paine:** 281; **Christopher Parsons:** 14, 15, 16, 17, 48, 51, 66, 96, 100, 105, 131, 134, 135, 144, 146, 147, 152, 167, 172, 196, 199, 202, 206, 208, 213, 214, 219, 225, 234, 240, 242, 243, 290, 293, 300, 303, 304, 305, 307, 317, 327, 328, 329, 332, 333, 340; **J. Prevost:** 63; *Radio Times:* 279, 285, 287; **Les Requins Associas:** 256; **M. Salisbury:** 351 *right*, 354 *bottom*; **J. Saunders:** 286; **Sir Peter Scott:** 56, 228, 232-3, 359 *top*; **G. Schimanski:** 35, 36; **H. Sielmann:** 33, 34, 44, 112; **Andrew Smith:** 156 and front cover; **L. H. Smith:** 157, 158-9; **T. Soper:** 50, 58, 97, 98; **South African Railways:** 288; **J. Sparks:** 351 *left*, 354 *top*; **Survival Anglia:** (A. Root) 258, (J. Root) 259; **N. Tinbergen:** 262; **Jane Trethowen:** 316; **Wildlife Picture Agency:** 174, 175, 320.

Index